P9-CLH-757

# HOUSING AND INCOME ______

# HOUSING AND INCOME



MARGARET G. REID

THE UNIVERSITY OF CHICAGO PRESS

*Library of Congress Catalog Card Number: 62-19628*

THE UNIVERSITY OF CHICAGO PRESS, CHICAGO & LONDON
The University of Toronto Press, Toronto 5, Canada


*Composed and printed by* THE UNIVERSITY OF CHICAGO PRESS, *Chicago, Illinois, U.S.A.*

# PREFACE

In the early stages of writing this monograph an appropriate title appeared to be "Housing and the Mysterious Income Variable." The economic literature indicated a wide range in the effect of income on housing, and various cross-sections of the same population showed quite different tendencies. For a long time various hunches failed to lead to a coherent set of causes accounting for this variation. Then its rationale seemed to be found.

A more appropriate title now is "Housing and Income: A Theme with Variations." The theme is that values and rents of dwelling units tend to rise markedly with normal or expected income of consumers. The variations on this theme are concerned with the effect of short-run or transitory change, of income change associated with age, and of other conditions that happen to be associated with the income variable.

The monograph is primarily an explanatory analysis concerned with what accounts for certain tendencies observed. It is not explicitly addressed to normative problems of the housing industry or of public-housing programs. However, in the final chapter some implications of findings bearing on these problems are briefly considered.

The monograph has been through many stages. It was begun in 1953. At the outset it was largely restricted to an examination of data of the Census of Housing of 1950. This census is the first to describe housing-income relations of many cross-sections of the population. Some tendencies observed early in the analysis left me with no doubt that American consumers tend to look upon high-quality housing as an important luxury. Clear indications were noted that, as normal income increases, the value and rent of dwelling units tend to increase at an even faster rate, so that housing-income ratios tend to rise with normal income. This is contrary to the long-standing notions that housing tends to take a declining percentage of increased income.

In view of this break with tradition it is not surprising that the new interpretation, even though accompanied by extensive evidence, was greeted with skepticism. As a consequence the investigation was extended to more sets of data, a longer period was covered, and additional techniques were used in an attempt to hold other things constant. In the later stages intertemporal comparisons were made. Dorothy S. Brady provided the stimulus for this. In reviewing what appeared to be the more reliable cross-section tendencies, she raised a question as to whether similar tendencies occurred through time. The intertemporal estimates shown in this monograph imply a high elasticity of housing with respect to secular increase in normal income.

The development of this monograph stems from notions about the income variable that have been long a matter of speculation. With the earliest consumption surveys, annual income was recognized as being an imperfect measure of ability to consume. This was obvious from the average dissavings observed among families low in the income distribution. At low current incomes something other than reported income must explain consumption. Papers by Dorothy S. Brady and by me presented at a session of the Conference on Research in Wealth and Income, held during 1950, examined several sets of cross-section relationships with a view to discovering the nature of income variables and their effect on tendencies observed. These dealt chiefly with total consumption and savings, and the tendencies observed implied the presence of short-run income change. A theory generalizing a wide range of tendencies was later developed by Milton Friedman and published in 1957. It is generally referred to as the permanent-income theory of consumption. At the outset this theory appeared to be useful for deriving hypotheses, the testing of which would expose the structure of demand for housing. The evidence of this monograph sustains this judgment. Its length testifies to the usefulness of the theory as well as to the mass of data awaiting analysts of housing and income.

My debt to Dorothy S. Brady and to Milton Friedman for advice in the development and testing of hypotheses and in the appraisal of findings is very great: Without their help this monograph would have been much more limited in scope. I also owe much to other persons who aided me on statistical techniques, debated with me the characteristics of data and their probable effects, or read and commented on portions of the manuscript at various stages. Among these are Martin J. Bailey, Gary S. Becker, Selma F. Goldsmith, Zvi Griliches, W. Lee Hansen, A. C. Harberger, H. Gregg Lewis, Jacob Mincer, Richard Muth, Albert Rees, and W. Allen Wallis. For assistance in the use of Univac I am indebted to Lilly Monheit. Many students shared in estimating coefficients of correlation and regression. Among these I am especially indebted to Ann C. Graff and Alan Fechter. The help I have received has been invaluable, but I am wholly responsible for imperfections that remain.

Contributions making feasible an extended investigation came from several sources. The first grant came from the Social Science Research Council for the initial exploration of the data of the Census of Housing of 1950. Another grant came from the Fund for the Republic, for the initial investigation of housing by race. A Ford Faculty Research Professorship permitting a year fully devoted to research was another source of help. Annual support came from the University of Chicago. This permitted time to integrate the findings from many sources, to speculate as to causes, and to trace intercorrelations that account for tendencies that initially appeared to be inconsistent. Much probing was necessary to get a firm basis for appraising which of various interpretations has greater validity.

The data utilized come chiefly from published sources. These were supplemented by unpublished tabulations of the Census of Housing of 1950 made available by the Fund for the Republic and the U.S. Bureau of the Census. The U.S. Bureau of Labor Statistics supplied unpublished information pertaining to the consumption survey of 1950 and the Consumer price Index. In addition, my research was facilitated by a gift from the U.S. Bureau of the Census of the volumes reporting the censuses of population and of housing of 1950 and by preliminary releases of the Census of Housing of 1960.

In presenting this monograph a word of warning seems to be called for. Readers of portions of the manuscript tell me that those unacquainted with or only vaguely familiar with the permanent-income hypothesis are likely to find the reading difficult, at least until they get a sense of how each part contributes to the whole. One reader recommends: "Read chapter i, the summaries of chapters ii through xiii, and then chapters xiv and xv." With this perspective the details of the main portions of chapters ii through xiii should not appear to be excessive or disconnected.

On the basis of suggestions from readers I have attempted to streamline the discussion describing the rationale of various hypotheses and to unify the findings from many sources. The findings are more than descriptions of sets of data. Attention centers on conditions influencing tendencies observed and the degree of their stability. Where the tendencies observed for various sets of households or types of cross-sections differ, an attempt was made to determine the cause or causes of the variation. Many technical facts are relegated to footnotes. However, a consideration of data from many sources and of many conditions does not make for easy reading. I can only hope that the discussion of various hypotheses and findings bearing on them will be worth the cost of reading to those seeking to understand the structure of demand for housing.

The monograph is primarily concerned with housing. Even so it has important implications for the analysis of other consumer products and of savings. For these also it seems important to make a distinction between the effect of normal or expected income, of short-run or transitory income, and of income change associated with the age of earners. The nature of income variables, as revealed in this monograph, also bears on the interpretation of annual income distributions as reported in various surveys. The monograph poses a question as to the meaning of variation in annual incomes if much of that variation represents short-run income change or change associated with age. Furthermore, the close relationship between housing and normal income poses a further question as to whether change in housing consumption may not prove useful for revealing secular change in the equality of distribution of normal incomes. Thus the monograph, although devoted to a single consumer product, seems to open the door to new insights into conditions affecting savings and consumption patterns in general, as well as to a better understanding of equality of economic status among consumers.

Margaret G. Reid
September, 1962

# CONTENTS

# TABLES

## FIGURES

Page

"We sense the rule of order over randomness, of pattern over chaos, of law over accident. The patterns we perceive are both of space and time. . . . What we admire as order and beauty is but a product and an index of the measured orderliness of the actions and interactions by which it has come about." Paul A. Weiss, "Life and Order," *The University of Chicago Magazine*, June, 1954

"The ultimate test of significance must consist of a network of conclusions and cross checks where theoretical considerations, intimate realistic knowledge of the data and refined statistical techniques concur." Ragnar Frisch, *Statistical Confluence Analysis by Means of Complete Regression Systems*, Oslo, 1943

# Chapter One

# ALPHA AND OMEGA: THE BEGINNING AND THE END

Over the past century many estimates have been made of housing-income relations of Western countries, and a wide range of tendencies has been observed. This monograph reviews some of these with special attention to urban households of the United States. It also adds appreciably to the stock of estimates and appraises their reliability.

## How Housing Has Been Viewed

In 1857 Engel summarized data with families in three[1] socioeconomic groups and observed that the percentage of total outlays for lodging or rent was much the same for the three groups. From this he concluded that housing tends to be a constant percentage of income. This conclusion was soon challenged by Schwabe. He classified families by income and observed that the higher the income, the lower the proportion of income going to housing. This tendency came to be referred to as the Schwabe law of rent. Engel, after classifying consumer units by income instead of socioeconomic class, accepted Schwabe's less precise law of rent. Stigler in commenting on it states: "The law seemed to contemporaries less obviously true than Engel's law."[2] It is of some interest that Marshall expressed the opinion that "house room satisfies the imperative need for shelter, but that need plays little part in the effective de-

1. These were families (a) dependent on public assistance, (b) just able to live without such assistance, and (c) in comfortable circumstances. It should be noted that such subsets seem unlikely to be homogeneous with respect to transitory income. See George Stigler, "The Early History of Empirical Studies of Consumer Behavior," *Journal of Political Economy*, April, 1954, p. 98.

2. *Ibid.*

mand for house room" and further judged that "where the condition of society is healthy, and there is no check on general prosperity, there seems always to be an elastic demand for house-room, on account both of the real conveniences and the social distinction it affords."[3] It seems probable that Marshall relied largely on extensive direct observation of housing among socioeconomic classes rather than on survey data with families classified by annual income.

Many investigators during the past one hundred years followed Schwabe's method of describing housing-income relations. In other words, they examined housing in relation to income, with consumer units classified by annual income. For the most part, they observed tendencies consistent with Schwabe's law. This law, however, admits a wide range in tendencies and applies equally to total consumption, consumption of food, and the use of other important products. It admits a wide range in tendencies, and a wide range has been observed, some of which indicate very little increase in housing with income.

By the late forties, uncertainty was coming to be expressed concerning this evidence. Grebler, for example, expressed the opinion that the growing volume of data on family income should be used with great discrimination if the relation of income to demand for housing is to be understood. He observed that "it has often been stated before and after the war that only a small percentage of the families have sufficient income to pay for new housing." He then goes on to point out that data for 1947 imply that "private enterprise has built homes within the reach of at least 75 per cent of the nation's families."[4]

In the middle fifties I took a quick look at average housing in relation to average incomes among census tracts within cities, as reported in the Census of Housing of 1950, and noted that housing-income ratios rise markedly with average income.[5] Then Muth,[6] using both time-series and cross-section data among cities, observed a similar tendency.

---

3. Alfred Marshall, Principles of Economics (8th ed.; New York: Macmillan Co., 1948), pp. 88, 107.

4. Leo Grebler, Production of New Housing (New York: Social Science Research Council, 1950), pp. 149-52.

5. Margaret G. Reid, "Value of Dwelling in Relation to Income," Journal of the American Statistical Association, June, 1954, pp. 337-38.

6. Richard Muth, "The Demand for Non-Farm Housing," in Arnold Harberger (ed.), The Demand for Durable Goods (Chicago: University of Chicago Press, 1960), pp. 29-98.

## Alternative Hypotheses

The new findings challenge the Schwabe law of rent. The diversity observed suggests two alternative hypotheses: (a) survey data merely provides descriptions of passing parades and makes little or no contribution to knowledge, or (b) the stability of housing-income relations is obscured in survey data by conditions that happen to be correlated with measured income. This monograph grew from an acceptance of the second hypothesis. It attempts to understand the diversity in housing-income relations observed and to discover the degree of their stability from place to place and through time. Fortunately, Univac came along to make estimates with many variables feasible.

Tenure and household type were obvious conditions to be held constant. The first additional condition to be dealt with is the random component of incomes. With its effect eliminated, the effect of a whole host of things could be identified. In the survey data, for example, cyclical change, the restrictions of a war economy, migration, the economic rise and decline of cities can be identified. In fact, as the probing continued it became more and more apparent that few important changes in the economy occur that do not leave their traces on the housing-income relations.

The monograph estimates the effect on housing-income relations of a great many conditions. The variables representing income and housing are discussed in chapters ii and iii, and those representing household types in chapter iv. Other variables are discussed later. For convenience the main variables used are summarized in the Appendix, together with symbols representing them.

## A Theory of Income Components

At the outset it was assumed that much of the variation observed in housing-income relations is likely to be a function of the heterogeneity of the income variable. Friedman's[7] permanent-income hypothesis provides a theory very useful for formulating testable hypotheses. It postulates that consumption tends to be a function of the permanent component of income, wealth possessed, the interest rate, and other conditions. Friedman's application of the theory concentrates attention on the per-

---

7. Milton Friedman, A Theory of the Consumption Function (Princeton, N. J.: Princeton University Press, 1957).

manent component of income or what this monograph refers to as norman income. This is the income that consumers have in mind when making decisions. Measured income of consumers, which is symbolized by y, is likely to be a very imperfect proxy for normal income, and its imperfections are so important to the interpretation of tendencies observed that chapter ii is largely devoted to a discussion of consumption theories with special attention to income variables.

## What Housing Represents

Housing consumption is defined as the services of residential structures and sites used during a period of time, particularly those occupied by private households. The U.S. Department of Commerce in its estimate of space rent attempts to approximate the market value of housing thus defined. Where the housing variable represents the market value of space at a point in time, it is symbolized by h. If price is held constant, this presumably represents housing consumption.

Not all measures of housing reported in surveys and censuses represent h. Rent paid may represent heat and light as well as space. For owner-occupants, housing expenditure reported makes no allowance for return on investment in dwelling unit occupied. Such heterogeneity and its possible effect on tendencies observed receive special attention in chapter iii.

## Sources Drawn On

The Census of Housing of 1950 is a chief source of data used. It permits a test of uniformity among places of housing-income relations. To test their stability through time, many other sets of data are used. These include the housing survey of 1933 and the census of 1960, as well as consumption of surveys of 1918-19, 1934-36, 1941, and 1950. For the most part, the evidence examined is confined to non-farm population of large cities or metropolitan areas or districts referred to as metro areas. However, there seems no reason to suppose that the findings to not apply to the population in general.

## Measures of Housing-Income Relations

Several types of cross-section estimates are presented. The customary method of describing housing with respect to income is the first used; in other words income of consumer units (y) is the explanatory variable. Other cross-section relations are also examined, many of them using an instrumental variable to minimize the effect on tendencies observed of the random component of measured income of consumer units. Other procedures are used to hold constant conditions that might affect housing-income relations observed. Wherever feasible, data of large-scale surveys are examined in a variety of ways.

Cross-section estimates of the relation of housing consumption to normal income are complicated by the correlation between normal income and other conditions that tend to affect housing-income ratios. These include size and composition of consumer units, the price of housing, and standard of housing desired by consumer units. A series of procedures, described in chapter ii, are used to standardize the observations. In addition, multivariate correlations are also used in an attempt to hold other conditions constant.

Change through time is also examined. Here one must consider price change and the adequacy of consumer price indexes to represent the behavior of consumers represented by the data. These are considered in chapters x and xi.

In this monograph housing-income relations are summarized in terms of coefficients of income elasticity of housing with respect to income. This is the ratio of the rate of increase in housing associated with the rate of increase in income. If the rate of increase in housing is less than the rate of increase in income, then the coefficient is less than 1.0, if the two rates are identical it is 1.0, and if the rate of increases in market value of housing exceeds that of income the coefficient is greater than 1.0. Throughout the monograph, where h and y represent the housing and income of households, this coefficient is symbolized by $\eta_{hy}$. Various subscripts and superscripts are used to denote variations among variables in housing and income represented. These are described later. The variables used and their symbols are summarized in the Appendix. This monograph is primarily devoted to an examination of conditions accounting for variation in coefficients of elasticity of housing with respect to income derived from various sets of data.

The purpose of this examination is to discover the relation of housing to normal income. To do so, it is necessary also to discover the effect on tendencies observed of things associated with income, such as the size and composition of consumer units, tenure of occupancy of the dwelling, price and standard of or preference for housing compared to other types of consumption. These are closely associated with y and hence they affect the tendencies observed.

The monograph as a whole is unique in the scope of observations used to test the stability of coefficients of elasticity of housing with respect to income and in the intensity of its investigation of conditions giving rise to variation in coefficients observed.

## Main Findings

Housing-income relations among consumer units observed for 1950 and 1960, as well as for earlier years, are consistent with Schwabe's law of rent. In other words they indicate that among consumer units the higher is the measured income the lower tends to be the housing-income ratio. The most common tendency of this type observed indicates that the income elasticity of housing among consumer units tends to be appreciably less than 1.0, being around 0.35 for 1950. From this evidence alone it follows that housing is suitably classed as a necessity. However, where measured income approximates normal income, different tendencies are observed. The monograph provides overwhelming evidence (a) that the tendencies observed by Schwabe, and by other persons using methods similar to his, understate the increase in housing accompanying increase in normal income, (b) that the random component in the income of consumer units contributes to this understatement, and (c) that the understatement is usually large.

Over the years for which data evidence has been assembled in this monograph, chiefly from 1918-19 to 1960, the elasticity of housing with respect to normal income appears to be between 1.5 and 2.0. In other words a 10 per cent rise in normal income has tended to be accompanied by a 15 to 20 per cent rise in housing. This tendency is observed in cross-section relations at a point in time and in estimates of intertemporal change. Thus, high quality housing in the American standard of living appears to be a luxury.

Several findings bearing on other conditions are also important: For example, the evidence presented indicates that housing-income ratios tend to be very high for consumer units with an aged or a female head. Thus, in estimating the relation of housing to normal income, it is important to hold constant difference in household types. The evidence also suggests that the price elasticity of demand for housing tends to be around -1.0—in other words that increase in the price of housing, relative to other consumer products, tends to decrease markedly housing consumption as represented by number of rooms, their facilities and quality. It also implies that increase in the relative price of housing has little effect on the percentage of income going to housing and that housing consumption tends to increase at about the same rate as the price of housing tends to fall.

Chapter xiv summarizes the findings of this monograph in some detail. The rejection of the Schwabe law of rent as describing response of housing to normal income is based on very substantial evidence. The evidence implies that high quality housing is one of the important luxury components of the American standard of consumption. With increase in normal income, other things being held constant, a marked rise in housing consumption is to be expected, but such rise will be checked if the price of housing rises faster than the price of other consumer products.

## In Pursuit of Highlights

This monograph consists of a series of very detailed and interlocked analyses. Successive stages in the evidence brought a reformulation of hypotheses and further testing. The analyses are designed to disclose, first, the nature of the conditions affecting housing-income relations commonly observed, and, second, how data available may be used in order to estimate the relation of housing to normal income. Much of the discussion will be of interest only to those who have wrestled with the complexities of similar data or who wish to scrutinize with care the data and the techniques on which the validity of the interpretation of the evidence rests.

Those without such experience may wish only to skim off the cream of the evidence and interpretation. This can be done by reading the introduction and concluding sections of the various chapters; chapter xiv, which provides a digest of the findings; and chapter xv, which presents some general implications of the evidence.

# Chapter Two

# CONSUMPTION THEORIES AND INCOME VARIABLES

The higher the income the higher tends to be consumption of housing in terms of space, facilities, their quality and market value. However, among sets of consumer units, such as are represented by various surveys, the tendencies observed differ widely. The main question considered in this monograph is whether such differences represent a fundamental aspect of consumer behavior or the nature of the income represented by the data or other conditions that happen to be associated with the income variable. This question can only be answered by ferreting out and holding constant the effect of these other conditions.

This chapter represents the first step. It reviews consumption theories and characteristics of income variables bearing on the tendencies observed. Its main topics are: (a) the form of the housing-income relationship; (b) the permanent-income theory of consumption; (c) other consumption theories; (d) methods of deriving estimates of housing with respect to normal income, and (e) the definition of income to be reported.

## The Form of the Housing-Income Relationship

It is assumed that the reliability of estimates is increased by expressing housing and income variables in log form. Where h represents the housing of owner-occupants[1] and y their incomes, the basic equation is:

$$\log h = a + b \log y. \qquad (2.1)$$

In other words, it is assumed that housing-income relationships tend to

1. See chap. iii for discussion of other variables representing housing.

be linear when the variables are expressed in log form.[2] It is of some interest to note that many housing-income curves representing h with respect to y among consumer units tend to be S-shaped, being asymptotic at both low and high incomes. It seems highly probable that such flattening of the curves represents a concentration at the extremes of the income distribution of negative and positive transitory income. The next topic describes such incomes.

Since variables are expressed in log form, the regression coefficient of income represents the elasticity of h with respect to y among consumers. It is symbolized by $\eta_{hy}$.

Other housing and income variables are used. These are described later. Unless otherwise specified all estimates of income elasticity of housing are derived from variables expressed in log form. In addition, other variables in multivariate estimates are also expressed in log form unless otherwise specified. These too are described later.

## The Permanent-Income Theory of Consumption

Friedman's permanent-income theory of consumption[3] pertains to the response of consumers to two quite different components of income, described by Friedman as permanent and transitory. The theory provides a useful frame of reference for understanding variation in tendencies observed in cross-section estimates of housing with respect to income and for formulating means of deriving reliable estimates of housing with respect to permanent income. In this monograph permanent income as defined by Friedman is referred to as normal income[4] and is symbolized by $y_n$ and transitory income is symbolized by $y_t$.

---

2. For discussion of the form of consumption-income curves in general, see S. J. Prais and H. S. Houthakker, The Analysis of Family Budgets (Cambridge University Press, 1955); and J. A. C. Brown, "A Synthesis of Engel-Curve Theory," Review of Economic Studies, XXII (1954-55), Part 1, 15-46.

3. A Theory of the Consumption Function (Princeton, N.J.: Princeton University Press, 1957).

4. This substitution in terminology is made because the term permanent has a connotation at variance with experience of consumers, at least those of the twentieth century. As defined by Friedman, $y_p$ is in a constant state of revision, being modified by changes in the economy at large and in conditions unique to particular consumers. Both such changes modify consumers' notions as to what is probably ahead of them. Hence $y_p$ is subject to continual revision. Under this condition the term normal seems more suitable than permanent.

The permanent-income theory of consumption is to be considered under the following topics: (a) the main features of the permanent-income theory, (b) the lack of correlation of h and $y_t$, (c) the two effects of $y_t$ uncorrelated with $y_n$, (d) circumstances where $y_t$ is correlated with $y_n$ and (e) the lag of housing behind change in $y_n$. Illustrations are given, some hypothetical and some real. They serve as an introduction to the more intensive examination of later chapters as to the effect of income characteristics and associated conditions.

Main Features of the Permanent-Income Theory.—The permanent-income theory has four postulates or tenets bearing on the analysis of this monograph: The first of interest is the conceiving of measured income of consumers as having two components. One is referred to by Friedman as the permanent component and to be referred to in this monograph as normal income and symbolized by $y_n$. This represents long-run expected income. It is an *ex ante* concept pertaining to the future. It may or may not be realized. Nevertheless, it represents expectation and presumably is the income that influences consumer decisions. The other is a transitory component, symbolized by $y_t$. It represents the difference between y and $y_n$. Hence $y_t$ may be zero,[5] negative, or positive. In other words

$$y = y_n \pm y_t. \tag{2.2}$$

The second postulate of interest is that $y_n$ and $y_t$ are uncorrelated. Under this condition the higher is y the greater is likely to be the importance of average positive $y_t$, and the lower is y the greater is likely to be the importance of average negative $y_t$. In addition, if circumstances for a group are normal, then the mean of y for that group of consumer units will tend to represent mean $y_n$ of the group. However, if conditions for the group in general are abnormal, as is likely at the turning points of cyclical change, the depression troughs and prosperity peaks, then mean y for a group of consumer units is likely to have a negative or a positive transitory component.

The third postulate is that consumption is a function of $y_n$, and that

5. The existence of a consumer unit implies that $y_n$ tends to be positive. It may represent income from earnings, pensions, or capital. Only under very rare conditions would the expectation be that future consumption was to be maintained solely through the use of assets that yielded no income. Where $y_n$ of an individual is zero, that individual is likely to be a member of a consumer unit with members having $y_n$ that is positive.

it is uncorrelated with $y_t$.[6] Under this condition the more the variance of y represents $y_t$ the lower will tend to be the income elasticity of consumption among consumers.

The fourth aspect of the theory of interest is that total consumption tends to be a constant percentage of $y_n$. In other words, it assumes that the elasticity of total consumption with respect of $y_n$ tends to be 1.0. This tenet is of interest in this monograph chiefly where total expenditure is used as a proxy for $y_n$, a substitution discussed later in this chapter.

The theory does not assume that $y_n$ is the only condition affecting total consumption. It recognizes that assets, the interest rate, and needs and preferences tend to affect behavior. Needs and preferences as related to the size and composition of consumer units are of considerable importance and so also may be climate and a variety of other conditions.

The theory as developed is primarily concerned with total consumption and savings. It is nevertheless applicable to the analysis of any consumer products, and its relevance for housing seems likely to be specially important. Friedman's examination of empirical evidence led him to conclude that consumer units tend to have a three-year horizon in gauging $y_n$. He does, however, point out that the length of such horizon may differ by type of products: ". . . there seems no reason why the horizon should be the same for all individual categories of consumption and some reason why it should differ systematically. For example, it seems highly plausible that housing expenditures are planned in terms of a longer horizon, and so a different concept of permanent-income, than expenditures on, say, food."[7]

Nerlove[8] in commenting on the concept of horizon states: "If both consumption and income are properly defined it does not seem reasonable that horizons for different categories of consumption should differ greatly from one another." One important difference between housing

6. For early discussion of the effect of transitory income on consumption-income relations observed, see Dorothy S. Brady, "Family Savings in Relation to Change in Level and Distribution of Income," in Conference on Research in Income and Wealth, Studies in Income and Wealth, XV (New York: National Bureau of Economic Research, 1952), 103-30; and Margaret G. Reid, "Effect of Income Concept upon Expenditure Curves of Farm Families," ibid., pp. 131-74.

7. Op. cit., pp. 207-8.

8. Marc Nerlove, in U.S. Department of Agriculture, Agricultural Economic Research, January, 1958, pp. 1-14.

and other consumer products is, however, obvious. An adjustment of housing consumption usually entails direct cost of moving. On the other hand, no direct cost is involved in reducing consumption of food or clothing. If the horizon is longer for housing than for total consumption, it seems highly probable that the effect of $y_t$ on coefficients of $\eta_{hy}$ is greater than the corresponding coefficients for total consumption.

Consumption as defined in the theory pertains to goods and services used rather than to expenditure made. If housing is described in terms of market value of dwelling unit or rent of space occupied, then within a given market these measures of housing seem likely to represent consumption. Much of the information on housing is of this type (see chap. iii). In fact, housing is one of the main consumer products for which much information is available for testing the permanent-income theory. Much of the housing data describe consumption, whereas for such things as furniture, equipment, automobiles, clothing, and other durable goods information is usually available only for expenditure currently made and little is known about additions to or utilization of stock on hand.

The Lack of Correlation of Housing and $y_t$.—At least one study presents direct evidence bearing on the correlation of housing with $y_t$. It describes behavior of consumers experiencing unemployment of a main earner. No mention is made of moving to another dwelling unit, although permitting rent to become delinquent is one of the adjustments to reduced income that is reported.[9]

Several types of indirect evidence testify to the lack of correlation between housing and $y_t$. One is stability of occupancy of dwelling units. In spite of the high mobility of the population of the fifties, compared to earlier decades, about 50 per cent of the non-farm households of 1954 had occupied their present residence at least five years. Change in residence tends to occur at time of marriage. Hence, among households, the stability of occupancy tends to increase with age of head and of children. Among households with head 45 years of age or more, and no children under 18 years of age, 71 per cent had occupied their present residence at least five years.[10]

---

9. See Philip A. Klein, "The Pattern of Credit and Expenditure Adjustment to Unemployment," in National Bureau of Economic Research, Annual Report, May, 1961, p. 58.

10. See Federal Reserve Bulletin, June, 1954, p. 583. The U.S. Bureau of the Census also reports duration of occupancy of dwelling unit

Stability of occupancy differs by tenure. With age of head held constant, it is appreciably higher for owners than for tenants. If the time-horizon of owners is longer than that of tenants, it seems probable that $y_t$, as it relates to housing, is more important for owners than tenants.

Variation in y Represented by $y_t$.—If h is uncorrelated with $y_t$, then the more the variation in y represents $y_t$ the lower will tend to be $\eta_{hy}$. Thus only if $y_t$ is unimportant can it be ignored, if reliable estimates of long-run housing-income relationships are desired.

A good deal of evidence implies that $y_t$ is likely to be important. For example, annual surveys of the Federal Reserve Board since the mid-forties have reported income change from one year to the next. Change reported by the survey of 1955 is fairly typical: Of all spending units[11] 34 per cent reported income of 1955 "about the same" as for last year, 46 per cent reported income larger, and 19 per cent reported income smaller.[12]

---

by tenure and age of head. See, for example, 1956 National Housing Inventory, Vol. III, Table 6.

11. This is the term used to describe the income and the consumer units of these surveys. The definition of pooled income resulted in a considerable percentage of the households and families being represented by more than one spending unit. For discussion of this fragmentation of households and families, see H. H. Lamale, Methodology of the Survey of Consumer Expenditures in 1950 (Processed report; Philadelphia: University of Pennsylvania, 1959).

12. See Federal Reserve Bulletin, June, 1956. The higher percentage reporting an increase rather than a decrease is in part related to the rise in average income. (Between these two years median income rose 7 per cent.) However, even if no such rise occurred, it seems not unlikely that a higher percentage of spending units of an annual survey would report an increase rather than a decrease. This expectation is based on the way in which income change experienced by people brings a change in the universe of spending units represented in successive years. For example, a rise in the income of an earner living with parents and getting established in the labor force might result in his being a spending unit in year B but not in year A. Thus, those reporting increase in income include those newly eligible as spending units. On the other hand, a person eligible as a spending unit in year A may, because of decline in income, now be a member of another spending unit. Consequently, this decline in income is not represented. In fact his income, even though less in year B than in year A, may serve to increase the income of the spending unit that he has joined and so swell the frequency of reports of increased income.

Several investigators have examined income change as reported in these surveys. See, for example, G. Katona and J. Fisher, "Income of Identical Spending Units," in Conference of Research in Income and Wealth, Studies in Income and Wealth, XIII (New York: National Bureau of Economic Research, 1951), 62-119; and Ralph B. Bristol, Jr., "Fac-

The U.S. Bureau of the Census through its Current Population Reports is now annually providing information on the frequency of part-year work by heads of families and conditions giving rise to this. For example, for 1960 only 62 per cent of the heads of families worked at full-time jobs at least 50 weeks during the year. Unemployment or layoffs was the main reason for part-year workers. These accounts for 31 per cent. Sickness or disability was second in importance.[13]

It seems likely that $y_t$ occurring because of unemployment, sickness, and disability has little correlation with $y_n$ if employment opportunities are normal. A consumer unit may one year have an atypically high income because weeks of unemployment, layoffs, and sickness were below normal and may, in another year, experience the opposite conditions, even though during both years the average experience of the labor force was identical.

Reporting error is another source of difference between y and $y_n$ and hence it contributes to the frequency and magnitude of $y_t$. There is evidence that reporting error is important and that much of it is random, in that some consumers tend to overstate and others to understate income received.[14] This reporting error will tend to increase the extent to which variation of y represents variation in $y_t$.

---

tors Associated with Income Variability," American Economic Review, Papers and Proceedings, May, 1958, pp. 279-90. Bristol reports, for example, a lower percentage of units with head "self-employed and managerial" or "unskilled" than those with head "professional and technical" or "clerical or sales" having income about the same from one year to the next.

13. See U.S. Bureau of the Census, Current Population Reports, P-60, No. 37, January, 1962, Tables 13 and 14.

14. See, for example, Herman Miller, "An Appraisal of the 1950 Census Income Data," Journal of the American Statistical Association, March, 1953, pp. 28-43, and his Income of the American People (New York: John Wiley & Sons, 1955). See also Conference on Research in Income and Wealth, "An Appraisal of the 1950 Census Data Income Data," in Studies in Income and Wealth, XXIII (Princeton, N. J.: Princeton University Press, 1958).

Not all reporting error is random. There is, for example, some evidence of systematic underreporting among those of high normal income, in that the dividend income reported understates appreciably dividend income distributed. Less is known of underreporting among those of low normal income. The possibility of this should not be ruled out. Several conditions make me suspect that such underreporting occurs. One is the great importance of part-time work among those of low economic status. This tends to result in failure to recall earnings received. A second is the portion of the income that comes from public

A gap between the period represented by consumption and by income is another condition tending to increase $y_t$. For some sets of data,[15] such as those of the census of housing, the housing pertains to the time of the interview and the income to the preceding year. For long-established households income of the preceding year may be just as good an indicator of $y_n$ as the annual income rate at the time of the census. However, for newly formed households the income of last year is likely on the average to understate greatly the income accounting for the housing occupied. This is the stage when many of the chief earners of consumer units are getting established in the labor force. The decision to establish a household and to occupy a dwelling unit of a given type may follow quickly the achieving of a full-time job or a pay rise. This experience tends to occur at all levels of $y_n$, and hence $y_t$, occurring because of the gap between the period represented by consumption and by income, seems likely to be randomly related to $y_n$.

The degree of equality of $y_n$ of consumer units is another condition influencing the extent to which $y_t$ explains the variance of y, and its effect is indirect and rather subtle. Even if the frequency and magnitude of short-run income change and of reporting error undergo no change, the importance of $y_t$ will increase if among consumers the equality of $y_n$ has increased. Hence the greater the equality of $y_n$ the more important tends to be $y_t$.

If consumer units are completely homogeneous with respect to $y_n$, then all difference in y represents $y_t$. Surveys, as usually designed, are unlikely to provide data for a group of consumers completely homogeneous with respect to $y_n$. Furthermore, groups seem likely to differ appreciably with respect to such homogeneity, as, for example, wage earners or households in slum housing versus all occupations or all households. If the homogeneity of consumer units with respect to $y_n$ differs, then one would expect to find difference among groups in the extent to which the variation in y represents $y_t$. Difference in the importance of $y_t$, that is

funds. Much of this is forthcoming only after a means test, demonstrating inability of private sources to provide a minimum of subsistence. Understating of income is common in these conditions, and it may well carry over to income reported in surveys, even though such information is presumably confidential.

15. For discussion of the comparability of the period represented by consumption and income in the general consumption surveys, see Helen H. Lamale, *op. cit.*

the combination of $y_n$ and positive and negative $y_t$, throughout the income distribution is referred to as the mixture of components in the income distribution. Such difference[16] contributes greatly to the variation observed in $\eta_{hy}$.

For cross-section surveys in general it seems likely that some of the variance in y represents $y_t$. Thus there seems reason to expect that $\eta_{hy}$ is likely to understate $\eta_{hy_n}$. This follows from the fact that housing appears to have no correlation with $y_t$, and some of the variation in y seems certain to represent $y_t$. The evidence of this and later chapters supports this judgment.

The Two Effects of $y_t$ Uncorrelated with $y_n$.—The most obvious effect of $y_t$ uncorrelated with $y_n$ has already been stated, namely its tendency to lower $\eta_{hy}$. It has another effect, namely its tendency, where y is held constant, to cause a difference in h to be observed between groups. The nature of this difference tends to depend on the difference in mean y between groups and on the extent to which it represents mean $y_n$. The bearing of the permanent-income theory on such tendencies is illustrated with hypothetical and real examples. Then some tendencies observed by investigators of data of the mid-thirties are noted and commented on.

A symbol is needed to represent housing now to be considered. The variable is h with y held constant. It is symbolized by $h_y$. This is to be compared with average y of various groups, to be symbolized by Y. This Y is assumed to represent $Y_n \pm Y_t$. In other words, average y of a group may have a transitory component that is zero or negative or positive. In addition, average h of groups is symbolized by H, and the ratio of H to Y by H/Y.

As a first step in considering tendencies likely to be observed, let us assume the following conditions: (a) There are two groups of consumers. For one all consumer units have a normal income of $5,000, and for the other all have a normal income of $3,500. (b) These two groups are homogeneous with respect to household type and preference for and market price of housing. (c) For some consumer units of each group $y_t$ is negative and for others it is positive, and for each group $Y_t$ is zero. Finally, (d), among consumer units housing is positively correlated with

16. An experiment with data to test this proposition for total expenditure is reported by Marilyn Dunsing and Margaret G. Reid, "Effect of Varying Degrees of Transitory Income on Income Elasticity of Expenditures," Journal of the American Statistical Association, June, 1948, pp. 348-59.

$y_n$ and uncorrelated with $y_t$. Under these conditions all variation in y represents $y_t$, and the two housing-income curves are horizontal, with the curve for the group with Y of $5,000 above that for the group with Y of $3,500.

For most surveys assumption (a) is unrealistic. However, the U.S. Bureau of the Census provides some data that appear to come close to illustrating such a condition, namely those for households in substandard and in other types of dwelling units. Gross rent-income curves for the city of Baltimore, as reported for 1950, are shown in Figure 1 for

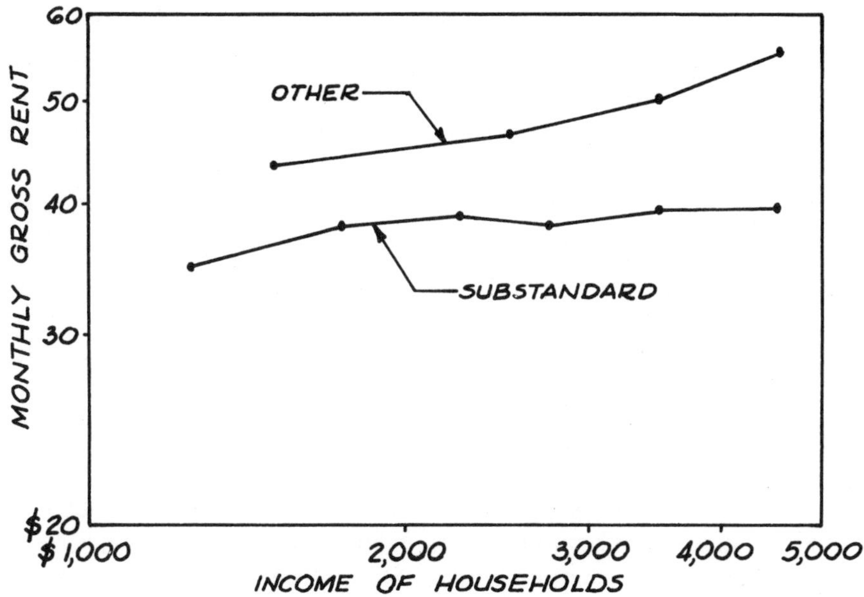


Fig. 1.—Monthly gross rent of dwelling unit with respect to annual income, tenant households in substandard (criteria are those of the U.S. Public Housing Administration) and other types of dwelling unit, city of Baltimore, Md., 1950. (Variables shown in log scale.)

Source of data: U.S. Bureau of the Census, U.S. Census of Housing: 1950, Vol. II: Nonfarm Housing Characteristics, chap. 21, Table B-3; and U.S. Bureau of the Census, Family Income and Rent Survey (Processed report; April, 1954).

two such groups of tenant households. Those in substandard dwellings represent 31 per cent of all tenant households. For each group the gross rent-income curve is quite flat: the coefficients of elasticity of gross rent with rexpect to income (y) are 0.101 and 0.205, respectively.[17] With y equal to $2,000, median gross monthly rent is $38 for the tenants in substandard dwellings and $45 for other tenant households. At the same time, the median income of tenants in substandard dwellings is $1,945 and that of other tenants is $2,979.

The examples shown in Figure 1 are consistent with the permanent-income theory as to direction of the relation of $h_y$ and Y likely to be observed where some of the variation of y represents $y_t$ and housing is uncorrelated with $y_t$. The correlation is very striking. Furthermore, it seems probable that the more $\eta_{hy}$ is lowered by $y_t$, and the greater the difference between groups in $Y_n$, the greater will tend to be the correlation between $h_y$ and Y. Offsetting conditions may of course be present.

Several conditions may affect the level of $h_y$. Among these is the size and composition of households. In addition, the relations described above will not be observed if the groups compared differ little with respect to $Y_n$ and markedly with respect to $Y_t$. For this reason it is necessary to consider conditions observed where assumption (c) stated above is relaxed. Under that assumption $Y_t$ for both groups is zero. Relaxing this assumption is immaterial if the importance of $Y_t$, whether negative or positive, is the same for all groups. It is, however, material if the direction and importance of $Y_t$ differ among groups, and such difference is especially important if the groups are similar with respect to $Y_n$.

Some variation in $Y_t$ among groups is to be expected, for example among groups of consumers representing cities at various stages of cyclical change. Difference in $Y_t$ may even occur between groups representing different economic strata within a city with abnormal employment opportunities, whether high or low. Furthermore, variation in $Y_t$ among groups is certain to be observed when consumer units are differentiated by the magnitude as well as the direction of income change that has occurred since the previous year.[18]

---

17. Casual inspection of data indicates similar difference for other cities in gross rent, where y is held constant.

18. This is strikingly illustrated by tendencies observed for families stratified by direction and extent of dollar income change from one year to the next. See Margaret G. Reid and Marilyn Dunsing, "The Effect of Variability of Incomes on Level of Income-Expenditure Curves of Farm Families," Review of Economics and Statistics, February, 1956, pp. 90-95; and Ruth P. Mack, "The Direction of Change in Income and the Consumption Function," Review of Economics and Statistics, November, 1948, pp. 239-58.

The probable effect of $Y_t$ on the correlation of $h_y$ with Y among groups at a point in time can be visualized by considering what tends to happen to the housing-income curve of a group of consumer units when $Y_t$ changes. When a group passes from a period of normal employment to a condition of considerable unemployment, such as occurs with the downturn of cyclical change, Y tends to fall as negative $Y_t$ increases. If at the same time housing consumption changes little, then the housing-income curve of consumers tends to shift down the income axis and H/Y ratios tend to rise. Thus under conditions of abnormally low employment, $h_y$ appears to be relatively high compared to a former state of normal employment where $Y_t$ was presumably zero. On the other hand, when a group passes from a period of normal employment to a condition of abnormally high employment, as may mark the peak of cyclical change, Y tends to rise as positive $Y_t$ increases. If at the same time housing consumption changes little, then the housing-income curve of the consumers tends to shift up the income axis and H/Y ratios tend to fall. Thus $h_y$ under conditions of abnormally high employment appears relatively low compared to a former state of normal employment.

The information available representing various phases of business cycles indicates tendencies consistent with the theory described. The implication is obvious. Valid interpretation of the relative level of housing-income curves of cross-section survey must take into account the probable effect of difference in $Y_t$ on tendencies observed among groups. Thus whether one observes $h_y$ to be positively correlated with Y among groups depends on whether Y represents $Y_n$ only or whether it is depressed by a negative $Y_t$ or augmented by a positive $Y_t$. If Y of one or more of the groups represented is depressed by a negative $Y_t$, then $h_y$ of such groups will appear relatively high compared to $h_y$ of other groups where negative $Y_t$ is less important or where $Y_t$ is zero or positive, provided groups are homogeneous with respect to $Y_n$.

The effect of difference in $Y_t$ can be illustrated by a hypothetical example. Let us assume two groups of consumers with the following characteristics: They are identical with respect to $Y_n$. The variance of y represented by $y_t$ is similar for the two groups, but consumer units within the groups differ with respect to $y_n$. In addition, they are alike in household types represented and in preference for and market price of housing. Where $Y_t$ of such groups is identical no difference is likely to be observed in $h_y$, thus the housing-income curves of the two groups coincide. If into this situation a difference in $Y_t$ is introduced, the tendencies observed change. If negative $Y_t$ of one group is greater than that of another or if positive $Y_t$ is greater for one group than that of another, then $h_y$ is observed to be negatively correlated with Y. Such effect of $Y_t$ on levels of consumption-income curves has been demonstrated where consumers are stratified by income change from one year to the next.[19] Thus the permanent-income theory provides explanations consistent with two opposite tendencies, namely a positive correlation of $h_y$ and Y and a negative correlation of $h_y$ and Y. The relationship observed depends on whether Y represents $Y_n$ or $Y_n$ plus or minus $Y_t$.

Much of the difference in transitory income of groups seems likely to be a cyclical phenomenon and its characteristics are considered further in the topic that follows. Before turning to it, some comments in the literature on difference in $h_y$ are noted.

A positive correlation among occupational groups between $h_y$ and Y was noted for families reporting in a large-scale survey of the mid-thirties:[20] "There appears to be some relationship between occupation and housing costs, wage earner families having the lowest expenditures at given income levels and independent professional and business families the highest."

For families stratified by race, the evidence of the surveys of the mid-thirties is mixed. The Consumer Purchases Study of 1935-36 representing all occupational groups shows for all southern cities and one northern city, where y is held constant, that rent of white families is higher than that of Negro families.[21] For the other northern city reporting data for both white and Negro families, namely New York, at most income levels the rent is slightly higher for Negro than white families. The official report interpreting this evidence for New York noted that more than 90 per cent of the Negro tenant families live in multifamily dwellings for which heat and light are likely to be included in the rent payment; hence the difference in rent by race, with y held constant, may

---

19. Reid and Dunsing, loc. cit.

20. U.S. Department of Labor, Bul. 648, I, 81. This bulletin reports housing data of the Consumer Purchases Study representing families with a native-born husband and wife. It is confined to those having received no relief during the year of the survey, that is some portion of 1935-36. (The comments quoted here pertain to white families only.)

21. Ibid., p. 25.

be caused by greater importance of utilities in the rent of Negro than white families.[22]

Other evidence of the mid-thirties suggests that the tendency for rent to be higher of Negro than white families, where y is held constant, was not unique to New York. A survey confined to families of wage earners and lower salaried clerical workers indicates that "at comparable income and consumption levels, it was generally found that in northern cities the Negroes actually paid higher rents than white families. . . . In Southern cities, on the other hand, Negro families generally paid lower rents than white families of similar financial status."

The official report ascribes these opposite tendencies, one with $h_y$ negatively correlated with Y of the two races and one with it positively correlated, to the same condition, namely to segregated housing markets. Concerning northern cities, it is noted that "Negroes are by custom restricted to certain sections of the city," and because of this "to obtain housing of quality comparable to the white families they must pay more." Concerning the southern cities, the report states: "The facilities of the dwellings they [the Negro families] occupied were . . . considerably below those of the white families, indicating again the operation of restriction on dwellings available for Negroes." These interpretations implicitly assume that a given dollar income, irrespective of race, represents equal ability and willingness to pay for housing, if segregation were not a factor.

The permanent-income theory contributes to an explanation of these tendencies. The difference described above between occupations, irrespective of region, and between races in the South are those to expect if $h_y$ tends to be positively correlated with $Y_n$ of groups. On the other hand, the negative correlation between $h_y$ and Y of Negro and white families in the North is the type expected if negative $Y_t$ was appreciably more important for the Negro than the white families represented. In other words, the tendency observed is that to be expected if negative $Y_t$, occurring be-

22. This difference is not very great, so it cannot be an important contributing factor. For example, the percentage of tenant families with heat and light included in contract rent was as follows:

| Race of persons | Heat | Light |
|---|---|---|
| Negro | 82 | 3 |
| White | 78 | 6 |

(Estimated from data shown in Bul. 648, I, 183.)

cause of widespread unemployment at the time of the survey, caused the housing-income curve to shift down the income axis more for Negro than for white families and if the difference in such shift offset any tendency under normal conditions for $h_y$ and $Y_n$ to be positively correlated. The possibility of such a combination of conditions determining tendencies observed is certainly greater for New York than for the cities of the South, merely because difference in $Y_n$ by race was less for New York than for southern cities.

One feature of the Consumer Purchases Study of 1935-36 makes it seem likely that $Y_t$ was more important for Negro than for white families. The Negro families of New York, on the average, reported for an earlier year than did the white families. In other words, Y of the Negro families reporting of New York represents a year closer to the depths of the Great Depression than does Y of the white families.[23] This difference by race in the year represented by this survey is doubtless an accident as to how the field work happened to be planned. Furthermore, it illustrates a type of condition that may be introduced when consumers represented in a single survey do not all report for the same year,[24] and especially if this period happens to involve important cyclical change.

That tendencies observed by race in the mid-thirties are caused by difference in $Y_t$ is also supported by data for 1950. For northern as well as southern cities, it shows a positive correlation between $h_y$ and Y by race. This evidence is presented in chapter vii.

Circumstances where $y_t$ is Correlated with $y_n$.—Friedman in formulating his permanent-income theory considered situations where $y_t$ tends to be uncorrelated with $y_n$. It seems highly probable that this lack of correlation of $y_n$ and $y_t$ represents characteristics of annual per capita national income, in that net positive or negative $y_t$ is as likely to occur in years when $y_n$ is high as when it is low. It probably also represents the characteristics of average income of geographic areas such as

23. For example, the report year of 67 per cent of the Negro families and 57 per cent of the white families was prior to the year ending May 31, 1936. Data on report year represented are reported by the U.S. Dept. of Labor, Bul. 643, I, 140, 204.

24. Variation among consumers in year represented was usual in large-scale surveys made prior to 1941. Beginning with that survey the year represented has been held constant, at least in making national surveys.

states and cities in that positive and negative cyclical change in income is as likely to occur in places of high as of low normal income. It seems likely also to describe much of $y_t$ of consumer units, such as that related to sickness, time off for changing jobs, extra vacation, various types of windfall gains or chance opportunities for extra earnings. There is, however, one type of $y_t$ that seems likely to be correlated with $y_n$ of consumer units, namely $y_t$ associated with cyclical employment opportunity. At least for the non-farm population, such $y_t$ seems likely to be positively correlated with $y_n$ on the downturn and negatively correlated on the upturn. In other words, it seems likely that cyclical downturn will bring a greater decrease and cyclical upturn a greater increase in y of consumer units with low than with high $y_n$.

That such correlations are likely is implied by the cyclical pattern of unemployment by occupation. In general, cyclical change in unemployment is greater among the unskilled than the skilled, and among the skilled than among the clerical and professional workers.[25] This implies that $y_t$ arising from cyclical change is unequally distributed among non-farm occupational groups. For some occupational groups cyclical change in $y_t$ seems likely to be small, notably for salaried business and professional workers, and for others it seems likely to be large, notably for unskilled workers. This distribution of cyclical $y_t$ among occupational groups will tend to affect coefficients of income elasticity where all occupational groups are represented. The main evidence pertaining to this correlation is presented in chapter vii.

Any correlation of $y_t$ with $y_n$ may also affect the correlation of $h_y$ with Y. In fact it may have contributed to the tendency observed for some northern cities during the mid-thirties for $h_y$ to be negatively correlated with Y between the races. In those years the degree of abnormal unemployment experienced by the Negro families was probably greater than that experienced by white families, and hence $Y_t$ was probably more important for Negro than white families, even where both races reported for the same year. This is to be expected so long as negative $y_t$ of the downturn of cyclical change tends to depress most

---

25. See, for example, Philip Hauser, "Differential Unemployment in the United States," in The Universities-National Bureau Committee for Economic Research, The Measurement and Behavior of Unemployment (Princeton, N.J.: Princeton University Press, 1957), p. 263. See also U.S. Bureau of Labor Statistics, Employment and Earnings, a monthly publication.

incomes of consumer units with low $y_n$.

The Lag of Housing Behind Change in Normal Income.—The lag of housing behind change in $y_n$ is another condition likely to affect tendencies observed. Several conditions probably combine to make such lag for housing longer than for other consumer products: Housing is quite important in the total budget, any change involving direct costs of moving, and the imperfections of the housing market are likely to necessitate considerable shopping around before making a decision. Any lag occurring seems likely, however, to affect tendencies observed in much the same way as $y_t$ uncorrelated with $y_n$. Hence techniques that hold constant the effect of such $y_t$ seem likely also to hold constant the effect of a lag of housing behind change in $y_n$.

## Other Consumption Theories

Three consumption theories other than Friedman's permanent-income theory are worthy of comment: that of Dorothy S. Brady and Rose D. Friedman,[26] that of Duesenberry,[27] and that of Modigliani and Brumberg.[28]

During the forties Brady and Friedman presented evidence that, where y is held constant, savings tend to be negatively related and consumption positively correlated with Y of groups compared. They extended their investigation to the position of families in the income distribution and observed that savings, and conversely total consumption, tend to be a function of the position of families in the income distribution. They observed among groups of families representing various cities of a national survey that savings as a percentage of income, and conversely consumption, tend to be similar if position in the income distribution is held constant. Furthermore, they found these tendencies quite stable through time. This interpretation of tendencies observed came to be referred to as the distributive theory of consumption and savings.

---

26. Dorothy S. Brady and Rose D. Friedman, "Saving and the Income Distribution," in Conference on Research in Income and Wealth, Studies in Income and Wealth, X (New York: National Bureau of Economic Research, 1947), 250-65.

27. James S. Duesenberry, Income Saving and the Theory of Consumer Behavior (Cambridge, Mass.: Harvard University Press, 1949).

28. Franco Modigliani and Richard Brumberg, "Utility Analysis and the Consumption Function," in K. K. Kurihari (ed.), Post Keynesian Economics (New Brunswick, N.J.: Rutgers University Press, 1954), pp. 388-436.

The consumption behavior observed by Brady and Friedman is that to expect where y has an important transitory component uncorrelated with consumption, and where $y_t$ is systematically related to y. Thus negative $y_t$ concentrating where y is low, tends to increase consumption-income ratios, and positive $y_t$, concentrating when y is high, tends to decrease consumption-income ratios, and the sign and the importance of $y_t$ causing this variation in ratios depends not on the dollar income but on the position of y in the income distribution.

During the forties Duesenberry also observed among groups of families representing places and occupations that total consumption, where y is held constant, tends to be positively correlated with Y. His observations led him to conclude that the "utility index is a function of relative rather than absolute consumption expenditure."[29] He interpreted the behavior observed as reflecting the effect on consumers of consumption of those with whom they came in contact, the effect, as it were, of trying "to keep up with the Jones." This explanation is commonly referred to as the standard of living theory. No one is likely to argue that consumption of one's associates does not affect one's sense of need. But the nature of such effect is likely to be a subject much debated. No attempt is made here to theorize as to the probable sequences of influences and resulting actions. Two things are, however, obvious: The income of each family exercises a very important constraint on its expenditure, and the standard of living theory does not explain deficit spending at low income—almost universal behavior as judged by general consumption surveys.

The permanent-income theory is not inconsistent with the hypothesis that standard of living is in large part shaped by environmental conditions, including the consumption of neighbors. Such standards may, however, have their effect primarily through their influence on earnings. There seems to be a growing appreciation that the higher the standard of living the higher is likely to be the income.

This monograph considers the probable effect of standards. For the purpose of clarity, the phrase "standard of living" or "standard of housing" refers to aspirations or a sense of need. Consumption as observed or measured, as represented by value or rent or quality of housing, is assumed to represent achievement. This is the result of the standard of

---

29. Op. cit., p. 112.

housing or the sense of need for housing, along with other conditions such as income or price of housing.

The consumption theory of Modigliani and Brumberg stresses the importance of income expectations not fully represented by current income. In this and other respects their theory is similar to that of Friedman. They give, however, greater attention than does Friedman to the lifetime horizon, to expected change in income with age, and to a balance between current income and the accumulation and use of assets.[30] This monograph considers conditions associated with age of head that seem likely to affect tendencies observed, including the accumulation of consumer capital in owner-occupied dwellings. Unfortunately, only very meager information is available on total assets.

### Methods of Deriving Estimates of Housing with respect to $y_n$

Investigators of family consumption from the outset have been concerned to minimize the effect of atypical situations, when knowledge of the usual situation was desired. Consequently, many surveys have confined their universe to families with at least one gainful worker with a specified minimum level of employment. As data accumulated, it became obvious that such a procedure did not insure that only typical incomes were represented. Surveys using these criteria reported total expenditure exceeding income of those consumers reporting very low income. Thus the low incomes did not explain current consumption or the accumulation of assets or other conditions that made deficit spending possible.

The effect of these and other techniques useful for reducing the im-

30. In conclusion the authors state: "We claim . . . that the proportion of income saved is essentially independent of income; and that systematic deviations of the savings ratio from the normal level are largely accounted for by the fact that short-term fluctuations of income around the basic earning capacity of the household, as well as gradual changes in this earning capacity, may cause accumulated savings to get out of line with current income and age. The common sense of our claim rests largely on two propositions: (a) that the major purpose of saving is to provide a cushion against the major variations in income that typically occur during the life cycle of the household as well as against less systematic short-term fluctuations in income and needs; (b) that the provisions the household would wish to make, and can afford to make, for retirement as well as for emergencies, must be basically proportional on the average, to its basic earning capacity, while the number of years over which these provisions can be made is largely independent of income levels. We have shown that our claim is strongly supported by budget data when these data are properly analyzed" (loc. cit., p. 430).

portance of effect of $y_t$ on income elasticities of housing are considered here. The techniques are: (a) to exclude consumers for whom $y_t$ is likely to be important; (b) to stratify consumers by $y_t$; (c) to use an instrumental variable; (d) to use differences in average housing and income between two subsets for a set of places; (e) to use the evidence of both regressions, and (f) to use total expenditure as a proxy for normal $y_n$ or $Y_n$. Each of these techniques is now to be briefly considered.

Exclude Consumers for Whom $y_t$ is Likely to be Important.—If negative $y_t$ tends to concentrate at low y and positive $y_t$ at high y, then presumably $\eta_{hy}$ will tend to be increased by the exclusion of very low and very high incomes. Consumption-income curves tend to be S-shaped even when variables are expressed in log form. Where curves have this form, the exclusion of the very low and the very high incomes is certain to increase the coefficients of income elasticity of consumption observed. The income elasticity of housing expenditure,[31] among all urban consumer units reporting in the 1950 consumption urban survey, is 0.472, and for the income range from $1,000 to $10,000 it is 0.552—an increase of 17 per cent. If consumer units with head not gainfully or self-employed are also excluded, the coefficient is increased to 0.579.

This simple method of minimizing the effect of $y_t$ may have some merit. Certainly for housing it makes a correction in the right direction.[32] Even so, much of the effect of $y_t$ remains. This judgment anticipates evidence presented later.

Another method of excluding consumer units high in $y_t$ is to revert to the practice of the earlier surveys and include wage earners with a minimum of employment and to exclude the self-employed.[33] The 1950

31. Including expenditure for housing away from home.

32. That such exclusion would permit reliable estimates was doubtless the hope that led Crochett and Friend in using the data of the 1950 urban consumption survey to confine their estimates of income elasticities chiefly to consumer units reporting incomes of $1,000 to $10,000. See Jean Crochett and Irwin Friend, "A Complete Set of Consumer Demand Relationships," in Irwin Friend and Robert Jones (eds.), Proceedings of the Conference on Consumption and Savings, (Processed report; Philadelphia: University of Pennsylvania, 1960) I, 1-92. For discussion of the effects of such exclusion, see Margaret G. Reid, "Discussion of 'A Complete Set of Consumer Demand Relationships,'" ibid., pp. 143-54.

33. There seems good reason to believe that $y_t$ of consumer units with heads not gainfully employed tends to be negative. These consumers concentrate low in the income distribution. In addition, there seems reason to believe, on the basis of probable reporting error alone, that

urban consumption survey provides evidence of the effect of such exclusion. The exclusion of these two subsets tends to increase by 15 per cent the income elasticity of housing expenditure among consumer units.[34]

The more precise the information on $y_t$ the more effectively can consumers where $y_t$ is important be excluded. The survey of 1950 attempted to get information indicative of the importance of $y_t$. It provides reports, made in the spring of 1951, of income in 1950, of whether income of 1949 was "about the same as that of 1950" or "higher" or "lower" and also as to whether income of 1951 was expected to be "about the same as that of 1950" or higher or lower. Friend and Kravis used this information to explore the effect of change thus indicated on income elasticity of housing. They identified what they called a three-year constant income set. Judgment as to constancy of income was based on reports of respondents in 1951 as to income change from 1949 to 1950 and expected income change from 1950 to 1951. They found only a slight difference between the coefficients of income elasticity of housing expenditure for this so-called constant income subset and for all urban units, irrespective of income change and expectation. The coefficients are 0.70 and 0.65, respectively.[35]

This small effect reported at first glance would seem to imply that $y_t$ is of minor importance. It should, however, not be overlooked that information as to income change used by Friend and Kravis came from judgments reported by a single survey as to direction and general magnitude of income change experienced and anticipated. Such judgments seem likely to be subject to a good deal of reporting error. Thus they seem likely to provide only a crude means of differentiating consumer

---

much of the variance of y of consumer units with a self-employed head represents $y_t$.

34. It increases the coefficient from 0.472 to 0.542. The excluded groups constitute 14.5 per cent of the entire set and for them the coefficient is 0.244. The data are shown in *Study of Consumer Expenditures Incomes and Savings. Statistical Tables, Urban U.S., 1950* (Philadelphia, Pa.: University of Pennsylvania, 1957), Vol. XVIII, Tables 2 and 4. Tabulated by the U.S. Bureau of Labor Statistics for the Wharton School of Finance and Commerce. The estimates shown relate to weighted regressions with variables expressed in log form. The housing variable is total expenditure for housing including housing away from home.

35. Irwin Friend and Irving Kravis, "Consumption Patterns and Permanent Income," *American Economic Review, Papers and Proceedings*, May, 1957, p. 548. The estimates shown pertain to urban families of three or four persons with head 35 to 55 years of age. Variables are expressed in log form.

units by $y_t$. In addition, this type of evidence does nothing to hold constant the reporting error of y, much of which is random.

Stratify Consumers by $y_t$.—Increasing the accuracy of information as to change in income from the preceding year would make it feasible to get strata of consumers with considerable homogeneity with respect to $y_t$. The greater this homogeneity, the more all $y_t$ would be represented by $Y_t$ of the various strata. The more this is achieved, the less the variance of y of the separate strata represents $y_t$. One means to more accurate data as to $y_t$ would be to survey identical consumer units for consecutive years. With such data, reporting error of the income for at least the earlier year seems likely to be less than when consumers are asked to recall income following a lapse of about two years. In addition, reports on income made in two consecutive years provide estimates of dollar change or percentage change. This is more precise evidence for gauging income stability than judgment that income of year A was about the same, higher, or lower than that of year B. There are, however, little survey data on incomes of identical consumer units in consecutive years, and the likelihood of having such data is limited by the cost of collection.[36]

Use an Instrumental Variable.—Where an explanatory variable such as y is subject to random error, an instrumental variable may be very useful. Valavanis[37] describes such a variable as one "exogeneous to the economy . . . not entering the particular equation, or equations, we want to estimate, nevertheless used by us in estimating these equations." Its main purpose is to eliminate or to minimize the random error of the explanatory variable. At the same time it tends to eliminate or minimize the random error of the dependent variable.

Thus, through the use of an instrumental variable, one may be able to derive observations for subsets of consumers where both the housing

---

36. For discussion of problems related to securing re-interview data, see Peter Vendome, "Aspects of the Dynamics of Consumer Behavior," Bulletin of the Oxford University Institute of Statistics, February, 1958, pp. 66-105.

37. Stefan Valavanis, Econometrics (New York: McGraw-Hill Book Co., 1959), p. 107. For further discussion of instrumental variables, see A. Madansky, "The Fitting Straight Lines When Both Variables Are Subject to Error," Journal of the American Statistical Association, March, 1959, pp. 173-205; and J. D. Sargan, "The Estimates of Economic Relationships Using Instrumental Variables," Econometrica, July, 1958, pp. 393-415.

and income variables have a zero random error. Average housing and income of subsets differentiated by means of an instrumental variable are to be symbolized in this monograph by H and Y, respectively,[38] and the income elasticity of housing estimated using such observations is symbolized by $\eta_{HY}$.

As a technique for deriving an explanatory variable with a minimum of random error, the term instrumental variable is relatively new in statistical literature. However, the type of observation thus provided has a long history in empirical investigation. Geographic areas probably represent the instrumental variable most widely used. Tendencies thus observed have commonly been referred to as interplace correlations. They are one type of interclass correlation used in this monograph.

My early explorations of the data of the Census of Housing of 1950 used census tracts of various metro areas as an instrumental variable. Observations thus derived showed an elasticity of housing with respect to average income around 2.0.[39] This preliminary evidence left no doubt in my mind that housing-income relations, as usually estimated, greatly understate the elasticity of housing with respect to normal income and that the random error in y is likely to be great.

At the outset the use of only tracts as an instrumental variable seemed insufficient, especially since it was necessary to confine the estimates to a highly selected set of tracts.[40] Quality of housing is another instrumental variable used to provide observations for interclass observations within metro areas (see chap. vii). Where it is used, or where tracts are used, one must consider whether tendencies observed are in part the result of a correlation of the standard of housing and Y, in accordance with the Duesenberry hypothesis.

---

38. In the study of housing, the usefulness of an instrumental variable is dependent first of all on its correlation with $y_n$ and its lack of correlation with $y_t$. Under these two conditions the mean income of the subsets derived through the use of an instrumental variable may represent variation in average $y_n$ for the groups of consumers represented. The extent to which it does depends on the size of the subsets. For each subset it must be sufficient so that $y_t$ randomly related to $y_n$ has a zero mean. The size needed is thus dependent on the variability of $y_t$. The higher its variability the higher is the number of consumer units needed per subset to insure that $y_t$ uncorrelated with $y_n$ has a zero mean for the subsets.

39. For a preliminary report of these findings, see Journal of the American Statistical Association, June, 1954, pp. 337-38.

40. For discussion, see chaps. vii and xiii.

Many sets of data also permit the use of widely dispersed geographic areas, such as cities, as an instrumental variable. With such a variable one does not escape the possibility that tendencies observed are influenced by a correlation of the standard of housing with Y. And one must also consider the possibility that tendencies observed are influenced by a correlation between the market price of housing and Y.

Three instrumental variables, census tracts and housing quality categories within places and geographic areas such as cities, are used to derive observations for interclass correlation representing data of the Census of Housing of 1950. For the urban consumption survey of 1950, city areas are the main instrumental variable feasible for this purpose. Data are reported by occupation of the head and by years of schooling. However, the observations are few, and the tendencies seem likely to be much influenced by the age distribution.[41]

Another type of instrumental variable is suggested by Friedman and Kuznets in their analysis of income from independent professional practice,[42] namely the income of the preceding year. If h and y represent year B, then y of year A would, under certain conditions, be a suitable instrumental variable for deriving observations for interclass correlations unaffected by $y_t$.[43] This would occur if $y_t$ of year B is uncorrelated with $y_t$ of year A. To the extent that $y_t$ has a duration beyond one year, $y_t$ of years A and B will be positively correlated. In addition there is some possibility, quite pronounced for the self-employed because of the definition of net income used, that $y_t$ of year B is negatively correlated with that of year A. The use of such an instrumental variable is handi-

41. In addition there seems likely to be some tendency for persons experiencing short-run income change to shift down and up the occupational ladder with change in their job opportunity. Some such shifting seems likely to be related to cyclical change and some to be independent of it.

42. Milton Friedman and Simon Kuznets, Income from Independent Professional Practice (New York: National Bureau of Economic Research, 1945). This study is basic to the formulation of the permanent-income theory.

43. Such income data would obviously serve another purpose, namely to provide estimates of income over two years. Some of the short-run income change and the reporting error of the separate years will be offsetting. Consequently, where y represents income of two years, $\eta_{hy}$ seems likely to be higher than where y represents income of one year. Whether use of two-year incomes represents a more effective method than use of income of year A as an instrumental variable to derive average incomes of subsets for year B remains to be tested.

capped by lack of income data of consecutive years for a set of consumer units for which information on housing is available.[44] However, even if such data were available their usefulness would be limited by the correlation between y of both years and age of earners—and age has a very important effect on the ratio of housing to income.

Use of Difference in Average Housing and Income between Two Sub-Sets for a Set of Places.—An instrumental variable correlated with h solely because of its correlation with $y_n$ may not be available. Furthermore, information as to other conditions affecting h that are correlated with the instrumental variable may be incomplete. Incomplete information occurs because no one thought of its being important at the time data were collected, or because their collection is expensive or difficult or looked upon as impossible. For example, average assets of families and the relative price of housing of a given quality are two conditions that might at great expense be measured for cities, but the relative standard of housing determining preference and sense of need for housing seem likely for long to be judged immeasurable. In addition, information on environmental conditions bearing on location and on cost of transportation as these affect housing is not available and is probably difficult to collect. Until such things can be held constant or are shown to be immaterial, intercity correlations, as well as census tracts and quality of housing as instrumental variables, are likely to be viewed with suspicion.

Using a second instrumental variable is one method of holding constant a variety of conditions that might affect interclass correlations. Places such as metro area or cities could represent one instrumental variable, and some criteria for differentiating subsets by mean $y_n$ within places could represent the other. The observations would be of differences between two subsets for a set of places. Such differences would under certain circumstances permit one to estimate the elasticity of $\eta_{hy_n}$, unaffected by a correlation of standard of housing or market price of housing with Y of intercity correlations.

Difference in average H and Y between environs and central cities for a set of metro areas illustrates the use of two instrumental varia-

44. A considerable body of data for farm families is available describing income and expenditure in consecutive years. However, for these families there is reason to believe that $y_t$ of consecutive years has a considerable correlation.

bles. The subsets represent two contiguous areas, symbolized here by E and C, and the metro areas are dispersed throughout the United States. If Y for E and for C represents $Y_n$, then difference in Y between E and C represents difference in $Y_n$. The difference in H between E and C may be wholly the result of difference in $Y_n$. On the other hand, it may be affected by other conditions, such as a tendency for the price of a given quality of housing to be less for E than for C. If this tendency is common among metro areas or if difference among metro areas is uncorrelated with difference in Y between E and C, then for the set of metro areas represented any difference in the market price of housing between E and C will not affect the elasticity of housing with respect to income derived from such observations. Any such effect will be registered solely in the level of the housing-income curves of these observations.

Observations representing difference of this type for a set of metro areas for housing and income are symbolized by $H^*$ and $Y^*$, respectively. Thus

$$H^* = \log H_E - \log H_C \tag{2.3}$$

$$Y^* = \log Y_E - \log Y_C. \tag{2.4}$$

And the correlation of $H^*$ and $Y^*$ for a set of metro areas will yield a coefficient of income elasticity of housing that will be unaffected by at least some conditions affecting housing, other than $y_n$, that differ between E and C or among metro areas.

Instrumental variables other than E and C are used to derive observations for a set of places representing difference between two subsets. For example, for cities of the 1950 urban consumption survey, observations are examined that represent difference in Y between two subsets of consumers units by years of schooling or by occupation of the head. The special characteristics of these observations are discussed later. Such observations are symbolized by $H^*$ and $Y^*$, as are any observations representing similar difference between subsets. The correlation of such variables is referred to as a correlation of differences. Such differences have been used by Duesenberry to estimate intertemporal price change. These have been considered in chapter xi.

Use the Evidence of Both Regressions.—How to derive reliable estimates of functional relationships where an explanatory variable such as income has a random error has been a matter of long-standing interest to statisticians.[45] The use of both regressions represents another method of investigating such relationship. The two regressions, for example the regression coefficient of h with respect to y and the reciprocal of the regression coefficient of y with respect to h, set the limits within which the functional relationship of h with respect to $y_n$ must fall, unless of course there are non-random conditions affecting the tendencies observed.

In this monograph some use is made of these two regressions. The coefficients of income elasticity of these regressions are referred to as income elasticity I and II, respectively. Coefficient I will be biased downward by any random error represented by y, such as $y_t$ correlated with y, and coefficient II will be biased upward by any random error represented by h,[46] such as variation among households in preference for housing or error in reporting value or rent of housing.

Where the variables are h and y the two coefficients are very different. For example, for owner households of metro areas of the United States as reported in the 1950 census of housing, the coefficients I and II are 0.30 and 1.99, respectively.[47] Such wide limits imply a large random element in either y or h or in both these variables. Where the functional relationship lies depends on the relative error of the two variables. If the error is equally important for the two variables, the average of the two coefficients comes close to representing the functional relation of housing to normal income. Accordingly, the coefficients presented above indicate an income elasticity of housing around 1.15. On the other hand, it will be higher if the error is less for housing than income, and lower if it is less for income than housing. Direct evidence as to the importance of the error component of these variable is not feasible. Evidence presented later implies that it is less for h than for y. The characteristics of these two regressions where variables are h and y are

---

45. See, for example, D. V. Lindley, "Regression Lines and the Linear Functional Relationship," Journal of the Royal Statistical Society, IX, Series B (1947), 218-44.

46. The second regression provides the coefficient $\eta_{yh}$. It will be biased downward by any random error in h. This downward bias will result in income elasticity II being biased upward, since it is the reciprocal of $\eta_{yh}$.

47. Estimated from data shown in U.S. Census of Housing: 1950. Vol. II, Nonfarm Housing Characteristics, chap. i, Table B-7. The estimates shown relate to weighted regressions with variables expressed in log form.

commented on later, notably in chapter vii.

Where an instrumental variable is used, there may be no need to use both regressions in order to get a satisfactory estimate of housing with respect to $y_n$. This depends on whether all $y_t$ is uncorrelated with $y_n$. If, however, these components are correlated, as seems likely if cyclical change is represented, then some of the variation in Y is likely to represent transitory income. Furthermore, there seems some likelihood that $Y_t$ is uncorrelated with $Y_n$. If so, the second regression is likely to be useful in deriving a reliable estimate where an instrumental variable is used, that is for observations where income is represented by either Y or $Y^*$.

Most of the estimates of income elasticity of housing shown in this monograph represent income elasticity I. Where it alone is considered no mention is made of the type of measure under consideration. Thus unless otherwise specified the explanatory variable of the relationship described is y or Y or $Y^*$.

Use Total Expenditure as a Proxy for $y_n$.—In studying consumption of various products, such as housing, total consumption has been used as a proxy for $y_n$. In many early studies this substitution was made because information on income was not available, and some investigators continued its use even where income was reported because the income variable seemed so unsatisfactory. One of the postulates of the permanent-income theory, namely that consumption tends to be uncorrelated with $Y_t$, revived an interest in this use of total expenditure. Consequently, it is of sufficient importance that chapter ix is devoted to tendencies observed where total expenditure is used as a proxy for $y_n$.

### Defining Income To Be Reported

Surveys differ in income concept. One question of considerable importance relates to business costs deducted in estimating net money income. Net income is commonly defined as gross receipts minus business and occupational expense. This concept is especially complex where an income recipient is self-employed. Reporting errors may be common because receipts and expenses are irregular. In addition, data collected tend to make only a crude distinction between current expense and change in capital. In the urban consumption survey of 1950, entrepreneurial income is gross receipts less outlays for current operation, including replacement of capital.[48] Thus income reported may deviate a good deal from a strict net income concept. Expenses for maintenance and replacement may increase the capital of some entrepreneurs and be insufficient to maintain that of others. Thus, for some, net income is understated and for others overstated, and what appears as variability from year to year of net income is in fact the variability of accretion to or depletion of capital.

Wage and salary income for the most part is classed as net income, even though some outlays can justly be classed as expense of acquiring income. Transportation to work is clearly such a cost, and so also is additional expense for food away from home because of a woman's being in the labor force. Women gainfully employed are likely to look upon some expenses for food at home and for care of children as a cost of acquiring income. However, in the sets of data, outlays for such expenses are not deducted in estimating net income. It seems probable that, the greater the number of earners in a family, the more income tends to overstate net income in a strict sense of gross receipts less expense of acquiring income and the more consumption other than housing tends to be overstated.

Money income tends to understate the total income of owner-occupants, in that it does not include the income in kind from the equity of owners in the dwelling occupied. Thus, where the housing variable represents consumption and the income variable represents money income, housing consumption with income held constant, that is $h_y$, is likely to be higher for owners than tenants unless some offsetting condition is present that tends to raise H/Y for tenants. The urban survey of 1941 gives some notion as to the degree to which money income understates total income of urban consumer units in owner-occupied dwellings. It shows income in kind from the equity in owner units to be \$9 per \$100 of money income.[49]

Difference in assets by tenure may also contribute to the tendencies observed. Owners have assets in the form of their owner-occupied dwell-

48. In some surveys, for example the large-scale survey of 1935-36 of non-farm families, entrepreneurial income is defined as funds withdrawn from business for consumption and non-business savings including life insurance. Such withdrawals are likely to be highly correlated with consumption expenditure, including atypical expenditures for durable goods and medical services, for example.

49. See U.S. Department of Labor, Bul. 822, Table 22.

ing. Do tenants equal in $y_n$ tend to have comparable assets of some other type? If not, one would expect housing-income ratios of owners to be relatively high compared to those of tenants, even if income as defined included return on the equity of owner-occupants.

These characteristics of economic status by tenure bear on the interpretation of some tendencies described in later chapters.

## A Summing Up

This chapter reviews consumption theories and considers characteristics of income variables and ways of deriving reliable estimates in spite of unsatisfactory survey data reported. In addition, it provides some notion of the range in the coefficients of income elasticity to be explained if in fact housing with respect to normal income tends to be similar from place to place and time to time. Most of the coefficients presented in this chapter are drawn from the economic literature. They show coefficients of elasticity of housing with respect to income, of cross-section data, ranging from 0.1 to 2.0. The preliminary examination of this variation gives reason to expect that the permanent-income theory of consumption will explain much of it. A question for later chapters is how much? And are tendencies indicated by cross-section data consistent with those indicated by change through time?

This chapter has given main attention to the permanent-income theory of consumption. It has examined in considerable detail two of its main postulates as they pertain to housing: (a) that consumption of housing (h) is positively correlated with normal income, symbolized by $y_n$, and is uncorrelated with transitory income, symbolized by $y_t$; and (b) that $y_n$ and $y_t$ are uncorrelated. The evidence reviewed bearing on housing-income relations is wholly consistent with postulate (a). However, there seems reason to believe that postulate (b) does not represent all situations, namely the tendency for $y_t$ associated with cyclical change to be correlated with $y_n$ of consumer units. It seems likely, however, that such $y_t$ is much, much less important than $y_t$ uncorrelated with $y_n$.

The evidence reviewed leaves no reason to doubt that $y_t$ uncorrelated with $y_n$ tends to be uncorrelated with h and that some of the variance of y of surveys is almost certain to represent $y_t$. As a consequence, coefficients of elasticity of housing with respect to income of consumers ($\eta_{hy}$) are almost certain to understate $\eta_{hy_n}$.

How to hold constant this effect of $y_t$ is the main problem posed.

The evidence presented indicates that it is important and that there are ways of minimizing its effect. The use of an instrumental variable represents one such technique. An ideal instrumental variable is correlated with $y_n$ and uncorrelated with $y_t$ and is only related to h through its relationship with $y_n$. Under these conditions the average income of subsets of consumers differentiated by such an instrumental variable will yield observations where average housing with respect to average income will represent $\eta_{hy_n}$.

The use of an instrumental variable is not new. Average consumption with respect to average income of cities and occupational groups has long been examined. Such relationships are referred to as interclass correlations. What is new is the explicit recognition of the usefulness of interclass correlations for holding constant the effect of random error of an explanatory variable. The rationale for using such variables is discussed in this chapter. One estimate of a tendency observed for an interclass correlation is presented: namely, that of a preliminary report made in 1954 of the investigation represented by this monograph. It shows where census tracts are used as an instrumental variable that the income elasticity of housing with respect to average income tends to be around 2.0. The more complete evidence derived through the use of instrumental variables is presented in chapters vi-viii, and xiii.

Average housing and income of subsets, derived through the use of an instrumental variable, are symbolized by H and Y, respectively. If the instrumental variable is ideal for its purpose, then the coefficient of income elasticity of housing derived through the use of these averages will represent $\eta_{hy_n}$.

One other type of observation seems likely to be useful if one instrumental variable is not ideal. It involves the use of two instrumental variables and represents differences in H and Y between subsets, such as environs and the central city, for a set of metro areas. Such variables are symbolized by $H^*$ and $Y^*$, respectively. These seem likely to hold constant group conditions, such as the standard of and market price of housing correlated or suspected of being correlated with instrumental variables used.

The effect of a correlation between $y_t$ and $y_n$ cannot be held constant through the use of an instrumental variable. Where this correlation is present, it seems probable that some of the variance of Y represents $Y_t$, and that this will tend to lower the estimate of income elasticity of housing derived from the interclass correlations. However, there seems some reason to expect that much of $Y_t$ is uncorrelated with $Y_n$. If so, $Y_t$ can be dealt with in another manner appropriate to random errors, such as the evidence of both regressions. These tend at least to set the limits of the probable relation of H with respect to Y, provided these variables are free from systematic effects of other conditions. The use of the evidence of both regressions is a technique long used by statisticians in dealing with a random error in an explanatory variable such as income.

The permanent-income theory of consumption also seems to explain variation in level of housing observed when income is held constant. Where observations represent the housing-income curve of h with respect to y, h with y held constant is symbolized by $h_y$. Among groups, $h_y$ is found to be positively correlated with the average income, if Y of groups represents $Y_n$. However, if groups are similar with respect to $Y_n$ and variation in Y represents $Y_t$, then $h_y$ will be found to be negatively correlated with Y. Both these types of correlation have been noted in various analyses of survey data presented in economic literature. Each type of correlation has brought forth a different interpretation. The first tendency as manifested in total consumption with income (y) held constant constitutes the basis for the distributive income theory of consumption of Dorothy Brady and Rose Friedman and the standard of living theory of Duesenberry. This tendency is consistent with the permanent-income theory, and many examples presented in later chapters demonstrate that the permanent-income theory explains this along with other phenomena.

The opposite tendency, namely the negative correlation between $h_y$ and Y, reflects the effect of variation in $Y_t$ of groups. It is very pronounced where consumer units are differentiated by direction and magnitude of income change. Thus a negative correlation of $h_y$ and Y is to be expected if groups compared differ markedly in $Y_t$. Situations of this kind are seldom to be observed except where consumer units are stratified using very reliable evidence on direction and magnitude of income change. Little such information is available and such evidence is not an important feature of this monograph. Nevertheless, the tendency of $Y_t$ to influence the correlation of $h_y$ with Y is shown.

This chapter thus presents the rationale of the many types of income variables and of the many cross-section regressions[50] examined later.

---

50. Herman Wold, Demand Analysis (New York: John Wiley & Sons,

Two other reviews are, however, essential for setting the stage for the main evidence as to income effects, namely the heterogeneity of the housing variable, to be considered in the chapter that follows, and tendencies associated with size and composition of consumer units, to be considered thereafter. These obviously must be held constant if income effect alone is to be estimated.

---

1953), discusses the problems arising because of errors in income and consumption as reported by families, and the usefulness of various types of regressions.

# Chapter Three

# WHAT HOUSING IS REPRESENTED

Housing consumption of main dwelling unit occupied by households is the prime interest of this monograph. This represents the use of structures and sites. Together these will be referred to as "space."[1] Unfortunately, much of the information provided by censuses and surveys do not describe housing consumption accurately. Unless they are confined to a single housing market, the housing variation may represent consumption times price. In addition, many measures of housing represent services other than space, such as are often included in contract rent.

This chapter is devoted to a consideration of the housing variables that are used. The main topics are as follows: (a) information reported; (b) the housing variables; (c) contract versus gross rent; (d) free versus controlled markets; (e) public versus private housing; (f) housing-income relations by tenure, and (g) owner-occupancy by income of consumer units. Special attention is given to the housing data reported by the Census of Housing of 1950 and the 1950 urban consumption survey.

## Information Reported

Information on housing differs by source of data. The Census of Housing of 1950 reports the value of one-unit[2] owner-occupied structures and contract[3] and gross rent of tenant units. The value of the units

1. The use of this term in chap. x is an exception. There housing space refers to all residential housing.

2. The Census of Housing of 1950 differs from that of 1940 in that no attempt was made to estimate the value of owner-occupied units in structures of two or more units or those attached to a place of business. In many cities of the Northeast these are an important part of the stock.

3. The Census of Housing of 1950 differs from that of 1940 in that

in owner-occupancy is estimated market value,[4] contract rent is the monthly contract rent of the dwelling occupied, and gross rent is contract rent adjusted to exclude cost of furniture and furnishings and to include outlays for heat and light not included in contract rent.[5] The consumption survey of 1950 reports expenditure for housing. For some strata of consumer units this information is reported by tenure. However, for many relationships examined, housing expenditure is reported only for consumer units irrespective of tenure. For these the housing variable is very heterogeneous, since housing expenditure represents a different portion of housing consumption of owner-occupants than of tenants.

The housing variables of the census and the consumption survey differ in other respects. For one thing, the census is confined to households, whereas the consumption survey of 1950 includes consumer units who were lodgers. The lodger subset of the consumption survey is likely to be important among consumer units of one person. The two sources also differ in the time represented. The census represents housing at the time of the census, that is around April 1, 1950, whereas the consumption survey represents the housing of the entire year of 1950. However, the coverage of a year rather than only the month of April does not seem to have affected appreciably tendencies later described.

---

no estimate is provided for tenant units for which rent is not directly charged, in other words for tenants units with so-called free rent. The Census of Housing of 1940 reports an estimated rent for these. For urban places their inclusion appears to have little effect on median rent reported. However, for rural non-farm places their exclusion tends to increase appreciably the median rent observed. For discussion of this difference between these censuses, see Margaret G. Reid, "Increase in Rent of Dwelling Units from 1940 to 1950," Journal of the American Statistical Association, July, 1959, pp. 358-76.

4. There has been a good deal of speculation as to the accuracy of values reported for owner-occupied units. One study indicates that considerable random reporting error occurs but that average values tend to be a good estimate, as judged by professional appraisers. See Leslie Kish and John B. Lansing, "Response Errors in Estimating the Value of Homes," Journal of the American Statistical Association, September, 1954, pp. 520-38.

5. The reporting error in contract rent seems likely to be very small, and much less than that of gross rent. For one thing, estimates of the rent represented by furniture and furnishings, excluded from estimated gross rent, are likely to be very crude and may well be affected by the degree of rent control prevailing. In addition, estimates of fuel and light bills are likely to be crude and are perhaps influenced by a seasonal condition.

## The Housing Variables

The main housing variable of this monograph is the value of one-unit owner-occupied structures. Its variation within a given market represents consumption. Where it represents a wide range in places, some of its variation seems likely to represent price. The effect of price on market value of dwellings is considered. However, value of dwelling unit, irrespective of any price effect, is symbolized by h. This symbol is also used to represent the estimated rental value of owner-occupied units. The 1940 census and some consumption surveys report such rental value,[6] and estimates of it are also made in order to compare the level of housing-income curves by tenure, as reported in the 1950 Census of Housing. Estimated rental value is assumed to be 10 per cent of the value reported[7] and to represent depreciation of and interest on capital including the equity of the owner, property taxes, and related costs. (The coefficients of income elasticity of housing are of course the same for value as for estimated rental value.) Thus h symbolizes either market value of dwelling units or a fixed percentage of that value. Where h also seems likely to represent consumption, this fact is noted.

For the purpose of this monograph, it would be desirable to have information on space rent of tenants. Contract rent of tenant units in one-unit structures comes fairly close to representing space rent, since it tends to have little additional services represented. The Census of Housing of 1950 reports such rent for such dwelling units. However, it does not report the income of tenants in such units. Thus these data do not serve the purpose of this monograph.

One large-scale study provides estimates of space rent, namely, the urban housing survey of 1933.[8] For it, space rent is defined as contract rent less the estimated cost of furnishings, refrigeration, gas, wa-

---

6. Some surveys, drawn upon in this monograph, notably those of 1935-36 and 1941, report rental value of owner units. The estimates come from the respondents, with perhaps some help from the interviewers. These provide no information as to value.

7. The Census of Housing of 1940 reports both the market value and the estimated rental value of owner units. For principal metropolitan districts, the estimated rental value of owner units is 11 per cent of their estimated market value (see U.S. Census of Housing: 1940).

8. See David Wickens, Financial Survey of Urban Housing (U.S. Bureau of Foreign and Domestic Commerce, 1937). (I failed to locate a precise statement as to how the cost of the additional services was estimated. The schedule did not provide for estimates by respondents.)

ter, heat, and the garage. Many of these costs are marginal, and during the Great Depression contract rent was probably much below average cost. Hence for this survey, representing the depths of the Great Depression, short-run supply conditions may have resulted in additional services being an abnormally high proportion of contract rent. Nevertheless, some tendencies indicated by these estimates of space rent are shown later. Space rent is symbolized by $h_s$.

Total expenditure for housing, reported by the consumption survey of 1950, includes expenditure for housing away from home. This represents expenditure for housing at school and for recreation. This type of housing expenditure tends to have a relatively high income elasticity among consumer units[9] and may well be positively correlated with transitory income. It is related to the age of head of consumer units. It reaches a peak at a time in the life cycle when children are most likely to be in college. Conditions affecting such expenditure seem likely to be different from those affecting expenditure for the main dwelling unit occupied. Unless otherwise specified, the housing variable of the consumption survey of 1950 used in this monograph is expenditure for the main dwelling unit.[10]

Housing expenditure is reported by tenure. That by tenants for their main dwelling unit, as reported in the consumption survey of 1950, seems to be quite comparable to contract rent as reported by the Census of Housing of 1950.[11] However, housing expenditure by owners constitutes

---

9. Expenditure for housing away from home constitutes 5.5 per cent of total housing. It has a relatively high income elasticity among consumer units, namely, 1.071 and its exclusion reduces the coefficient of income elasticity of housing expenditure from 0.472 to 0.436, a drop of 8 per cent.

10. This is reported in Vol. IV, op. cit., but not in Vol. II.

11. The consumption survey of 1950 reports expenditure by tenants for fuel, light, and refrigeration other than that included in contract rent. Expenditure for these utilities plus contract rent for the dwelling overstates gross rent as defined in the census to the extent that furnishings are paid for in contract rent.

There also seems some possibility that the consumption survey and the census differ in the treatment of rent-free units. I am under the impression that where rent is provided in lieu of wages that some allowance for rent is included in housing as reported in the consumption survey. (The published definitions provide no information.) Rent-free units are likely to be more important in the consumption survey than in the census in that the consumption survey represents consumer units who are domestic workers and the census represents only households. Domestic workers may be of considerable importance among one-person

a very different variable than estimated rental value as derived from the census of housing. It makes no allowance for the market value of the owner's equity. The gap thus created between consumption and expenditure is considered later.

The housing variables examined in this monograph are sufficiently different that it seems best to use different symbols. The main variables and their symbols are:

| Housing Represented | Symbol |
|---|---|
| Market value of or estimated rental value of owner units | $h$ |
| Contract rent of tenant units[12] | $h_r$ |
| Gross rent of tenant units | $h_{gr}$ |
| Housing expenditure of[13] | |
| a) owners | $h_e$ |
| b) consumer units irrespective of tenure | $h_{er}$ |

Of these variables, h is likely to be the most and $h_{er}$ the least homogeneous measure of housing consumption. The variable $h_{er}$ is, however, the main variable reported for the consumption survey of 1950. Estimates shown in chapter v make extensive use of this survey because of the scope of the information it provides for consumer units stratified by age of head, number of persons, occupation, and race as well as by income. Wherever feasible, estimates derived from this source are supplemented by estimates from the Census of Housing of 1950, where households are stratified by tenure and where the housing variable, especially that for owner-occupants, is fairly homogeneous.

## Contract versus Gross Rent

Contract rent represents more than space. Gross rent gives some

---

consumer units. This is of course only one of many conditions that may affect tendencies observed, especially when consumer units are stratified by number of persons.

12. The tenant units may be either households, the consumer units represented by the census data, or households plus lodgers, the consumer units represented by the housing data of the urban consumption survey of 1950. (The large-scale consumption surveys prior to 1941 were confined to families with husband and wife both present, and few of these are likely to have been lodgers.)

13. With few exceptions, expenditure for housing away from home is excluded.

indication of the things provided beyond space that are represented. As reported by the census, gross rent includes expenditure by tenants for utilities such as water, electricity, gas and other fuels, in addition to those included in contract rent. However, this amount is not added to contract rent reported. Instead it is added to contract rent less an estimate[14] of rent of furniture and furnishings included in contract rent.

It is not surprising that the gap between contract and gross rent varies among cities. In some cities contract rent is about one-half of gross rent, and in others it exceeds gross rent. The first condition seems likely to occur in cities with low winter temperature and with little heat and light represented in contract rent. These two conditions tend to coincide in New England. Contract rent in excess of gross rent tends to occur in cities with high winter temperature and where furnishings represented in contract rent are quite important, conditions that appear to coincide in cities where winter tourists are important, for example, Phoenix, Arizona, and Miami, Florida.[15]

Because contract rent of many units represents additional services, there seemed at the outset some possibility that gross rent might be better than contract rent as a proxy for housing consumption. The likelihood of this turns on whether the additional services in gross rent have much the same relation to normal income as the consumption of space. If they have, then gross is likely to be preferable to contract rent. But if they have not, increasing the importance in the housing variable of additional services may worsen rather than improve the housing variable as a means of estimating demand for space by tenants.

The consumption survey of 1950 reports expenditure for housing utilities, that is, fuel, light, and refrigeration. Among 49 cities such average expenditure by owner-occupants is positively correlated with average income. Measures of correlation are as follows:

$$x_{Fl} = -.625 + .801\, x_Y \qquad r^2 = .145 \qquad (3.1)$$

where Fl and Y are mean expenditure for housing utilities and income of owner-occupants, as reported in the consumption survey of 1950, with

---

14. This was presumably provided by tenants with or without the help of census enumerators. No information on it is provided in the published reports.

15. For example, median gross rent per $100 of contract rent in Boston and Providence is $138 and $156, respectively, whereas in Phoenix and Miami it is $94 and $91, respectively.

variables expressed in log form. Thus Y explains only 15 per cent of the variation among cities in Fl.

On the other hand 30 per cent of the variation in Fl is explained by mean January temperature. When this variable, symbolized by Jt for owners, is added to those of equation (3.1) the following correlation is observed:

$$x_{Fl} = .879 + .556\, x_Y - .402\, x_{Jt} \qquad R^2 = .361. \qquad (3.2)$$

Thus Y and Jt explain 36 per cent of the variation in Fl among cities, and Jt explains much more of it than Y. In addition, equation (3.2) indicates an elasticity of expenditure for housing utilities with respect to average income among cities of 0.556.[16] This is much less than that indicated for housing space (see chapts. vi ff.). In addition, the amount people are willing to pay for space seems little affected by climate, whereas housing utilities are much affected. Accordingly, in this monograph, contract rent is the principal housing variable used in an attempt to discover the relation of housing of tenants to normal income. Some attempts are made to hold constant the importance of additional services in contract rent. One variable used for this purpose is the ratio of gross to contract rent, that is, gross per $100 of contract rent. This is symbolized by g/c.[17] It seems likely to be no more than a very crude means of holding constant the extent to which contract rent overstates housing consumption.

---

16. This approximates the elasticity of food with respect to normal income. (Estimates from my unpublished manuscript entitled "Food and Income.") It may well be that food and housing utilities comprise much the same mixture of necessities and luxuries, as judged by consumer units.

17. To the extent that contract rent includes furnishings and furniture not represented in gross rent, this ratio tends to be lowered. Some indication of the extent of this lowering is provided by a comparison of the ratios of gross to contract rent as indicated by the data of the census and the consumption survey of 1950. Gross rent as reported by the consumption survey includes payment for furniture and furnishing represented by contract rent, whereas the census does not. For 47 places the mean g/c of the census is 116 and of the consumption study 123. This evidence implies that the exclusion of payment for furnishings and furniture from the estimate of gross rent as reported in the Census of Housing of 1950 lowered g/c by 6 per cent. The degree of lowering differs markedly among places represented. Among 47 cities the $r^2$ of the ratios is only 0.547. This $r^2$ suggests that if g/c is a good proxy for the importance of additional services in contract rent for the census it is a poor proxy for the consumption survey.

Some use is also made of the percentage of tenants[18] reported to have heat and other specified services paid for in contract rent, around the time of the Census of Housing of 1950. Variation in such percentage among places is discussed in chapter xi.

## Free versus Controlled Markets

Estimates of housing of 1950 seem likely to be influenced by rent control and restrictions on construction associated with World War II. These caused (a) a lag in the improvement of housing behind income change, and (b) contract rent understating market rent of existing stock. This monograph does not attempt to make a direct estimate of the effect of either of these conditions. Indirect estimates indicate that they are appreciable for tenant units of 1950. For owner-occupants, a free market for stock prevailed throughout the forties and the volume of construction during the late forties was high.[19] Tenant housing seems likely to have been affected by Federal controls imposed on contract rents in 1942, and continued to 1949, and by local controls in effect in some states and cities during 1950.[20]

Places undoubtedly differed in the extent to which tenant housing of 1950, in terms of either quality or rent paid, had adjusted to rise in demand occurring with increased income. In some places a considerable volume of new construction occurred during the late forties, and market demand determined the initial rent of these new units. New construction was especially important in places with increasing population. In other places, the volume of new construction from 1945 to the time of the census was small, and meager improvement in the stock constructed earlier seems not unlikely. Rent control may well have checked such improvement. Tenants may have been willing, in spite of increased income, to

18. The consumption survey of 1950 reports the percentage of tenants with expenditure for fuel, light, or refrigeration. Examination of the variation among cities in average expenditure by tenants for fuel, light, and refrigeration not included in contract rent gave no reason to suppose that this percentage is useful for holding constant the importance of additional services in contract rent in estimating the relation of housing consumption to income.

19. In metro areas of the United States, units constructed in 1945 or later constituted 17.2 per cent of the stock of owner units occupied in 1950. See U.S. Census of Housing, Col. II, Part 1, Table B-4.

20. For discussion of the federal rent act of 1949 and early increases in rent occurring with federal decontrol, see Monthly Labor Review, March, 1950, pp. 253-56.

accept low-quality housing at below market price rather than to pay the market price for a higher quality. In other words, if markets had been free, tenants probably would have demanded a higher quality even at a higher price.

### Public versus Private Housing

In relation to income of occupants, free market rents seem likely to differ from rents in public housing. Certainly they are subject to a different set of conditions. This monograph does not explore this difference. Comment is, however, made later on the possibility that public housing may account for certain tendencies observed among places differing markedly in the importance of tenant housing, the rent of which was determined by a public administrator. In 1949 its difference among places was appreciable. The U.S. Department of Labor reports that publicly financed units constituted 19 per cent of all tenant units of Seattle.[21] In many cities no such units existed or were a minor portion of the stock.

### Housing-Income Relations by Tenure

This section describes difference in housing-income ratios by tenure and how housing variables, peculiar to owner-occupants, affect the income elasticity of housing observed. It provides a frame of reference for the interpretation of tendencies described in later chapters.

Housing-Income Ratios by Tenure.—For the spring of 1950, the median annual estimated rent of owner-occupied units[22] of metro areas of the United States was $891, and the median annual contract rent of tenant units was $463. Owners, of course, had higher average income than tenants, median incomes being $3,884 and $3,044, respectively.[23] Annual rents per $100 of income, to be referred to as a housing-income ratio, are $22.9[24] and $15.2. Thus the tenure with the higher income devoted a higher percentage of income to housing. If rent control depressed average contract rent during the spring of 1950, it seems likely to have height-

21. See Monthly Labor Review, July, 1949, p. 46.

22. Those in 1-unit structures.

23. See Census of Housing: 1950. Vol. II, Nonfarm Housing Characteristics, chap. i, Table B-7.

24. Income is represented by money only. This tends to understate the total income of owners compared to tenants. Under the assumption that the net income from owner equity tends to be one-half of the estimated rental value of the owner units, this ratio is lowered to 20.6.

ened the difference observed between tenures for 1950.

The consumption survey of 1941 permits a similar estimate in a free market, with estimates of rental value of owner dwelling units provided by respondents. That survey indicates housing-income ratios of owner and tenant units of $16.6 and $15.1, repsectively.[25] Here also the tenure with the higher income has the higher housing-income ratio[26] in spite of the fact that contract rent of tenants includes additional services, tending thus to overstate housing consumption. However, the difference by tenure is much, much less than that observed for 1950. It raises the question as to whether rent control was responsible for this difference by tenure between years or something else. An increase occurred between 1940 and 1950 in the importance of services included in rent. This, in a free market, would be expected to raise the rent-income ratio of tenants compared to that of owners.

Housing Expenditure-Income Ratios by Tenure.—The consumption survey of 1950 reports housing expenditure for four types of owners as well as for tenants. Data for these are shown in Table 1. Average income of the four categories of owner-occupants is quite similar, when account is taken of variation in the age of head of consumer units. Yet the ratio of housing to income, namely housing expenditure per $100 of income, ranges from $8 to $17. The longer the period of time that had elapsed since acquiring the dwelling unit, the lower is this ratio. Thus, among these four sets of owner-occupants, the housing expenditure-income ratio is least for owners with the lowest income and the highest average age of head. This seems likely to reflect the fact that the older the head the less are the interest payments on the mortgage, because of the greater importance of owners' equity. It may also reflect the lag in taxes on residential property during inflation. In such a situation it would not be surprising to find that the more recent the purchase the higher tends to be the tax-value ratio.[27]

The housing expenditure of owners in general is less than that of tenants in spite of their much higher income. The consumption survey

---

25. See U.S. Bureau of Labor Statistics, Bul. 822, Table 22. The estimates shown represent full-year owners and tenants exclusive of lodgers.

26. The ratio for owner falls from 16.6 to 15.3, where income of owners is represented by money income plus income in kind from owner-occupied dwelling.

27. Data to test this supposition are not available.

Table 1

Housing Expenditure-Income Ratios and Related Characteristics, Urban Consumer Units, by Tenure, Consumption Survey, 1950

| Tenure | Per cent of all consumer units (1) | Disposable income (2) | Housing expenditure[a] | | Age of head (years) (5) | Persons (6) | Full-time earners (7) |
|---|---|---|---|---|---|---|---|
| | | | As reported (3) | Per $100 of income (4) | | | |
| 1. Owner all year | | | | | | | |
| a. Bought in 1950 | 1.2 | $4,695 | $764 | $16.3 | 45 | 3.5 | 0.9 |
| b. Bought in 1946-49 | 16.5 | 4,647 | 412 | 8.9 | 43 | 3.5 | 1.0 |
| c. Bought before 1946 | 27.5 | 4,356 | 326 | 7.5 | 55 | 3.1 | 0.9 |
| 2. Owner end of year, renter earlier | 3.2 | 4,437 | 684 | 15.4 | 38 | 3.2 | 0.9 |
| 3. All owners | 48.4 | 4,469 | 390 | 8.7 | 50 | 3.3 | 0.9 |
| 4. Renter, end of year | 51.5 | $3,384 | $438 | $12.9 | 43 | 2.8 | 0.9 |

Source: Study of Consumer Expenditures Incomes and Savings. Statistical Tables, Urban U.S., 1950 (Philadelphia, Pa.: University of Pennsylvania, 1956), Vol. XVIII, Table 6. Tabulated by the U.S. Bureau of Labor Statistics for the Wharton School of Finance and Commerce.

a. Housing expenditure pertains to the main dwelling unit.

of 1950 shows average income of owners exceeding that of tenants by 32 per cent.

These ratios imply several things: (a) that housing expenditure greatly understates the consumption of owners compared to that of tenants because housing expenditure of owners omits the housing represented by the equity of owners; (b) that the degree of the understatement varies among owners; (c) that the understatement tends to increase with lapse of time since purchase, and (d) that it is likely to be greatest among owners with an aged head.

The Gap for Owners between Housing Expenditure and Consumption.— The urban consumption survey of 1941 reports both housing expenditure and estimated rental value of owner units. If the latter represents market value, then this survey provides an estimate of the extent of the gap between housing expenditure and market value. For owner-occupants, this survey shows housing expenditure to be about 48 per cent of the estimated rental value of owner units.[28] Estimated rental value is $17.7 and housing expenditure $8.0 per $100 of income.

The extent of this gap varies with measured income (y). For urban owner-occupants the higher is y, the smaller tends to be the gap. For example, housing expenditure per $100 of estimated rental value of the dwelling units is $29 for owner-occupants with y under $1,000 and $64 for those with y of $5,000 or more.

Because of this variation by y in the gap between housing consumption and expenditure, $\eta_{h_e y}$ is much higher than $\eta_{hy}$. For the urban owner-occupants of the survey of 1941; these coefficients are 0.672 and 0.418, respectively. Thus $\eta_{h_e y}$ is 64 per cent higher than $\eta_{hy}$. This is the kind of difference to expect[29] if the purchase of the dwelling and the early

28. Estimated from data of Bul. 822, Table 22, op. cit. Only owner-occupants throughout the entire survey year are represented. The Consumer Purchases Study of 1935-36 show a similar difference. The publications of this survey are cited in the bibliography.

29. It is also the tendency to expect if the gap between housing expenditure and consumption of owner-occupants tends to be less in places of high than of low income. Two conditions could contribute to this: the period of acquiring full equity is longer or the tax rate on residential property is higher in places of high than of low income. No attempt is made in this monograph to estimate the likelihood of these conditions. The evidence presented does demonstrate, however, that some of the tendencies observed are a function of income change with age and the timing of payment for owner units. It is sufficient to sound a warning note about hasty interpretation of tendencies observed where housing of owners is represented by expenditure.

stage of ownership, when interest payment is high, tend to occur during years of high income, or if expenditure for repairs and replacement tend to be positively correlated with $y_t$.[30]

## Owner-Occupancy by Income of Consumer Units

Where the housing variable is expenditure, irrespective of tenure, tendencies observed may be influenced by the distribution of owner-occupancy by income. In general, owner-occupancy is relatively high at low income, falls from low to moderate income, and then rises from moderate to high income. This non-linear relationship with income is related to the distribution of age by income, a characteristic of consumer units considered in the chapter that follows. With age of head held constant, owner-occupancy is more important among consumer units of high than low income.

The distribution of owner-occupancy by income is described by the number of owner-occupants above the median income of all consumer units per 100 owner-occupants below such median income. This index is symbolized by $o_y$. For all urban consumer units of 1950, $o_y$ is 147. This is one of the explanatory variables used in later chapters. In general, the higher $o_y$ the greater tends to be the gap, at high compared to low incomes, between housing value and expenditure.

## A Summing Up

Information on housing consumption comes from many sources. In them, housing is described in a variety of ways. Some difference in definition has an important bearing on tendencies observed. Thus, in making comparison among sources, it is of the utmost importance to take into account what is represented by the housing variable. Tendencies observed may represent merely lack of comparability in housing represented: additional services in contract rent differ markedly from place to place and have had an upward trend.

If prices are held constant, the potential rental value of owner-occupied units probably may come fairly close to describing housing consumption or at least representing difference in housing within a given market. The contract rent of households, as reported by censuses and

---

30. Such a correlation is consistent with the expectation that outlays for consumer capital tend to be positively correlated with $y_t$.

various surveys, rates second in its suitability. Its usefulness is impaired by additional services, beyond space, paid for in contract rent. Even so, it seems likely that contract rent is a better variable than gross rent for estimating the demand of tenants for housing space. This conclusion rests on evidence that the elasticity of demand for housing utilities, such as heat, fuel, and light, with respect to normal income is much lower than that for housing space and that demand for housing utilities is much affected by climate. Hence, the less the additional services represented by the housing variable, the more likely is it to be a good proxy for space.

Housing expenditure by tenants approximates contract rent and thus has the same defects as contract rent. For owners, housing expenditure tends greatly to understate market value of such housing, and furthermore the gap between housing expenditure and such market value tends to be especially marked among consumer units with an aged head and consequently with low current income. The size of the gap is large because households with an aged head tend to concentrate at low incomes. The owner-occupants at the low point on the age-income cycle tend to have their mortgage almost or entirely paid off, so interest payments tend to be low. Hence housing expenditure tends greatly to understate their consumption. At higher incomes the owner-occupants are likely to be in the early stages of payment for their dwelling unit. Hence, for owner-occupants, the higher is measured income, the less the gap between housing expenditure and consumption. Consequently, among owner-occupants the income elasticity of housing expenditure is higher than that of market value.

In general, housing expenditure is not so useful a measure of market value of housing as either estimated rental value of owner units or contract rent of tenant units. Nevertheless, extensive use is made of this variable in this monograph because of the large volume of data available on housing expenditure and the need of understanding tendencies observed in such data. (They are widely used for estimating housing-income relations.)

Tendencies observed where markets are free and where they are controlled seem likely to vary. Conditions that may need to be taken into account include rent control, in the process of being relaxed in 1950, restrictions on residential construction during much of the forties, and the growth of tenant housing financed by public funds and its variation among cities. There seems no doubt that these conditions affect some of the tendencies observed for tenant housing. They probably had little effect on those observed for value of owner-occupied units.

# Chapter Four

# WHAT PERSONS ARE REPRESENTED

Housing-income ratios differ by size and composition of consumer units. These are reviewed in this chapter. Its main topics are: (a) the gap between persons represented by housing and by income; (b) age of head of consumer unit; (c) normal versus non-normal households; (d) number of persons per consumer unit; (e) consumer units by age of children; (f) number of full-time earners per consumer unit, and (g) demographic characteristics by income of consumer units.

Housing observed differs with number of persons and age and sex of members, and housing-income ratios differ even more. The number of persons per consumer unit, commonly referred to as size, is the information most frequently available as to persons represented by housing as measured. Where it refers to separate consumer units it is symbolized by s, and where it refers to the average size of a group, such as the consumer units of a city, it is symbolized by S. Sex of head and age of members are other characteristics of persons that affect housing-income ratios, and the permutations and combinations of age, sex, and number of persons reaches astronomical magnitudes.

## The Gap between Persons Represented by Housing and by Income

To appreciate the gap between the persons represented by the housing and the income, it is necessary to review definitions of consumer and income units. The consumer unit of the census data is a household. It consists of all persons occupying a dwelling unit.[1] There may be one

1. Dwelling units are confined to living quarters with less than five lodgers.

person or two or more persons. Each household has a head and the income reported is that of the head and of all persons in the household related to the head. There may be other persons with income present, such as lodgers and domestic workers. Their income is not represented by the income reported for the household, although their consumption is.

For the census of housing, the presence of lodgers in dwelling units is the main condition accounting for a gap between persons represented by housing and by income. These have been declining in importance. For the United States, from 1940 to 1950, lodgers per 100 private households fell from 12.8 to 8.5. Still they are of sufficient importance and differ among groups within the population so that they are likely to influence some tendencies observed.

For urban places of 1950 there were 10 lodgers per 100 households[2] (see Table 2). This ratio differs by race, being 9 for white and 29 for non-white households. Measured in terms of lodgers per 100 persons in private households, a similar difference by race is observed. Thus one would expect that the housing variable reported for non-white households overstates appreciably the housing of primary units represented by income.

Table 2

Number of Lodgers per 100 Urban Households and Persons by Race and Region

| Region | Per 100 households | | | Per 100 persons | | |
|---|---|---|---|---|---|---|
| | All (1) | White (2) | Non-white (3) | All (4) | White (5) | Non-white (6) |
| 1. All | 10.4 | 8.6 | 29.1 | 3.2 | 2.6 | 8.1 |
| 2. Northeast | 9.7 | 8.0 | 38.7 | 2.9 | 2.4 | 10.6 |
| 3. North Central | 10.9 | 9.2 | 36.1 | 3.3 | 2.8 | 9.9 |
| 4. South | 11.8 | 9.0 | 23.0 | 3.5 | 2.7 | 6.4 |
| 5. West | 8.7 | 7.9 | 26.5 | 2.9 | 2.7 | 7.6 |

Source: U.S. Census of Population: 1950, Vol. II, Tables 107 and 148.

2. No private household has more than 5 lodgers who are unrelated to the head of the house. Where more lodgers are present the place of living is classed as a quasi-household. This definition may have resulted in much of the extreme overcrowding, through doubling up of potential households, being unrepresented by the Census of Housing of 1950.

Lodgers per household head also vary by region, especially those of urban non-white households. For these the range per 100 households is from 23 in the South to 39 in the North Central region. The greater importance of lodgers in non-white households of the North and West than the South seems likely to be related to the net migration of non-white population from the South to the North and West. Lodging is one of the stages on the way to getting established in a new place. Furthermore, lodgers are a very mobile segment of the population and their importance may well be indicative of cyclical employment opportunity.

The value and rent of dwelling units reported by censuses represent space occupied by all members of households, including lodgers. On a pro rata basis, the housing of persons represented by income tends to be overstated by 3 per cent of white and 9 per cent for non-white households.

Consumption survey of 1950 represents a somewhat different universe than a census of housing. It includes persons in quasi-households, such as hotels and lodging houses, whereas the census of housing is confined to dwelling units. The consumption surveys also differ in that some of the consumer units represented are lodgers in dwelling units. The gap between persons represented by the housing and the income variables can best be seen by noting how a household with lodgers is represented. The head of such a household reports gross[3] expenditure made for housing, and each lodger unit within the household also reports any housing expenditure made. The total expenditure reported by persons living in the household is the sum of such expenditures. Thus, between subsets of the population differing with respect to lodgers, double counting of housing may vary appreciably in that it represents expenditure reported by the primary unit and by lodgers. The extent of double counting will depend on the degree to which expenditure by lodgers represents service other than space. For the consumption survey of 1950, double counting seems likely to be appreciable for non-white households.

The heterogeneity of the housing variable introduced by the presence of lodgers is only one of many conditions that confound estimates of demand for housing with respect to income as derived from survey and census data.

3. Some consumption surveys deduct from the housing expenditure of consumer units with household status a pro rata share of space occupied by lodgers. This practice is followed in some surveys made in the United Kingdom.

## Age of Head of Consumer Unit

Several conditions would lead one to expect housing consumption-income ratios to vary with age of head: In the first place, income tends to change with age; this change is likely to be anticipated, and housing decisions seem likely to have a long horizon, if only because changing a dwelling unit entails economic and, perhaps, social cost also. In the second place, change in income with age of head tends to be positively correlated with change in number of persons per consumer unit, and, with increase in number of persons, an increased percentage of total expenditure tends to go to things other than housing, such as food and clothing. This would tend to restrict any increase in housing associated with increase in income from youth to middle years and also to minimize any decrease in housing associated with the decrease in income after the peak of income or of family size is passed. A further condition is present where housing is represented by expenditure, namely the increasing gap with greater age between housing consumption and expenditure, since with higher age the frequency of owner-occupancy and the extent of the equity of owners both tend to increase.

Three sets of data describing housing and income by age of head are shown in Tables 3, 4, and 5. Those of Table 3 come from the Census of Housing of 1950. They describe estimated rental value of owner units, contract rent of tenant units, and the income of the primary units of the respective sets.[4] Those of Tables 4 and 5 come from the consumption survey of 1950. The first represents all consumer units irrespective of tenure, and the second shows data by tenure as well as age.

All sets of data have one thing in common; income first increases with age of head and then decreases. The peak income tends to occur where head is around 50 years of age.[5] For all consumer units of the

---

4. The households represented by the census data shown in Table 3 are not strictly comparable to those represented by the data of Tables 4 and 5 from the consumption survey: the census data shown include no broken families or single consumer units nor any with unrelated persons present, whereas data of the consumption survey represent all consumer units.

5. The Consumer Finance Survey of the Federal Reserve Board shows the peak income of 1950, among spending units of the spring of 1951, occurring when head is around 40 years of age. This lower level seems likely to be due to the division of families resulting from the definition of spending unit, for example the tendency to report sons and daughters living with parents as separate spending units, whereas the

consumption survey, average income of such units is about 50 per cent higher than average income of consumer units with head under 25 years,

Table 3

Rent and Income, Normal[a] Households, Metro Stratum of the United States, by Tenure and Age of Head, Census of Housing, 1950[b]

| Age of head of household[c] (in years) | Estimated or contract rent[b] (1) | Income[d] (2) | Rent per $100 of income (3) | Number of persons (4) |
|---|---|---|---|---|
| | A. Owner-occupants | | | |
| Under 35 | $850 | $3,738 | $22.7 | 3.7 |
| 35 - 45 | 943 | 4,273 | 22.1 | 4.0 |
| 45 - 55 | 978 | 4,587 | 21.3 | 3.4 |
| 55 - 65 | 907 | 4,106 | 22.1 | 2.7 |
| 65 or more | 788 | 2,525 | 31.2 | 2.4 |
| Mean[e] of subsets | 893 | 3,846 | 23.2[f] | 3.2 |
| | B. Tenant-occupants | | | |
| Under 35 | 471 | 3,296 | 14.3 | 3.1 |
| 35 - 45 | 470 | 3,653 | 12.9 | 3.6 |
| 45 - 55 | 488 | 3,843 | 12.7 | 3.0 |
| 55 - 65 | 482 | 3,552 | 13.6 | 2.5 |
| 65 or more | 445 | 2,162 | 20.6 | 2.3 |
| Mean[e] of subsets | $471 | $3,301 | $14.8[f] | 2.9 |

Source: Vol. II, chapter 1, Tables B-1, B-2, B-7, and B-8.

a. The data represent all standard metropolitan areas of the United States, referred to here as the U.S. metro stratum. All averages represent medians.

b. For owners this is 10 per cent of the median value of one-unit structures. For tenants it is median monthly contract rent expressed at an annual rate.

c. Households with a husband and wife and with no non-relatives present. For other households, information is reported for only three age categories (see Table 6).

d. Money income of 1949, before taxes, of primary units of the 1950 households. For owners, income represents those in all types of structure, whereas the estimated rent shown represents only one-unit structures.

e. Each subset has a weight of one.

f. Computed from the estimated means of the subsets.

and more than twice that of consumer units with head 75 years of age or more.[6]

The difference with age in rent of or expenditure for housing is positively correlated with the difference in income. It first rises with age and then falls (see Table 3). However, the difference in expenditure for housing with age of head is minor compared to difference in income.

Where housing is represented by expenditure, difference in housing and income with age has a greater positive correlation for owners than tenants. It has already been noted in chapter iii that the peak of expenditure for interest on mortgages probably occurs at an age when income tends to be relatively high.

The interaction of income and housing is such that housing-income ratios tend to be high for households or consumer units with an aged head, moderately high for those with a young head, and relatively low for those with a middle-aged head. This pattern is apparent[7] for the sets of data shown in Tables 3, 4, and 5. It is also of interest to note that the rise in housing expenditure-income ratios between consumer units with head around 50 and 65 years of age or more is appreciably less for owners than tenants and is less for owners who bought before 1946 than for those who bought during 1946 through 1949 (see Table 5).

The small variation in housing with age of head of households, in spite of an appreciable variation in income, is not surprising if consumers tend to have a relatively long horizon in planning their housing. The failure of housing to rise more than slightly with increase in income from youth to middle age may be the result of a rise in number of persons per consumer unit. The addition of another person to a household changes the allocation of the total expenditure among various products: Expenditure for food and clothing tends to increase much more than ex-

---

census reports them as part of the primary units of households. (Data are shown in Federal Reserve Bulletin, August, 1951, Table 17.) A similar tendency is shown for other years in the United States and also in the United Kingdom for 1953. See Harold Lydall, "The Life Cycle on Income, Savings and Asset Ownership," Econometrica, April, 1955, p. 139.

6. Thus difference in income with age of head accounts for much of the inequality of incomes observed among consumer units in general.

7. There is one exception. The housing expenditure-income ratios of consumer units with head under 35 years of age, and buying during 1946 through 1949, are relatively low. They may well reflect the lower interest rate available for veterans, and their heavy concentration in this age category.

Table 4

Housing Expenditure, Income[a] and Related Characteristics, Urban Consumer Units, by Age of Head, Consumption Survey, 1950

| Age of head of consumer units (years) | Per cent all consumer units (1) | Disposable income (2) | Housing expenditure | | Per cent with owner occupancy (5) | Persons (6) | Full-time earners (7) |
|---|---|---|---|---|---|---|---|
| | | | As reported (3) | Per $100 of income (4) | | | |
| Under 25 | 3.8 | $3,050 | $386 | $12.7 | 13 | 2.5 | 0.8 |
| 25 - 35 | 21.8 | 3,876 | 446 | 11.5 | 34 | 3.3 | 0.9 |
| 35 - 45 | 23.1 | 4,464 | 458 | 10.3 | 50 | 3.6 | 1.0 |
| 45 - 55 | 20.4 | 4,500 | 431 | 9.6 | 54 | 3.1 | 1.0 |
| 55 - 65 | 16.4 | 3,850 | 384 | 10.0 | 59 | 2.6 | 0.9 |
| 65 - 75 | 10.4 | 2.687 | 322 | 12.0 | 59 | 2.1 | 0.5 |
| 75 or more | 4.1 | 2,161 | 298 | 13.8 | 60 | 1.9 | 0.3 |
| 65 or more | 14.5 | 2,538 | 315 | 12.4 | 59 | 2.0 | 0.4 |
| All | 100.0 | $3,910 | $414 | $10.6 | 48 | 3.0 | 0.9 |

Source: Vol. XVIII, Table 1.

a. All averages are means.

Table 5

Housing Expenditure and Income, Consumer Units in Large Cities and Suburbs, by Tenure and Age of Head, Consumption Survey, 1950[a]

| Tenure and age of head of consumer unit (years) | Per cent of all consumer units[b] (1) | Income[c] (2) | Expenditure for housing: As reported (3) | Expenditure for housing: Per $100 of income (4) |
|---|---|---|---|---|
| | A. Owners: Bought before 1946 | | | |
| 1. Under 35[d] | 1.0 | $4,313 | $333 | $7.7 |
| 2. 35 - 45 | 4.0 | 5,075 | 348 | 6.9 |
| 3. 45 - 55 | 5.7 | 5,337 | 372 | 7.0 |
| 4. 55 - 65 | 5.4 | 4,350 | 337 | 7.7 |
| 5. 65 or more | 5.0 | 2,986 | 285 | 9.5 |
| 6. Mean of 5 subsets[e] | . . . | 4,412 | 335 | 7.6 |
| | B. Owners: Bought 1946 through 1949 | | | |
| 1. Under 25 | 0.5 | 3,807 | 341 | 9.0 |
| 2. 25 - 35 | 3.9 | 4,577 | 406 | 8.9 |
| 3. 35 - 45 | 4.4 | 5,323 | 486 | 9.1 |
| 4. 45 - 55 | 2.5 | 4,912 | 440 | 9.0 |
| 5. 55 - 65 | 1.5 | 4,541 | 359 | 7.9 |
| 6. 65 or more | 0.9 | 2,404 | 291 | 12.1 |
| 7. Mean of 5 subsets[f] | . . . | 4,334 | 395 | 9.1 |
| | C. Tenants: End of Year | | | |
| 1. Under 25 | 3.0 | 2,910 | 394 | 13.5 |
| 2. 25 - 35 | 12.0 | 3,628 | 468 | 12.9 |
| 3. 35 - 45 | 10.0 | 3,742 | 469 | 12.5 |
| 4. 45 - 55 | 8.0 | 3,708 | 491 | 13.2 |
| 5. 55 - 65 | 5.8 | 3,238 | 470 | 14.5 |
| 6. 65 or more | 4.8 | 2,049 | 380 | 18.6 |
| 7. Mean of 5 subsets[f] | . . . | $3,240 | $453 | $14.0 |

Source: Vol. IV, Table 19, for large cities and suburbs of the three regions.

a. Data of small cities are omitted because of the additional computation necessitated for their inclusion. There seems no reason to suppose that tendencies for large cities and suburbs of the three regions do not represent consumer units in general. In addition confining the estimates to large cities and suburbs increases the comparability between the estimates shown in this table and those of Table 3 of the metro stratum.

b. The data shown here represent 78 per cent of all urban units.

c. Disposable income.

d. There are very, very few consumer units under 25 years of age in this category.

e. Each subset has a weight of one.

f. For these averages, consumers units with head under 35 years of age are combined. This procedure increases the comparability among the tenure subsets. Each subset has a weight of one.

penditure for or consumption of housing. Similarly when income declines from middle to old age, number of persons per consumer unit tends to decline. This reduces the demand for food and clothing, and leaves a larger percentage of the total budget for housing.

These things by no means include all conditions that may contribute to variation in housing-income ratios with age of head. Another is the variation with age of head in number of earners and the fact that job-related expenses classed as consumption may result in net income's overstating the extent of change in net income with age of head. This type of expense is discussed later in this chapter (see pp. 80-83).

Even though, on the average, housing-income ratios tend to be high for consumer units with an aged head, they vary widely among such consumer units. The extent of labor force participation of family members, including that of the head, may be a contributing factor. Age as an index of the stage reached in the family-income cycle is complicated by the tendency for the income cycle to vary among occupations. For example, where head is a salaried professional, peak income of families tends to be reached around 60 years of age and where he is an unskilled worker it tends to be reached around 40 years of age.[8]

### Normal versus Non-normal Households

Data shown in Table 3 describe difference in housing and income by age of head for five categories representing normal households. (A normal household is one with a male head having his wife but without a non-relative present.) For the U.S. metro stratum these are 77 per cent of owner and 69 per cent of tenant households. Information is also provided for three age-of-head categories for two types of non-normal households:[9] (a) those with a male head with wife absent or a non-relative

---

8. Estimates derived from data shown in Study of Consumer Expenditures Incomes and Savings: Statistical Tables, Urban U.S.—1950 (Processed report; Philadelphia: University of Pennsylvania, 1957), Vol. XVIII, Table 9.

9. Data for these household types are not reported for the 1950 urban consumption survey. It does report for the 9 urban areas average income and housing expenditure by sex of head. For large cities in the North, the housing expenditure-income ratios of consumer units with a male head is 10.5 and with a female head, 16.2. A smaller percentage of owner-occupants among consumer units with a female rather than a male head, and a higher average age of female than male head, probably contributes to this difference. In general, consumer units with a female

present, and (b) those with a female head, with or without a non-relative present. Characteristics associated with non-normal households appear to differ from those of normal households, within specified age-of-head categories. Some of these differences are now briefly reviewed.

Average rental value of owner units (H), contract rent of tenant units ($H_r$) and income of the primary unit of households (Y) are shown in Table 6 for two age-of-head categories of non-normal households with a male or a female head, together with averages for normal households of comparable categories. In general, housing tends to be somewhat lower and Y appreciably lower for non-normal than for normal households. By comparison, housing-income ratios are high for non-normal households. Between the two types of non-normal households, housing is somewhat less for those with a female than a male head, and income is very much less. Hence housing-income ratios of households with a female head tend to be especially high.

Data available do not permit a further breakdown of these categories for the purpose of testing the effect of conditions suspected of contributing to the tendencies shown in Table 6. A definitive analysis would probably involve one in a host of conditions. Some non-normal households represent households on their way to becoming normal. Such a change occurs when a husband-wife household feels that income has reached a point where it is no longer necessary to have a lodger present. Other non-normal households are fragments of former normal households which may or may not return to the normal category. For any one household, the stage of being non-normal seems more likely to be associated with a negative than a positive $y_t$, as when the absence of a wife makes a household non-normal and at the same time puts the income below its former norm. One thing is obvious: these categories are unstable in the life history of consumers and of income recipients.

Speculation and a little indirect evidence are all I have to offer to explain the differences in housing-income ratios between normal and non-normal households shown in Table 6. They bear on four points: the presence of lodgers, special circumstances of female heads, age difference not held constant, and lag of housing behind change in $y_n$.

a) Housing of non-normal households tends to overstate the con-

---

head concentrate at low income levels and thus tend to lower the slope of housing-income regressions among consumer units in general. (For data on housing expenditure by sex of head, see ibid., Vol. IV, Table 12.)

sumption of persons represented by income. Among non-normal owner and tenant households of two or more persons, 40 and 70 per cent, respectively, had a non-relative present, and many of these undoubtedly were lodgers sharing indirectly in the cost of the dwelling unit occupied. The presence of lodgers may account for the fact that for owner households with male head the average number of persons per household is

Table 6

Rent and Income of Normal[a] and Non-normal Households,[b] Metro Stratum of the United States, by Tenure and by Sex and Age of Head, Census of Housing, 1950[a]

| Sex and age of head and household type | Estimated or contract rent[c] (1) | Income[c] (2) | Rent per $100 of income (3) | Number of persons (4) |
|---|---|---|---|---|
| | A. Owner-Occupants | | | |
| 1. Male | | | | |
| a) 45 - 65 years | | | | |
| 1) Normal | $949 | $4,379 | $21.6 | 3.0 |
| 2) Non-normal | 896 | 3,654 | 24.5 | 3.2 |
| b) 65 years or more | | | | |
| 1) Normal | 788 | 2,525 | 31.2 | 2.4 |
| 2) Non-normal | 806 | 1,990 | 40.5 | 2.6 |
| 2. Female | | | | |
| a. 45 - 65 years | 844 | 2,074 | 40.7 | 2.3 |
| b. 65 years or more | 781 | 968 | 80.7 | 2.0 |
| | B. Tenant-Occupants | | | |
| 1. Male | | | | |
| a) 45 - 65 years | | | | |
| 1) Normal | 486 | 3,740 | 13.0 | 2.8 |
| 2) Non-normal | 409 | 2,617 | 15.6 | 1.9 |
| b) 65 years or more | | | | |
| 1) Normal | 445 | 2,162 | 20.6 | 2.3 |
| 2) Non-normal | 338 | 1,021 | 33.1 | 1.5 |
| 2. Female | | | | |
| a) 45 - 65 years | 446 | 1,881 | 42.2 | 1.8 |
| b) 65 years or more | $401 | $ 817 | $15.1 | 1.4 |

Source: Vol. II, chapter 1, Tables B-1, B-2, B-7, and B-8.

a. Normal households only are represented in Table 3.

b. Non-normal households are those with a female head or a male head without wife present or with a non-relative present.

c. For definitions, see Table 3.

higher for non-normal than normal households. For these, the higher is the number of persons the higher is H/Y, whereas the opposite tendency is more usual. (Tendencies by household size are considered below.)

b) A variety of conditions seems likely to contribute to the unusually high housing-income ratio of households with a female head. For them, lodgers seem more likely to be present than for non-normal households with a male head. The income of some female heads is depressed by inability to earn because of the presence of small children. This tends to be a temporary condition, and average income is, as it were, depressed by negative $Y_t$. In addition, it seems not unlikely for female heads that average error in reporting income tends to be negative. Probable behavior indicated by some reports makes this seem likely. For all age-of-head categories, income from public funds is important for female heads, and such income becomes available only by meeting a means test. Understatement of income in such a situation seems likely, and such behavior may well carry over to the reporting of income whatever the situation.

c) The income reported by non-normal more than normal households seems likely to understate $y_n$ at the time the decision was made to occupy the present dwelling unit, in that the non-normal households are further past the peak of the age-income cycle than are normal households. The age-of-head categories of the census are much too broad to exclude variation in age of head between non-normal and normal households within the same category. Within an age-of-head category, the higher the age of head the greater tends to be the importance of non-normal households. For the category 45 to 65 years the number of non-normal households per 100 normal households by age and sex of head is given in Table 7.[10]

The tendency for non-normal households to rise in importance with higher age of head is very striking for heads 65 years of age or more (Table 8).[11] Thus it seems probable that some of the tendency for a housing-income ratio to be higher for non-normal than normal households is an age phenomenon.

d) It seems highly probable that the fragmentation of normal households such as occurs with the death of a spouse or separation or divorce

10. See Census of Population: 1950, Tables 105 and 107.

11. As of 1950 life expectancy at 60 years was 15.8 for males and 18.6 for females. See Historical Statistics of the United States, (Washington, D.C.: Government Printing Office, 1960).

of spouses is more likely to bring a decline than an increase in income. Furthermore, the decline experienced seems likely on the average to be greater where the emergent non-normal household has a female than where it has a male head. In addition, it seems highly probable that much of the fragmentation involved in the break-up of a family was not antici-

Table 7

Number of Non-normal Households by Age and Sex of Head per 100 Normal Households, by Age of Head (45-65 yrs.)

| Age of head (years) | Male | Female |
|---|---|---|
| 45 - 50 | 8 | 21 |
| 50 - 55 | 10 | 25 |
| 55 - 60 | 12 | 30 |
| 60 - 65 | 15 | 39 |

Source: U.S. Census of Population: 1950, Tables 105 and 107.

Table 8

Number of Non-normal Households by Age and Sex of Head per 100 Normal Households, by Age of Head (65-85 yrs. or more)

| Age of head (years) | Male | Female |
|---|---|---|
| 65 - 70 | 21 | 56 |
| 70 - 75 | 28 | 75 |
| 75 - 80 | 39 | 98 |
| 80 - 85 | 55 | 129 |
| 85 or more | 85 | 183 |

Source: U.S. Census of Population: 1950, Tables 105 and 107.

pated in judging $y_n$ at the time when the dwelling unit was chosen. Taking lodgers represents one way to continue in the dwelling unit chosen earlier. But even where a change in dwelling unit seems unavoidable because of decline in $y_n$, a delay may occur. This may represent a hope that something will turn up, perhaps best described as hope that $y_n$ will rise, or it may represent the time needed to make other suitable living arrangements.

Estimates shown later in this monograph provide some evidence as to the effect of age and sex of head and presence of lodgers on coefficients of income elasticity of housing observed. The variables used are described later. They tend to be crude and may well serve as proxies for other conditions not directly represented.

## Number of Persons per Consumer Unit

Variation in housing-income ratios with number of persons is to be expected if only because an additional person in the consumer unit is more likely to bring higher food than higher housing consumption. Such difference might be interpreted in terms of economies of scale, in that two or more persons can take turns sharing the same bathroom, or even the same bed. The effect of an additional person on consumption of food and housing can of course be otherwise interpreted. An additional person without a corresponding increase in income represents a lower $y_n$. If high-level housing consumption has a higher luxury component than high-level food consumption, then fall in housing consumption and rise in food consumption with an additional person present would not be surprising.

Two sets of data, shown in Tables 9 and 10 describe housing and income by number of persons. Those of Table 9 come from the Census of Housing of 1950[12] and represent rental value of owner units, contract rent of tenant units, and income of primary units of the respective households. Those of Table 10 come from the consumption survey of 1950 and represent all consumer units, irrespective of tenure.[13] These show housing expenditure and income together with some characteristics of consumer units associated with number of persons.

The two sets of data have much in common. Income tends first to rise with number of persons, then, after a certain size is reached, it tends to decline. The decline for tenants may in part be related to a shift to owner-occupancy of tenants with higher income. Housing shows a positive correlation with income, although the rise in housing with number

12. The number represents all persons living in the dwelling unit at the time of the census, irrespective of their relationship to the household head or their representation in the income reported.

13. The number of persons is confined to those represented by income, and it measures persons on a full-year equivalent basis. Lodgers, domestic servants living in, and visitors are not included.

of persons is not so persistent as the rise in income, and, after a certain point, there are obvious signs of a decline in housing. Among owner households, income as shown in Table 9, reaches its peak at five persons, and at this size housing is a little past its peak. For consumer units of six or more, income is 0.5 and housing 19 per cent lower than for consumer units of five persons.

The net effect of variation in income and housing is a marked decline in housing-income ratios with increase in number of persons. Fur-

Table 9

Rent and Income of Households, Metro Stratum of the United States, by Tenure and Number of Persons, Census of Housing, 1950[a]

| Number of persons per household | Annual estimated or contract rent (1) | Income (2) | Rent per $100 of income (3) |
|---|---|---|---|
| | A. Owner Units[b] | | |
| One | $675 | $1,816 | $37.2 |
| Two | 886 | 3,335 | 26.6 |
| Three | 913 | 3,878 | 23.6 |
| Four | 934 | 4,161 | 22.5 |
| Five | 906 | 4,190 | 21.6 |
| Six | 856 | 4,145 | 20.7 |
| Seven or more | 732 | 4,190 | 17.5 |
| Six or more | 804 | 4,171 | 19.3 |
| | B. Tenant Units | | |
| One | 412[c] | 1,534 | 26.9 |
| Two | 502[c] | 3,087 | 16.3 |
| Three | 474 | 3,265 | 14.5 |
| Four | 459 | 3,404 | 13.5 |
| Five | 433 | 3,348 | 12.9 |
| Six | 405 | 3,203 | 12.6 |
| Seven or more | 360 | 2,905 | 12.4 |
| Six or more | $384 | $2,989 | $12.8 |

Source: Vol. II, chapter 1, Tables B-1, B-2, and B-7.

a. See footnotes of Table 3 for definitions. All averages are medians.

b. Income data are available only for households in all types of structure and information on value of dwelling is available only for households in one-unit structures. This gap seems likely to raise slightly the rent-income ratios of owners shown here.

c. For these, the proportion of newly formed households is likely to be high. If so, the relaxing of rent control seems likely to have its greatest effect here.

thermore, with measured income held constant, the more persons per consumer unit the lower tends to be housing expenditure[14] (see Table 10, column 5).

For tenants, some of the decline in housing-income ratios with increase in number of persons seems likely to represent the decreased importance of additional services in contract rent. This is to be expected, since with increasing number of persons a higher percentage of the tenants is likely to be in one-unit structures[15] and additional services tend to be of minor importance for such units.[16] However, a common pattern is observed for owners and tenants, and, for owners, housing-income ratios are unaffected by variation in services represented.

One interpretation of the decline in rent-income ratios with number of persons is that it represents the correlation of number of persons per household and income by age of the head of consumer units. The tendency can then be rationalized in terms of a long horizon in planning housing consumption and greater economies of scale for housing than for other consumer products. Such a correlation undoubtedly explains some of the decline in housing-income ratios with increase in number of persons, shown in Tables 9 and 10. It seems probable, however, that another condition contributes, especially to the decline in housing as such. Table 9 indicates a drop in the estimated rent of owners from $934 for households of four persons to $732 for those of seven or more, and a drop in contract rent of tenants from $474 for those of three persons[17] to $360 for those of seven or more. These are drops of 22 and 24 per cent, respectively. It may well be that some, if not all, of such drops

14. Schiff examined contract rent of households with measured income held constant, as reported in the Census of Housing of 1940, and noted a similar tendency (Eric Schiff, "Family Size and Residential Construction," American Economic Review, March, 1946, pp. 97-112).

15. As reported by the Census of Housing: 1940, Vol. III.

16. Gross rent is reported, by number of persons per household, only for households of husband and wife with no non-relatives present (see Census of Housing: 1950, Vol. II, Table 10). For metro areas of the United States, such as are represented in Table 9, gross rent-income ratios are not systematically related to number of persons—ranging from two to five persons. However, when data are standardized for region there appears to be a systematic tendency for gross rent-income ratios to decline with number of persons.

17. Contract rent of households of two persons was even higher. These, however, may have been heavily weighted with new households which in 1950 may have been paying relatively high rent because of getting little or no benefit from rent control.

Table 10

Housing Expenditure, Income and Related Characteristics, Consumer Units by Number of Persons, Consumption Survey, 1950[a]

| Number of persons | Per cent of consumer units | Income[b] | Housing expenditure | | | Per cent with owner-occupancy | Age of head | Persons | Number of full-time earners |
|---|---|---|---|---|---|---|---|---|---|
| | | | As reported | Per $100 of income | With measured income of consumer units held constant[c] | | | | |
| | (1) | (2) | (3) | (4) | (5) | (6) | (7) | (8) | (9) |
| 1. One | 13.5 | $1,895 | $321 | $16.9 | $484 | 25 | 55 | 1.0 | 0.5 |
| 2. Two | 32.1 | 3,601 | 420 | 11.7 | 492 | 47 | 50 | 2.0 | 0.8 |
| 3. Three | 23.2 | 4,221 | 441 | 10.4 | 462 | 50 | 43 | 3.1 | 1.0 |
| 4. Four | 17.3 | 4,793 | 439 | 9.2 | 438 | 59 | 42 | 4.1 | 1.1 |
| 5. Five | 8.2 | 4,901 | 429 | 8.6 | 413 | 58 | 41 | 5.1 | 1.1 |
| 6. Six or more | 3.7 | $4,942 | $402 | $ 8.1 | $366 | 59 | 44 | 6.9 | 1.2 |

Source: Vol. XVIII, Table 1.

a. All averages are means.

b. Disposable income.

c. This is the mean of the eight income categories under $10,000, each category having a weight of one.

are the result of a negative correlation between number of persons and normal lifetime income. In other words, it does not describe what tends to happen when persons are added to a given household, but rather it represents difference among economic groups where usual number of persons tends to be negatively correlated with normal income. Under this condition the higher the average number of persons, represented by the data shown in Tables 9 and 10, the higher the percentage of the households with low normal income.

Table 11

Birth Rate of Women 15 to 44 Years of Age, by Occupation of Husband, and Median Income of the Male Labor Force, by Occupation, 1952[a]

| Non-farm occupation[a] | Median income of males in the labor force (1) | Children ever born per woman 15 to 44 years, married, husband present (standardized for age) (2) |
|---|---|---|
| 1. Professional, technical workers | $4,876 | 1.653 |
| 2. Managers, officials, and proprietors except farm | 4,402 | 1.759 |
| 3. Clerical workers | 3,448 | 1.574 |
| 4. Sales workers | 3,662 | 1.535 |
| 5. Craftsmen and foremen | 3,792 | 1.932 |
| 6. Operatives | 3,263 | 2.076 |
| 7. Service workers except private household | 2,516 | 1.805 |
| 8. Laborers except farm and mine | $2,325 | 2.380 |

Source: U.S. Bureau of the Census, Current Population Reports, P-60, No. 14, 1953, Table 4, and P-20, No. 84, 1958, Table 4.

a. Each of these categories includes "kindred" workers.

The relation of birth rate to normal income supports this hypothesis. Birth rate of women by occupation of the husband in relation to average income of the male labor force, also by occupation, is shown in Table 11 and Figure 2 A. The relationship shown there implies that around 1950, among occupations, the higher the average income the low-

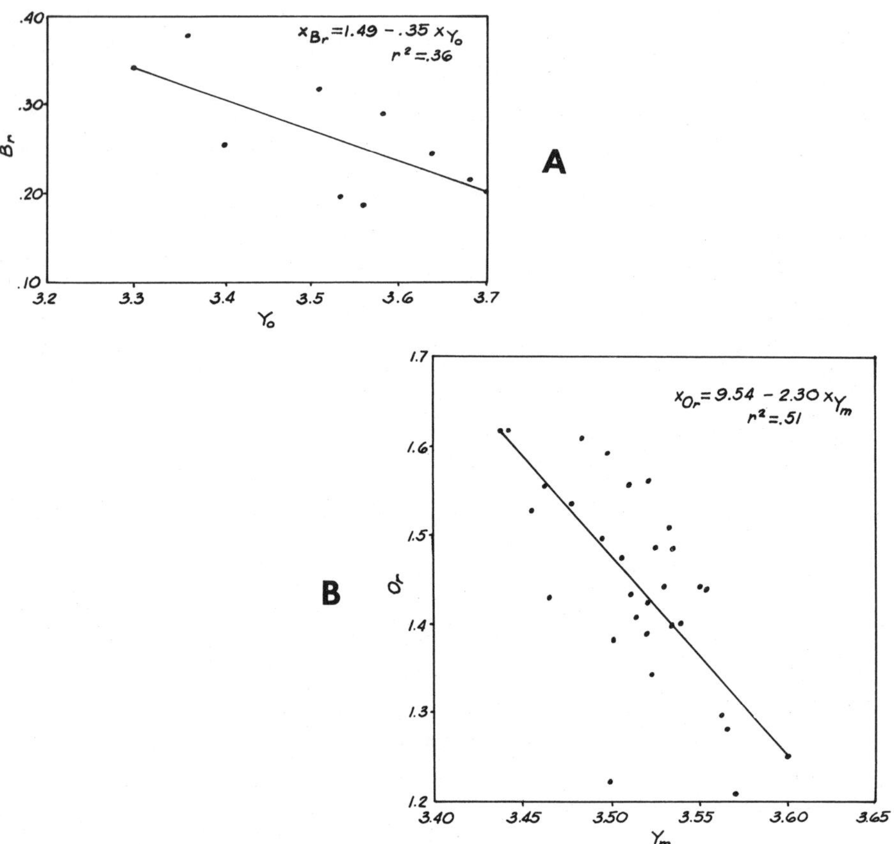


Fig. 2.—Birth rate (see Table 11 for definition) and doubling up of potential households,[a] in relation to average income of the male labor force, by occupation or by city (the cities included are those represented in Table 21). (Variables in log form.)

Panel A: Birth rate (Br) of women by occupation of husband, in relation to average income of the male labor force, by occupation.

Panel B: Number of "other relatives" per 100 households (Or) in relation to median income of fully employed males ($Y_m$), among metro areas, 1949.

Source of data: U.S. Bureau of the Census, Current Population Reports, P-20, No. 84, 1958, and P-60, No. 14, 1953, Table 4; and Census of Population: 1950, Vol. II, Tables 59 and 78, and states' reports.

a. This is measured in terms of the number of persons in households related to the head apart from his spouse and children. These are referred to as other relatives. This measure of doubling up is plotted against the median income of the male labor force employed at least 50 weeks during 1949.

er tended to be the birth rate. The correlation is significant at about .10 probability level.

One other piece of evidence also supports the hypothesis that the higher the number of persons in a household, at a given point in time, the higher the proportion that comes from strata of low normal income. This evidence pertains to doubling up of potential households. For example, among cities the higher the average income[18] of the male labor force the lower tends to be the average number of other relatives[19] in the household. This relationship is illustrated in Figure 2 B with data of the Census of Population of 1950. The tendency shown is significant at the .01 probability level.

If number of persons per household in part represents change with age and in part the economic stratum of the population represented, it is indeed a complex variable. The change in number of persons with age of head tends to have some positive correlation with change in income with age of head, on the other hand, with age of head held constant, number of persons is negatively correlated with normal income.

## Consumer Units by Age of Children

Three characteristics of consumer units have just been considered, namely age and sex of head and the number of persons. In addition, age of persons other than the head appears to be of considerable importance. It affects the allocation of expenditure among consumer products, and even more important it bears on the labor-force participation of members of consumer units, and this affects the importance of $y_t$. The older the children and the greater the number of adults in a consumer unit, the higher is likely to be the number of earners. However, the composition of consumer units tends to be in such a state of flux that it seems probable that the higher the number of earners the higher is likely to be the percentage of earners who are transitory. Thus their earnings are unlikely to be looked upon as a part of the expected income of the con-

18. This represents male labor force with 50 to 52 weeks of work during 1949. This measure of relative income among cities has been used rather than the income of families or of primary units of households in order to avoid the positive correlation between income and the contribution to income of primary units occurring because of the doubling up of related persons.

19. This is doubling up exclusive of the presence of lodgers unrelated to the household head.

sumer unit and hence are unlikely to influence housing consumption observed.

Table 12 shows housing expenditure, income, and related characteristics of consumer units, for eight types of consumer units in large cities of three regions. The consumer units are differentiated by age of the oldest child and by marital status of the head. A considerable variation occurs among the eight types in average age of head (Ag), number of persons (S) and full-time earners (Ea) and in the importance of owner-occupancy (O)—all things likely to be systematically related to housing expenditure-income ratios.

The 24 observations, with consumer units differentiated by region and by number and age of children, have several things in common with those for consumer units by age of head and by number of persons. One is the much greater variation among the types in average income than in housing expenditure. The respective ranges are from \$1,999 to \$5,551 for average income and from \$308 to \$525 for housing expenditure. As a result there is a wide range in housing-income ratios—namely, from 7.5 to 18.6. Another thing is the positive relationship between average income and average number of earners: among types of consumer units 83 per cent of the variation in average income (Y) is explained by average number of full-time earners (Ea). The correlation is as follows:

$$x_Y = 3.633 + .769x_{Ea} \qquad r^2 = .832 \qquad (4.3)$$

where Y is mean income and Ea the mean number of full-time earners per consumer unit, by type of consumer unit, with variables expressed log form. Thus, much of the variation in average income by type of consumer unit is a function of Ea.

Housing expenditure-income ratios, symbolized by $H_{er}/Y$, are negatively correlated with S, Ea, and O. The simple correlations of $H_{er}/Y$ with these three variables are shown in Table 13. The dominant variable is Ea. It explains 87 per cent of the variation in $H_{er}/Y$, and this percentage is increased little by taking into account S or O.

The relation of $H_{er}/Y$ to Ea for consumer units stratified by age of children and by number of persons is shown in Figure 3. The two sets of strata have a common pattern.[20] They pose forcibly the question as to

20. Similar observations by age of head, shown in Tables 3 and 4, tend to fall within the general pattern. There is one exception: $H_{er}/Y$ is relatively low where the head of consumer units is 65 years of age

Table 12

Housing Expenditure, Income and Related Characteristics, Consumer Units by Marital Status of Head and Age of Children, Large Cities by Region, Consumption Survey, 1950[a]

| Type of consumer unit | Per cent of consumer units (1) | Income[b] (Y) (2) | Housing expenditure[c] ($H_{er}$) | | Per cent with owner-occupancy (O) (5) | Age of head (Ag) (6) | Persons (S) (7) | Full-time earners (Ea) (8) |
|---|---|---|---|---|---|---|---|---|
| | | | As reported (3) | Per $100 of income (4) | | | | |
| | **A. Large Cities in the North** | | | | | | | |
| 1. Husband and wife | | | | | | | | |
| a) No others | 7.1 | $3,867 | $441 | $11.4 | 40 | 52 | 2.0 | 0.89 |
| b) Oldest child | | | | | | | | |
| 1) Under 6 | 4.1 | 3,890 | 480 | 12.3 | 29 | 31 | 3.3 | 0.85 |
| 2) 6 - 16 | 4.9 | 4,512 | 491 | 10.9 | 43 | 39 | 4.2 | 0.91 |
| 3) 16 - 18 | 0.9 | 4,291 | 429 | 10.0 | 53 | 46 | 4.2 | 0.93 |
| 4) 18 or more | 3.3 | 5,529 | 443 | 8.0 | 60 | 54 | 3.9 | 1.36 |
| 2. One parent only | 0.6 | 2,157 | 401 | 18.6 | 12 | 37 | 2.9 | 0.32 |
| 3. Other adults[d] | 7.5 | 2,884 | 401 | 13.9 | 29 | 53 | 1.7 | 0.72 |
| 4. All others[e] | 2.5 | 4,676 | 415 | 8.9 | 52 | 46 | 5.0 | 1.10 |
| | **B. Large Cities in the South** | | | | | | | |
| 1. Husband and wife | | | | | | | | |
| a) No others | 3.7 | 3,546 | 392 | 11.1 | 42 | 48 | 2.0 | 0.92 |
| b) Oldest child | | | | | | | | |
| 1) Under 6 | 2.1 | 3,433 | 442 | 12.9 | 31 | 29 | 3.3 | 0.84 |
| 2) 6 - 16 | 2.3 | 4,124 | 428 | 10.4 | 46 | 38 | 4.2 | 0.83 |
| 3) 16 - 18 | 0.4 | 4,651 | 434 | 9.3 | 43 | 44 | 4.2 | 1.06 |
| 4) 18 or more | 1.4 | 4,989 | 378 | 7.6 | 61 | 53 | 4.0 | 1.28 |
| 2. One parent only | 0.4 | 1,999 | 305 | 15.3 | 14 | 34 | 3.2 | 0.47 |
| 3. Other adults[d] | 3.3 | 2,550 | 332 | 13.0 | 38 | 53 | 1.7 | 0.74 |
| 4. All others[e] | 1.8 | $3,455 | $334 | $ 9.7 | 47 | 46 | 4.6 | 0.98 |

Table 12 (continued)

| Type of consumer unit | Per cent of consumer units (1) | Income[b] (Y) (2) | Housing expenditure[c] ($H_{er}$) As reported (3) | Housing expenditure[c] ($H_{er}$) Per $100 of income (4) | Per cent with owner-occupancy (O) (5) | Age of head (Ag) (6) | Persons (S) (7) | Full-time earners (Ea) (8) |
|---|---|---|---|---|---|---|---|---|
| | **C. Large Cities in the West** | | | | | | | |
| 1. Husband and wife | | | | | | | | |
| a) No others | 4.4 | $4,024 | $441 | $11.0 | 52 | 50 | 2.0 | 0.90 |
| b) Oldest child | | | | | | | | |
| 1) Under 16 | 2.3 | 3,940 | 489 | 12.4 | 45 | 30 | 3.3 | 0.79 |
| 2) 6 - 16 | 2.8 | 4,700 | 477 | 10.1 | 62 | 38 | 4.2 | 0.95 |
| 3) 16 - 18 | 0.5 | 5,189 | 496 | 9.6 | 66 | 46 | 4.4 | 1.11 |
| 4) 18 or more | 1.5 | 5,551 | 417 | 7.5 | 78 | 53 | 4.1 | 1.22 |
| 2. One parent only | 0.3 | 2,582 | 376 | 14.6 | 32 | 41 | 3.0 | 0.45 |
| 3. Other adults[d] | 4.7 | 2,527 | 367 | 14.5 | 30 | 54 | 1.4 | 0.53 |
| 4. All others[e] | 1.0 | $4,462 | $479 | $10.7 | 67 | 45 | 4.5 | 1.02 |

Source: Vol. IV, Table 14.

a. No summary is provided for urban consumer units in general. All averages are means.

b. Disposable income.

c. Exclusive of expenditure for housing away from home.

d. These are adult groups other than husband and wife and include one-person consumer units.

e. This includes all consumer units with children in which an adult other than a parent is present.

why housing-income ratios tend to be negatively correlated with Ea. Some conditions likely to bear on this relationship have already been considered. They are discussed further in the section that follows.

Table 13

Coefficients of Correlation of Housing Expenditure-Income Ratios ($H_{er}/Y$) with Number of Full-time Earners (Ea), Number of Persons (S) and Percentage of Owner-Occupied Units (O), in Large Cities among Types of Consumer Units, 1950[a]

| Variables | $H_{er}/Y$ (1) | Ea (2) | S (3) | O (4) | Coefficient of determination (5) |
|---|---|---|---|---|---|
| | A. Coefficient of Simple Correlation | | | | |
| 1. $H_{er}/Y$ | 1.000 | -0.933 | -0.572 | -0.866 | .... |
| 2. Ea | .... | 1.000 | 0.460 | 0.876 | .... |
| 3. S | .... | .... | 1.000 | 0.406 | .... |
| 4. O | .... | .... | .... | 1.000 | .... |
| | B. Coefficients of Regressions, $H_{er}/Y$ the Dependent Variable | | | | |
| Equation | | | | | |
| (4.4) | 0.999[b] | -0.612 | .... | .... | 0.871 |
| (4.5) | 1.220 | .... | -0.346 | .... | 0.327 |
| (4.6) | 1.741 | .... | .... | -0.431 | 0.749 |
| (4.7) | 1.058 | -0.557 | -0.109 | .... | 0.897 |
| (4.8) | 1.174 | -0.493 | .... | -0.103 | 0.881 |

a. The variables are shown in Table 12, and for estimates shown here they are expressed in log form.

b. The constant term of the equations is shown in this column.

## Number of Full-time Earners per Consumer Unit[21]

The preceding section demonstrates that average housing-income ratios of consumer units, stratified by age of children and by number of

---

or more. This may well be the effect of high equity of owner-occupants. This would tend to increase the gap between housing expenditure and consumption.

21. As defined in the consumption survey this describes "members of consumer units employed 48 weeks or more during 1950." This comes close to being what the U.S. Bureau of the Census defines as a "year-round full-time worker." See, for example, _Current Population Reports_, P-60, 1959.

persons, tend to be negatively correlated with Ea. Many conditions, if present, could contribute to those tendencies: for example, (a) Ea is positively correlated with $y_n$, and housing-income ratios tend to decline with increase in $y_n$; (b) Ea is positively correlated with job-related expense so that the higher is Ea the more Y overstates income available for consumption, apart from job-related expense; (c) Ea is positively correlated with S and the higher is S the less consumer units of a given income can spend on housing because of the greater need for food and other consumer goods, or because economies of scale for these are not so great

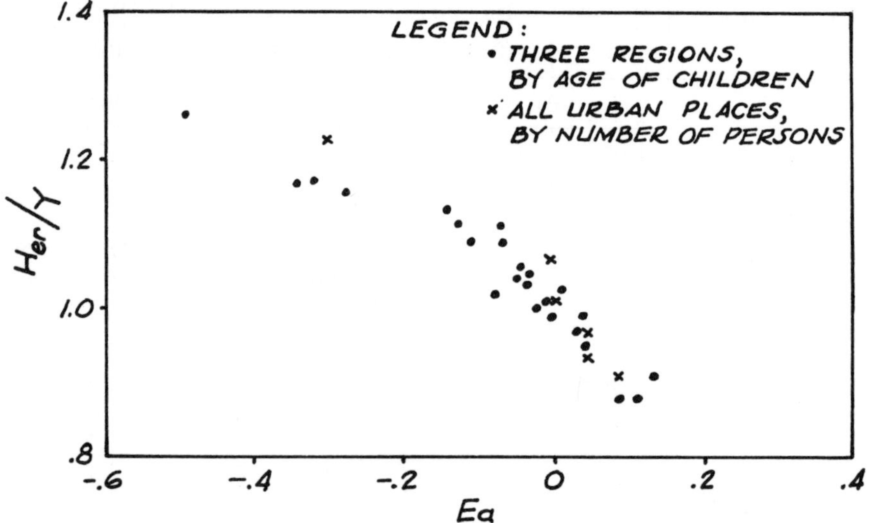


Fig. 3.—Housing expenditure-income ratios ($H_{er}/Y$) in relation to average number of full-time earners (Ea), consumer units, by age of children, and by number of persons, large cities of three regions,[a] 1950. (Ratios expressed in log form.)

a. The North, the South, and the West, as these are defined in the consumption survey of 1950.

as for housing; (d) Ea is positively correlated with $Y_t$, and housing has little or no correlation with it. Hence the higher Ea the lower tends to be $H_{er}/Y$; and (e) Ea of any one year is negatively correlated with $y_n$ of consumer units and the lower $Y_n$ the lower tends to be $H_{er}/Y$.

Information available permits an appraisal of these possibilities. Evidence presented in later chapters makes condition (a) seem very unlikely. In other words, they indicate that the higher is $y_n$, the higher tends to be housing-income ratio of consumers. Various scraps of evidence support the likelihood that job-related expense is of considerable importance, such as transportation to and from work,[22] some additional meals away from home, some extra clothing costs,[23] and outlays to replace services that would be rendered by family labor full-time in the household.[24]

Evidence of the preceding section supports the likelihood that condition (c) may be important. The marked correlation between S and Ea complicates interpretation as to causation. However, evidence shown in Table 13 by equations (4.4) and (4.5), implies that Ea rather than S is the important condition explaining valuation in $H_{er}/Y$.

A large stock of evidence[25] supports the likelihood that the higher Ea the more measured income overstates expected future income. Evidence of Table 12 is very striking. Husband-wife families, stratified by age of the oldest child, in large measure represent a succession of stages through which families in general tend to pass. For such families

---

22. One study shows that where family income is held constant the proportion of car buyers is greater among husband-wife families in which the wife is an additional worker than among households where there is only one worker. In addition, purchases of cars tend to be relatively low in households where the head is unemployed or on a reduced work schedule (see Board of Governors of the Federal Reserve System, Consumer Installment Credit, Vol. II, Part I, 1957, pp. 191-92).

23. The U.S. Department of Labor has observed that among males and females, standardized for age, that those at work spend much more for clothing than those not at work. See, for example, U.S. Department of Labor, Bul. 640, p. 690. Such evidence poses the question as to whether clothing expenditures go up because of increased income or because gainful employment increases the sense of need for additional clothing or decreases the time available for consumer production to maintain or to increase the stock of clothing.

24. Emma Holmes has made an estimate of job-related expenditure of wives who lived with husbands and had gainful employment. She estimates that about half of the income earned by wives went to job-related expenditure (see paper presented at the Annual National Agricultural Outlook Conference, U.S. Department of Agriculture, No. 19, 1958).

25. For studies bearing on this, see Dorothy S. Brady, "Individual Income and the Income Structure of Consumer Units," American Economic Association, Papers and Proceedings, May, 1958, pp. 269-79; Jacob Mincer, "Labor Supply, Family Income and Consumption," American Economic Association, Papers and Proceedings, May, 1960, pp. 581-82; Herman P. Miller, Income of the American People, 1955 (New York: John Wiley & Sons, 1955); Richard N. Rosett, "Working Wives: An Econometric Study," Studies in Household Behavior (New Haven: Yale University Press, 1951), pp. 53-99; and various issues of Current Population Reports, Series P-50, published by the U.S. Bureau of the Census.

Ea,[26] by age of oldest child, is given in Table 14.

Many studies have shown that the younger her children the less likely is a mother to be employed. Her increased employment when children are old enough to go to school undoubtedly contributes to the rise of Ea with age of the oldest child. The relatively high Ea for consumer units with the oldest child 18 years of age or more undoubtedly occurs because in some consumer units the child is a full-time earner. However, much of the income from such a supplementary earner may be looked upon as transitory. These earners are likely to be, as it were, on their way to membership in other households.

Table 14

Average Number of Full-time Earners (Ea) of Husband-Wife Families, by Age of the Oldest Child, Urban Places, Consumption Survey,[a] 1950

| Age of the oldest child (in years) | Ea |
|---|---|
| Under 6 | 0.83 |
| 6 to 16 | 0.90 |
| 16 to 18 | 1.09 |
| 18 or more | 1.29 |

Source: Vol. II, Table 14.

a. These are consumer units that include both a husband and wife without adults present other than their grown children.

Evidence bearing on full-time earners in relation to normal income indicates that condition (e) probably should be rejected. In other words, there is little reason to suppose that the higher Ea the lower tends to be $Y_n$. In fact, the opposite tendency seems more probable. Among occupational subsets of the consumption survey of 1950, Ea is highest where the head is self-employed and Y is high, and Ea is lowest where head is unskilled worker and Y is low. For these Ea is 1.1 and 0.8, respectively. To be sure there is extensive evidence that the lower the income of the

26. Each region has a weight of one. For husband-wife families with no children, Ea is 0.89. Many of these have an aged head retired from the labor force.

husband the more likely is the wife to be gainfully employed.[27] However, the lower an occupation in the economic hierarchy, the higher the percentage of males who are less than full-time earners.[28] This condition probably applies also to supplementary earners low in the occupational hierarchy. Where the count of earners describes the number of persons earning, as does that of the U.S. Bureau of the Census, it may well be that the lower $y_n$ the higher the number of earners.[29] However, the tendency with respect to number of full-time earners appears to be different.[30]

The evidence thus suggests that conditions (b) and (d), certainly, and condition (c), probably, contribute to the negative correlation between $H_{er}/Y$ and Ea shown in Figure 3. In other words, it is a function of a positive correlation between Ea and job-related expense and the transitory component of average income, and probably also with the decreased proportion of the total budget allocated to housing because of additional persons in the consumer unit.

The consumption survey reports average income and housing expenditure for subsets of consumer units by Ea. These data, together with related variables, are shown in Table 15. They indicate nothing not suggested by the interclass correlations already described. For example, increase in number of earners is accompanied by a marked increase in income and a slight increase in housing expenditure, and a marked fall in $H_{er}/Y$. In addition, number of earners is positively correlated with number of persons, and if the no earner subset is excluded, it is positively correlated with average age of head and hence with the age of other members in the unit.

---

27. See, for example, Current Population Reports, P-60, No. 12, June, 1953.

28. Ibid., P-60, No. 23, November, 1956, p. 5.

29. For example, among urban families a lower percentage of white than Negro families reports more than one earner (see Current Population Reports, P-60, No. 12, June, 1953, p. 7).

30. With age of head held constant, the average number of full-time earners of consumer units where head is an unskilled worker is appreciably less than where the head is a salaried professional or official. For the seven age categories the averages are 0.769 and 0.956, respectively, with each age category having a weight of one. (These estimates are derived from Vol. XVIII, Table 9.)

Table 15

Housing Expenditure, Income and Related Characteristics, Urban Consumer Units by Number of Full-time Earners, Consumption Survey of 1950[a]

| Full-time earners | Per cent of consumer units | Income (Y) | Housing expenditure ($H_{er}$) | | Per cent with owner-occupancy (O) | Age of head (Ag) | Persons (S) | Full-time earners[b] (Ea) |
|---|---|---|---|---|---|---|---|---|
| | | | As reported | Per $100 of income | | | | |
| | (1) | (2) | (3) | (4) | (5) | (6) | (7) | (8) |
| None | 26.0 | $2,248 | $331 | $14.7 | 43 | 53 | 2.4 | 0 |
| One | 61.8 | 4,229 | 441 | 10.4 | 49 | 43 | 3.2 | 1.0 |
| Two[b] | 11.0 | 5,638 | 456 | 8.1 | 56 | 46 | 3.4 | 2.0 |
| Three or more | 1.2 | $7,826 | $486 | $ 6.2 | 71 | 53 | 5.2 | 3.1 |

Source: Vol. XVIII, Table 1.

a. See Table 12 for definitions.

b. It is of interest to note that the U.S. Bureau of the Census reports two-fifths of the families with two or more earners in 1951. See Current Population Reports, P-60, No. 12, June, 1953, p. 6. The number of earners is appreciably higher than the number of full-time earners.

## Demographic Characteristics by Income of Consumer Units

The demographic characteristics reviewed contribute much to the variation in housing-income relations observed, and no consumption survey has yet been made sufficiently large to provide subsets homogeneous with respect to the housing variable and, in addition, with respect to the size and composition of consumer units and their labor-force participation. Thus indirect methods must be used in an attempt to take account of their probable effects.

These demographic characteristics are especially troublesome when y is the explanatory variable. Rise in income is accompanied by an appreciable rise in the number of persons, a rise in the average age of persons other than the head and his spouse, a marked rise in the average number of full-time earners, and a marked fall and later some rise in the age of head. (The correlation of these characteristics of consumer units with Y of cities, for example, is very much less.)

Three variables are used to describe these demographic characteristics by income of consumer units. The first is the number of persons above per 100 persons below median y, symbolized by $s_y$. The second is ea per consumer unit above minus ea per consumer unit below median income, symbolized by $ea_y$. And the third is the average age of head of consumer units below the first quartile of the income distribution, with average age of all heads equal to 100. This is symbolized by $ag_y$.

The magnitude of these variables for urban consumer units in general is as follows:

| | |
|---|---|
| $s_y$ | 138 |
| $ea_y$ | 0.56 |
| $ag_y$ | 115 |

In other words, there are 38 per cent more persons in consumer units above than below median income. This distribution occurs in spite of the fact that the lower is normal income the higher tends to be the birth rate and the doubling up of potential households. In addition, there are 0.56 more full-time earners per consumer unit above than below the median income. This by itself gives some reason to suspect that the incomes of consumer units have a transitory component of considerable importance. In addition, for urban consumer units $ag_y$ is 115. This indicates an appreciable concentration at low incomes of consumer units with an aged head. The distribution of each of these characteristics by income is such as to lower the income elasticity of housing expenditure among consumer units.

All these variables, that is, $s_y$, $ea_y$, and $ag_y$, are complex. For example, at some point in the income distribution the rise in number of persons with increased income is associated with a rise in the ratio of adults to children. Thus $s_y$ as well as describing number of persons per consumer unit may serve as a proxy for family composition. For some consumer units, two full-time earners may be a norm of considerable duration, and housing may be adjusted to the resulting income, when allowance is made for job-related expense. For other consumer units, two full-time earners put them well up the income scale but is a condition not likely long to endure. For still other consumer units one full-time earner may be unusual. The normal may be one or more part-time earners.

For consumer units in general it seems highly probable that variation in labor-force participation of members is an important cause of transitory income. However, there seems no reason to suppose that for consumer units $ea_y$ is the best proxy for $y_t$. It is merely the best available from the consumption survey of 1950. Other variables used for interplace and intertemporal estimates are described in later chapters.

The variable $ag_y$ is also likely to represent a host of conditions. In spelling these out, one should consider the question as to why some aged heads are low in the income distribution and others are high. Heads are likely to be low in the income distribution if the decline in their income with age has not been offset by a rise in the income of other persons present. Low income where the head is aged is the most common experience. Furthermore, consumption surveys directly identify only those aged who have managed to maintain their headship. This implies that they have enough income or assets to make headship possible. Some of them may of course be in a stage preparatory to merging with another consumer unit or transferring to the institutional population.[31] Because of such shifts, the data available probably do not represent the aged with very low income receipts. Many of these may be members of other

31. This population is not represented by the consumption survey nor by the census of housing.

consumer units where the head is a son or a daughter or another relative.[32]

Some consumer units with an aged head are relatively high in the income distribution. Some of these are heads whose peak income comes relatively late, and others have experienced a decline in income[33] which has been offset by the increase in the income of one or more other persons present. The presence of such earners is in part related to age of marriage and the doubling up of potential households. These tend to be a function of social custom and may well vary with the economic strata of the population represented.

A full investigation of these characteristics is beyond the scope of this monograph. However, probing into various interactions, which is continued in chapter v, is sufficient to indicate that the mixture of income components by age of head is likely to be very heterogeneous.

### A Summing Up

The mixture of household types for a nation tends to be much the same from year to year. Thus, estimates derived from time series are likely to be little affected by it. However, the mixture of household types together with associated conditions tends to differ greatly with measured income of consumer units (y), and these tend to have an important bearing on cross-section housing-income relations observed.

Age of head is associated with marked difference in housing-income ratios. Income varies markedly with age of head, while housing differs only slightly. Thus housing-income ratios tend to be high when income is low in the age-income cycle and tend to be low when income is high. Housing-income ratios tend to be especially high for households with an

32. In urban places of the United States in 1950 for every 100 household heads there were 6.7 persons classed as parents of the head (see Census of Population: 1950, Vol. II, Table 106).

33. The individual income of some household heads high in the income distribution may be quite low, compared to that of other persons in the unit. This likelihood raises the question as to conditions determining the designation of headship. If children are the main earners and father is present, he seems likely to be the head where patriarchial custom dominates. Headship assigned to an aged mother with small income receipts seems likely to be less frequent. Headship may also go with ownership of the dwelling unit occupied. For comment on the interpretation of headship of consumer units, see my review of American Housing and Its Use, by L. Winnick, published in the Journal of Political Economy February, 1959, pp. 101-3.

aged female head. They are at the very low point on the age-income cycle. Such households tend to concentrate very low in the income distribution. The effect of this is to lower the elasticity of housing with respect to income of a sample of all consumer units.

Increase in income tends to be accompanied by an increase in number of persons per household, and vice versa. However, housing is only slightly higher for households of four than of two persons and tends to be lower for households of seven or more persons than for those of four persons. Some of this difference is related to change in household size with age of head, and some of it relates to the higher birth rate and greater doubling up of potential households among those of low than of high normal income. Many conditions affecting housing-income relations appear to be associated with variation in number of persons. Their net effect is a decline in housing-income ratios with increase in number of persons per household.

Increase in income is accompanied by a rise in number of earners per consumer unit. This rise seems to be a fairly good index of a positive correlation between transitory ($y_t$) and measured income ($y$). In general, the expectation is that the greater the rise in number of earners with $y$, the more $y_t$ explains the variation of $y$.

The combinations and permutations of size and composition of households and number of earners are numerous. No survey has yet been of sufficient size to provide strata of consumer units completely homogeneous with respect to all of these characteristics. The data for 1950 are, however, sufficient to demonstrate their probable effect on tendencies observed. Estimates are presented in chapter v for strata fairly homogeneous in type of consumer unit. The effect of size and composition of household and number of earners on tendencies observed is a recurring theme throughout this monograph.

Throughout the monograph an attempt is made to trace the interplay of conditions that cannot be directly dealt with. Some of these seem to be inextricably intercorrelated, such as age of head, size and composition of the units, and the earning of members. The sequence of analyses and the synthesis of findings seem, however, to have resolved many paradoxes observed. Not the least of these is the puzzle of a negative correlation between birth rate and normal income and positive correlation between number of persons and measured income of consumer units.

# Chapter Five

# HOUSING WITH RESPECT TO INCOME AMONG CONSUMER UNITS

The customary method of estimating the relation of housing to income is to classify consumer units by measured income (y) and to estimate the increase in housing with respect to such income. The discussion of chapter ii pointed out that transitory components of income ($y_t$), uncorrelated with housing, result in such a measure understating the increase in housing with respect to normal income ($y_n$). Several examples are given in chapter ii to illustrate this likelihood: Furthermore the evidence of chapter iv indicates that the increase in number of persons and earners with y, symbolized by $s_y$ and $ea_y$, and the concentration of aged heads of consumer units where y is low, symbolized by $ag_y$, tend to lower coefficients in income elasticity of housing between consumer units. In addition, chapter iii gives reason to expect, where housing is represented by expenditure, irrespective of tenure, that is by $h_{er}$, that increase in the importance of owner-occupancy with y, symbolized by $o_y$, tends to lower $\eta_{h_{er}y}$.

This chapter explores in more detail housing-income relations where y is the explanatory variable. The estimates represent the entire range of incomes reported, and an examination is made of the variation in coefficients of income elasticity of housing observed. In addition, variation in housing is examined among places and between subgroups of consumer units, where y is held constant.

## Data Examined

Three main sources are drawn upon, namely the Census of Housing of 1950, the consumption survey of 1950, and the housing survey of 1933.[1]

1. These are the principal surveys representing consumer units in general and reporting data for a considerable set of places. Data from

Each of these sources provides data for a set of urban places. Many estimates pertain to cities or metro areas. In addition, housing with respect to income indicated by national urban surveys of 1941 and 1950 is compared. Estimates pertain chiefly to the urban population. There seems no reason, however, to suppose that the findings are not applicable to residential housing in general.

The data examined represent diverse economic conditions. For example, those for 1950 represent high employment levels, and those for 1933 the depths of the Great Depression. Thus tendencies under high and low employment can be compared. Other conditions, at least with respect to rental housing, differ between periods represented. In 1950 a lag of housing behind income change seems likely to have been present because of rent control and restrictions on building during the late forties. A different kind of lag may have been present in 1933, i.e., a lag in the decline of value and rent of dwellings behind decline in income as the depression deepened.

Economic conditions represented by the sets of data differ. So also do the housing variables. The estimates presented relate to: (a) the value or estimated rental[2] value of units in owner-occupancy in the spring of 1950 and the year of 1933, symbolized by h; (b) contract rent of tenants during the spring of 1950 and the years 1950 and 1933, symbolized by $h_r$; (c) expenditure during 1950 for the main dwelling by consumer units with owner-occupancy, symbolized by $h_e$, and (d) expenditure during 1950 of consumer units, irrespective of tenure, symbolized by $h_{er}$. Tendencies are described in terms of coefficients of elasticity of housing with respect to y. This is the ratio of the rate of increase in h, for example, to the rate of increase in y. Such coefficients are symbolized by $\eta_{hy}$.

The income variable, that is, y, differs somewhat by source of data although not enough to seem to justify a variation in notation. The income variable of the consumption survey of 1950 is disposable income for the same period as is represented by the housing variable. On the other hand, the census of housing reports housing for the spring of 1950 and income before taxes for the year 1949, of persons in households of

---

the Census of Housing of 1960 will permit additional estimates.

2. This is 10 per cent of the reported value of the owner-occupied units in the one-unit structures.

1950. Where y represents income before taxes, $\eta_{hy}$ tends to be less than where it represents income after taxes. In addition, the gap in the census data between the period represented by housing and the income seems likely to increase the importance of $y_t$ and to lower $\eta_{hy}$.[3]

All estimates are made using grouped data. The housing and income variables of the consumption survey and the housing survey of 1933 represent means. The income variable of the census of housing represents midpoints of income intervals between $1,000 and $10,000. The lowest and the highest income intervals are represented by mean income before taxes as reported in the consumption survey of 1950. The housing variable of the census of housing is median housing by income interval.[4] Estimates shown represent weighted regressions with housing and income variables expressed in log form. Hence the assumption is that income elasticities of housing tend to be the same at all levels of y.

This chapter is mainly devoted to an examination[5] of coefficients of income elasticity of housing among consumer units. The historic role that this type of evidence has played in conclusions as to income elasticity of demand for housing justifies careful consideration. The evidence supports the initial hypothesis that coefficients of income elasticity of housing, where y is the explanatory variable, tend to be biased downward by $y_t$.

The main topics that follow are: (a) coefficients representing consumer units of all regions; (b) holding constant tenure, normal income, and type of consumer unit; (c) variation among places in income elasticity of housing among consumer units; (d) variation among places in the mixture of income components and its effect; (e) coefficients of $\eta_{h_{er}y}$ of strata differentiated by normal income and other conditions; (f) variation in $\eta_{hy}$ among places with race held constant, and (g) variation in housing among subgroups with y held constant.

The main findings of the chapter are summarized on pages 135-38. Those familiar with the implications of the permanent-income hypothesis

---

3. For discussion of this, see chapter ii.

4. The use of midpoints and medians for the data of the Census of Housing of 1950 was largely a matter of computation cost.

5. For a pioneer study of variation in coefficients of elasticity among expenditure with respect to income among consumer units, see H. Gregg Lewis and Paul H. Douglas, "Studies in Consumer Expenditures," Journal of the School of Business, Vol. XX, No. 4, Part 2 (October, 1947).

may want to turn directly to these and to skip the intervening pages that explore the data in considerable detail.

## Coefficients Representing Consumer Units of All Regions

Where the housing variable is expenditure for the main dwelling, the income elasticity of housing expenditure among all urban consumer units of 1950 is 0.436. This coefficient of $\eta_{h_{er}y}$ provides a kind of benchmark for many of the estimates shown later. Some are higher, some are lower.

The consumption survey and the Census of Housing, both of 1950, permit estimates by tenure. These are given in Table 16.

Table 16

Two Estimates of Elasticity of Housing with respect to Income among Consumers, by Tenure, 1950

| Tenure | Urban consumer units, 1950[a] $\eta_{h_e y}$ or $\eta_{h_r y}$ | Households of metro areas, census of housing, 1950[b] $\eta_{hy}$ or $\eta_{h_r y}$ |
|---|---|---|
| Owners | 0.527 | 0.314 |
| Tenants | 0.431 | 0.261 |

a. *Study of Consumer Expenditures*, Vol. XVIII. Tenure is that as of the end of 1950.

b. *U.S. Census of Housing: 1950*, Vol. II, chapter 1, Table B-7. Tenure is that at the time of the census, namely April, 1950.

The coefficients for owners are higher than those for tenants. The difference is especially striking for the consumption survey. For it, the housing variable of the owners is confined to expenditure, and, as was noted in chapter iii, urban housing of 1941 so represented tends to have a relatively high income elasticity among consumer units, that is higher than where housing is represented by rental value of the dwelling units (h).

The coefficients indicated by the census data are lower than those from the consumption survey. For owners the difference in the housing variable undoubtedly contributes to this. In other words, $\eta_{h_e y}$ tends to be higher than $\eta_{hy}$. This difference seems likely to occur because $h_e$ represents expenditure for the main dwelling unit occupied and h represents its estimated rental value, and, where y is low, $h_e$ is much, much less than h, because of the concentration there of owners with the mortgage on the dwelling now occupied paid off and hence with low current expenditure for housing.

For tenants also the income elasticity of housing indicated by the census is lower than that indicated by the consumption survey. Difference in treatment of income tax appears to have little effect. When income taxes are added to disposable income, the coefficient for tenants of the consumption survey is lowered from 0.431 to 0.429. Thus the use of income before taxes for the estimate derived from the census seems unlikely to account for $\eta_{h_r y}$ being lower for the census than for the consumption survey.[6]

The importance of $y_t$ may have differed between these two sources. It seems highly probable that error in reporting income is greater for the data of the census than for the consumption survey, if only because of the lesser attention given to income by the census schedule. The gap between the periods represented by the housing and the income variable by the data of the census is another factor likely to lower the coefficients observed for that source (see chapter ii). In addition, the use of midpoints and medians to represent income and rent of the census data may account for some of the difference observed.

In spite of the fact that the coefficients differ by source of data and manner of estimating averages, it is very important to note that $\eta_{h_r y}$ for each of these sources is very low.

Change appears to have been occurring in coefficients of income elasticity of housing. The urban consumptions surveys of 1950 and 1941 represent similar universes, housing variables, and state of the economy. Yet the coefficients of income elasticity indicated for 1950 are appreciably lower than those of 1941. By tenure they are given in Table 17. These coefficients pose questions as to whether housing in 1950 tended to improve less with increase in $y_n$ than in 1941. Before accepting such an interpretation of this evidence, it should be noted that the difference between the coefficients of 1941 and 1950 is the type to be expected if $y_t$ was more important in 1950 than in 1941. Such a change would not be surprising in view of the increased equality of $y_n$. The forties brought

6. In making this comparison the income tax is that of consumer units of the consumption survey grouped by disposable income. Thus the random component of the income tax tends to be minimized.

a narrowing of wage rates among regions and among occupations as well as highly progressive income taxes. These seem likely to have increased the equality of $y_n$ among consumer units in the nation in general. And, other things being equal, such as frequency in reporting error and the relative magnitude or frequency of shortrun income change, the greater the equality of $y_n$ the greater is likely to be the importance of $y_t$.

Table 17

Elasticity of Housing Expenditure and Rent with respect to Income among Consumers, 1941 and 1950

| | Owners $\eta_{h_e y}$ | Tenants $\eta_{h_r y}$ |
|---|---|---|
| 1950[a] | 0.517 | 0.431 |
| 1941[b] | 0.672 | 0.591 |
| 1950 with 1941 equal to 1.0 | 0.77 | 0.73 |

a. See Study of Consumer Expenditures, Vol. XVIII, Table 6. The estimates represent owner-occupants throughout the survey year and those who were tenants at the end of the survey year. Those who became owner-occupants during the survey year are not represented here.

b. See U.S. Department of Labor, Bul. 822, Table 22. The estimates pertain to full-year owners and renters.

It is also of interest to note that between 1941 and 1950 the coefficient declined more for tenants than for owners. This is the type of difference to be expected if rent control depressed rent more in places of high than of low income.

Evidence presented later in this chapter as well as in later chapters is consistent with these interpretations of change.

## Holding Constant Tenure, Normal Income, and Type of Consumer Unit[7]

The consumption survey of 1950 provides data by income of consumer units stratified by characteristics correlated with normal income as

7. This analysis is confined to the data of the consumption survey of 1950. To use the census data in this manner, the mean of the housing variable would have had to be estimated. Furthermore, the census of housing does not report data by demographic characteristics. Hence it does not serve the purpose of this section.

well as by tenure and by type of consumer units. This section explores the effect of various types of stratification on the coefficient of income elasticity of housing expenditure observed. This effect is tested by comparing coefficients of income elasticity of combined strata with the weighted mean coefficients of respective strata. Estimates are shown in Table 18, A-I, with consumer units stratified by tenure, occupation, years of schooling, race and age of head and number and age of children.[8] And in Table 19 estimates are shown with consumer units stratified by urban area, and then by urban area and tenure and by urban area and race. (Urban areas of this survey are the large cities, suburbs, and small cities of the North, South, and West.)

The discussion of chapters ii, iii, and iv provides a basis for predicting certain effects. Chapter ii, for example, gives reason to expect that stratification by a condition correlated with $y_n$, such as occupation and years of schooling, race and urban areas, will increase the importance of $y_t$ and consequently lower the income elasticity of housing.[9] It also gives reason to suppose that stratification by some characteristics representing $y_t$ will tend to decrease the importance $y_t$. Evidence of chapter iv implies that number of persons per consumer unit is correlated with $y_t$, insofar as it is represented by number of earners. Consequently, stratification by number of persons per consumer unit seems likely to increase the coefficient of income elasticity of housing observed.

Chapter iii also gives reason to expect that difference in owner-occupancy among strata will affect the income elasticities of housing expenditure. The greater the importance of owner-occupancy, the more housing expenditure tends to understate rental value. Hence, if owner-occupancy is correlated with $y_n$ of the strata, holding tenure constant seems likely to increase the income elasticity of housing expenditure observed, and, if it is negatively correlated, the opposite tendency is likely to be observed.

---

8. This term refers to consumer units differentiated by the age of the oldest child and the relationship of all adults to the head. The interclass relationships among such types are considered in chapter iv.

9. For further discussion of this characteristic of incomes, see my "Comments" on the paper by Jean Crochett and Irwin Friend, "A Complete Set of Consumer Demand Relationships," in Irwin Friend and Robert Jones (eds.), Consumption and Saving (Philadelphia: University of Pennsylvania Press, 1960), I, 1-92. "Comments" on pp. 143-54.

However, if the housing variable represents consumption equally well for the two tenures, such as estimated rental value of the owner units and contract rent of the tenant units, holding tenure constant presumably tends in part to hold $y_n$ constant, and accordingly the income elasticity of housing will tend to decline.

All the sets of strata examined differ in average income (Y). However, some types of stratification tend to lower and others to raise the income elasticity of housing. The intercorrelation of conditions affecting housing-income ratios of the various types of stratification tends to be quite complex.[10] For example, stratification by occupation, race, and age is in part a stratification by tenure, and stratification by age is in part stratification by number of persons and earners and by owner-occupancy. Published data for various strata do not permit directly holding constant all of these conditions. This is not surprising in view of their number. The estimates shown go no further than stratification by two conditions, for example age of head and number of persons, urban area and tenure, or urban area and race. However, in interpreting the evidence the probable effect of other conditions is noted.

Holding Constant Tenure.—Chapter iii indicates that housing expenditure of owner-occupants tends to understate rental value of dwelling unit and that, in general, owner-occupancy tends to be more important among consumer units of high than of low $y_n$. Under these conditions it would not be surprising to find that holding tenure constant increases income elasticity of housing expenditure.

The income elasticity of housing expenditure for all consumer units is 0.436, and the weighted mean for the four tenure subsets is 0.473, an increase of 8 per cent (see Table 18 A). The tendency observed is the type to expect if increasing the homogeneity of the housing variable more than offsets any tendency for the coefficient to be lowered by the greater importance of $y_t$ for the separate[11] than for the combined tenures.

Holding Constant Occupation, Years of Schooling, and Race of Head of Consumer Unit.—Each of these characteristics seems likely to differentiate consumer units to some extent by $y_n$. In addition, such strata seem likely to be fairly similar with respect to several conditions

10. The importance of some of these is indicated by data shown in Tables 1, 3, 4, 10, 12, and 15.

11. Average income of owners is $132 per $100 of average income of tenants.

Table 18

Coefficients of $\eta_{h_{er}y}$ and Related Characteristics, All Urban Consumer Units, by Tenure and Demographic Characteristics, Consumption Survey, 1950[a]

| | Percentage of consumer units (1) | $\eta_{h_{er}y}$ [b] (2) | $V_y^2$ [c] (3) | Index of distribution by income of | | | |
|---|---|---|---|---|---|---|---|
| | | | | Age of head[d] ($ag_y$) (4) | Persons[e] ($s_y$) (5) | Earners[f] ($ea_y$) (6) | Owner-occupancy[g] ($o_y$) (7) |
| | | | | A. By Tenure | | | |
| 1. All tenures | 100.0 | 0.436 | 0.080 | 115 | 138 | 0.56 | ... |
| a. Owners bought | | | | | | | |
| 1) Before 1946 | 27.6 | 0.474 | .100 | 116 | 155 | .70 | ... |
| 2) 1946 through 1949 | 16.5 | 0.619 | .058 | 116 | 135 | .44 | ... |
| 3) 1950 | 4.4 | 0.530 | .036 | 113 | 115 | .40 | ... |
| b. Tenants | 51.5 | 0.431 | .071 | 114 | 136 | .53 | ... |
| 2. Weighted mean[h] | | | | | | | |
| a. Absolute | 100.0 | 0.473 | ... | ... | ... | ... | ... |
| b. Ratio[i] | ... | 1.08 | ... | ... | ... | ... | ... |
| | | | | B. By Occupation of Employed Heads | | | |
| 1. All with head employed | 86.3 | 0.471 | .056 | 104 | 130 | .48 | 157 |
| a. Self-employed | 9.8 | 0.374 | .130 | 112 | 131 | .34 | 134 |
| b. Salaried professional and official | 13.6 | 0.470 | .049 | 100 | 132 | .29 | 177 |
| c. Clerks | 13.1 | 0.367 | .044 | 102 | 143 | .38 | 182 |
| d. Skilled | 17.8 | 0.391 | .025 | 100 | 122 | .47 | 126 |
| e. Semiskilled | 17.1 | 0.485 | .028 | 102 | 127 | .47 | 155 |
| f. Unskilled | 14.9 | 0.422 | 0.060 | 108 | 145 | 0.52 | 158 |
| 2. Weighted mean[h] | | | | | | | |
| a. Absolute | 86.3 | 0.412 | ... | ... | ... | ... | ... |
| b. Ratio[i] | ... | 0.87 | ... | ... | ... | ... | ... |

Table 18 (continued)

| | Percentage of consumer units (1) | $\eta_{h_{er}y}$ [b] (2) | $V_y^2$ [c] (3) | Index of distribution by income of: Age of head[d] ($a_{gy}$) (4) | Persons[e] ($s_y$) (5) | Earners[f] ($e_{ay}$) (6) | Owner-occupancy[g] ($o_y$) (7) |
|---|---|---|---|---|---|---|---|
| **C. By Years of Schooling of the Head** | | | | | | | |
| 1. All heads | 100.0 | 0.436 | 0.080 | 115 | 138 | 0.56 | 147 |
| a. 8 years or less | 40.4 | 0.377 | .085 | 114 | 154 | .68 | 146 |
| b. 9 through 11 years | 41.3 | 0.347 | .058 | 112 | 132 | .50 | 155 |
| c. 12 through 15 years | 15.7 | 0.399 | .086 | 105 | 133 | .41 | 177 |
| d. 16 years or more | 2.6 | 0.492 | .061 | 95 | 132 | .23 | 187 |
| 2. Weighted mean[h] | | | | | | | |
| a. Absolute | 100.0 | 0.374 | . . . | . . . | . . . | . . . | . . . |
| b. Ratio[i] | . . . | 0.86 | . . . | . . . | . . . | . . . | . . . |
| **D. By Race** | | | | | | | |
| 1. All races | 100.0 | 0.436 | .080 | 115 | 138 | .56 | 147 |
| a. White | 90.2 | 0.401 | .079 | 116 | 140 | .53 | 136 |
| b. Negro | 9.4 | 0.621 | .068 | 105 | 137 | .57 | 134 |
| c. Other | 0.4[k] | 0.502 | .029 | 118 | 146 | .75 | 228 |
| 2. Weighted mean[h] | | | | | | | |
| a. Absolute | 100.0 | 0.419 | . . . | . . . | . . . | . . . | . . . |
| b. Ratio[i] | . . . | 0.96 | . . . | . . . | . . . | . . . | . . . |
| **E. By Age of Head (In Years)** | | | | | | | |
| 1. All consumer units | 100.0 | 0.436 | .080 | . . . | 138 | .56 | 147 |
| a. Under 25 | 3.8 | 0.653 | .020 | . . . | 104 | .33 | 548 |
| b. 25 - 35 | 21.8 | 0.527 | .033 | . . . | 106 | .32 | 184 |
| c. 35 - 45 | 23.1 | 0.523 | .050 | . . . | 119 | .38 | 173 |
| d. 45 - 55 | 20.4 | 0.429 | .075 | . . . | 134 | .59 | 153 |
| e. 55 - 65 | 16.4 | 0.363 | .101 | . . . | 149 | .71 | 140 |
| f. 65 - 75 | 10.4 | 0.359 | .115 | . . . | 156 | .62 | 136 |
| g. 75 or more | 4.1 | 0.373 | 0.092 | . . . | 155 | 0.41 | 128 |
| 2. Weighted mean[h] | | | | | | | |
| a. Absolute | 100.0 | 0.426 | . . . | . . . | . . . | . . . | . . . |
| b. Ratio[i] | . . . | 0.98 | . . . | . . . | . . . | . . . | . . . |

Table 18 (continued)

| | Percentage of consumer units (1) | $\eta_{h_{er}y}$ [b] (2) | $V_y^2$ [c] (3) | Index of distribution by income of: Age of head[d] ($ag_y$) (4) | Persons[e] ($s_y$) (5) | Earners[f] ($ea_y$) (6) | Owner-occupancy[g] ($o_y$) (7) |
|---|---|---|---|---|---|---|---|
| | **F. By Age of Head, Consumer Units of Two Persons (In Years)** | | | | | | |
| 1. All two person units | 32.20 | 0.453 | 0.073 | . . . | . . . | 0.52 | 103 |
| a. Under 25 | 1.78 | 0.542 | .023 | . . . | . . . | .39 | 205 |
| b. 25 - 35 | 5.63 | 0.481 | .035 | . . . | . . . | .60 | 169 |
| c. 35 - 45 | 4.37 | 0.484 | .046 | . . . | . . . | .42 | 139 |
| d. 45 - 55 | 6.10 | 0.355 | .070 | . . . | . . . | .46 | 133 |
| e. 55 - 65 | 7.24 | 0.416 | .088 | . . . | . . . | .44 | 117 |
| f. 65 - 75 | 5.12 | 0.352 | .075 | . . . | . . . | .47 | 109 |
| g. 75 or more | 1.96 | 0.504 | .091 | . . . | . . . | .32 | 116 |
| 2. Weighted mean[h] | | | | | | | |
| a. Absolute | 32.20 | 0.414 | . . . | . . . | . . . | . . . | . . . |
| b. Ratio[i] | . . . | 0.91 | . . . | . . . | . . . | . . . | . . . |
| | **G. By Number of Persons, All Consumer Units** | | | | | | |
| 1. All sizes | 100.0 | 0.436 | .080 | 115 | . . . | .56 | 147 |
| a. One person | 13.5 | 0.427 | .090 | 120 | . . . | .50 | 59 |
| b. Two persons | 32.1 | 0.453 | .073 | 118 | . . . | .52 | 103 |
| c. Three persons | 23.2 | 0.511 | .044 | 100 | . . . | .44 | 150 |
| d. Four persons | 17.3 | 0.539 | .042 | 95 | . . . | .36 | 154 |
| e. Five persons | 8.2 | 0.680 | .043 | 95 | . . . | .48 | 146 |
| f. Six or more persons | 5.7 | 0.726 | 0.038 | 93 | . . . | 0.68 | 152 |
| 2. Weighted mean[h] | | | | | | | |
| a. Absolute | 100.0 | 0.492 | . . . | . . . | . . . | . . . | . . . |
| b. Ratio[i] | . . . | 1.13 | . . . | . . . | . . . | . . . | . . . |

Table 18 (continued)

| | Percentage of consumer units (1) | $\eta_{h_{er}y}$ [b] (2) | $V_y^2$ [c] (3) | Index of distribution by income of: Age of head[d] ($a_{gy}$) (4) | Persons[e] ($s_y$) (5) | Earners[f] ($e_{ay}$) (6) | Owner-occupancy[g] ($o_y$) (7) |
|---|---|---|---|---|---|---|---|
| | H. By Number of Persons, Consumer Units with Head (45 to 55 Years of Age) | | | | | | |
| 1. All sizes with head 45 to 55 years | 20.43 | 0.429 | 0.075 | . . . | . . . | 0.59 | 153 |
| a. One person | 2.38 | 0.414 | .075 | . . . | . . . | .38 | 58 |
| b. Two persons | 6.10 | 0.355 | .070 | . . . | . . . | .46 | 133 |
| c. Three persons | 4.96 | 0.450 | .058 | . . . | . . . | .54 | 140 |
| d. Four persons | 3.90 | 0.543 | .056 | . . . | . . . | .43 | 135 |
| e. Five persons | 1.64 | 0.582 | .053 | . . . | . . . | .65 | 135 |
| f. Six or more | 1.45 | 0.740 | .042 | . . . | . . . | .88 | 114 |
| 2. Weighted mean[h] | | | | | | | |
| a. Absolute | 20.43 | 0.452 | . . . | . . . | . . . | . . . | . . . |
| b. Ratio[i] | . . . | 1.05 | . . . | . . . | . . . | . . . | . . . |
| | I. By Type of Consumer Unit, Large Cities in the North[l] | | | | | | |
| 1. All types | 100.0 | 0.372 | .075 | 114 | 155 | .58 | 168 |
| a. Husband-wife | | | | | | | |
| 1) no children | 22.8 | 0.409 | .073 | 119 | 101 | .55 | 102 |
| 2) oldest child (years) | | | | | | | |
| a) Under 6 | 13.2 | 0.484 | .026 | 103 | 104 | .15 | 163 |
| b) 6 - 16 | 15.9 | 0.619 | .030 | 101 | 100 | .25 | 178 |
| c) 16 - 18 | 3.0 | 0.349 | .021 | 102 | 102 | .29 | 127 |
| d) 18 or more | 10.7 | 0.304 | .052 | 103 | 112 | .73 | 108 |
| b. One parent | 2.0 | 0.895 | .027 | 95 | 113 | .29 | 231 |
| c. Other adults | 24.1 | 0.384 | .104 | 117 | 158 | .71 | 137 |
| d. All others | 8.3 | 0.270 | 0.042 | 98 | 124 | 0.63 | 172 |
| 2. Weighted mean[h] | | | | | | | |
| a. Absolute | 100.0 | 0.405 | . . . | . . . | . . . | . . . | . . . |
| b. Ratio[i] | . . . | 1.09 | . . . | . . . | . . . | . . . | . . . |

Source: Vol. IV and Vol. XVIII, various tables.

a. Except for Panel I, estimates pertain to all urban consumer units.

b. The housing variable is housing expenditure apart from that for housing away from home. The coefficient is $\eta_{h_{er}y}$ except where strata by tenure are described. For these the coefficient is $\eta_{h_e y}$ for owners and $\eta_{h_r y}$ for tenants.

c. This is the squared variance of the log of $y_o$. See fn. h, below, for information on the relevance of this variance to estimates made.

d. This is the mean age of head of consumer units in the first quartile of the income distribution, with the average age of head of all consumer units equal to 100. (Age of head tends first to decrease with higher income and then to increase, and housing expenditure-income ratios tend to be high where the head is aged and the income low.)

e. The number of persons above median income of all consumer units per 100 persons below such income.

f. The number of earners per consumer unit above the median income of all consumer units minus the corresponding mean of consumer units below such income.

g. The number of consumer units with owner-occupancy above median income of all consumer units, with number of owner-occupants below such income equal to 100.

h. The method of weighting is as follows:

$$\bar{\eta} = \frac{\Sigma\, n_o\, v_o^2\, \eta_o}{\Sigma\, n_o\, v_o^2}$$

where $n_o$, $v_o^2$, and $\eta_o$ are, respectively, the number of observations, the squared variance of the logs of measured income, and the computed coefficients of $\eta_{h_{er}y}$ for minor cell o, and $\bar{\eta}$ is the weighted mean coefficient of elasticity of the minor cells. I am indebted to Dr. Milton Friedman for this formula. For discussion of its applicability, see Robert Eisner, "The Permanent Income Hypotheses," American Economic Review, December, 1958, pp. 972-90.

i. The coefficient shown on line 1 of the respective panels equals 1.00.

j. This coefficient may have been biased upward somewhat by free rent among those of low money income. Of Negro consumer units with incomes under $1,000, 7 per cent did not report expenditure for either an owned or rented dwelling unit. For white consumer units with such incomes, 1 per cent did not report such expenditure.

k. The number is small, around 50 consumer units. In addition, the weights provided in the published reports are very inadequate since only 4 income intervals are represented by these estimates.

l. See Table 12 for description of the distinguishing features of types c and d.

Table 19

Coefficients of $\eta_{h_{er}y}$ and Related Characteristics, All Consumer Units and by Tenure, Race and Urban Area, Consumption Survey, 1950

| | Percentage of consumer units[a] (1) | $\eta_{h_{er}y}$[b] (2) | $V^2_y$[c] (3) | $ag_y$[d] (4) | $s_y$[d] (5) | $ea_y$[d] (6) | $o_y$[d] (7) | $Y_{ov}$[e] (8) |
|---|---|---|---|---|---|---|---|---|
| | A. Urban Owners and Tenants Combined | | | | | | | |
| 1. All urban consumer units | 100.0 | 0.436 | 0.080 | 115 | 138 | 0.56 | 147 | 0.094 |
| a. North | | | | | | | | |
| 1) Large cities | 36.3 | .372 | .075 | 114 | 155 | .58 | 168 | .085 |
| 2) Suburbs | 10.8 | .532 | .074 | 114 | 129 | .56 | 134 | .099 |
| 3) Small cities | 9.2 | .379 | .084 | 119 | 148 | .52 | 141 | .096 |
| b. South | | | | | | | | |
| 1) Large cities | 8.5 | .530 | .075 | 113 | 126 | .50 | 177 | .106 |
| 2) Suburbs | 2.2 | .485 | .062 | 109 | 121 | .43 | 126 | .103 |
| 3) Small cities | 6.2 | .688 | .081 | 114 | 124 | .61 | 122 | .130 |
| c. West | | | | | | | | |
| 1) Large cities | 14.0 | .366 | .084 | 120 | 148 | .58 | 157 | .085 |
| 2) Suburbs | 4.0 | .360 | .082 | 121 | 128 | .59 | 129 | .093 |
| 3) Small cities | 8.8 | .395 | .088 | 124 | 139 | .49 | 132 | .098 |
| 2. Weighted[f] mean | | | | | | | | |
| a. Absolute | 100.0 | .425 | ... | ... | ... | ... | ... | ... |
| b. Ratio[g] | ... | .97 | ... | ... | ... | ... | ... | ... |
| | B. Urban Owners,[h] Bought before 1946 | | | | | | | |
| 1. All | 27.60 | .474 | .100 | 116 | 155 | .70 | ... | na |
| a. North | | | | | | | | |
| 1) Large cities | 8.88 | .438 | .090 | 115 | 155 | .71 | ... | na |
| 2) Suburbs | 4.03 | .547 | .091 | 120 | 145 | .65 | ... | na |
| 3) Small cities | 2.90 | .476 | .108 | 117 | 155 | .61 | ... | na |
| b. South | | | | | | | | |
| 1) Large cities | 2.13 | .385 | .090 | 115 | 136 | .68 | ... | na |
| 2) Suburbs | 0.66 | .349 | .081 | 114 | 135 | .56 | ... | na |
| 3) Small cities | 1.96 | .385 | .103 | 111 | 145 | .80 | ... | na |
| c. West | | | | | | | | |
| 1) Large cities | 3.62 | .406 | .102 | 119 | 154 | .66 | ... | na |
| 2) Suburbs | 1.10 | .526 | .110 | 123 | 142 | .62 | ... | na |
| 3) Small cities | 2.32 | .481 | .123 | 117 | 141 | .54 | ... | na |
| 2. Weighted[f] mean | | | | | | | | |
| a. Absolute | 27.60 | .402 | ... | ... | ... | ... | ... | ... |
| b. Ratio[g] | ... | .85 | ... | ... | ... | ... | ... | ... |
| | C. Urban Tenants,[i] End of the Survey Year | | | | | | | |
| 1. All | 51.50 | .431 | .071 | 114 | 138 | .53 | ... | na |
| a. North | | | | | | | | |
| 1) Large cities | 22.30 | .470 | .069 | 117 | 142 | .53 | ... | na |
| 2) Suburbs | 3.97 | .546 | .068 | 113 | 118 | .51 | ... | na |
| 3) Small cities | 4.27 | .298 | .077 | 126 | 156 | .52 | ... | na |
| b. South | | | | | | | | |
| 1) Large cities | 4.95 | .622 | .068 | 113 | 120 | .43 | ... | na |
| 2) Suburbs | 0.77 | .734 | .050 | 103 | 117 | .42 | ... | na |
| 3) Small cities | 2.99 | .738 | .066 | 108 | 109 | .38 | ... | na |
| c. West | | | | | | | | |
| 1) Large cities | 6.95 | .418 | .078 | 126 | 153 | .59 | ... | na |
| 2) Suburbs | 1.44 | .285 | .072 | 122 | 127 | .55 | ... | na |
| 3) Small cities | 3.86 | .475 | 0.062 | 126 | 135 | 0.43 | ... | na |
| 2. Weighted[f] mean | | | | | | | | |
| a. Absolute | 51.50 | .479 | ... | ... | ... | ... | ... | ... |
| b. Ratio[g] | ... | 1.11 | ... | ... | ... | ... | ... | ... |

Table 19 (continued)

| | Percentage of consumer units[a] (1) | $\eta_{h_r y}$ [b] (2) | $V^2_y$ [c] (3) | $ag_y$ [d] (4) | $s_y$ [d] (5) | $ea_y$ [d] (6) | $o_y$ [d] (7) | $Y_{ov}$ [e] (8) |
|---|---|---|---|---|---|---|---|---|
| | D. By Urban Area,[j] Negro Consumer Units | | | | | | | |
| 1. All Negro consumer units | 9.4 | 0.621 | 0.068 | 105 | 137 | 0.57 | 134 | na |
| a. North | | | | | | | | |
| 1) Large cities | 4.0 | .458 | .054 | 113 | 151 | .70 | 151 | na |
| 2) Suburbs | 0.3 | .402 | .063 | k | k | k | k | na |
| b. South | | | | | | | | |
| 1) Large cities | 2.4 | .425 | .059 | 111 | 143 | .55 | 150 | na |
| 2) Suburbs | 0.3 | .503 | .065 | k | k | k | k | na |
| 3) Small cities | 1.6 | .464 | .055 | 115 | 152 | .38 | 129 | na |
| c. West | | | | | | | | |
| 1) Large cities | 0.5 | .479 | .059 | 110 | 104 | .57 | 125 | na |
| 2. Weighted[f] mean | | | | | | | | |
| a. Absolute | 9.1 | .451 | ... | ... | ... | ... | ... | ... |
| b. Ratio[g] | ... | .73 | ... | ... | ... | ... | ... | ... |
| | E. By Urban Area, White Consumer Units | | | | | | | |
| 1. All | 90.2 | .401 | .079 | 116 | 140 | .53 | 136 | na |
| a. North | | | | | | | | |
| 1) Large cities | 32.3 | .363 | .076 | 116 | 143 | .55 | 159 | na |
| 2) Suburbs | 10.5 | .531 | .073 | 113 | 128 | .56 | 132 | na |
| 3) Small cities | 9.1 | .379 | .084 | 119 | 148 | .52 | 141 | na |
| b. South | | | | | | | | |
| 1) Large cities | 6.1 | .457 | .065 | 110 | 124 | .53 | 146 | na |
| 2) Suburbs | 1.9 | .379 | .053 | 112 | 123 | .47 | 116 | na |
| 3) Small cities | 4.5 | .611 | .069 | 113 | 126 | .64 | 119 | na |
| c. West | | | | | | | | |
| 1) Large cities | 13.3 | .360 | .086 | 120 | 158 | .59 | 156 | na |
| 2) Suburbs | 4.0 | .360 | .082 | 121 | 128 | .59 | 129 | na |
| 3) Small cities | 8.5 | .395 | 0.088 | 124 | 139 | 0.49 | 132 | na |
| 2. Weighted[f] mean | | | | | | | | |
| a. Absolute | 90.2 | .402 | ... | ... | ... | ... | ... | ... |
| b. Ratio[g] | ... | 1.00 | ... | ... | ... | ... | ... | ... |

Source: Vol. IV and XVIII, various tables.

a. The weights represented here relate to consumer units represented, as reported in Vol. XVIII, p. xiii, rather than to the number of consumer units reporting.

b. Housing variable is expenditure for housing apart from housing away from home of all consumer units irrespective of tenure.

c. This is an estimate of squared variance of y expressed in log form. It is used in estimating the weighted mean of income elasticity of the various strata. See Table 18, fn. h, for a description of the method of weighting.

d. See Table 18, footnotes d - g, for a description of these variables.

e. This is an estimate of the variance of average incomes of occupational groups where head of the consumer unit is employed. Average income is expressed in log form. See pp. 118-19, "The Mixture of Income Components," for an interpretation of this variable. In this column "na" symbolizes "not available."

f. See Table 18, fn. h, for a description of the method of weighting.

g. The coefficient of income elasticity of housing shown on line 1 of the respective panels equals 1.0.

h. The housing variable of this panel is h and the coefficient of income elasticity shown in column 2 is $\eta_{hy}$.

i. The housing variable of this panel is $h_r$ and the coefficient of income elasticity shown in column 2 is $\eta_{h_r y}$.

j. Three urban areas are omitted because of the small number reporting. This omission excludes only 37 Negro consumer units that reported, or 3 per cent of all Negro units.

k. Omitted because variability error is likely to be very high for these areas. Less than 75 consumer units reported.

affecting housing-income ratios, such as age of head and of children and number of persons per consumer unit. One would thus expect stratification by these characteristics to increase the importance of $y_t$ and lower the coefficient of income elasticity observed.

Such is the effect observed (see Table 18 B, C, and D). Furthermore, the degree of reduction appears to be related to the extent to which occupation, years of schooling, and race represent difference in $y_n$. The average income of the high stratum per $100 of that of the low stratum and the ratio of the mean $\eta_{h_{er}y}$ of the separate stratum to $\eta_{h_{er}y}$ of the combined strata are given in Table 20.

Table 20

Effect on Coefficients of Income Elasticity of Housing Expenditure among Consumers, Holding Constant Occupation, Schooling and Race of Head and the Range in the Average Income among the Strata Represented, Urban Consumer Units 1950

| Strata differentiated by | Ratio of incomes, stratum with lowest income equal to $100 (1) | Weighted $\eta_{h_{er}y}$ with coefficient of combined strata equal to 100 (2) |
|---|---|---|
| Occupation of employed head[a] | $191 | 0.87 |
| Schooling of the head | $196 | 0.86 |
| Race | $156 | 0.96 |

Source: Study of Consumer Expenditures.

a. Estimates are confined to consumer units with an employed head. In other words consumer units with head not employed are excluded. The difference observed in holding "occupation" constant is somewhat less if consumer units with head not employed are included. However, the inclusion of this group merely introduces another condition to be considered, namely, a stratum with negative transitory income.

Thus the tendencies observed are those to be expected: The weighted mean of the coefficients of the strata is lower than the coefficient of the combined strata, and the more the strata differ in average income the more is the income elasticity of housing lowered. Stratification by occupation and by race is, in part, stratification by tenure. For these two types of strata the importance of owner-occupancy is positively correlated with average income.[12] Hence holding occupation or race of head constant would tend to increase the income elasticity of housing. However, such effect appears to have been more than offset by the greater importance of $y_t$ of the separate strata than of the combined set.

Holding Constant Urban Area.—Urban areas presumably differentiate consumer units by $y_n$. Estimates with urban area held constant are shown in Table 19 A for all consumer units. Holding urban area constant lowers $\eta_{h_{er}y}$ by 3 per cent. In view of the wide range in y among plces, this difference appears small: The mean income of the highest per $100 of the lowest urban area is $159. The small reduction in $\eta_{h_{er}y}$ observed, where urban area is held constant, may in part occur because, among the areas, the importance of owner-occupancy is positively correlated with y. This condition seems likely to offset, in part, any tendency for increased importance of $y_t$ of the separate areas to lower mean $\eta_{h_{er}y}$.

Another condition may influence the tendencies observed, namely the positive correlation between Y of areas and the lag of tenant housing behind income change.

For owner-occupants who bought prior to 1946,[13] holding urban area constant brings a marked decline in the coefficient of $\eta_{h_e y}$, a decline of 15 per cent (see Table 19 B). This substantial decline is not surprising, since the mean income is $150 for the area of the highest income per $100 of the area with the lowest income.

On the other hand, holding area constant tends to increase the coefficient of $\eta_{h_r y}$ for tenant units, an increase of 11 per cent (see Table 19 C). This occurs in spite of the fact that the mean income is $148 for the urban area of highest income per $100 for the area of the lowest income. A greater lag of rents behind income change in areas of high than of low income would contribute to the effect observed. (So also could a greater

---

12. The percentage of consumer units with owner-occupancy in the strata of lowest and of highest average income is as follows:

| | Lowest | Highest |
|---|---|---|
| Occupation of employed head | 36 | 51 |
| Schooling of the head | 49 | 49 |
| Race | 32 | 50 |

13. Data available permit an estimate for owners who bought from 1946 through 1949. However, the evidence of Table 19 B and C, seems sufficient to indicate the probable bearing of the distribution of owner-occupancy and interest payments on tendencies observed.

importance of additional services in contract rent of places of low than of high income. The distribution of multi-unit structures together with their relationship to additional services represented by contract rent makes it seem unlikely that the distribution of additional services represented by contract rent contributes to the tendencies just described.)

Holding urban area constant shows a striking difference by race. For Negro consumer units it lowers the coefficient by 27 per cent and for white consumer units no change occurs. Difference among strata in average income and in the importance of owner-occupancy undoubtedly contributes to these tendencies. The range in income represented among the strata is much greater for the Negro than the white consumer units: For example, the stratum with the highest income per $100 of that with the lowest is $196 to Negro and $135 for white consumer units. In addition, among the strata of Negro consumer units, the importance of owner-occupancy is negatively correlated with Y, and among strata of white consumer units it is positively correlated.[14] Thus for the Negro consumer units, the relation of owner-occupancy to Y augments the effect of the increased importance of $y_t$ of the strata, whereas for white consumer units these two conditions tend to have offsetting effects.

Another interplace condition differing by race may have contributed to these tendencies, for example interarea migration. For white consumer units the importance of recent migration probably differed only slightly among areas. On the other hand, for Negro consumer units, at the time of the 1950 survey, recent in-migrants were heavily concentrated in the large cities of the North. In other words, among areas for Negro consumer units the importance of recent in-migrants is positively correlated with Y. Hence, where Y is high, there is a concentration of conditions associated with recent in-migration that tends to increase rent-income ratios. For one thing, high rents are often accepted on a temporary

---

14. The percentage of consumer units with owner-occupancy in the area of lowest and highest income is as follows:

| | Area with Income | |
|---|---|---|
| Consumer Units | Lowest | Highest |
| All | 51 | 63 |
| Negro | 49 | 41 |
| White | 53 | 63 |

The correlation coefficient of average income and percentage of owner-occupancy of the nine areas is .474 for all and -.211 for the Negro consumer units.

basis, while in-migrants are "looking around for something we can afford." In addition, sharing of households is common where in-migration is important, and where lodgers are present housing reported tends to overstate the housing of the primary unit of the household for which income is reported.[15] Another condition was present in 1950, namely the relaxing of rent control, and it tends to bear heavily on in-migrants.

Whatever the combination of circumstances, with urban area held constant, the coefficient of $\eta_{h_{er}y}$ is only slightly higher for Negro than for white consumers.

Holding Constant Age of Head of Consumer Unit.—For urban consumer units, holding average age of head constant tends to decrease the income elasticity of housing. A decrease of 2 per cent occurs (see Table 18 E). The intercorrelation of age and tenure makes it seem likely that the tendency observed is compounded of several conditions. There is, for example, a marked positive correlation between age of head and the importance of owner-occupancy and a slight negative correlation between the importance of owner-occupancy and average income by age of head.[16] The confluence of these conditions seems likely to lower average $\eta_{h_{er}y}$ of the strata by age. This effect may have been augmented by the increasing gap for owner-occupants with age of head of consumer units between rental value of the dwelling unit occupied and current housing expenditure. An offsetting condition seems likely, however, to

15. Table 2 describes the greater importance of lodgers in non-white households of North and West than of the South. This difference is common to both tenures. Data by tenure are provided by a special tabulation of the Census of Housing of 1950 for white and non-white households. Los Angeles, Detroit, and Birmingham are among the metro areas included. These data indicate the following percentage of households with non-relatives present:

| | Owners | | Tenants | |
|---|---|---|---|---|
| | White | Non-White | White | Non-White |
| Detroit | 7 | 31 | 7 | 24 |
| Los Angeles | 7 | 19 | 6 | 15 |
| Birmingham | 5 | 9 | 4 | 11 |

Thus the difference shown here between the South and the North is much greater for non-white than white households. (These estimates are included in the Fund for the Republic's Housing and Minorities: Final Report to the Commission on Race and Housing, chap. iv [Margaret G. Reid, "Housing in Relation to Income"] processed report; June, 1957).

16. The variables are shown in Table 4. The relationship is hyperbolic.

be present, namely a positive correlation between average income and number of earners. This would, it seems probable, tend to increase $\eta_{h_{er}y}$. However, the net effect of holding age of head constant is its decline.

Where age of head is held constant for consumer units of two persons, $\eta_{h_{er}y}$ is lowered by 9 per cent (see Table 18 F). For this set of strata, there is the relatively high negative correlation between average income of the strata and the importance of owner-occupancy: It is -0.670 (or a $r^2$ of the variables of .449). The effect of greater importance of owner-occupancy for strata of low than of high income seems likely, however, to be in part offset by a positive correlation between average income and average number of earners.

Holding Constant Number of Persons per Consumer Unit.—Evidence presented in chapter iv indicates that with income held constant the higher the number of persons the lower tends to be housing expenditure. Hence it is not surprising that holding number of persons constant tends to increase $\eta_{h_{er}y}$ by 13 per cent (see Table 18 G). However, stratification by number of persons also differentiates strata by number of earners and by owner-occupancy. Both of these are positively correlated with the average income by number of persons, hence both tend to raise $\eta_{h_{er}y}$ for the strata. It may be that number of earners, rather than number of persons, as such, accounts for the increase in the income elasticity observed where number of persons is held constant.

Where age of head as well as number of persons is held constant, the increase in the income elasticity is reduced somewhat, at least for consumer units with head 45 to 55 years of age. For this age category, holding number of persons constant increases the income elasticity by 5 per cent (see Table 18 H). For such strata, also, there is a very marked positive correlation between average income and number of earners and also percentage of owner-occupants.

The indirect effect of these two correlations may account for the increase observed in the mean coefficient of $\eta_{h_{er}y}$. Other evidence is needed to determine whether the number of persons as such has a direct effect.

Holding Constant Age of Children.—Holding constant age of children tends to increase the income elasticity of housing. For large cities in the North the increase is 9 per cent (see Table 18 I). This increase is not surprising since among these strata variation in income is largely explained by number of full-time earners.[17] The effect of holding age of children constant is very similar to that of holding number of persons constant, and both of these characteristics seem likely to serve as proxies for number of earners and hence for $y_t$.

A Summing Up.—Four important tendencies anticipated in chapters ii, iii, and iv have been demonstrated: (1) Where consumer units are stratified by a proxy for normal income, the mean elasticity of housing with respect to income among consumer units of the separate strata tends to be less than the income elasticity of housing of all consumer units combined. This is the effect to expect since such stratification tends to increase the importance of $y_t$, which in turn lowers the coefficient of income elasticity of housing. A similar effect is noted in the review of economic literature presented in chapter ii. (2) Where consumer units are stratified by a characteristic that directly or indirectly represents $y_t$, the income elasticity of housing tends to be increased; number of persons per consumer unit and age of children seem to serve as its proxies. (3) Stratification by tenure tends to increase $\eta_{h_{er}y}$ observed. There is, however, no reason to expect such a tendency if the housing variable is h. Stratification by tenure then seems likely to decrease income elasticity of housing among consumer units observed. This is to be expected if (a) average $y_n$ is higher for owners than for tenants or if (b) owners tend to have a higher standard of housing than tenants. (4) The effect of stratification by tenure on tendencies observed where housing is represented by $h_{er}$ depends on whether the importance of owner-occupancy is negatively or positively correlated with average income of the respective strata. If it is positively correlated with the average income of strata, the mean coefficient of income elasticity of housing expenditure of the strata is likely to be higher than the coefficient of the combined strata, whereas if owner-occupancy is negatively correlated with the income of the strata the opposite tendency is likely to be observed.

These tendencies seem likely to be quite universal. One tendency observed probably is not: With urban area held constant, and transitory income presumably increased in importance, the coefficient of $\eta_{h_r y}$ of 1950 is increased. This, however, is the effect to be expected if market rents of 1950 understated market demand more in areas of high than of low income.

---

17. An estimate of this relationship is shown in chap. iv.

Testing the effect of holding constant tenure and demographic characteristics such as age and number of persons is complicated by their intercorrelation. The intercorrelation is, in fact, so extensive that a much larger sample of consumer units than that of the consumption survey of 1950 would be necessary to permit a direct test of the effect of holding constant the set of conditions just reviewed.

From an examination of the effect on average income elasticity of housing of holding constant various conditions, we turn now to an examination of variation among places in coefficients of income elasticity of housing where all types of consumer units are represented.

### Variation among Places in Coefficients of Income Elasticity of Housing among Consumer Units

Wide difference exists among places in coefficients of income elasticity of housing among consumer units. These are illustrated in Figure 4 using census data of 1950 for owner units in the metro areas of New York, Des Moines, and Mobile. Conditions likely to contribute to such difference are explored in this and the next section using data of the Census of Housing of 1950 as well as data of the consumption survey of 1950 and of the housing survey of 1933. For the consumption survey, the housing variable is expenditure for the main dwelling unit, irrespective of tenure. It is symbolized by $h_{er}$. For the Census of Housing of 1950 and the housing survey of 1933, estimates are made for both owners and tenants, and housing variables are symbolized by h and $h_r$.

The Range.—For each set a wide range in the coefficient of income elasticity of housing is observed. These are as follows:

1. Consumption survey, 1950 ($\eta_{h_{er}y}$)
   a) Urban areas[18] . . . . . . . . . . 0.360 - 0.688
   b) Cities[19] . . . . . . . . . . . . . . . . 0.133 - 0.753
2. Census of Housing, 1950[20]
   a) Owners ($\eta_{hy}$) . . . . . . . . . . . 0.185 - 0.614
   b) Tenants ($\eta_{h_r y}$) . . . . . . . . . . 0.109 - 0.639

18. See Table 19 A, column 2.
19. See Table 21, column 2.
20. See Table 22, columns 1 and 2.

3. Housing, survey, 1933[21]

a) Owners ( $_{hy}$) . . . . . . . . . . . 0.168 - 0.407
b) Tenants ( $_{h_r y}$) . . . . . . . . . . 0.255 - 0.466

With different housing variables and economic conditions represented, perhaps the most surprising thing about these ranges is their similarity.[22]

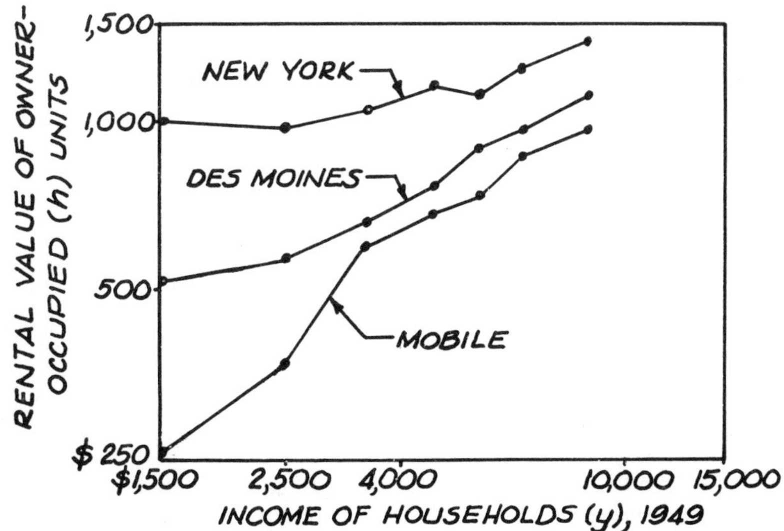


Fig. 4.—Estimated annual rental value of owner units in relation to annual income, three metro areas, Census of Housing, 1950.[a] (Variables shown on log scale.)

Source of data: U.S. Census of Housing: 1950, Vol. II, Table A-7.

a. Estimated rental value of owner units is 10 per cent of the median market value of dwelling units. They represent owners in one-unit structures. Income is represented by the midpoint of income intervals, and housing by the median estimated rent by income interval. Consumer units with incomes below $1,000 and of $10,000 or more are not represented. For estimates of coefficients of elasticity of housing with respect to income, consumer units are shown in Table 22.

21. See Table 23.

22. It should be noted that all regions of the country are represented by each of these sets.

Common Variation of Tenures.—They have, however, another characteristic: within places the coefficients are similar by tenure. This similarity is apparent for both 1950[23] and 1933. The correlation between

Table 21

Coefficients of $\eta_{h_{er}y}$ and Related Characteristics, 30 Cities, Consumption Survey, 1950

| City[a] (1) | $\eta_{h_{er}y}$[b] (2) | $ag_y$[c] (3) | $s_y$[c] (4) | $ea_y$[c] (5) | $o_y$[c] (6) |
|---|---|---|---|---|---|
| 1. Atlanta, Georgia | 0.517 | 113 | 112 | 0.516 | 211 |
| 2. Baltimore, Maryland | .239 | 113 | 121 | .562 | 147 |
| 3. Birmingham, Alabama | .514 | 110 | 121 | .423 | 234 |
| 4. Boston, Massachusetts | .268 | 116 | 146 | .681 | 219 |
| 5. Canton, Ohio | .306 | 114 | 131 | .555 | 166 |
| 6. Chicago, Illinois | .261 | 112 | 163 | .614 | 227 |
| 7. Cincinnati, Ohio | .472 | 118 | 140 | .493 | 185 |
| 8. Cleveland, Ohio | .344 | 113 | 130 | .382 | 138 |
| 9. Hartford, Connecticut | .401 | 118 | 140 | .599 | 219 |
| 10. Indianapolis, Indiana | .291 | 113 | 140 | .561 | 144 |
| 11. Kansas City, Mo.-Kansas | .716 | 118 | 152 | .495 | 152 |
| 12. Los Angeles, California | .248 | 124 | 145 | .678 | 169 |
| 13. Louisville, Kentucky | .590 | 115 | 130 | .408 | 134 |
| 14. Miami, Florida | .519 | 107 | 140 | .365 | 148 |
| 15. Milwaukee, Wisconsin | .133 | 117 | 143 | .545 | 158 |
| 16. Minneapolis-St. Paul, Minnesota | .325 | 113 | 179 | .511 | 208 |
| 17. New Orlenas, Louisiana | .443 | 109 | 133 | .527 | 186 |
| 18. New Jersey, Northern Area | .370 | 112 | 125 | .538 | 170 |
| 19. New York, New York | .432 | 117 | 135 | .649 | 191 |
| 20. Norfolk-Portsmouth, Virginia | .618 | 114 | 131 | .390 | 122 |
| 21. Omaha, Nebraska | .327 | 115 | 146 | .625 | 147 |
| 22. Philadelphia, Pa.-Camden, New Jersey | .477 | 110 | 145 | .617 | 185 |
| 23. Pittsburgh, Pennsylvania | .465 | 106 | 127 | .524 | 178 |
| 24. Portland, Oregon | .366 | 129 | 186 | .665 | 163 |
| 25. Providence, Rhode Island | .279 | 115 | 130 | .632 | 140 |
| 26. St. Louis, Missouri | .473 | 119 | 146 | .641 | 180 |
| 27. San Francisco-Oakland, California | .446 | 116 | 145 | .538 | 148 |
| 28. Scranton, Pennsylvania | .448 | 121 | 141 | .498 | 136 |
| 29. Seattle, Washington | .265 | 123 | 148 | .524 | 183 |
| 30. Youngstown, Ohio | .461 | 110 | 141 | .520 | 144 |
| 31. Mean[d] of 30 cities | 0.400 | 115 | 140 | 0.543 | 171 |

Source: Vols. I and II.

a. The cities include 30 of the 31 cities with at least 150 consumer units reporting. Jackson, Miss., had this number but is excluded since information on income by occupation is not reported in the Census of Population of 1950. Estimates derived from such income are shown in Table 22.

b. The housing variable is expenditure of the tenures combined, excluding expenditure for other housing.

c. See Table 18, footnotes d - g, for a description of these variables.

d. Each city has a weight of one.

23. $\eta_{h_{er}y}$ for urban areas, shown in Table 19 B and C, are an exception. These coefficients are much influenced by the gap between housing expenditure and consumption that differs by tenure, and among owners the gap is also a function of age. Some characteristics of these relationships are illustrated in Fig. 8.

the coefficients by tenure, as indicated by the Census of Housing of 1950, is shown in Figure 5. Something close to a one-to-one relationship is indicated.[24]

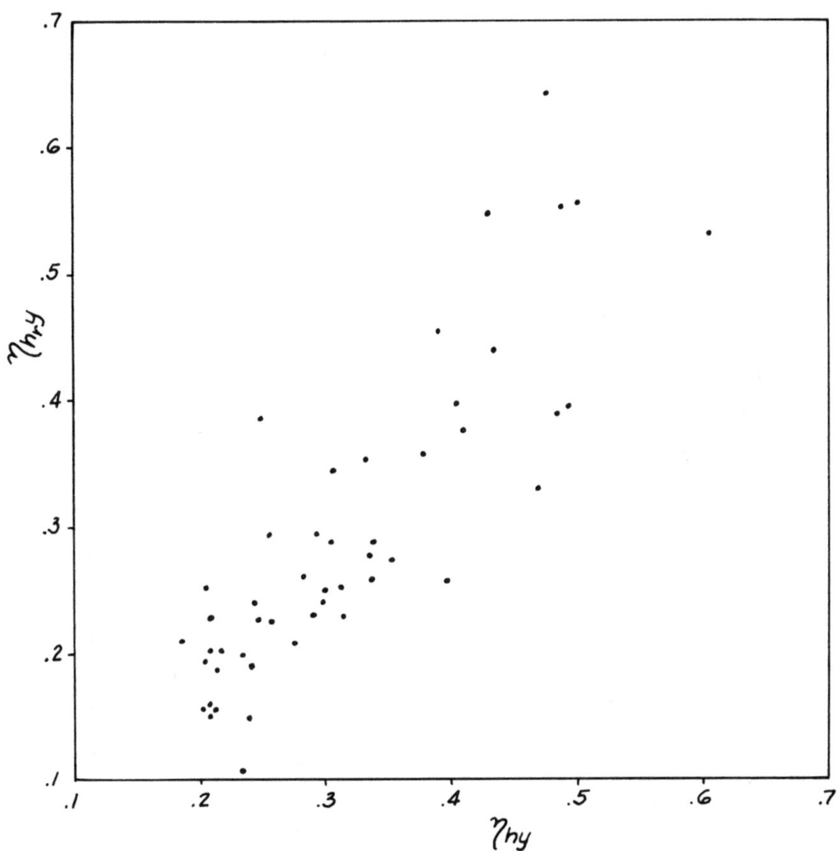


Fig. 5.—Coefficients of $\eta_{h_r y}$ in relation to coefficients of $\eta_{hy}$, 49 metro areas, Census of Housing, 1950 (coefficients are shown in Table 22).

24. This is not inconsistent with a longer planning horizon for housing for owners than for tenants. Such a difference would tend to make $\eta_{hy}$ lower than $\eta_{h_r y}$, but it would not tend to affect the correlation of these coefficients among places.

Table 22

Coefficients of $\eta_{hy}$ and $\eta_{h_r y}$, and Related Characteristics, 50 Metro Areas, Census of Housing, 1950[a]

| Metro area[b] | $\eta_{hy}$[c] (1) | $\eta_{h_r y}$[d] (2) | $\eta_{hry}$[e] (3) | O[f] (4) | $Y_{ov}$[g] (5) |
|---|---|---|---|---|---|
| 1. Atlanta, Georgia | 0.388 | 0.451 | 0.419 | 50.6 | 0.145 |
| 2. Baltimore, Maryland | .259 | .291 | .273 | 55.0 | .092 |
| 3. Birmingham, Alabama | .500 | .560 | .530 | 50.7 | .119 |
| 4. Boston, Massachusetts | .242 | .186 | .211 | 44.5 | .077 |
| 5. Canton, Ohio | .218 | .169 | .202 | 68.2 | .072 |
| 6. Charleston, West Virginia | .468 | .329 | .395 | 47.6 | .091 |
| 7. Chicago, Illinois and Indiana | .185 | .212 | .201 | 41.8 | .082 |
| 8. Cincinnati, Ohio | .250 | .387 | .320 | 49.1 | .087 |
| 9. Cleveland, Ohio | .212 | .201 | .207 | 53.5 | .081 |
| 10. Dallas, Texas | .412 | .370 | .394 | 57.3 | .129 |
| 11. Denver, Colorado | .290 | .293 | .291 | 55.5 | .093 |
| 12. Des Moines, Iowa | .328 | .262 | .306 | 66.7 | na |
| 13. Detroit, Michigan | .233 | .109 | .186 | 61.8 | .073 |
| 14. Hartford, Connecticut | h | h | h | 44.5 | .083 |
| 15. Houston, Texas | .398 | .254 | .334 | 55.5 | .116 |
| 16. Indianapolis, Indiana | .300 | .250 | .279 | 58.5 | .091 |
| 17. Jacksonville, Florida | .393 | .404 | .398 | 55.8 | .129 |
| 18. Kansas City, Kansas and Missouri | .351 | .272 | .318 | 58.3 | .091 |
| 19. Knoxville, Tennessee | .483 | .383 | .439 | 56.3 | .115 |
| 20. Los Angeles, California | .222 | .204 | .214 | 54.1 | .080 |
| 21. Louisville, Kentucky | .360 | .372 | .365 | 55.6 | .095 |
| 22. Memphis, Tennessee | .470 | .639 | .558 | 48.0 | .139 |
| 23. Miami, Florida | .216 | .178 | .198 | 53.9 | .119 |
| 24. Milwaukee, Wisconsin | .222 | .150 | .186 | 49.8 | .063 |
| 25. Minneapolis-St. Paul, Minnesota | .249 | .226 | .240 | 60.3 | .079 |
| 26. Mobile, Alabama | .614 | .533 | .576 | 53.4 | na |
| 27. New Orleans, Louisiana | .491 | .397 | .434 | 38.9 | .130 |
| 28. New York, New York and New Jersey | .212 | .230 | .224 | 31.7 | .087 |
| 29. Norfolk-Portsmouth, Virginia | .433 | .442 | .438 | 42.7 | .122 |
| 30. Oklahoma City, Oklahoma | .333 | .278 | .310 | 58.5 | .096 |
| 31. Omaha, Nebraska | .317 | .251 | .293 | 63.4 | .084 |
| 32. Peoria, Illinois | .299 | .243 | .279 | 63.9 | .075 |
| 33. Philadelphia, Pennsylvania, and New Jersey | .201 | .251 | .220 | 61.9 | .084 |
| 34. Phoenix, Arizona | .313 | .347 | .328 | 57.0 | .099 |
| 35. Pittsburgh, Pennsylvania | .304 | .276 | .291 | 54.8 | .078 |
| 36. Portland, Oregon | .260 | .224 | .248 | 65.6 | .077 |
| 37. Providence, Rhode Island | .204 | .153 | .176 | 45.3 | .077 |
| 38. Richmond, Virginia | .430 | .548 | .483 | 54.7 | .128 |
| 39. Rochester, New York | .211 | .154 | .189 | 60.9 | .070 |
| 40. St. Louis, Missouri and Illinois | .329 | .353 | .341 | 51.4 | .086 |
| 41. Salt Lake City, Utah | .288 | .231 | .266 | 61.9 | .081 |
| 42. San Antonio, Texas | .481 | .552 | .511 | 57.5 | .133 |
| 43. San Diego, California | .238 | .149 | .196 | 52.7 | .065 |
| 44. San Francisco, California | .204 | .192 | .198 | 49.1 | .080 |
| 45. Scranton, Pennsylvania | .231 | .199 | .216 | 52.6 | .070 |
| 46. Seattle, Washington | .274 | .212 | .251 | 63.2 | .077 |
| 47. Wheeling, West Virginia-Steubenville, Ohio | .333 | .276 | .309 | 58.6 | .079 |
| 48. Wichita, Kansas | .317 | .228 | .279 | 57.5 | na |
| 49. Wilmington, Delaware | .285 | .269 | .278 | 57.6 | .109 |
| 50. Youngstown, Ohio | .244 | .237 | .242 | 68.5 | .063 |
| 51. Mean[i] for the metro areas | .316 | .293 | .307 | 54.7 | .093 |

Source: U.S. Census of Housing: 1950, Vol. II, Table A-7, and U.S. Census of Population: 1950, Vol. II, Table 78.

Stability through Time.—Another characteristic of interest is the positive correlation among places between the coefficients observed for 1933 and 1950. The relationship for tenants of 16 places is shown in Figure 6. The correlation is quite pronounced. However, the regression of the coefficients for 1950 with respect to those for 1933 is quite steep. Abnormalities of the rental market in either year could have contributed to this. It is, however, the tendency to expect if rent control tended to lower $\eta_{h_r y}$ for 1950, and if its effect was greatest in places that, with normal markets, tend to have a low coefficient. Evidence shown above as well as that of later chapters implies this likelihood.

The positive correlation among places between the coefficients for the two tenures suggests the presence of influences common to the two tenures. Furthermore, the correlation among places of the coefficients over a span of 17 years suggests that conditions contributing to variation

---

Footnotes to Table 22 (continued)

a. The housing variable is the median value or contract rent, by income interval, and the income is the midpoint of the income intervals, except for incomes below $1,000 and $10,000 or more. For these intervals, income is represented by mean income before taxes as reported in the consumption study of 1950. The estimates shown represent weighted regression coefficients with variables expressed in log form.

b. The following criteria determined the selection of metro areas of this set: (a) Places represented by the Consumer Price Index of the U.S. Bureau of Labor Statistics. (It seems probable that these give a fair representation of large cities and metro areas.) (b) Places included in the consumption survey of 1950. (Some information is provided by comparison between the tendencies indicated by the Census of Housing of 1950 and the consumption survey of 1950.) (c) Places represented in the housing survey of 1933. (These were included to permit a test of the stability of relationships.) And (d) additional places in the South in order to have more adequate representation of this region. (Two such places were added, namely Knoxville, Tenn., and San Antonio, Tex.) With few exceptions the metro areas are those with population of 250,000 or more. Only for these is information on average income by occupation reported. The variance of such average incomes appears to explain much of the variation in coefficients of income elasticity of housing shown in columns 1, 2, and 3.

c. The housing variable is median value of the one-unit owner-occupied units.

d. The housing variable is median contract rent of tenant-occupied units.

e. This is the weighted mean of the coefficients shown in columns 1 and 2. The weights are the percentage of units with owner- and tenant-occupancy as indicated by estimate shown in column 4.

f. Percentage of all occupied units with owner-occupancy.

g. This is the standard deviation of average income of eight main occupational groups of the male labor force, with average income expressed in log form. The data come from the Census of Population: 1950, Vol. II, Table 78. The occupational groups are as follows: (1) professional, technical, and kindred workers; (2) managers, officials, and proprietors exclusive of farm; (3) clerical and kindred workers; (4) sales workers; (5) craftsmen, foremen, and kindred workers; (6) operatives and kindred workers; (7) service workers except private household, and (8) laborers, except farm and mine. For further comment on this index see text, pp. 118-19.

h. No estimate was made for this place. The median value of dwelling units of owner-occupants with incomes of $10,000 or more is above $20,000. The variable $Y_{OV}$ is shown, however, because Hartford is in the set shown in Table 21.

i. Each metro area has a weight of one.

among places have considerable stability.

The Puzzle.—These characteristics of the coefficients were early noted in exploring the housing-income relations reported in this monograph. There seemed no reason to suppose that they were a function of $s_y$ or $ag_y$, since these tend to be fairly similar among places. One of two explanations seemed reasonable: (a) The variation represents the effect of conditions varying among places, such as standard or living or price; or (b) it represents variation among places in the importance of

Table 23

Coefficients of $\eta_{hy}$ and $\eta_{h_r y}$, by Tenure, 16 Cities, Urban Housing Survey of 1933[a]

| City | $\eta_{hy}$ (1) | $\eta_{h_r y}$ (2) |
|---|---|---|
| 1. Atlanta, Georgia | 0.407 | 0.466 |
| 2. Birmingham, Alabama | .328 | .441 |
| 3. Cleveland, Ohio | .215 | .255 |
| 4. Dallas, Texas | .236 | .306 |
| 5. Des Moines, Iowa | .286 | .340 |
| 6. Indianapolis, Indiana | .260 | .337 |
| 7. Minneapolis, Minnesota | .233 | .306 |
| 8. Oklahoma City, Oklahoma | .270 | .284 |
| 9. Peoria, Illinois | .224 | .376 |
| 10. Providence, Rhode Island | .209 | .318 |
| 11. Richmond, Virginia | .356 | .466 |
| 12. Salt Lake City, Utah | .259 | .353 |
| 13. San Diego, California | .168 | .270 |
| 14. Seattle, Washington | .289 | .317 |
| 15. Wheeling, West Virginia | .213 | .311 |
| 16. Wichita, Kansas | .243 | .366 |
| 17. Mean[b] for 16 cities | 0.262 | 0.344 |

Source: Financial Survey of Urban Housing.

a. The survey included 22 cities. Two conditions led to the exclusion of six cities: (a) Data are not available for a similar estimate in the Census of Housing of 1950, and (b) a large percentage of owner-occupancy in structures of two or more units. This study reports the value of owner-occupied structures by income, and it seems probable that the greater the importance of such structures having two or more units the greater the likelihood that the estimate of $\eta_{hy}$ for the owners would be biased. The housing variable for the owners is mean value of structure occupied at the end of the year, and for tenants it is mean annual contract rent. The contract rent of tenants and the income pertain to 1933.

b. Each city has a weight of one.

$y_t$. At the outset there seemed some reason to expect that $y_t$ varied among places, merely because equality of $y_n$ seems likely to differ. Under this condition variation among places in the coefficients is to be expected. To test the effect of $y_t$ necessitates having some measure of its importance, or conversely some measure of the extent to which variation in y represents variation in $y_n$. The measure used is discussed and tested in the section that follows.

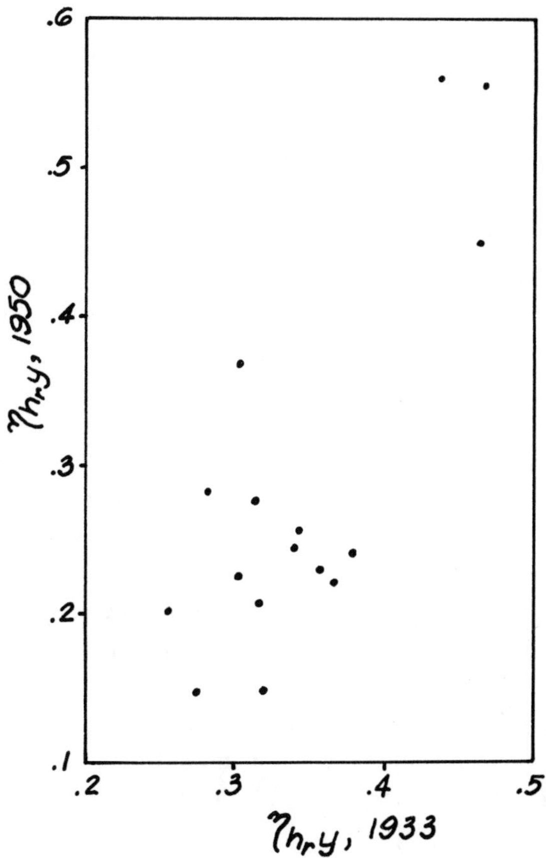


Fig. 6.—Coefficients of $\eta_{h_r y}$ Census of Housing, 1950, in relation to $\eta_{h_r y}$, urban housing survey, 1933, 16 places (coefficients are shown in Tables 22 and 23).

### Variation among Places in the Mixture of Income Components and Its Effect

In chapter ii it was noted that measured income tends to be the sum of two components, a positive permanent or normal component ($y_n$) and a negative or positive transitory component ($y_t$). It was also noted that the greater the importance of $y_t$ the lower is likely to be $\eta_{hy}$.

A good deal of evidence has already been presented to support this hypothesis, and several crude measures of the mixture of income components have been considered. For example, it seems probable that $y_t$ is more important for self-employed workers than for those whose main income comes from wages and salaries. If so, then the greater the importance of self-employed workers the more the variation in y represents $y_t$. In addition, it has been demonstrated that stratifying consumer units by a proxy for $y_n$, such as occupation of the head, tends to lower $\eta_{h_{er}y}$.

This section presents a more direct estimate of the mixture of income components, one that provides a measure that goes beyond merely indicating greater or less importance of $y_n$. It is first described, and then it is compared with coefficients of income elasticity of housing among consumer units of various places.

A Measure[25] of the Mixture of Income Components.—The variance of average incomes among occupational groups seems likely to provide an index of the variation of $y_n$ of consumer units.[26] The presumption is that the greater the difference in average income among occupational groups the more likely is y to approximate $y_n$. Otherwise stated, the greater the difference in average income among occupational groups the less of the variation of y represents $y_t$. Thus it is reasonable to expect that the greater the variance of average income among occupations the higher is likely to be $\eta_{hy}$, for example.

The estimated variance of average income of main occupational groups, with average income expressed in log form, is used as index of the extent to which y represents $y_n$. It is symbolized by $Y_{ov}$.

---

25. Coefficients of correlation of the income of subsets of consumer units in successive years presumably provide another measure. For an example of the use of such a measure, see Margaret G. Reid, "Savings by Family Units in Consecutive Periods," in Walter W. Heller et al. (ed.), Savings in the Modern Economy (Minneapolis: University of Minnesota Press, 1953), pp. 218-20.

26. See fn. 28 below for comment on characteristics of the basic data used.

The consumption survey of 1950 reports average income for 6 occupational groups. Estimates of $Y_{ov}$ for the 9 urban areas[27] using these average incomes are shown in Table 19. They range from 0.085 to 0.130.

For other places, data from the Census of Population of 1950 are used. They represent the median income of the male labor force of the 8 main occupational groups.[28] Estimates for 49 metro areas are shown in Table 22.

They range from 0.063 to 0.145. This difference implies a marked difference among places in the equality of $y_n$ of consumer units.

Association between Coefficients of Income Elasticity of Housing and $Y_{ov}$.—For the nine urban areas $Y_{ov}$ is closely and positively correlated with coefficients of $\eta_{h_{er}y}$: 84 per cent of their variation is explained. This relationship is shown in Figure 7 A.

Panel B shows a similar relationship for estimates derived from

---

27. Similar data are reported for many cities. However, the number of consumer units is small, so the sampling variability of average income by occupation is likely to be high.

28. These are the eight non-farm occupational categories of the male labor force designated by boldface type in the reports, apart from the category "private household workers." Data are shown by Census of Population: 1950, Vol. II, Table 78.

Such measures may be far from perfect as measures of the relative importance of $y_n$. Certainly many conditions seem likely to contribute to their imperfections: (a) Considerable variation in average income occurs for occupations within the main categories; (b) some shifting around of persons among occupations occurs and some of it is probably associated with $y_t$; (c) variation occurs in employment opportunity of metro areas, and this seems likely to bring greater variation in the annual income of those low than those high in the occupational hierarchy. Consequently, some of the variation represented by $Y_{ov}$ is likely to reflect cyclical $y_t$ correlated with $y_n$ of consumer units. And (d) $Y_{ov}$ does not take into account variation in income directly related to the age distribution of the population.

Many of such imperfections may be common to various places. This may account for the fact that in spite of them tendencies indicated are those expected if $Y_{ov}$ is a fairly good index among places of the inequality of $y_n$.

Some tests were made of the adequacy of the eight main occupational categories to represent the income variance of average income among occupations in general. Estimates were made for 34 metro areas of the variance of average income among occupations using the full detail for all non-farm occupations of the male labor force reported by the U.S. Census of Population, exclusive of private household workers. The occupational categories included all with at least 200 persons represented. Estimates of $Y_{ov}$ thus derived were found to be very closely correlated with $Y_{ov}$ derived from the data for the eight main occupational groups. In addition, some evidence bearing on condition (c) is presented in chapter vii.

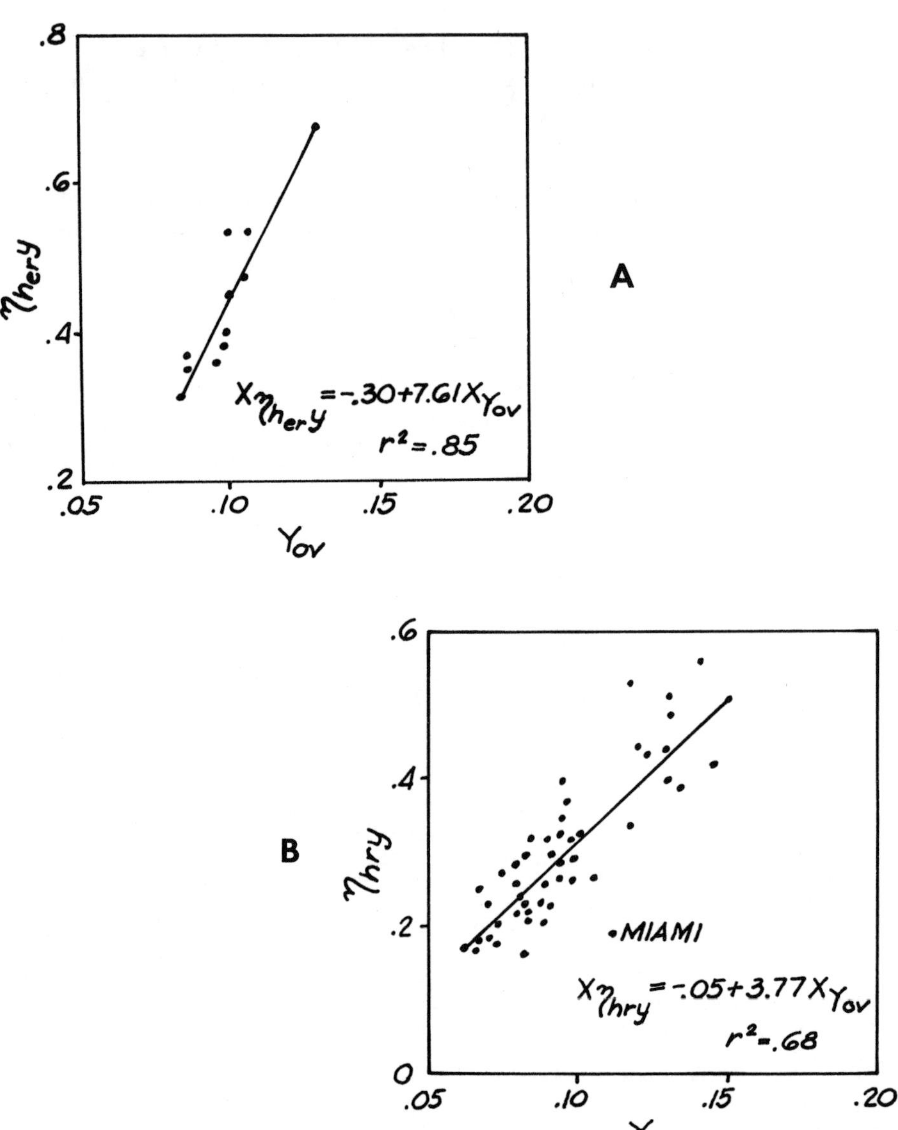


Fig. 7.—Coefficients of income elasticity of housing among consumer units in relation to variation of average income among occupations ($Y_{OV}$), nine urban areas, consumption survey, 1950, and 47 metro areas, Census of Housing, 1950 (coefficients are shown in Tables 19 and 22).

Panel A: $\eta_{h_{er}y}$ in relation to $Y_{OV}$, nine urban areas.

Panel B: $\eta_{h_{r}y}$ (an average of the coefficients for the two tenures) in relation to $Y_{OV}$.

the Census of Housing of 1950. The elasticity coefficients shown represent the average of the respective coefficients of the two tenures which is symbolized by $\eta_{hry}$. $Y_{ov}$ explains 68 per cent of its variation. One place only falls markedly outside the general pattern. This is the metro area of Miami, a place renowned for its tourists, and having a rapid expansion[29] around the time of the census of 1950.

The variable $Y_{ov}$, derived from the census data of incomes for 1949, also explains an appreciable part of the variation in $\eta_{h_{er}y}$ of the 29[30] cities of the consumption survey of 1950. The coefficient of correlation is shown in Table 24, equation (5.3). The small size of the city samples seems likely to have introduced some random error in the coefficient of

Table 24

Coefficients of Correlation of $\eta_{h_{er}y}$ in relation to Characteristics of the Income Distribution, 29 Cities, Consumption Survey, 1950[a]

| Equation number | Regression Coefficients | | | | | $r^2$ or $R^2$ |
|---|---|---|---|---|---|---|
| | $Y_{ov}$ (1) | $ag_y$ (2) | $s_y$ (3) | $ea_y$ (4) | $o_y$ (5) | (6) |
| (5.3) | 3.356 | | | | | .256 |
| (5.4) | .... | -1.446 | | | | .043 |
| (5.5) | 3.291 | -0.186 | | | | .256 |
| (5.6) | .... | .... | -0.594 | | | .044 |
| (5.7) | 3.495 | .... | 0.123 | | | .257 |
| (5.8) | .... | .... | .... | -0.901 | | .268 |
| (5.9) | 2.277 | .... | .... | -0.635 | | .362 |
| (5.10) | .... | .... | .... | .... | -0.241 | .021 |
| (5.11) | 3.565 | .... | .... | .... | -0.371 | .301 |
| (5.12) | 2.326 | .... | 0.283 | -0.745 | 0.151 | .365 |

a. Variables used are shown in Table 21. All variables except $Y_{ov}$ are expressed in log form.

29. In this metro area about one-tenth of the population of 1950, one year of age or more had been in a different county in 1949 and one-third had been in a different house. This makes it seem probable that incomes reported for 1949 had a considerable $y_t$ related to migration during 1949 or to early stages of household formation (for discussion see chap. ii).

30. The Northern New Jersey area is excluded since there is no estimate of $Y_{ov}$ that is strictly applicable to this area.

$\eta_{h_{er}y}$. In addition, a gap of a year existed between the population represented in the consumption survey and by the incomes[31] represented by $Y_{ov}$. This may also have had some bearing on the tendency observed.

Other Conditions Associated with $Y_{ov}$.—Several conditions associated with income of consumer units are also associated with $Y_{ov}$. For the 29 metro areas the following correlation between $Y_{ov}$ and specified variables has been observed:

| Variables | Coefficient of Correlation |
|---|---|
| $ag_y$ | -0.366 |
| $s_y$ | -0.480[32] |
| $ea_y$ | -0.446 |
| $o_y$ | 0.143 |

The relatively high correlation between $Y_{ov}$ and $s_y$ and $ea_y$ may well occur because the greater the equality of $y_n$, that is the lower $Y_{ov}$, the more the y is positively correlated with earners per consumer unit, and the increase in earners with y, symbolized by $ea_y$, is positively correlated with $s_y$. Thus the negative correlation between $Y_{ov}$ and $s_y$ and $ea_y$ may merely signify that these are proxy variables for the mixture of the income components and other conditions related thereto.

The simple correlation of each of these variables with $\eta_{h_{er}y}$ for the 29 cities, is shown in Table 24, and also relationships with $Y_{ov}$ held constant. Of the four variables only $ea_y$ has a significant simple relationship with $\eta_{h_{er}y}$ (see equation 5.8). It explains about the same amount of the variation in $h_{er}y$ as does $Y_{ov}$, the $r^2$ of the respective relationships being .256 and .268. The variables $ea_y$ and $Y_{ov}$ together explain 36 per cent of its variation, and the partial regression coefficients of $ea_y$ are higher than the simple coefficient (see Table 24, eq. [5.9]).

On the other hand, the addition of $s_y$ to the variable $Y_{ov}$ adds nothing to the explanation of $\eta_{h_{er}y}$. Furthermore, the addition of $ag_y$ adds nothing to the explanation of $\eta_{h_{er}y}$. However, the partial regression coefficient of $ag_y$ is negative, the sign to be expected (see Table 24, eq.

31. A gap also occurs between the universes represented. That of $\eta_{h_{er}y}$ presumably is the urbanized portion of some areas and that of $Y_{ov}$ is the entire metro area.

32. For the nine urban areas the corresponding coefficient is -0.779 (data are shown in Table 19 A, columns 5 and 8).

[5.5]). In other words, the more the aged concentrate at low incomes the higher tends to be housing-income ratios at low incomes and the lower tends to be $\eta_{h_{er}y}$.

The addition of $o_y$ to equation (5.3) adds somewhat to the explanation of $\eta_{h_{er}y}$. The $r^2$ of the variables is increased from .256 to .301 (see eq. [5.11]). However, the partial regression coefficient of $o_y$ is negative, the sign expected. In other words, the higher $o_y$, that is the more owner-occupancy increases with income, the lower tends to be $\eta_{h_{er}y}$.

The relationship of $ea_y$ and $s_y$ with $\eta_{h_{er}y}$, for the nine urban areas, is also of interest.[33] The respective correlations are .06 and -.68. In other words for the nine areas $\eta_{h_{er}y}$ has little or no relationship with $ea_y$ whereas it has a negative[34] correlation with $s_y$.

It may be well that $ea_y$ is a fairly good proxy of the importance of $y_t$ of consumer units within a given city but that interplace correlations of one kind or another tend to reduce its usefulness as such an index among areas. The characteristics of $ea_y$ as an index of $y_t$ unquestionably need further consideration, including the testing of other measures of the irregularity of labor-force participation of members of consumer units.

A Brief Summing Up.—The evidence is overwhelming that where y is the explanatory variable, a marked downward bias in $\eta_{hy}$ occurs because of $y_t$. This arises from reporting error or short-run income change. Even the highest coefficient observed among various metro areas, namely, 0.753, is likely to be biased downward. No sets of consumer units seem likely to be entirely free from random short-run income change and all incomes reported seem likely to be subject to reporting error. Furthermore, much of the variation among places in income elasticity is explained by $Y_{ov}$, a measure of the extent to which y represents $y_n$. Hence there seems no reason to suppose that conditions among places, such as standard of living or price, cause much, if any, of the variation in the coefficients observed. Until further evidence is forthcoming it seems reasonable to ascribe most of variation among places of income elasticity of housing among consumer units to the mixture of income components.

---

33. Variables are shown in Table 19 A, columns 2, 5, and 6.

34. Significant at the .05 probability level.

## Coefficients of $\eta_{h_{er}y}$ of Strata Differentiated by Normal Income and Other Characteristics

The variation in one other set of coefficients of income elasticity of housing calls for comment, namely those of strata by tenure, occupation, years of schooling, race, and age of head and by number of persons and age of children shown in Tables 18 and 19. The coefficients shown range from 0.270 to 0.895.[35] Some of this variation has been considered above: it was noted that the coefficient of $\eta_{h_{er}y}$ for all urban places combined is much higher for Negro than white consumer units but that much of this difference disappears where area is held constant. However, some of the variation in the coefficients of various strata has not been reviewed and a few of the patterns noted provide further evidence as to the intercorrelation of conditions that tend to be associated with y.

No index of the importance of $y_n$ is available for most of these strata. Thus, in seeking an explanation of variation in $\eta_{h_{er}y}$ among strata, one is dependent on the evidence of other characteristics. Among the strata the range in four of the variables is as follows:

| Variable | Range |
|---|---|
| $ag_y$ | 93 - 124 |
| $s_y$ | 95 - 158 |
| $ea_y$ | 0.15 - 0.88 |
| $o_y$ | 58 - 548 |

In other words, the various strata represent a very great difference in conditions associated with y that seem likely to affect the income elasticity of housing observed. With very, very few exceptions these variables suggest the presence of conditions likely to lower $\eta_{h_{er}y}$. Their diversity renders difficult any test of their effect. Furthermore, there is a great deal of correlation among them. For example, for several sets of strata $s_y$ and $ea_y$ have a marked positive correlation. In addition, when the strata by number of persons is excluded, there is a marked positive correlation between $ag_y$ and $ea_y$.

_Two Important Tendencies._—The patterns that emerge depend on

35. The estimates shown omit strata where the relevant characteristic is held constant and those where sampling variability seems likely to be high (see Table 18, fn. k).

what characteristic differentiates the strata. Two tendencies seem of special interest:

1) When tenure is held constant, the coefficients of income elasticity among the areas appear to be a function of $ag_y$. However, a difference by tenure occurs. For owner units who bought before 1946, the higher is $ag_y$ the higher tends to be $\eta_{h_e y}$, and for tenants the higher $ag_y$ the lower tends to be $\eta_{h_r y}$. These tendencies are illustrated in Figure 8. They provide further evidence on the heterogeneity of the housing variable represented by $h_{er}$, as well as why $ag_y$ and $o_y$ explain so little of the variation in $\eta_{h_{er} y}$. The positive slope for the owner-occupants shown in Figure 8 A seems reasonable when one recalls that the higher the age of head the more likely is current housing expenditure to be low because equity in the dwelling occupied is high or because property tax of 1950 was relatively low for the aged. On the other hand, the tendency shown for tenants is the type to be expected if rent-income ratios tend to rise as income declines with age of head.

2) Among strata by number of persons, the higher the number of persons in the stratum the higher tends to be $\eta_{h_{er} y}$ (see Table 18 G and H). For both sets of strata, these coefficients are closely and positively correlated with the number of persons in the stratum. Thus the coefficients are relatively low for consumer units of one or two persons and relatively high for consumer units of five or six or more persons. The respective mean coefficients are 0.412 and 0.707.

The high coefficients for strata where number of persons is high seem in some measure to be the result of $o_y$ being relatively low for such units. However, for these strata $o_y$ explains only a little of the variation in $\eta_{h_{er} y}$. Furthermore, among these strata by number of persons, the coefficient is positively rather than negatively correlated with $ea_y$. This raises the question as to whether there may be some unique condition associated with measured income where consumer units are stratified by number of persons.

One condition described in chapter iv is not directly represented by the variables $ag_y$, $s_y$, $ea_y$, or $o_y$, namely the negative correlation between $y_n$ and the birth rate and doubling up of potential households, that is the negative correlation between s and $y_n$. A positive correlation between number of persons represented by the various strata and the coefficient of $\eta_{h_{er} y}$ is to be expected under the following conditions: (a) The higher the number of persons in a stratum the more consumer units

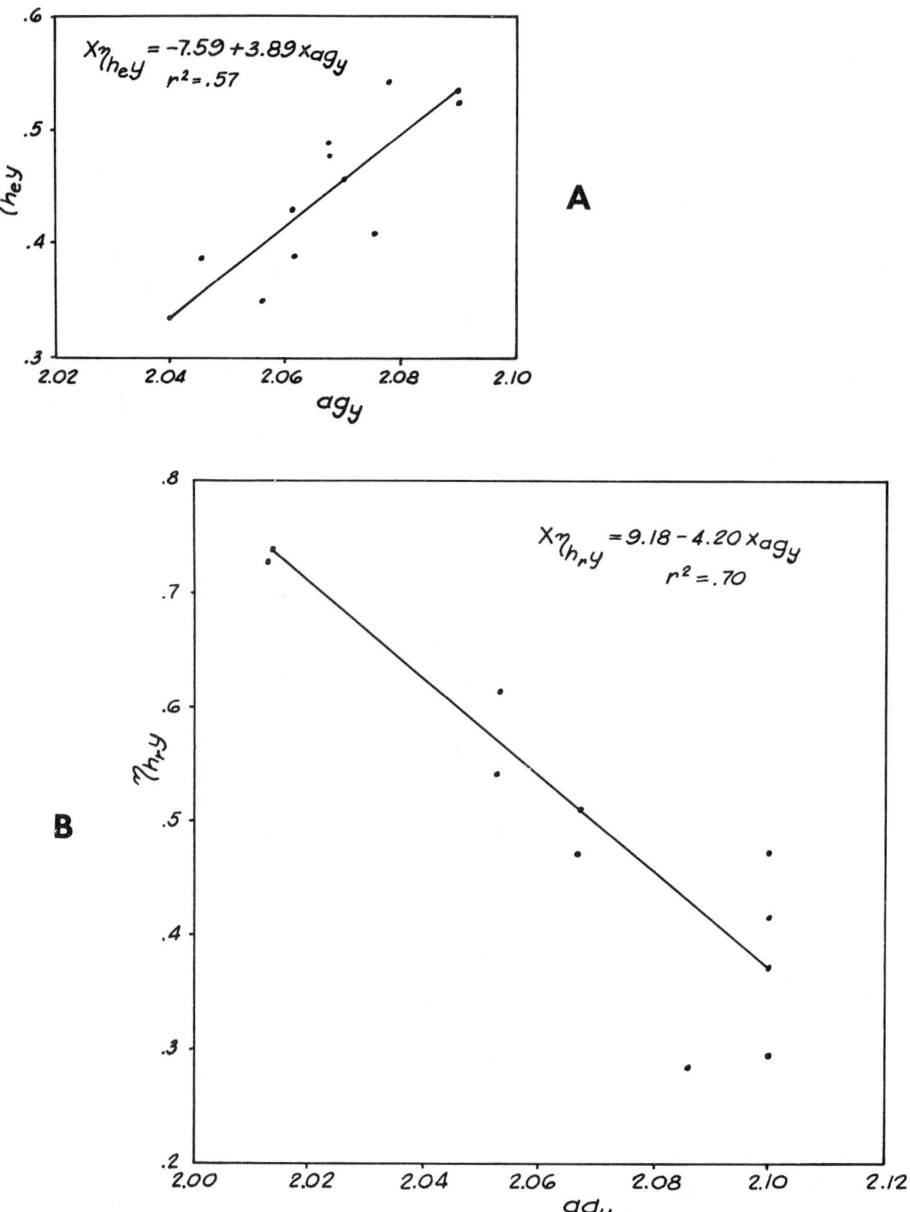


Fig. 8.—Coefficients of $\eta_{h_e y}$ and $\eta_{h_r y}$ in relation to distribution of age of head by income ($ag_y$), urban areas by tenure, consumption survey, 1950 (coefficients and ratios are shown in Table 19, B and C).

Panel A: Owners, before 1946.

Panel B: Tenants at the end of the survey year.

where y is low represent those of low $y_n$, and the more consumer units where y is high represent a phase in the life cycle of those high $y_n$; and (b) housing is little affected by number of persons when $y_n$ is held constant. I know no way of directly testing this interpretation. However, other tendencies noted are consistent with it. For example, among the strata of Table 18 H, that is among strata by number of persons with age of head held constant, the higher $ea_y$ the higher tends to be $\eta_{h_{er}y}$. This is the effect to be expected if the higher the number of persons the more likely are those at low income to represent consumer units that have few, if any, full-time earners in spite of large number of persons.

An Appraisal.—There seems no reason to suppose that $\eta_{h_{er}y}$ shown in Tables 18 and 19, for various strata of the urban universe, yield reliable estimates of the relation of housing to $y_n$. It is true that holding one or more things constant does affect the tendency observed. However, none of the estimates shown here, nor any that I have observed in other similar attempts,[36] reduce much the heterogeneity of the tenure and demographic variables. Furthermore, stratification by place and by occupation tends to increase the importance of $y_t$, to accentuate the downward bias in the coefficients of income elasticity observed and to yield estimates with only a faint resemblance to housing with respect to $y_n$.

Nevertheless, this exploration into holding a few things constant has thrown light on the structure of the intercorrelations that need to be taken into account, and it should contribute to a heightened appreciation of the difficulty through this type of procedure of holding constant such things as size and composition of consumer units, tenure, and standard of housing.

## Variation in $\eta_{hy}$ among Places with Race Held Constant

Holding race constant within metro areas tends to lower the $\eta_{hy}$. (Estimates are shown in Table 25 for seven metro areas.) This is the effect to be expected since stratification by race tends to increase the equality of $y_n$ within strata and hence to increase the importance of $y_t$. However, the mean coefficient is much the same for the two races, and furthermore the variation in coefficients among places appears to be no

36. For extensive estimates of this type, see Jean Crochett and Irwin Friend "A Complete Set of Demand Relationships," op. cit., pp. 1-92.

greater for the white than for non-white households.

The main implication of this similarity is that the equality of $y_n$ within places tends to be much the same for white as for Negro consumer units. Although the coefficients are much the same for the two races, it seems highly unlikely that they represent the coefficient of elasticity of housing with respect to normal income.

Table 25

Coefficients of $\eta_{hy}$ Households Stratified by Race, Seven Metro Areas, Census of Housing, 1950[a]

| Metro area | All (1) | White (2) | Non-white (3) |
|---|---|---|---|
| 1. Birmingham | 0.500 | 0.341 | 0.266 |
| 2. Chicago | .185 | .199 | .231 |
| 3. Detroit | .233 | .232 | .078 |
| 4. Houston | .398 | .330 | .241 |
| 5. Los Angeles | .222 | .221 | .130 |
| 6. New Orleans | .491 | .380 | .368 |
| 7. St. Louis | .329 | .294 | .372 |
| 8. Mean[b] | 0.337 | 0.285 | 0.241 |

Source: Unpublished tabulations from the Census of Housing, 1950.

a. For characteristics of variables, see Table 22, fn. a.

b. Each place has a weight of one.

### Variation in Housing among Subgroups with y Held Constant

Transitory income tends to distribute consumer units at random. Hence, with y held constant, one should expect to find housing, symbolized by $h_y$, or some variant thereof, to be positively correlated with average income (Y) of subsets, if such Y represents average $y_n$. In Chapter ii it is noted that this phenomenon has been otherwise interpreted, namely as a tendency for consumer units with a common place of residence or occupation or tenure to have a common standard of housing shaped by group standards.

Final judgment as to the validity of these alternative interpretations must be postponed until the evidence of later chapters is reviewed. This section is concerned solely with the association between $h_y$ and Y among various places, and occupations and tenures for 1950 and for urban places between 1941 and 1950.

Difference among Places.—Figure 4 shows h with respect to y for three metro areas. For these the higher is Y of the areas[37] the higher tends to be h where y is held constant. A positive correlation between average price of housing and average income might have contributed to this tendency as well as a positive correlation between standard of housing and Y.

Difference by Occupation.—The consumption survey permits a comparison between occupational groups within urban places of the United States, so that any effect from difference in average market price and standard of housing among places tends in considerable measure to be held constant. Examples of housing-income curves are shown in Figure 9 for two occupational subsets quite similar in the importance of owner-occupancy[38] and quite different in average income.[39] Between occupations, the higher is Y the higher tends to be $h_{er}$ where y is held constant.

Difference by Tenure.—Difference in housing, where y is held constant, is observed between tenures. This tendency is illustrated in Figure 10, using data for the metro stratum areas of the United States for 1950. The difference in level of housing where y is held constant is very great indeed. In other words, where y is held constant the housing of owners is much, much higher than that of tenants. This difference occurs in spite of the fact that housing of tenants is represented by contract rent which tends to overstate housing consumption, whereas the

---

37. The median income and value of dwelling of these three metro areas are as follows:

| | Income | Value of Dwelling |
|---|---|---|
| Des Moines | $3,783 | $7,249 |
| Mobile | 2,733 | 4,511 |
| New York | 4,704 | 12,339 |

38. The percentage of owner-occupancy is 51 for salaried professional and 43 for the semiskilled subgroup. Thus, this difference in owner-occupancy tends to narrow the relative level of the two intraclass regressions shown in Fig. 9.

39. The mean income and expenditure for housing of these two occupational groups are as follows:

| | Income | Expenditure for Main Dwelling Unit |
|---|---|---|
| Salaried professional and officials | $5,406 | $571 |
| Semiskilled wage earners | 3,673 | 367 |

estimated rental value of the owners presumably represents only market value of space.

Several things could have contributed to the marked difference observed: (a) Owners may have a higher standard of housing than tenants;

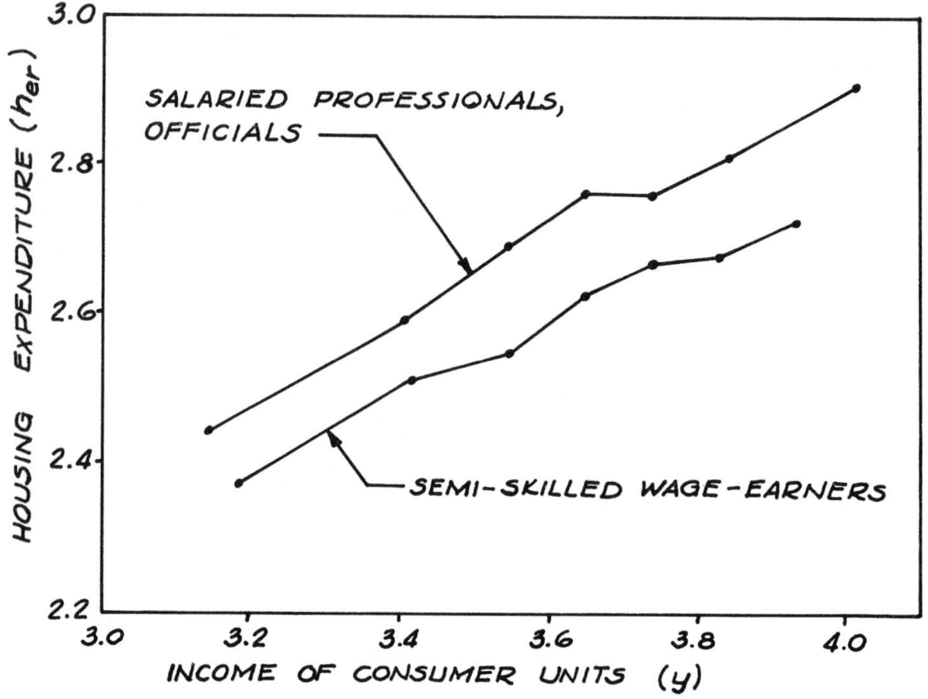


Fig. 9.—Housing expenditure in relation to income of consumer units, two occupational groups, consumption survey, 1950.[a] (Variables in log form.)

Source of data: Study of Consumer Expenditures Incomes and Savings, Vol. XVIII.

a. The lowest incomes shown represent all consumer units with income under $2,000 and the highest all those with incomes of $7,500 or more.

(b) 10 per cent of the estimated market value of owner-occupied units may overstate the market rental of owner units; (c) money income understates the total income of owner units because it does not include income in kind from the equity of the owner-occupant (such omission tends to shift to the left the housing-income curve of owners and thus appears to raise its level compared to the housing-income curve of tenants). In addition, the total income including income in kind on the form of owner's

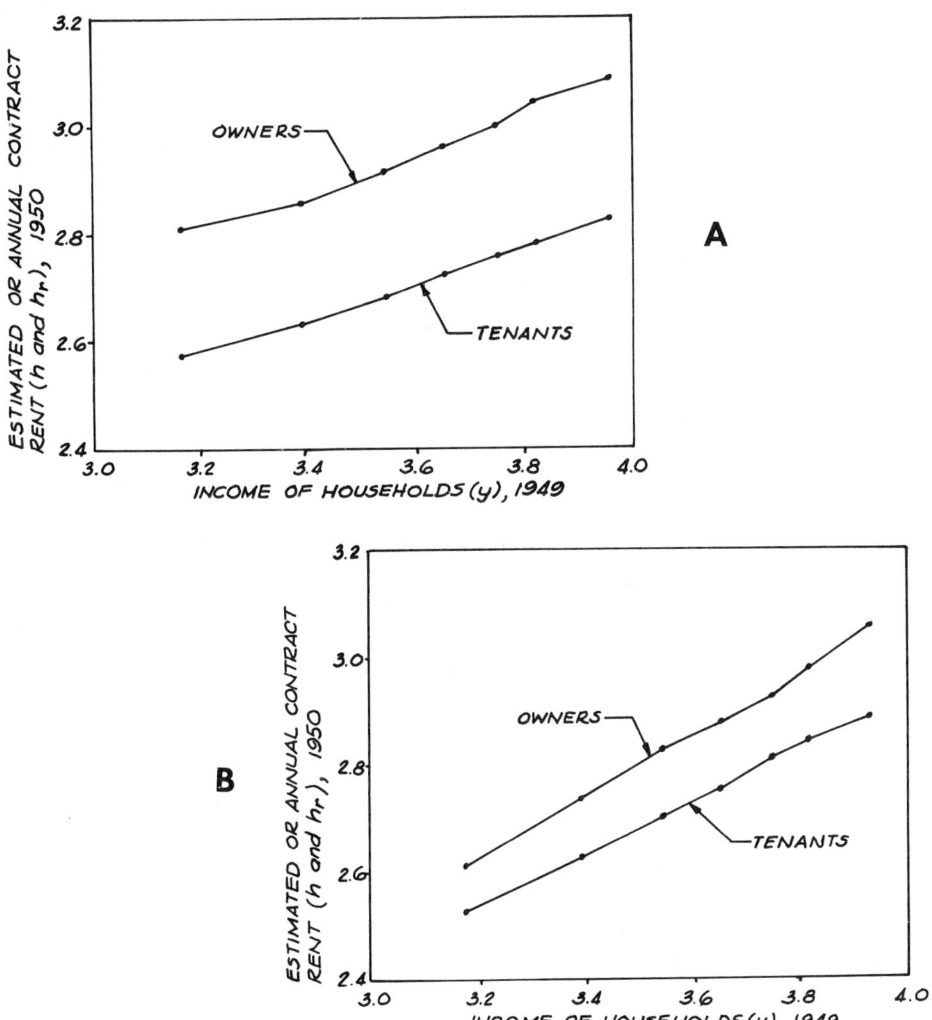


Fig. 10.—Estimated annual rental value of owner units and contract rent of tenant units in relation to annual income of consumer units, metro stratum of United States and of the West South Central region, Census of Housing, 1950.[a] (Variables in log form.)

Panel A: Owners and tenants, metro stratum of the United States, 1950.

Panel B: Owners and tenants, metro stratum of West South Central region, 1950.

a. See Table 22, fn. a, for source of census data and method of estimating rental value of owner units, annual contract rent of tenant units, and annual income by interval. Observations for the lowest and the highest income intervals are omitted.

equity may understate the demand of owner- compared and to tenant-occupants if owner-occupants tend to have a higher ratio of assets to income than tenants. Assets as well as $y_n$ tend to influence consumption decisions; and (d) the contract rent of tenants may understate appreciably the demand of tenants in a free market.

The possibility of condition (a) being important is dealt with in later chapters. A direct test of condition (b) does not seem feasible. It seems probable, however, that the effect of condition (c) is appreciable. This is indicated by the tendency shown in Figure 11. This shows estimated rent-

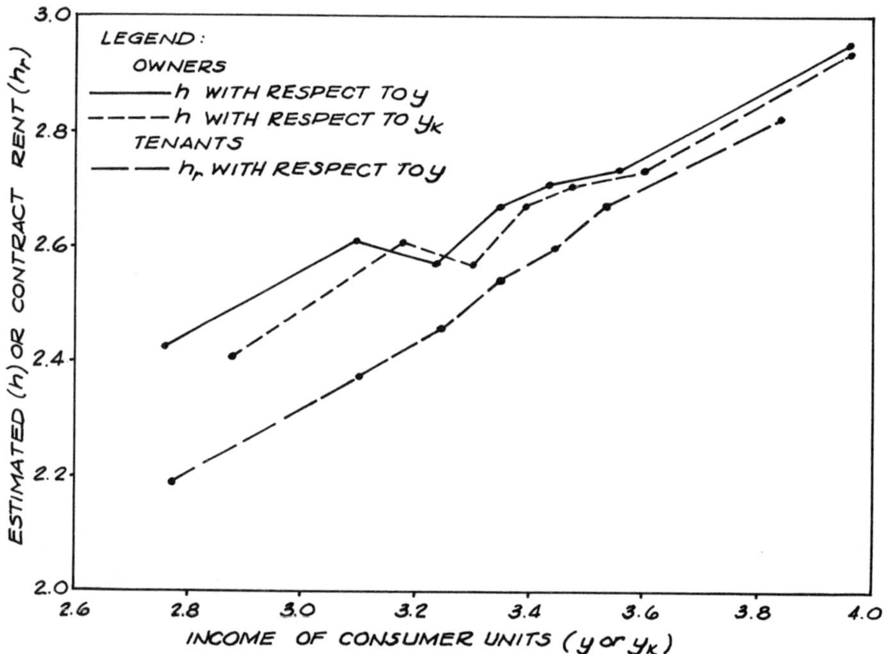


Fig. 11.—Estimated annual rental value of owner units and contract rent of tenant units[a] in relation to income[b] of consumer units, urban consumption survey, 1941.

Source of data: U.S. Department of Labor, Bul. 822, Table 22.

a. The owner set is confined to consumer units in owner dwellings throughout the entire year and the tenant set to those who were tenants throughout the entire year. The lowest incomes shown represent all those with income under \$1,000 and the highest income all those with income of \$5,000 or more.

b. Both money income (y) and money income plus income in kind ($y_k$). The income in kind represents rental value of the owner dwelling unit minus housing expenditures.

al value of owner units in 1941 in relation to money income. It also shows such rent in relation to total income that includes income in kind from the equity in the dwelling unit occupied symbolized by $y_k$: The substitution of $y_k$ for y narrows somewhat the gap between the level of owner and tenant housing, with income held constant. This narrowing is especially marked at low income levels where the aged with high equity in the dwelling unit occupied tend to concentrate.

Several types of evidence suggest that condition (d) is probably quite important, namely that contract rent of 1950 understates the demand of tenants in a free market. One is that, where a considerable volume of new construction of tenant units had occurred or where the Consumer Price Index indicates little effect from rent control on the prewar stock,[40] the difference in housing observed, where y is held constant, is much less than that for the United States in general (see Fig. 10 B as compared to Fig. 10 A). Where y is \$3,500, $y_h$ per \$100 of $y_{h_r}$ is \$173 for metro areas of the United States and \$137 for those of the West South Central region. On the other hand, difference in average income between tenures would lead one to expect less difference by tenure for the United States than for the West South Central region. (Average income of owners per \$100 of income of tenants is \$128 for the United States and \$141 for the West South region.) Thus it seems reasonable to conclude that difference in housing by tenure, shown in Figure 10 A, where y is held constant, has been increased by rent control.

1950 versus 1941.—If conditions affecting housing of owners and tenants had been the same in 1950 as in 1941, one would expect to observe a similar pattern between tenures for these years. Similarity is not observed. Relationships are shown in Figure 12 using data for urban places. Panel A shows housing expenditure of owners with respect to income for 1941 and 1950, and Panel B shows the corresponding relationships for tenants. All the data are expressed in current dollars. In other words, no attempt is made to adjust for change in the purchasing power of the dollars. The position of median income is, however, indicated.

Where dollar income is the same, housing expenditure of owners is higher for 1950 than for 1941. There are no exceptions, although the difference between years is small at the highest income level. The tendency

40. For discussion of the effect of these conditions, see Margaret G. Reid, "Increase in Rent of Dwelling Units from 1940 to 1950," Journal of American Statistical Association, June, 1959, pp. 358-76.

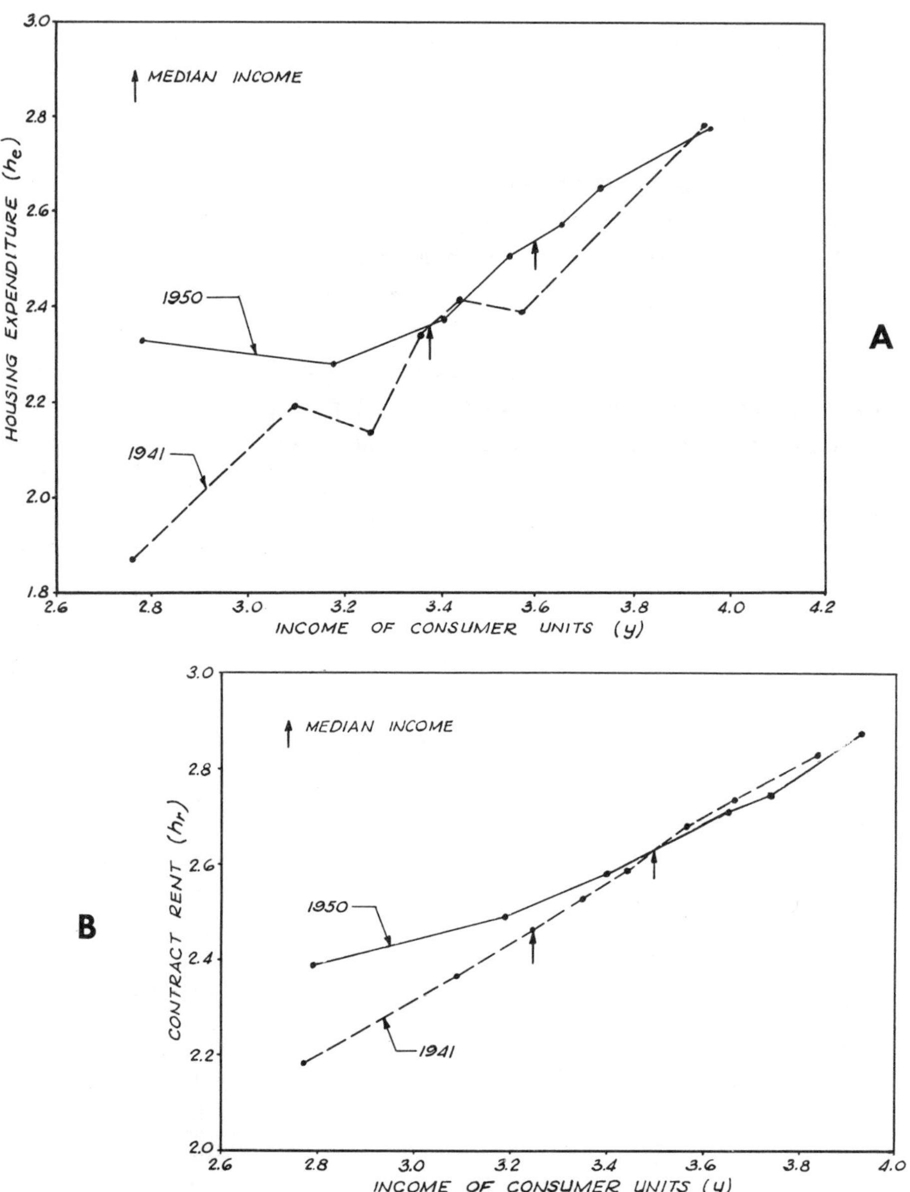


Fig. 12.—Annual expenditure for housing, by tenure, urban surveys, 1941 and 1950.[a] (Variables in log form.)
Panel A: Owners.
Panel B: Tenants.

a. Only full-year owners are represented. Data of the survey of 1941 also represent full-year tenants, whereas those of the consumption survey of 1950 represent consumer units who were tenants at the end of the survey year.

observed between years for owners is the type to expect if increase in real income and/or inflation appreciably raised expenditure for housing, and if $y_t$ is important for each year. Thus, between years where y is held constant, housing tends to be positively correlated with average income of all owners (Y). On the other hand, where y is held constant, contract rent of tenants is relatively high in 1950 at low dollar incomes and relatively low at high incomes. The two regressions intersect at about the median income of tenants of 1950. The tendencies observed are the type to be expected (a) if rents rose more in places of low than of high income, and (b)[41] if the lag of rental tenant housing behind income change in places of high income was rather large.[42]

A Concluding Comment.—There seems little doubt that difference among subsets in level of housing observed where y is held constant is in part a result of $y_t$, and that some of it for 1950 is also the result of rent control. Whether some of it is also the result of the housing standards and the price of housing must be judged in the light of tendencies observed where $y_t$, standard of housing, and market price of housing are all held constant. Tendencies observed with such constraints are considered in chapter viii.

## A Summing Up

In the past, descriptions of housing-income relations have chiefly utilized measured income of consumer units (y) as the explanatory variable. Hence, this chapter presents a customary type of evidence. The tendencies observed have, however, been scrutinized in several non-conventional ways. A search has been made for conditions giving rise to variation in tendencies observed. Friedman's permanent-income hypothesis, discussed in chapter ii, provides the frame of reference. In addition, an attempt has been made to take into account demographic characteristics of the population and how these may affect tendencies observed.

---

41. It is also the type to be expected if additional services in contract rent fell between 1941 and 1950. The reverse of this occurred, so this possibility can be dismissed. For information on change of services in rent see Monthly Labor Review, July, 1954.

42. The National Housing Inventory of 1956 does not permit a comparison between 1941 and 1956 of contract rent with income held constant. It does report gross rent by income level. However, the consumption survey of 1941 does not report gross rent of tenants.

The coefficients of income elasticity of housing among consumer units observed, using data of the consumption survey and the census of 1950, are all well below 1.0, and for the most part appreciably below 0.5. They thus seem to confirm the Schwabe law of rent, namely that housing takes a decreasing percentage of income. However, these coefficients, even the highest observed, seem likely to be biased downward by the transitory component of incomes ($y_t$).

Wide difference in coefficients is observed. For example, for 49 metro areas the range for owner-occupants is from 0.185 to 0.614 (see Table 22). Much of this difference appears to be a function of the mixture of normal ($y_n$) and transitory income ($y_t$). Variation in coefficients observed for consumer units, irrespective of place, tenure, and year, appears to be explained by this mixture. In general, the more $y_t$ influences the position of consumer units in the income distribution, the lower tends to be the income elasticity of housing. One measure of the importance of $y_n$ explains a large part of the variation in coefficients observed. This evidence gives no reason to suppose that coefficients of elasticity of housing with respect to $y_n$ differ by tenure or by place or through time. This is the main finding of this chapter. Thus this chapter amplifies a type of evidence presented in chapter ii and demonstrates more fully the effect on tendencies observed of the variables used to represent housing and of various conditions correlated with y. It isolates and measures the effect of the main condition that causes variation among places in elasticity of housing with respect to y. It does not, however, provide evidence as to the magnitude of the coefficient of elasticity of housing with respect to $y_n$. Chapters vi-viii, x, and xiii deal more directly with this.

Several findings of lesser importance and some qualifications of the main findings are now summarized: (1) The years represented by the coefficients differ greatly in stage of the cyclical change represented and in degree of lag of housing behind income change. Difference ascribed to these conditions have not been identified with great precision. It seems probable, however, that the effect of these is minor compared to the effect of $y_t$ uncorrelated with $y_n$. As more data become available, this hypothesis can be tested further.

2) There is little doubt that the coefficient of income elasticity of contract rent of 1950 for the United States in general tends to be biased downward by a lag of tenant housing behind income change and the concentration of this lag in areas of relatively high income. This likelihood

is supported by two pieces of independent evidence: (a) the tendency of average income elasticity of contract rent to increase where urban area is held constant, and (b) the tendency, where y is held constant, for contract rent to be lower at high y of 1950 than of 1941 (Fig. 12 B), whereas, where y is held constant, h for owners is in general higher in 1950 than in 1941 (see Fig. 12 A). In view of regional policies with respect to rent control, the tendency observed is not surprising. It should be noted, however, that consumer behavior under rent control is unlikely to provide a reliable indication of free market behavior.

3) Coefficients of income elasticity of housing among consumer units, those for owners as well as tenants, seem likely to have declined during the forties. Evidence of such decline comes from the consumption surveys of 1941 and 1950 representing similar universes and housing variables. The downward trend in the coefficient may, however, be the result of the increased importance of $y_t$ because of increased equality of $y_n$ rather than to a change in demand for housing with respect to $y_n$.

4) The more the variation in y represents $y_n$ the higher tends to be the income elasticity of housing observed. Hence the average coefficient of the separate occupations and races is less than that of groups combined. This difference seems likely to be due to the increased importance of $y_t$ with decrease in the range of $y_n$ represented.

5) Some of the variation observed in the coefficients of income elasticity of housing is related to the variable used to represent housing. Where housing of owner-occupants is represented by expenditure rather than by rental value, the income elasticity observed tends to be higher than where their housing is represented by the rental value of the dwelling unit. This difference appears to occur because owners with high equity in their dwelling units, and hence with low current expenditure, are the aged who concentrate where y is low.

6) The combination of tenures also affects the tendencies observed. Where housing is represented by expenditure, such combination tends to lower the income elasticity of housing expenditure observed. This lowering occurs because of the increasing gap between housing expenditure and consumption with rise in the importance of owner-occupancy accompanying rise in y.

7) Evidence examined in chapter iv indicates that where y is held constant housing expenditure tends to decline with increase in number of persons per consumer unit. It is noted there that this tendency may

be caused by the negative relationship between $y_n$ and the birth rate and the doubling up of potential households, and the consequent likelihood that the higher the number of persons per consumer unit the greater the importance of consumer units with low $y_n$. Evidence presented in this chapter supports this conclusion. In addition, it gives some reason to suppose, with $y_n$ held constant, that the addition of children to a household does not tend to decrease housing. Increase in income to its peak on the age-income cycle is positively correlated with number of persons.

8) Since $y_t$ appears to be very important, it is not surprising, where y is held constant, that housing is correlated with the average income ($Y_n$) of respective subsets. Whether it is also influenced by price of housing and standard of living is considered in later chapters. The difference in housing between tenures with y held constant is greater in 1950 than in 1941. This is the type of difference to be expected if the lag of tenant housing behind income change was greater in 1950 than in 1941.

9) A wide range in coefficients of income elasticity of housing among consumer units has been observed, some as high as 0.90. Nevertheless, it seems not improbable that all such coefficients tend to be biased downward by $y_t$. Later chapters provide evidence as to the magnitude of this bias.

# Chapter Six

# AVERAGE HOUSING IN RELATION TO AVERAGE INCOME OF PLACES

Where average income differs among cities and the difference represents normal income, in dollars of constant purchasing power, then the elasticity of average housing with respect to average income tends to provide an estimate of the relation of housing consumption to normal income. A necessary condition is, of course, that other things are held constant, such as age of persons in consumer units, the cost of housing relative to other products, the standard of housing, additional services included in contract rent, and such things as rent control and lag of housing behind change in normal income.

This chapter describes interclass correlations among places. The main variables are average housing and income of households or of other consumer units. The variables used correspond to those examined in chapter v, with symbols here being shown in upper-case letters. As in previous estimates the housing and income variables are expressed in log form, hence the regression coefficient of the interplace correlation represents the income elasticity of housing. Where housing is symbolized by H, the interplace[1] coefficient of income elasticity is symbolized by $\eta_{HY}$.

The main topics of this chapter are: (a) the sets of data used; (b) characteristics of variables; (c) elasticity of housing with respect to average income among places; (d) difference by tenure in average housing where Y is held constant; and (e) holding construction cost constant.

1. For such estimates, unless otherwise specified, each place has a weight of one.

## The Sets of Data Used

Estimates shown utilize data of the Census of Housing of 1950, the consumption survey of 1950, and the housing survey of 1933,[2] sources utilized for estimates shown in chapter v. In addition, some estimates are shown for the 1956 National Housing Inventory, and the consumption survey of 1935-36. Thus the estimates presented span 20 years.

The consumption survey of 1935-36, like that of 1950, reports housing expenditure ($H_e$). In addition, it reports the estimated rental value of owner units (H). It is similar to the housing survey of 1933 in that it represents behavior in a free market. However, the degree of depression represented by the consumption survey of 1935-36 is less than that represented by the housing survey of 1933. Other features of the consumption survey of 1935-36 seem likely to affect tendencies observed. These are commented on later. The sets of data examined represent a variety of conditions. Each contributes something to an understanding of tendencies that are likely to be observed among places under different conditions.

The Census of Housing of 1950 provides a very large stock of data on which to draw. Estimates are shown for three sets of places: (a) metro areas of the nine geographical divisions of the United States; (b) 30 metro areas represented by the Consumer Price Index; and (c) nine metro areas represented by the 1956 National Housing Inventory. These are referred to as the division, the index, and the inventory sets, respectively. The first describes tendencies among large cities and their environs

---

2. The estimates shown in this chapter come close to utilizing the full stock of data available for urban places where information by tenure is reported. However, there are some data for 1929. These come from the housing survey of 1933, and the housing and income of 1929 were reported by households of 1934, classified by tenure as of that period. For each tenure there is a considerable gap between the number reporting income and the number reporting housing. It is the type of a gap to be expected if an appreciable number of households passed from owner to tenant status during the period and if more households formed between 1929 and 1934 were tenants than owners. Conditions such as these make it unlikely that estimates of 1929 for these data would be especially reliable.

In addition, the Census of Population of 1940 provides some data. Rent of dwelling units is reported by income and by tenure for eleven metropolitan districts. However, the manner of tabulating the rent makes very difficult an estimate of median rent for the set for which income is reported. Hence, estimates from this source are not included in this monograph (see U.S. Bureau of Census, *Census of Population and Housing: 1940*, Special Report: *Families, Income and Rent* [1943]).

throughout the United States. The second describes tendencies among a fairly representative set of large metro areas and permits a test of the effect of inflation and rent control. The third permits a comparison between 1950 and 1956 for a constant set of metro areas. An intensive examination has been made of a subset of the index set, namely 14 metro areas with no more than 5 per cent of the tenant dwelling units constructed in 1945 or later. This subset will be referred to as the low-new subset.

## Characteristics of Variables

The characteristics of average housing and average income of consumer units are considered in this section together with some of the variables used in an attempt to hold constant the effect of conditions correlated with Y.

Average Housing of Places.—Because of rent control, the tenant market of 1950 was abnormal. Three variables are used in the hope of holding constant its effect. The first is the rise in the rent index from December, 1941,[3] to April, 1950. In other words, the measure of rent change used is rent of April, 1950, with that of December, 1941, equal to 100. It is symbolized by $P_r''$. Among the cities represented it ranges from 101 for Norfolk to 133 for Houston.

The other two variables represent the importance of new construction. The importance of housing built during 1945 or later is symbolized by $B_1$, and that built during 1940 through 1944 by $B_2$. These vary widely among metro areas. For example, $B_1$ ranges from 1 to 26 per cent. If contract rent of 1950 of some places was depressed by rent control and if the units entering the market during the late forties had rents above those of similar quality under rent control, as was permitted by the regulations, one would expect that the higher $B_1$ the higher would tend to be $H_r$ where Y is held constant.

The expectation as to the effect on contract rent of 1950 of units built during the early forties has a more speculative base. The variable $B_2$ has been used because of the likelihood that some inflation occurred during the early forties and that its effect on rent tended to be more pronounced for new than for existing stock. Accordingly, the expectance is,

3. The rent index of this period was unaffected by rent control.

where Y is held constant, that among cities the higher $B_2$ the higher tends to be $H_r$.

Average Income of Places.—Ideal data would represent places differing in average normal income ($Y_n$), and Y observed would equal $Y_n$. However, even when sample size is very large, Y may have a transitory component ($Y_t$) because of cyclical change being represented. If $Y_t$ is the same for all places, it will affect only the level of the interplace regression. On the other hand, if $Y_t$ tends to be uncorrelated with $Y_n$, as seems probable, and hence positively correlated with Y, it will tend to lower $\eta_{HY}$.

General principles considered in chapter ii with respect to the importance of $y_t$ apply also to $Y_t$: The importance of $Y_t$ will be influenced by two things, namely (a) the occurrence of conditions giving rise to $Y_t$ and (b) the extent of the variation among places in $Y_n$. The greater the uniformity among places in the normality of employment opportunity the less likely is the variation in Y to represent that of $Y_t$, and conversely the greater the variation in $Y_n$ among places the more likely is variation of Y to represent that of $Y_n$.

Forces in the economy, including high mobility of the population, inflation, and income tax, have tended to reduce the variation among places in $Y_n$. Thus one should expect, with other conditions held constant, that the earlier the period represented, that is, 1933 as compared to 1960, the more likely is Y to represent $Y_n$. The evidence presented in this chapter deals chiefly with average incomes of 1949 and 1950 and the mid-thirties. Presumably, normal income differed more among places in the mid-thirties than in 1949. However, widespread unemployment of the thirties makes it seem likely that $Y_t$ of cities accounted for much of the variation of Y of those years.

Unfortunately, there is little direct evidence bearing on the relative importance of the $Y_t$ of places, although the state of the economy in general provides clues as to what to expect. The sets of incomes examined include those of 1933, of 1949,[4] and of 1950, and employment levels of 1933 were undoubtedly very abnormal. Accordingly, it would not be surprising if $Y_t$ accounted for more of the variation of Y of places of the 1933 than of the places of the 1949 or the 1950 set.

---

4. The year represented by the income reported for the Census of Housing of 1950.

However, as judged by postwar standards, 1949 represents a year of relatively low employment levels, so that it would not be surprising if $Y_t$ of places for 1949 is of some importance. The Census of Population of 1950 reports the distribution of the labor force by weeks worked in 1949. A wide variation occurs among cities. It seems not improbable that the higher the percentage of the labor force very low in weeks worked during 1949 the greater the likelihood that $Y_t$ is negative, and the lower this percentage the greater the likelihood that it is positive.

The percentage of the male labor force of 1950 that worked less than 26 weeks during 1949 has been used as a proxy for the degree of abnormality of employment opportunity among metro areas. It is symbolized by Le, referring to the importance of low employment among males in the labor force. The assumption is that the higher Le the greater the likelihood that $Y_t$ is negative, and the lower is Le the greater the likelihood that $Y_t$ is positive. However, Le seems likely to be only a crude proxy for $Y_t$, since it will also reflect variation among places in the usual age at which males enter the labor force. This may well be negatively correlated with $Y_n$.[5] If so, the higher Le the lower will tend to be H or $H_r$, because high Le is serving as a proxy for low $Y_n$. This possibility should not be overlooked in interpreting tendencies observed.

Size and Composition of Consumer Units.—The size and composition of consumer units vary markedly among places, and the evidence of chapter iv indicates that housing-income ratios tend to be especially high for households with an aged or a female head. Consequently, it would seem advisable in estimating the relation of housing to $Y_n$ to hold constant their importance among places. This is feasible for estimates using census data of 1950 and 1956. The main variable used is the number of all households per 100 households, exclusive of those with a male head 65 years of age or more or a female head. The variable is symbolized by Af. The expectation is that the higher Af the higher will tend to be housing where Y is held constant.[6]

---

5. This will occur if there is a tendency, under normal employment conditions, for the weeks worked per year to be less for unskilled and semiskilled than for skilled and professional and managerial workers.

6. The usefulness of Af may, however, be reduced by conditions related to the negative correlation among places between normal income and the doubling up of potential households. Evidence on this is presented in chap. iv, Fig. 2. To the extent that this occurs there seems likely to be a positive correlation among places between Af and $Y_n$. This cor-

## Income Elasticity of Average Housing among Places

Coefficients of income elasticity of housing among places by tenure have been estimated for several sets of data. Simple coefficients are shown in Table 26 for the housing survey of 1933 and the consumption surveys of 1935-36 and 1950. And simple and partial coefficients of income elasticity of housing are shown in Table 27 for estimates derived from census data of 1950 and 1956.

The secondary variables used in examining the data of the Census of Housing of 1950 are Af, Le, $B_1$, $B_2$, and $P_r''$. With the exception of Le the expectation is that the partial regression coefficient of each of these five variables will be positive. In other words, where Y is held constant the greater the importance of households with an aged or female head (Af), the greater the importance of tenants units built during the forties ($B_1$ and $B_2$), and the greater the increase in rent from 1941 to 1950 ($P_r''$) the higher will tend to be $H_r$ of cities. If Le represents $Y_t$, its coefficient seems likely to be positive, whereas if it represents only the percentage of casual workers in the labor force where employment is normal its partial coefficient seems likely to be negative.

The characteristics of the coefficients shown are discussed as follows: (a) general characteristics of coefficients; (b) coefficients of $\eta_{HY}$; (c) coefficients of $\eta_{H_eY}$; (d) coefficients of $\eta_{H_rY}$ derived from census data of 1950 and 1956; (e) coefficients of $\eta_{H_rY}$ derived from the consumption study of 1950, and (f) further characteristics of coefficients.

General Characteristics of Coefficients.—The interplace coefficients of income elasticity are appreciably higher than those considered in chapter v, where y is the explanatory variable. This is not surprising. Chapter v demonstrates that $y_t$ random among consumer units is important and that it tends to lower the coefficient of income elasticity of housing where y is the explanatory variable. Such $y_t$ tends to have a zero mean for places so that it does not affect $\eta_{HY}$, for example.

A wide range in interplace coefficients of income elasticity of housing is observed. Six simple coefficients of $\eta_{HY}$ are shown in Tables 26 and 27. They range from 1.03 to 2.63. There are 10 simple coefficients of $\eta_{H_rY}$. They range from 0.62 to 1.25. These two sets of coefficients

---

relation seems likely because the undoubling of households tends to increase the percentage of households with a female head in places where $Y_n$ is relatively high.

represent years ranging from 1933 to 1956. They imply that interplace coefficients tend to be far from stable. This wide difference presents a marked contrast to the similarity of the coefficients of 1933 and 1950 shown in Figure 6, page 117, where y is the explanatory variable. It seems likely, however, that interplace regressions are very sensitive to a number of conditions and that the effect of these tends to be obscured where y is the explanatory variable. This chapter considers whether the variation between years in interplace coefficients represents change in the relation of housing to normal income or in other conditions.

For the two tenures the coefficients of income elasticity of housing of the thirties are very similar, i.e., 1.03 for owners and 1.14 for tenants. On the other hand they are very different for 1950. For example, the division set of 1950 indicates a simple coefficient of $\eta_{HY}$ of 1.95 and of $\eta_{H_rY}$ of 0.78 (see Table 27). Rent control is one obvious condition that separated the markets by tenure for 1950. Its effect is considered in more detail below.

Coefficients of $\eta_{HY}$.—Two of the six coefficients of $\eta_{HY}$ are below 1.50. These two represent 1933 and 1935-36, for which because of widespread unemployment or underemployment much of the variation in Y seems likely to represent that of $Y_t$.

For the sets of places representing 1933 and 1935-36, the coefficients of $\eta_{HY}$ are almost identical (see Table 26). If abnormal employment were the only condition likely to cause variation in $\eta_{HY}$, one would expect it to be higher for the set of 1935-36 than of 1933. However, the universe represented differs between these surveys. For the set of 1935-36 there is a very marked negative correlation among places between average age of head of consumer units and average income. This would tend to lower $\eta_{HY}$ for this survey. A similar correlation is not present for the 1933 survey.[7] Thus a combination of conditions probably ac-

7. The survey of 1933 includes all households, a full range in normal incomes within places thus being represented. On the other hand, the data for 1935-36 pertain to native white, husband-wife families that had received no relief during the year. Confining the universe to nonrelief families may have reduced somewhat the importance of $y_t$. This likelihood cannot be tested. One thing seems certain, however: Confining the estimate to native white families reduced the range among places in $Y_n$. Its reduction tends to increase the importance of $y_t$ associated with variation among places in employment opportunity. It also seems likely to have increased the proportion of Y represented by the age-in-

Table 26

Coefficients of Correlation of Average Housing with respect to Average Income among Sets of Urban Places, by Tenure, Housing Survey of 1933 and Consumption Surveys of 1935-36 and 1950[a]

| Source of data and year represented | Owners | | | Tenants | | Number of places[g] | Type of consumer unit[h] |
|---|---|---|---|---|---|---|---|
| | $\eta_{HY_k}$[c] (1) | $\eta_{HY}$[c] (2) | $\eta_{H_eY}$[d] (3) | $\eta_{H_rY}$[e] (4) | $\eta_{H_sY}$[f] (5) | (6) | (7) |
| | **A. Income Elasticity of Average Housing among Places[b]** | | | | | | |
| 1. Housing survey, cities,[i] 1933 | .... | 1.025 | .... | 1.138 | 1.007 | 22 | All households |
| 2. Consumption survey cities 1935-36 | 1.087 | 1.036 | 1.491 | 1.516 | .... | 16[j] | Native, white, nonrelief, husband-wife families |
| 3. Urban consumption survey, 1950[k] | | | | | | | |
| a. Urban areas | | | | | | | |
| 1. All | .... | .... | 1.398 | 1.254 | .... | 9 | All consumer units |
| 2. Large cities and suburbs | .... | .... | 1.628 | 0.623 | .... | 6 | All consumer units |
| b. Large cities | .... | .... | 1.553 | 0.767 | .... | 43[l] | All consumer units |
| | **B. Coefficients of Determination ($r^2$)** | | | | | | |
| 1. Housing survey, cities,[i] 1933 | .... | 0.529 | .... | 0.587 | 0.423 | 22 | All consumer units |
| 2. Consumption survey cities 1935-36 | 0.845 | 0.834 | 0.720 | 0.839 | .... | 16 | Native, white, nonrelief, husband-wife families |
| 3. Urban consumption survey, 1950[k] | | | | | | | |
| a. Urban areas | | | | | | | |
| 1. All | .... | .... | 0.780 | 0.813 | .... | 9 | All consumer units |
| 2. Large cities and suburbs | .... | .... | 0.897 | 0.600 | .... | 6 | All consumer units |
| b. Large cities | .... | .... | 0.676 | 0.408 | .... | 43[l] | All consumer units |

Source: Financial Survey of Urban Housing; U.S. Department of Labor, Bul. 648, Vol. I, and Study of Consumer Expenditures, Vol. IV.

a. All variables represented by the estimates shown in this table are means and are expressed in log form.

b. With one exception the income variables represent money income. The exception is represented by the coefficient shown in column 1. For this the income variable is total income, including income in kind from the equity in the owner-occupied unit. It is symbolized by $Y_k$. Except for the consumption survey of 1950, average income represents income before taxes. However, for the periods represented, income tax was unimportant prior to 1950.

c. The housing variable is average estimated rental value of owner units. For the survey of 1933 this is 10 per cent of the reported value of the dwelling unit. The estimate for the survey of 1935-36 is that reported by respondents.

d. The housing variable is annual housing expenditure for the main dwelling unit. This type of variable is confined to consumption surveys.

e. The housing variable is or approximates the contract rent of the main dwelling unit occupied. For the consumption survey of 1950 it represents contract rent for the main dwelling unit occupied plus fees paid in acquiring occupancy rights and expenditure by tenants for repairs and maintenance of the units occupied. Contract rent represents a very, very large proportion of such expenditure.

f. The housing variable is an estimate of space rent of tenants. See chap. iii for a discussion of this variable.

g. Unless indicated, the number of places includes all places represented in the set for which data by tenure are reported.

h. In housing surveys the consumer unit is usually referred to as a household. This practice is followed here. The housing variable describes the housing of all persons in the dwelling and the income variable describes the income of the primary unit of the household. This tends to be the income of the head together with that of related persons sharing the dwelling unit. For the consumption survey the consumer unit is identified in terms of degree of pooling of income. The group with a pooled income tends to approximate the related persons of a household.

i. The estimates for owners pertain to those in one-unit structures.

j. These are the large and middle-sized cities included in this survey and the small-sized cities of two regions for which the U.S. Bureau of Labor Statistics reports data. Further urban data for small cities, from the survey of 1935-36, are reported by the U.S. Department of Agriculture (see U.S. Department of Agriculture, Misc. Pub. 396).

k. For the set of estimates shown here, the owner units exclude those who during 1950 purchased the units occupied at the time of the survey. This exclusion was made because of the high variability of the expenditure of these units and the likelihood that the level of such purchase was unusually high in 1950 compared to that of 1935-36.

l. This estimate is confined to cities in which at least 50 consumer units were represented in both the owner and the tenant subsets. This criteria was used to minimize somewhat the sampling variability. Compared to other sources represented it is likely to be high for this set.

counts for the similarity of the interplace coefficients of these two surveys. Both seem likely to understate $\eta_{HY_n}$, although conditions giving rise to such understatement probably differ between the sets.

There are three simple coefficients of $\eta_{HY}$ derived from the Census of Housing of 1950. Their range is small—from 1.57 to 1.95 (see Table 27). Holding Af and Le constant increases the coefficients somewhat. In addition, the sign of the partial regression of Af is positive, the sign to expect. The sign of Le is also positive, implying that it is serving as a proxy for abnormally low employment and hence for negative $Y_t$.

The coefficient of $\eta_{HY}$ for the inventory set for 1956 is very high (2.63). It provides, however, little reason for concluding that an important change has occurred in the relation of housing to $Y_n$. The estimate may be unreliable in spite of the fact that the coefficient of determination of the variables indicates significance at the .01 level. One element of unreliability is the much lower variation of Y of the metro areas for set of 1956 than of 1950. The standard deviations of Y are 0.0391 and 0.0296,[8] respectively. In other words, for the nine metro areas the standard deviation of Y fell by 24 per cent between 1949 and 1955.[9] Does this represent the trend toward greater equality of $Y_n$? If so, it should have no effect on the estimate of $\eta_{HY}$. Or does it represent variation in employment opportunity during the 1955, such as very high employment opportunity in metro areas with where $Y_n$ is low? The Census of Housing of 1960 should help to answer these questions. (Data by place for

---

come cycle; and the more the variation in Y is a function of age of head the lower is likely to be $\eta_{HY}$.

Information as to distribution of age of head is not reported by tenure. It is reported, however, for the tenures combined, and the greater the importance of heads 65 years of age or more the lower tends to be the average income of places. Among the 22 cities the correlation is as follows:

$$x_Y = 13.02 - 4.70\, x_{A_m} \qquad r^2 = .45 \qquad (6.1)$$

where Y is the mean income per family and $A_m$ is an estimate of the importance of male heads 65 years of age or more, with variables expressed in log form. It explains 45 per cent of the variation in Y. It is significant at the .01 level. ($A_m$ is the number of all families with those with male head less than 65 years of age equal to 100.) Data for this estimate come from Volume I of the series of bulletins of the U.S. Department of Labor reporting this survey. They are listed in the bibliography.

8. Y represents median income of households of various places expressed in log form.

9. The years represented by the income of the respective sets.

Table 27

Coefficients of Correlation of Average Housing with respect to Average Income and Related Conditions, by Tenure, among Places, 1950 and 1956[a]

| Set of metro areas | Regression coefficients | | | | | | | Number of places |
|---|---|---|---|---|---|---|---|---|
| | Y[b] (1) | Af[c] (2) | Le[d] (3) | $B_1$[e] (4) | $B_2$[f] (5) | $P_r''$[g] (6) | $R^2$[h] (7) | (8) |
| | A. Dependent Variable: Estimated Average Rental Value of Owner Units (H) | | | | | | | |
| 1. The division set | .... | .... | .... | .... | .... | .... | ... | 9[i] |
| a) | 1.952 | .... | .... | .... | .... | .... | 0.821 | ... |
| b) | 1.952 | 0.343 | .... | .... | .... | .... | .847 | ... |
| 2. The index set | .... | .... | .... | .... | .... | .... | ... | 30[j] |
| a) | 1.568 | .... | .... | .... | .... | .... | .735 | ... |
| b) | 1.663 | 0.571 | .... | .... | .... | .... | .746 | ... |
| c) | 1.766 | 0.349 | 0.179 | .... | .... | .... | .753 | ... |
| 3. The inventory set | .... | .... | .... | .... | .... | .... | ... | 9[k] |
| 3' 1950 | | | | | | | | |
| a) | 1.626 | .... | .... | .... | .... | .... | .681 | ... |
| b) | 1.902 | 1.659 | .... | .... | .... | .... | .826 | ... |
| 3'' 1956 | | | | | | | | |
| a) | 2.625[l] | .... | .... | .... | .... | .... | .833 | ... |
| b) | 2.743 | 1.610[m] | .... | .... | .... | .... | .909 | ... |
| | B. Dependent Variable: Contract Rent of Tenant Units ($H_r$) | | | | | | | |
| 1. The division set | .... | .... | .... | .... | .... | .... | ... | 9 |
| a) | 0.776 | .... | .... | .... | .... | .... | .420 | ... |
| b) | 0.785 | -0.118 | .... | .... | .... | .... | .420 | ... |
| c) | 1.453 | .... | .... | 2.148 | .... | .... | .861 | ... |
| 2. The index set | .... | .... | .... | .... | .... | .... | ... | 30 |
| a) | 0.995 | .... | .... | .... | .... | .... | .470 | ... |
| b) | 1.002 | 0.450 | .... | .... | .... | .... | .478 | ... |
| c) | 0.860 | 0.586 | -0.333 | .... | .... | .... | .520 | ... |

Table 27 (continued)

| Set of metro areas | Regression coefficients | | | | | | | Number of places |
|---|---|---|---|---|---|---|---|---|
| | $Y^{b}$ | $Af^{c}$ | $Le^{d}$ | $B_1^{e}$ | $B_2^{f}$ | $P_r''^{g}$ | $R^{2\,h}$ | |
| | (1) | (2) | (3) | (4) | (5) | (6) | (7) | (8) |
| d) | 0.877 | 0.558 | -0.306 | 0.558 | .... | .... | .538 | ... |
| e) | 1.126 | .... | .... | 1.385 | .... | .... | .579 | ... |
| f) | 1.024 | 0.446 | -0.236 | 0.229 | .... | 1.274 | 0.612 | ... |
| The low-new subset[n] | .... | .... | .... | .... | .... | .... | ... | 14 |
| a) | 1.201 | .... | .... | .... | .... | .... | 0.747 | ... |
| | (0.202) | .... | .... | .... | .... | .... | ... | ... |
| b) | 1.383 | 1.310 | .... | .... | .... | .... | .834 | ... |
| | (0.187) | (0.546) | .... | .... | .... | .... | ... | ... |
| c) | 1.352 | 1.270 | -0.0241 | .... | .... | .... | .834 | ... |
| | (0.312) | (0.653) | (0.190) | .... | .... | .... | ... | ... |
| d) | 1.267 | 1.186 | 0.0049 | 1.960 | .... | .... | .856 | ... |
| | (0.315) | (0.645) | (0.188) | (1.651) | .... | .... | ... | ... |
| e) | 1.395 | 1.366 | 0.0347 | 1.641 | 1.360 | .... | .892 | ... |
| | (0.300) | (0.604) | (0.174) | (1.531) | (0.811) | .... | ... | ... |
| f) | 1.586 | 1.622 | 0.258 | 2.021 | 2.329 | 0.815 | .924 | ... |
| | (0.291) | (0.560) | (0.202) | (1.389) | (0.934) | (0.472) | ... | ... |
| 3. The inventory set | .... | .... | .... | .... | .... | .... | ... | 9 |
| 3' 1950 | | | | | | | | |
| a) | 0.675 | .... | .... | .... | .... | | .484 | ... |
| b) | 0.669 | -0.095 | .... | .... | .... | | .530 | ... |
| 3'' 1956 | | | | | | | | |
| a) | 0.973 | .... | .... | .... | .... | | .629 | ... |
| b) | 0.954 | -0.274[m] | .... | .... | .... | | .646 | ... |

Source: U.S. Census of Housing: 1950, Vol. II, state reports, and Table 72; 1956 National Housing Inventory; U.S. Department of Labor, Bul. 699, and various issues of Monthly Labor Review.

a. The average of housing and income are medians. All variables are expressed in log form.

b. Median money income before taxes.

c. Estimate of the importance of households with an aged or a female head. For description see p. 143.

d. The percentage of the male labor force of 1950 reporting less than 26 weeks of work during 1949.

e. The number of all dwelling units per 100 dwelling units built prior to 1945.

f. The number of all dwelling units per 100 of those in the stock exclusive of units built 1940 through 1944.

g. This is the rent index of April, 1950, with that of December, 1941, equal to 100.

h. This is the coefficient of determination of the variables.

i. The divisions are New England, Middle Atlantic, East North Central, West North Central, Atlantic, East South Central, West South Central, Mountain, and Pacific.

j. Four places for which an index is reported are excluded. These are small places for which census data for cities are not reported. The initial investigation of the effect of rent change was made using the data of cities. It shows essentially the same characteristics as are indicated for metro areas.

k. These are all the metro areas for which data are reported from the *1956 National Housing Inventory*.

l. See comment in the text on characteristics of income that may account for this very high coefficient.

m. Reports for the housing inventory of 1956 do not describe, for owner units in one-unit structures, the number of households with a female head. Hence, an index of the importance of owner units with a head 65 years of age or more was used as a substitute for Af. This is symbolized by $A_h$.

n. This includes the one metro area, namely Portland, Me., not included in the main index set of 30 metro areas. Estimates shown in brackets are the standard errors of the regression coefficients.

1960 are, however, not available at the time of writing.)

Coefficients of $\eta_{H_eY}$.—For these coefficients, housing is represented by the expenditure for housing of owners. The distribution of the gap between H and $H_e$ is likely to affect tendencies observed. It was noted above that this gap tends to increase with age of the head of household.[10]

There are four coefficients of $\eta_{H_eY}$: one represents 1935-36 and three represent various combinations of the population of the consumption survey of 1950. These coefficients are very similar: Those for 1950 range from 1.40 to 1.63 and that for 1935-36 is 1.49. This similarity between the periods is surprising in view of the probable difference between them in the importance of $Y_t$. However, the eligibility criteria of the survey of 1935-36 resulted in a negative correlation between average age of head and average income and this tends to increase the gap at low incomes between H and $H_e$ and to increase $\eta_{H_eY}$ observed. Thus the age-income relationship, peculiar to the survey of 1935-36, seems likely to have offset the effect of the greater importance of $Y_t$ for the 1935-36 set.[11]

There seems no reason to expect that $\eta_{H_eY}$ for the consumption survey of 1950 is much, if at all, affected by a correlation between age of head and income.[12] Its main feature of interest is its similarity to the

10. The older the head the higher is likely to be the equity in the dwelling unit occupied and the lower the payments for interest on the mortgage—a main component of housing expenditure of owners. Hence the older the head the more $H_e$ understates H.

11. This age-income relationship is described by equation (6.1), shown in fn. 7, above. This seems likely to have accounted for the marked difference between $\eta_{HY}$ and $\eta_{H_eY}$, observed for the set of places of the survey of 1935-36. The coefficients are 1.04 and 1.49. This is the type of difference to expect. A heavy concentration of aged heads in places of low incomes would increase the gap there between H and $H_e$, and the wider such difference at low compared to high average incomes the more $\eta_{H_eY}$ tends to exceed $\eta_{HY}$.

There seems no reason to suppose, for this period, that the correlation among places between average age of head and average income was important for a representative sample of consumer units. Evidence to support this conclusion comes from the Census of Population of 1930. It reports the distribution of owner households by age of male head. Among cities the importance of owner households with head 65 years of age or more is not related to the average income reported in the housing survey of 1933. See U.S. Bureau of the Census, Census of Population: 1930, Vol. VI, Families.

12. Average income of owner units who purchased their dwelling unit prior to 1950 was compared with the percentage of owner households with head 65 years of age or more, as indicated by the Census of Housing of 1950.

coefficient of $\eta_{HY}$ of the census data. For example, for the index set of metro areas the single coefficient of $\eta_{HY}$ is 1.57, and for the set of 43 places[13] of the consumption survey $H_{H_eY}$ is 1.55. This evidence implies that among places in 1950 $H_e$ tends to be a good proxy for H.

Coefficients of $\eta_{H_rY}$ Derived from Census Data of 1950 and 1956.— For the various sets of places the simple coefficient of $\eta_{H_rY}$ tends to be low. The tendencies observed are the type to expect if change in tenant housing during much of the forties was uncorrelated with change in average income or if the lag of tenant housing behind income change was somewhat greater in places of high than of low income (see Table 27 B).

For the division set of 1950, $\eta_{H_rY}$ is 0.78. This is lower than its closest counterpart for the survey of 1933 when widespread unemployment seems likely to have brought conditions tending to lower $\eta_{H_rY}$: For the set of places of 1933, $\eta_{H_rY}$ is 1.14 (see Tables 26 and 27).

The low coefficient of the division set of 1950 seems likely in part to reflect the effect of a negative correlation between $B_1$[14] and Y. This correlation is as follows:

$$x_{B_1} = 3.12 - .313\, x_Y \qquad r^2 = .420. \qquad (6.2)$$

This correlation seems likely to be responsible for the fact that for the division set, with $B_1$ held constant, the partial coefficient of income elasticity of $H_r$ among divisions is 1.45: In other words holding $B_1$ constant doubles $\eta_{H_rY}$ (see Table 27 B, line 1[c]). This increase may well be a function of conditions peculiar to the division set.[15]

---

13. Twenty-two of these cities are in the index set of the census (see Table 27).

14. This is the number of all tenant units per 100 units exclusive of those built in 1945 or later.

15. Some evidence points to a fairly high positive correlation among the divisions between $B_1$ and $P_r''$. See, for example, Margaret G. Reid, "Increase in Rent of Dwelling Units from 1940 to 1950," Journal of the American Statistical Association, June, 1959, pp. 358-76. Among the metro areas of the index set, the correlation of these variables is positive, but rather low. It is .224, and is significant at the .25 probability level. Excluding the five metro areas having considerable new construction in the late forties from public funds increases the correlation to .379. This is significant at about .02 probability. Such a difference is not surprising. There seems no reason to expect that contract rents in the public and the private economy are affected by the same conditions. (The metro areas excluded are Norfolk-Portsmouth, Portland, Oregon, San Francisco, Seattle and Washington, D.C. This exclusion was based on some in-

The index set includes a considerable range in the variable $B_1$. Yet holding $B_1$ constant increases $\eta_{H_r Y}$ only slightly from 1.00 to 1.13—an increase of 13 per cent. Holding constant Af, Le and $P_r''$ as well as $B_1$ has little effect on the coefficient of $\eta_{H_r Y}$ observed. Furthermore, under these conditions the regression coefficient of Le has a negative rather than a positive sign.

A more intensive examination has been made of observations for 14 metro areas of the index set with less than 5 per cent of units constructed in 1945 or later. Findings are summarized in Table 27 B. The simple coefficient of $\eta_{H_r Y}$ is relatively high, i.e., 1.20, and Y explains 75 per cent of the variation of $H_r$. With Af, Le, $B_1$, $B_2$, and $R_p$ held constant the partial coefficient of $\eta_{H_r Y}$ is 1.59, the $R^2$ of the variables is .92. In addition, the regression coefficient of all variables has the sign expected,[16] and several of them are twice their standard errors. In view of this evidence it would not be surprising, where rental markets tend to reflect willingness of consumers to pay, that the interplace income elasticity of housing as of 1950, under normal housing market conditions, differed little by tenure.

The 1956 National Housing Inventory provides meager evidence for a later period. A period of six years would seem to be sufficient to eliminate any effect of rent control, except in such places as New York where rent control was formally continued. For the nine metro areas represented by the 1956 National Housing Inventory, the simple coefficient of $\eta_{H_r Y}$ is appreciably higher for 1956 than 1950. Even so it is somewhat lower than the interplace coefficient observed for 1933. Furthermore, the partial regression coefficient of Af has a negative rather than a positive sign. One feature of the set of nine metro area is worth noting, namely the low variation in average income among the metro areas, appreciably lower for the set of 1956 than 1950. The standard deviations of tenant incomes are 0.0445 and 0.0538,[17] respectively. The possible bearing on interplace coefficients of this reduction in the variation of Y has already been commented on. In general, it reduces the reliability of the estimates, since

---

formation provided by the U.S. Housing and Home Finance Agency, reports on emergency housing by the U.S. Bureau of Labor Statistics, and information in the census of housing as to percentage of the tenant stock of 1950 reported built in 1940 through 1945. For the metro area of Norfolk-Portsmouth, 29 per cent were built in those years.)

16. That is under the assumption that Le is a proxy for $Y_t$.

17. Y is expressed in log form.

they tend to be much influenced by any abnormality of employment or variation in the mixture of household types. For this estimate abnormality of employment is not represented, and the variable representing mixture of household types is crude.

Coefficients of $\eta_{H_rY}$ of the Consumption Study of 1950.—$\eta_{H_rY}$ is much the same for the consumption study as for the Census of Housing of 1950. For the division set of metro areas the simple coefficient is 0.78, and, for the set of large cities and suburbs of the three areas as delineated in the consumption survey, it is 0.62, and for the set of 43 large cities it is 0.77 (see Table 26).

The inclusion of the small cities in the universe represented increases $\eta_{H_rY}$ from 0.62 to 1.25.[18] This inclusion increases the range of $Y_n$[19] represented and also the range in $H_r$ represented prior to the imposition of rent control. The latter seems likely to minimize the effect of rent control on tendencies observed.

This interpretation is supported by the fact that the inclusion of the three urban areas representing small cities does not increase $\eta_{H_eY}$ for owners. In fact, by this inclusion it is decreased slightly. This may well be the effect of a higher percentage of owner households with a female head in small cities than in large cities and suburbs. Such a distribution of households with a female head is indicated by the Census of Housing of 1950.[20]

Further Characteristics of Coefficients.—Other characteristics of the coefficients shown in Tables 26 and 27 worthy of note are as follows:

a) Residuals of equations of the index sets for owners, with Af and

---

18. A similar increase in $\eta_{H_rY}$ is observed using the data of the Census of Housing of 1950 by combining the observations for metro areas. The increase is from 0.78 to 1.06. On the other hand, such a combination reduces $\eta_{HY}$ for owners from 1.95 to 1.40. This drop may well be the result of the great importance in urban places outside of metro areas of households with an aged or a female head. Their greater importance in urban places outside of metro areas where Y is low tends to lower $\eta_{HY}$. On the other hand, for tenants, Af is much the same for the urban as the metro stratum of the various divisions.

19. The inclusion of the three urban areas representing small cities increases the variation of the log of average incomes from 0.0360 to 0.0474.

20. For example, in 1950 in metro areas 13.4 per cent and in urban places outside of metro areas 17.8 per cent of the owner households had a female head. In addition, among the female heads those 65 years of age or more were more important in metro areas than in places outside of metro areas.

Le held constant, show no indication that climate or importance of recent in-migration affects tendencies observed.

b) The coefficients of $\eta_{HY}$ and of $\eta_{H_rY}$ of the housing survey of 1933 are quite similar. This survey represents a random sample of both owners and tenants in a free market. The similarity thus supports the hypothesis that, where markets are free, interplace coefficients tend to be much the same for owners and tenants. However, for the consumption survey of 1935-36, $\eta_{HY}$ is appreciably lower than $\eta_{H_rY}$. It seems highly probable that both of these coefficients are lowered by $Y_t$, and it seems not unlikely that the importance of this component was greater for owners than tenants. This supposition is based on the probable selectivity of one of the eligibility criteria of this survey. All families receiving any relief during the report year were excluded. For this criterion to be neutral by tenure, it would be necessary for relief to be granted according to the importance of $y_t$. Two differences by tenure make it seem probable that the eligibility for relief was determined at a higher level of negative $y_t$ for owners than tenants. This supposition is based on the fact that eligibility for relief was based on a means' test. Owners on the average have a higher $y_n$ than tenants, and hence they would have to have had a greater negative $y_t$ to be eligible for relief. Furthermore, in some places, equity in an owner-occupied dwelling was judged to be grounds for denying relief assistance, since it represented reserves that could be drawn upon. Thus a combination of conditions may account for the much lower percentage[21] of owners than tenants receiving relief.

c) For the set of places represented by the housing survey of 1933, additional services represented by contract rent tend to be positively correlated with Y. This tends to increase $\eta_{H_rY}$ observed. Where rent represents space, the coefficient is lowered: $\eta_{H_sY}$ for tenants is 1.01, whereas $\eta_{H_rY}$ is 1.12. Thus, for this set of places, holding additional services constant reduces by 12 per cent the coefficient of income elasticity of tenant housing observed. In applying this rate to other situations, possible change in distribution of additional services needs to be taken into account. Additional services paid for by contract rent have been increasing. If the increase has been fairly uniform among places, the relationship indicated for 1933 may be fairly representative. On the other hand,

21. For the 16 cities the mean percentage of families excluded because of having received relief during the report years was 7.4 and 18.2 of owners and tenants, respectively.

if the increase in their importance has been greater in places of low than of high $Y_n$, the positive correlation between additional services and Y observed for 1933 may have disappeared. Under this condition, the importance of additional services may no longer be correlated with Y. If so, their effect on $\eta_{H_rY}$ would depend solely on the income elasticity of additional services. This appears to be lower than that of space (see chapter iii). A full investigation of the distribution of additional services among places is not feasible with information currently available.

d) For the owners, $\eta_{HY}$ for the set of 1935-36 is much the same whether the income variable represents total income or money income. The respective coefficients shown in Table 26 are 1.09 and 1.04. Thus the money income reported for the main sets of data appears at least as satisfactory as total income for estimating interplace income elasticity of housing.

## Average Housing by Tenure where Y is Held Constant

Chapter v demonstrated, where income of consumer units (y) is held constant, that housing of owners (h) tends to be higher than that of tenants ($h_r$). This tendency is illustrated in Figure 10, using data of the Census of Housing of 1950, and in Figure 11, using data of the consumption survey of 1941. Such tendencies are to be expected if much of the variation in y represents $y_t$. If this is a correct interpretation, then, where Y is held constant, such difference between H and $H_r$ of the tenures, under normal market conditions, will not be observed.

The housing and income variables of the housing survey of 1933 and the Census of Housing of 1950 have much in common, in that the income variable represents money only and the housing of owners is H and that of tenants is $H_r$. They are different in that (a) the housing survey of 1933 represents a much lower employment level than that of 1950, and (b) the housing of owners and tenants of 1933 were both subject to much the same conditions, whereas the rental market of 1950 was just emerging from rent control.

Interplace regressions by tenure, representing these two periods, are shown in Figure 13. Panel A represents 22 cities of the housing survey of 1933, and panel B the division set of metro areas of 1950. Difference between periods observed is very striking. For the set of 1933 the regression of the two tenures is similar in level as well as in slope, in

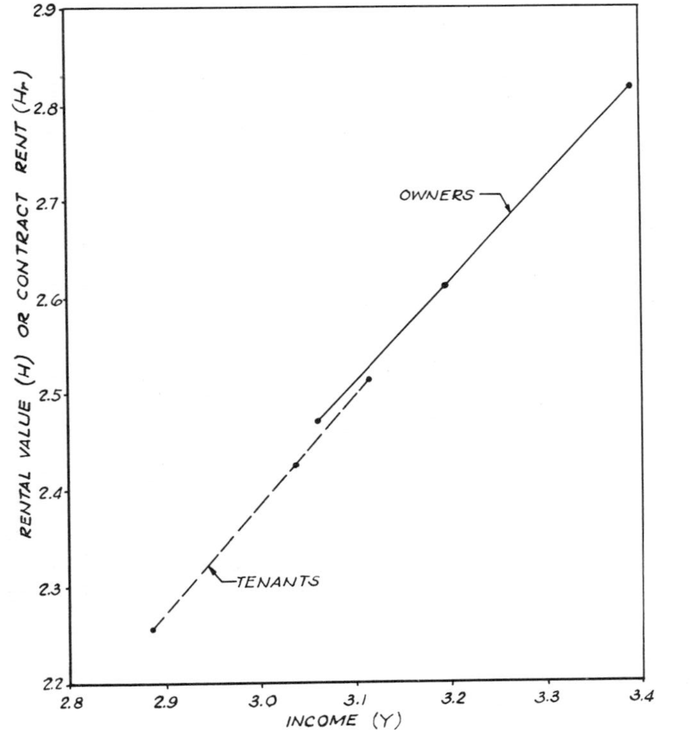


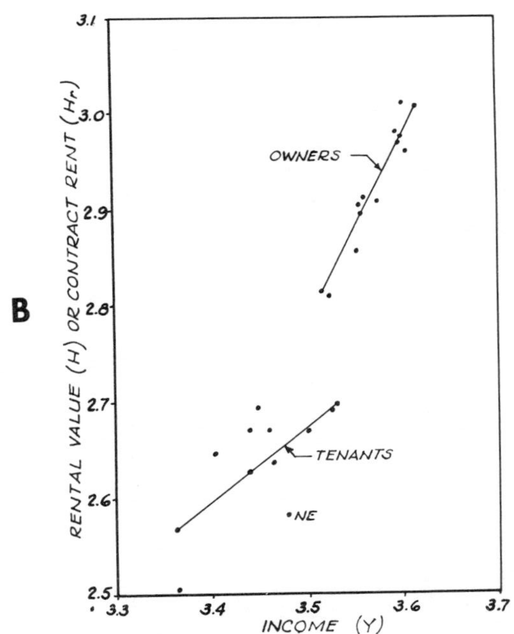


Fig. 13.—Average annual estimated rental value of owner units (H) and contract rent of tenant units ($H_r$) in relation to average income of consumer units (Y),[a] 1933 and 1950. (Variables in log form.)

Panel A: Housing survey, 22 cities, 1933.

Panel B: Census of Housing, metro areas of nine divisions, 1950.

a. Coefficients of correlation are shown in Table 26 as well as the source of data used and definitions of housing and income variables.

spite of the fact that Y of tenants is much below that of owners. The two regressions are close where average income is common to the two tenures.[22] This similarity occurs even though the consumer units represented, where Y is similar for the two tenures, are the owners of places of low Y and the tenants of places of high Y.

Under the assumption that the relation of housing consumption to $Y_n$ is independent of tenure, it would seem reasonable to expect, where $Y_n$ is the same, that $H_r$ would tend to be higher than H, because of the additional services represented by $H_r$. For the 1933 set of places, where Y is held constant, H is observed to be slightly higher than $H_r$. This is, however, the difference to expect if $Y_t$ is important and is uncorrelated with $Y_n$. Under this condition, $Y_t$ is positively correlated with Y, and such correlation tends to lower the interplace regression and to cause the difference in level observed. At the same time it tends to make average housing where Y is held constant appear higher for the tenure with the higher $Y_n$.[23]

On the other hand, for the division set of 1950, the interplace regressions by tenure are very different in both level and slope. At the range of average income common to the two tenures, contract rent of tenants is much, much below the estimated rental value of the owner units. This occurs in spite of the fact that $H_r$ of 1950 represents a considerable amount for additional services other than space and that a marked increase in the importance of such services occurred between 1933 and 1950.

An extrapolation of the regression for the owners indicates, in places where Y is low, $H_r$ including additional services exceeds H (see Figure 13). This is the relationship to be expected for normal markets if housing in relation to $Y_n$ is independent of tenure.

## Holding Constant Construction Cost

If market price is correlated with Y, it may be one of the conditions affecting $\eta_{HY}$ and $\eta_{H_rY}$. The nature of the effect will depend on the price elasticity of demand for housing. If the price elasticity of demand for

22. The regressions shown are interpolations, their limits being marked by the lowest and the highest Y of places represented.

23. One other condition tends to contribute to this: Y tends to understate total income more for owners than tenants. If income in kind is included, the interplace regression shifts more to the right for owners than for tenants.

housing is between 0.0 and -1.0, the higher the price of housing the higher will tend to be H or $H_r$. The more the coefficient of price elasticity approaches -1.0 the less will be the effect of price on value or rent. If the coefficient is lower than -1.0, then the higher the price of housing the less consumers will tend to spend for housing.

Muth examined variation among cities in H with respect to Y and the Boeckh index of construction cost. He observed a partial coefficient of $\eta_{HY}$ of 1.68 and a partial coefficient of elasticity of housing with respect to construction cost of -1.59.[24] The partial coefficient of $\eta_{HY}$ of 1.68 is much the same as the simple coefficients of $\eta_{HY}$ shown in Table 27. In addition, the partial coefficient for the cost variable, observed by Muth, gives no reason to expect that a positive correlation between Y and market price of housing tends to increase H.

## A Summing Up

This chapter examines average housing in relation to average income of places (Y). In other words, it is concerned with interplace regressions. For most places the number of consumer units is large so that $y_t$ uncorrelated with $y_n$ tends to have a zero mean. Y may of course have a transitory component ($Y_t$) arising from abnormal employment opportunity. Under extreme conditions of cyclical change for the nation in general, it seems not unlikely that $Y_t$ uncorrelated with $Y_n$ is quite important. Such $Y_t$ tends, of course, to be positively correlated with Y. Consequently it tends to lower the elasticity of average housing with respect to Y. (The coefficient is symbolized by $\eta_{HY}$ where H represents value and Y the average income of owner households of various places.)

The elasticity of average housing with respect to average income among places is high. For owner-occupants for 1950 $\eta_{HY}$ falls between 1.5 and 2.0. This stands in marked contrast to mean $\eta_{hy}$ of metro areas shown in Table 22, namely 0.32. The corresponding estimates for tenants for 1950 are 0.94 and 0.29, respectively. Thus for both tenures the income elasticity of housing observed among places is much, much higher where Y rather than y is the explanatory variable.

Wide difference in interplace coefficients is observed for the various periods. Some of this seems to be related to the state of the econo-

---

24. Richard Muth, "The Demand for Non-Farm Housing," in Arnold Harberger (ed.), The Demand for Durable Goods (Chicago: University of Chicago Press, 1960), p. 72.

my in general. When unemployment is widespread, coefficients tend to be low, probably because among cities unemployment tends to be uncorrelated with $Y_n$.

The interplace coefficients of income elasticity of contract rent are unusually low for 1950. However, there seems good reason to believe that rent control is an important contributing factor.

The much higher coefficients of elasticity of housing with respect to Y than y raise a question as to whether some condition associated with Y is a contributing factor. An upward bias is likely to be imparted, if the price of housing is positively correlated with Y and if the price elasticity of demand for housing is greater than -1.0, that is between 0.0 and -1.0. An estimate by Muth implies, however, that the price elasticity of housing is at least as low as -1.0. This evidence does not support the hypothesis that $\eta_{HY}$, for example, tends to be biased upward by a positive correlation between Y and price of housing.

The interplace coefficients may also be biased upward by a positive correlation between standard of housing and Y. Tests of this possibility are presented in later chapters.

Where Y is held constant, the average housing of owners and tenants of 1933 is quite similar. On the other hand, where Y of 1949 is held constant the estimated rental value of owner units is much, much higher in 1950 than contract rent of tenants. Rent control undoubtedly accounts for some of the difference in level observed for 1950.

Interplace regressions are much influenced by conditions affecting the economy in general, such as unemployment and rent control. These have only minor effects on coefficients of income elasticity where y is the explanatory variable. This is not surprising since the overwhelming condition affecting such coefficients is the marked positive correlation between y and $y_t$. Such correlation tends to be much, much less, where Y is the explanatory variable.

The usefulness of interplace regressions for revealing the relation of housing to $Y_n$ will be reduced if equality of $Y_n$ among places has increased. As this equality increases, tendencies observed among cities will to an increasing extent depend on the mixture of household types and phase of cyclical change represented.

# INTERCLASS CORRELATIONS WITHIN PLACES

The observations examined in this chapter are averages of subsets of consumer units within places derived through the use of instrumental variables. Two instrumental variables are used: (a) quality of housing as defined in the Census of Housing of 1950[1] and (b) sub-areas within metro areas and cities, such as census tracts. The interclass coefficients of elasticity of average housing with respect to average income among such subsets within places will be unaffected by climate and presumably affected little, if at all, by variation in the price of housing or standard of housing of cities. (These factors, in general, are referred to as environmental.) The tendencies observed within places seem likely to represent the relation of housing to normal income if they are unaffected by such things as variation in household type or cyclical change or by a correlation between consumer preferences for housing and the instrumental variable used.

The variables representing the average of subsets within places are symbolized by upper-case letters, as are the averages for places examined in chapter vi. In addition, superscripts are used to differentiate the

1. Averages of five quality categories are used. These categories are:

Not dilapidated

- With private toilet and bath, and hot running water
- With private toilet and bath, and only cold water
- With running water, lacking private toilet or bath
- No running water

Dilapidated (Information is reported for two categories of dilapidated dwelling units. However, since in many metro areas the number of dwelling units represented is very small, in most of the estimates shown all dilapidated dwelling units are represented by one subset.)

observations by type of instrumental variable used. Where it is by quality of housing the superscript q is used, and where it is by sub-area, such as a census tract, the superscript *a* is used. Thus average value of dwelling of subsets by quality of housing is symbolized by $H^q$ and that of census tracts or other sub-area of places by $H^a$. The corresponding symbols for income are $Y^q$ and $Y^a$. In addition, Y continues to be used as a general symbol representing average income of places and of groups or subsets within places irrespective of instrumental variables used.

The main sources of data utilized are the Census of Housing of 1950 and the housing survey of 1933, and attention centers on owner-occupants. The greater simplicity of the housing variable for owners than tenants accounts for this concentration. However, some estimates are shown for tenants. In addition, evidence presented in this chapter for 1950 and 1933 is supplemented by that shown in chapter xiii for 1960.

The main topics are as follows: (a) conditions associated with the instrumental variables; (b) correlations among subsets by quality of housing; (c) correlations among tracts within metro areas, 1950; (d) correlations among areas within cities, 1933; (e) income elasticity of housing with h as the explanatory variable; (f) variation among groups in $H^q$ with $Y^q$ held constant; and (g) variation among groups in $Y^q$ with $H^q$ held constant.

## Conditions Associated with the Instrumental Variables

The two main requirements of a suitable[2] instrumental variable are its correlation with $y_n$ and its lack of correlation with $y_t$ uncorrelated with $y_n$. Subsets by quality of housing and by areas within metro areas and cities seem likely to meet these requirements. Where instrumental variables are used, Y of subsets will tend to represent $Y_n$, if among consumer units $y_t$ is uncorrelated with $y_n$. Another requirement of an ideal instrumental variable is that it has no direct relationship with the variable to be explained. Hence for this analysis an ideal instrumental variable has no association with h other than through its association with $y_n$ of consumer units. Thus one must consider whether those who occupy

2. The consumption survey of 1950 reports data by occupation and years of schooling of the head of consumer units. Neither of these characteristics appears to represent an instrumental variable especially suitable for interclass correlations. Their characteristics are discussed in chap. viii.

dwelling units of high quality do so because $y_n$ is high, or because of high preference for housing compared to other consumer products, and similarly whether households in census tracts where $H^a$ is high are there because they are willing to cut the consumption of other products in order to live in an area of high quality housing or because $y_n$ is high. Evidence bearing on the probable association of preference for housing with the instrumental variables used is reported later in this chapter and also in chapter viii.

Various conditions affecting housing-income ratios, other than $y_n$, may be correlated with the instrumental variable. These need to be held constant if interclass regressions are to yield an unbiased coefficient of elasticity of housing with respect to $y_n$. Among the conditions considered in this chapter are household type, cyclical change, and importance of new construction of tenant dwelling units represented. Where quality of housing is the instrumental variable, considerable information is available.

Distribution of Household Types.—Households with an aged or a female head tend to have high housing-income ratios.[3] If they concentrate in subsets where Y is low, they will tend to increase housing-income ratios there and thus tend to lower the coefficient of income elasticity observed. On the other hand, if they concentrate on subsets where Y is high their distribution tends to have the opposite effect.

Data available permit estimates of the importance of households with an aged or a female head by quality category. This importance is symbolized by Af.[4] The distribution of Af with respect to $H^q$ or to $Y^q$ is measured by Af of dwelling units of high[5] quality with Af of low[6] quality equal to 100. The resulting ratio is symbolized by $Af^q$. A considerable range is observed among places. For owner units represented in Table 28, the range among places is from 86 to 90, and for those in Table 29 from 78 to 98. The higher is $Af^q$ the more the distribution of households with an aged or a female head tends to increase housing-income ratios

3. See chap. iv for description of housing-income ratios by age and sex of head of households.

4. This is all consumer units per 100 consumer units exclusive of those with an aged or a female head.

5. These are dwelling units not dilapidated and with private bath and toilet and hot running water.

6. These are dwelling units not dilapidated but lacking cold running water and all dilapidated units.

for dwelling units of highest quality, and hence the higher is likely to be the elasticity of average housing with respect to average income among quality subsets. If $Af^q$ equals 100, presumably the distribution of these

Table 28

Coefficients of Correlation of Average Housing with respect to Average Income and Related Characteristics, among Quality Subsets, by Degree of Urbanization, United States and Divisions, 1950[a]

| | Regression coefficients[b] | | $r^2$ [c] | $Af^q$ [d] | $Lo^q$ [d] | $B_1{}^q$ [e] |
|---|---|---|---|---|---|---|
| | Constant | $HY^q$ | | | | |
| | (1) | (2) | (3) | (4) | (5) | (6) |
| A. Inside metro areas | | | | | | |
| 1. Owners | -4.407 | 2.051 | .99 | 89.8 | 100.9 | ... |
| 2. Tenants | -1.393 | 1.162 | .98 | 90.7 | 96.7 | 105.2 |
| B. Urban outside metro areas | | | | | | |
| 1. Owners | -2.413 | 1.490 | .99 | 86.9 | 101.0 | ... |
| 2. Tenants | -0.703 | 0.950 | .99 | 82.0 | 98.3 | 106.4 |
| C. Rural outside metro areas | | | | | | |
| 1. Owners | -1.988 | 1.367 | .97 | 86.2 | 102.1 | ... |
| a) New England | -3.326 | 1.774 | .99 | 87.8 | 98.3 | ... |
| b) East South Central | -1.584 | 1.249 | .99 | 85.6 | 101.9 | ... |
| 2. Tenants | -1.108 | 1.061 | 1.00 | 84.8 | 100.3 | 115.8 |

Source: U.S. Census of Housing: 1950, Vol. II, chapters 1, 2, and 7.

a. Information on value and contract rent of dwelling units is reported for dwelling units not dilapidated and for those dilapidated. There are four subcategories of the first and two for the second. The subcategories differ in plumbing facilities (see text, p. 162 n.). For the owner units the value reported is that of one-unit structures and the income is that of primary units of owner households in all types of structures. The gap between the households represented by the housing and the income variables seems likely to lower only slightly the coefficient of $\eta_{HY^q}$. For tenants there is no such gap.

b. The estimates are weighted by the number of households reporting. All variables are used in log form. The regression coefficient of $Y^q$ provides an estimate of the income elasticity of average housing with respect to average income among subsets.

c. This is the coefficient of determination of $H^q$ and $Y^q$ of the quality subsets.

d. See Appendix A for description of these variables representing distribution of household types among quality subsets.

e. This is a variable representing the importance of new construction among dwelling units of the highest quality with the importance of such construction in dwelling units of low quality equal to 100. The new construction pertains to that built in 1945 or later.

Table 29

Coefficients of Elasticities of Average Housing with Respect to Average Income and Related Characteristics, Owner-Occupants, among Quality Subsets, 50 Metro Areas, 1950

| Metro areas [a] | $\eta_{HY^q}$ [b] | $Af^q$ [c] | Le [d] |
|---|---|---|---|
| 1. Atlanta, Georgia | 1.60 | 90.3 | 12.9 |
| 2. Baltimore | 1.69 | 89.0 | 12.6 |
| 3. Birmingham | 1.70 | 84.8 | 14.7 |
| 4. Boston | 2.03 | 81.0 | 12.7 |
| 5. Canton | 1.98 | 90.5 | 14.0 |
| 6. Charleston, West Virginia | 1.99 | 93.3 | 20.3 |
| 7. Chicago | 2.28 | 91.0 | 10.7 |
| 8. Cincinnati | 2.29 | 88.7 | 12.5 |
| 9. Cleveland | 2.00 | 85.3 | 11.8 |
| 10. Dallas | 1.49 | 94.1 | 11.5 |
| 11. Denver | 2.24 | 96.6 | 12.7 |
| 12. Des Moines | 2.44 | 96.5 | 10.5 |
| 13. Detroit | 2.27 | 92.9 | 11.4 |
| 14. Hartford | 1.72 | 80.1 | 11.4 |
| 15. Houston | 1.46 | 86.0 | 12.3 |
| 16. Indianapolis | 2.15 | 92.7 | 11.4 |
| 17. Jacksonville | 1.49 | 83.5 | 14.1 |
| 18. Kansas City | 2.07 | 83.9 | 11.2 |
| 19. Knoxville | 1.46 | 93.1 | 18.2 |
| 20. Los Angeles | 1.56 | 86.4 | 15.9 |
| 21. Louisville | 1.86 | 89.3 | 12.7 |
| 22. Memphis | 1.33 | 82.1 | 13.3 |
| 23. Miami | 1.91 | 83.0 | 18.6 |
| 24. Milwaukee | 2.19 | 98.4 | 9.6 |
| 25. Minneapolis-St. Paul | 2.40 | 94.0 | 10.9 |
| 26. Mobile | 1.50 | 91.9 | 17.9 |
| 27. New Orleans | 1.88 | 87.1 | 13.6 |
| 28. New York | 1.47 | 79.1 | 14.0 |
| 29. Norfolk-Portsmouth | 1.55 | 81.8 | 11.7 |
| 30. Oklahoma City | 1.67 | 82.5 | 12.0 |
| 31. Omaha | 2.14 | 88.4 | 10.2 |
| 32. Peoria | 2.57 | 94.6 | 12.1 |
| 33. Philadelphia | 1.66 | 86.4 | 13.1 |
| 34. Phoenix | 1.58 | 87.1 | 20.0 |
| 35. Pittsburgh | 2.14 | 88.9 | 15.8 |
| 36. Portland, Oregon | 1.51 | 86.2 | 16.6 |
| 37. Providence | 1.66 | 79.9 | 17.1 |
| 38. Richmond | 1.77 | 86.2 | 11.2 |
| 39. Rochester, New York | 1.65 | 87.8 | 11.4 |
| 40. St. Louis | 2.33 | 87.4 | 11.7 |
| 41. Salt Lake City | 2.39 | 85.9 | 12.3 |
| 42. San Antonio | 1.73 | 96.7 | 15.9 |
| 43. San Diego | 1.50 | 95.6 | 14.2 |
| 44. San Francisco | 1.68 | 84.1 | 14.0 |
| 45. Scranton | 1.62 | 81.9 | 19.1 |
| 46. Seattle | 1.55 | 87.0 | 14.7 |
| 47. Wheeling-Steubenville | 2.18 | 90.4 | 16.3 |
| 48. Wichita | 1.65 | 84.5 | 11.1 |
| 49. Wilmington | 1.57 | 77.8 | 11.2 |
| 50. Youngstown | 2.26 | 92.3 | 11.9 |
| Mean | 1.86 | 88.0 | 13.5 |

Source: Census of Housing, 1950, Vol. II, various chapters, Tables A-1 and A-4, and Census of Population, Vol. II, various chapters, Table 72.

a. These are the metro areas represented in Table 22.

b. These estimates pertain to five quality categories. They are the four subcategories of dwelling units judged to be not dilapidated, and the entire category of units classed as dilapidated. (For detailed description see p.162, n. 1.) The categories are weighted by the number of households reporting. This is done in the hope of minimizing the sampling error because for some metro areas the number represented in some of the quality categories is small. However, the simple coefficients of correlation of $H^q$ and $Y^q$ are uniformly high so that the weighting is of only minor importance.

c. See p. 164 for description of this variable.

d. Percentage of the male labor force with less than 26 weeks of employment during 1949.

households by quality of dwelling unit will not affect income elasticity of housing observed. However, since $Af^q$ tends to be less than 100, the distribution of households with an aged or a female head seems likely, on the average, to lower $\eta_{HY}q$. The variable $Af^q$[7] is used in the examination of variation in $\eta_{HY}q$.

The distribution of lodgers in households by quality of housing is also of some importance, since the presence of lodgers tends to be associated with relatively high housing-income ratios. Under this condition their concentration in housing of high quality tends to increase $\eta_{HY}q$ observed, and conversely their concentration in housing of low quality tends to have the opposite effect.

The Census of Housing reports the number of households with persons not related to the head. Since these persons are primarily lodgers,[8] their distribution serves as a proxy for the distribution of lodgers. For owner households of the U.S. metro stratum, lodgers appear to be equally likely in housing of low as of high quality. On the other hand, for tenant households lodgers tend to concentrate in housing of low quality. For this reason alone one would expect $\eta_{H_rY}q$ to be lower[9] than $\eta_{HY}q$.

It was noted in chapter iv that lodgers tend to be more important for non-white than white households and that their importance appears to be positively correlated with in-migration. Taking into account the distribution of lodgers is thus of special importance where an attempt is made to discover whether housing with respect to normal income tends to differ by race when household type is held constant. Lodgers are more important for non-white than white households, even when in-migration is held constant. Furthermore, among non-white households lodgers tend to be

7. The small number of subsets by quality of housing and the marked correlation among such subsets between average income and the importance of households with an aged or a female head preclude the use of multivariate correlation in estimating housing-income relation with household type held constant.

8. The Census of Population of 1950 reports, for private households of urban places, eight resident employees per 100 lodgers.

9. For the 50 metro areas represented in Table 29 the mean percentage of households with non-relatives present in dwelling units of the highest and the lowest quality, for which information is provided, by tenure, is as follows:

| Tenure | Highest Quality | Lowest Quality |
|---|---|---|
| Owners | 7.7 | 6.6 |
| Tenants | 6.2 | 9.2 |

more important in dwelling units of high than of low quality. This concentration tends to increase $\eta_{HY}$ observed.

The measure representing the distribution of lodgers by quality categories is similar to Af. It is the ratio of the importance of lodgers[10] for the top quality with their importance for low quality equal to 100. This variable is symbolized by $Lo^q$. Estimates of $Lo^q$ are shown in Tables 28 and 30.

Transitory Income Caused by Cyclical Change.—In chapter ii it was pointed out that within a given labor market $y_t$ caused by cyclical change is likely to be positively correlated with $y_n$ during the trough of the depression and negatively correlated with $y_n$ at the peak of prosperity. In other words, the lower is $y_n$ the more likely is it to be depressed by negative $y_t$ when employment opportunities in general are low and increased by positive $y_t$ when employment opportunities are high.

The effect of such a distribution of $y_t$ is tested in this chapter with Le, that is the percentage of the male labor force with less than 26 weeks of work during 1949, serving as proxy for variation among places in the cyclical change represented. If the expectations described above are valid, Le will be negatively correlated with $\eta_{HY}q$.

## Correlations among Subsets by Quality of Housing,[11] 1950

Coefficients of $\eta_{HY}q$ and of $\eta_{H_rY}q$ for strata of the United States by degree of urbanization, where quality of housing is the instrumental variable, are shown in Table 28 together with related characteristics. Similar coefficients for owner-occupants of a large set of metro areas are shown in Table 29, and Table 30 shows such coefficients for seven metro areas for households stratified by race.

Owner and Tenant Units by Degree of Urbanization.—Three strata of the non-farm population of the United States as described by the Census of Housing of 1950 are metro areas and urban and rural non-farm places outside of metro areas. These are to be referred to as the metro, urban, and rural non-farm strata, respectively. Unless otherwise indicated the strata discussed represent the entire United States. Coefficients for these strata are shown in Table 28.

---

10. This is the number of all households per 100 households without a non-relative present.

11. See fn. 1, above, for description of the categories.

Table 30

Coefficients of Elasticity of Average Housing with respect to Average Income and Related Characteristics, among Quality Subsets, Owner-Occupants Stratified by Race, Seven Metro Areas, 1950[a]

| Metro area and race | Regression coefficient of $Y^q$ [b] | | Distribution of household types[c] | |
|---|---|---|---|---|
| | Constant (1) | $\eta_{HY^q}$ (2) | $Af^q$ (3) | $Lo^q$ (4) |
| 1. Birmingham | | | | |
| a) White | -4.952 | 2.174 | 93.5 | 102.3 |
| b) Non-White | -3.940 | 1.949 | 91.4 | 100.6 |
| 2. Chicago | | | | |
| a) White | -4.225 | 1.988 | 88.7 | 101.7 |
| b) Non-White | -5.219 | 2.314 | 90.7 | 116.2 |
| 3. Detroit | | | | |
| a) White | -4.231 | 1.969 | 94.3 | 101.5 |
| b) Non-White | -5.211 | 2.294 | 98.3 | 112.8 |
| 4. Houston | | | | |
| a) White | -3.435 | 1.751 | 88.8 | 102.4 |
| b) Non-White | -3.370 | 1.805 | 90.9 | 105.7 |
| 5. Los Angeles | | | | |
| a) White | -2.593 | 1.557 | 83.1 | 100.4 |
| b) Non-White | -2.275 | 1.500 | 83.1 | 98.0 |
| 6. New Orleans | | | | |
| a) White | -3.455 | 1.802 | 92.1 | 101.7 |
| b) Non-White | -3.678 | 1.913 | 98.3 | 105.3 |
| 7. St. Louis | | | | |
| a) White | -3.690 | 1.851 | 91.9 | 103.0 |
| b) Non-White | -5.205 | 2.341 | 87.4 | 113.7 |
| 8. Mean[d] | | | | |
| a) White | . . . | 1.870 | 90.3 | 101.9 |
| b) Non-White | . . . | 2.017 | 89.9 | 107.5 |
| c) Both | . . . | 1.944 | 90.1 | 104.7 |

Source: Unpublished tabulations of the Census of Housing of 1950 furnished through the courtesy of the Fund of the Republic.

a. All variables shown represent households in owner-occupied dwellings in one-unit structures.

b. These are weighted by number of households reporting and all variables are expressed in log form.

c. See p. 164 for description of these variables.

d. Each place has a weight of one.

The first thing to be noted is that these coefficients are relatively high. By tenure they are as follows:

| Stratum | $\eta_{HY^q}$ | $\eta_{H_rY^q}$ |
|---|---|---|
| Metro | 2.05 | 1.16 |
| Urban | 1.49 | 0.95 |
| Rural non-farm | 1.37 | 1.06 |

These stand in striking contrast to estimates for the same metro areas shown in chapter v, where income of consumer units (y) is the independent variable: For the metro stratum $\eta_{hy}$ is 0.314, and $\eta_{h_ry}$ is 0.261. In other words, for the same universe $\eta_{hy}$ is 15 per cent of $\eta_{HY^q}$, and $\eta_{h_ry}$ is 22 per cent of $\eta_{H_rY^q}$. If this difference is wholly the effect of $y_t$ randomly related to $y_n$, it does indeed have a marked tendency to lower $\eta_{hy}$ and $\eta_{h_ry}$.

The within-place interclass coefficients $\eta_{HY^q}$ and $\eta_{H_rY^q}$ of the metro stratum are higher than the corresponding interplace coefficients describing tendencies among the nine divisions of the stratum: $\eta_{HY^q}$ and $\eta_{H_rY^q}$ are 2.05 and 1.16, whereas $\eta_{HY}$ and $\eta_{H_rY}$ are 1.95 and 0.78, respectively. Thus $\eta_{HY^q}$ is slightly higher than $\eta_{HY}$, and $\eta_{H_rY^q}$ is appreciably higher than $\eta_{H_rY}$—that is higher by 49 per cent. The difference for the owner set can be dismissed as immaterial—it is about 5 per cent. The difference for the tenants cannot be so dismissed. However, it seems likely to be caused by a somewhat different correlation between Y of metro areas and rent control than Y of quality categories of the metro stratum and rent control.

Table 28 shows six coefficients of $\eta_{HY^q}$. They range from 1.24 to 2.05. This variation is positively correlated with $Af^q$. Thus the less households with an aged or a female head concentrate in dwelling units of low quality the higher is $Af^q$, and the higher is $\eta_{HY^q}$. Since $Af^q$ in general is less than 100, this correlation gives no reason to suppose that 2.05 overstates the elasticity of housing with respect to $y_n$. Further evidence on this relationship is considered below.

The income elasticity of housing indicated by the quality subsets of each of the three strata is higher for owners than tenants, and the difference is especially marked for the metro stratum. Difference by tenure for this stratum is shown in Figure 14. The lower coefficient for tenants than owners may be closely related to the distribution of the relaxing of rent control and the importance of new tenant dwelling units. For exam-

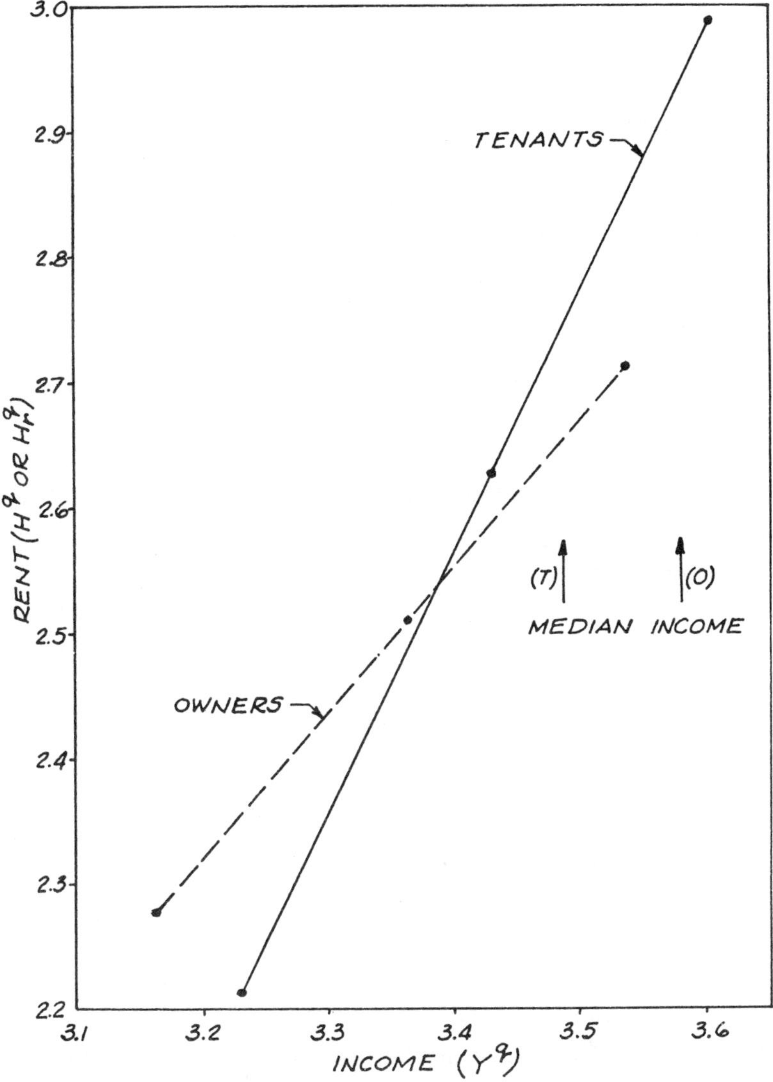


Fig. 14.—Average annual estimated or contract rent of nonfarm dwelling units in relation to average income, by tenure, subsets of households by quality of housing, metro stratum of the United States, 1950.[a] (Variables in log form.)

a. See Table 28 for source of data represented and equations used in estimating the regressions shown. The estimates are interpolations. The arrows indicate the median incomes of owners (O) and tenants (T).

ple, among metro areas the rent index, symbolized by $P_r''$, is negatively correlated with percentage of tenant units of the top quality. From this it seems reasonable to infer that the relaxing of rent control was lagging more in the cities of the North and West where quality of tenant housing was relatively high, than in the South where its quality was relatively low.

Among the three strata the difference between $\eta_{HY}q$ and $\eta_{H_rY}q$ tends to decrease with decrease in urbanization. In fact the gap is very slight for the rural non-farm stratum (see Table 28). The common pattern for the tenures in $Af^q$ may be a contributing factor, as well as the greater importance of new housing of high quality for tenants of the rural non-farm stratum than the urban and metro strata (see Table 28, column 7).

Owner-Occupants within Metro Areas.—Estimates of $\eta_{HY}q$ for owner-occupants, by quality of housing, are shown in Table 29 for 50 metro areas. These are the places represented in Table 22 where y of consumer units is the explanatory variable.

For these 50 metro areas the mean $\eta_{HY}q$ is 1.86. This stands in marked contrast[12] to mean $\eta_{hy}$ of Table 22 which is 0.316. Thus for the same places the mean $\eta_{HY}q$ is six times higher than mean $\eta_{hy}$. Or, in other words, $\eta_{hy}$ is 17 per cent of $\eta_{HY}q$. This contrast poses two main questions. Does it represent entirely the magnitude of the random transitory component of income of consumer units? Or does it in part represent an independent correlation between housing and the instrumental variable? Several sets of evidence to be considered later bear on these questions.

The mean $\eta_{HY}q$ of the 50 metro areas, namely, 1.86 is very similar to the interplace coefficient of $\eta_{HY}$ of the metro areas of the nine divisions of the United States (see Table 27). It is 1.95. This similarity adds to the stock of evidence that implies the absence of environmental conditions associated with Y of metro areas tending to increase $\eta_{HY}$.

$\eta_{HY}q$ varies appreciably among the 50 metro areas—the range is from 1.33 to 2.57 (see Table 29). A wide range among metro areas is also observed in $\eta_{hy}$, where income of consumer units is the explanatory

12. There is one difference in that the income variable, $Y^q$, represents all owner-occupants and the housing variable, $H^q$, represents only those in one-unit structures. This gap for quality subsets between the consumer units represented by value and those represented by income seems more likely to decrease than increase $\eta_{HY}q$.

variable (see chapter v, Table 22). However, among metro areas coefficients of $\eta_{HY^q}$ and of $\eta_{hy}$ are not correlated. This is not surprising since variation in coefficients of $\eta_{hy}$ among metro areas appears to be largely a function of $y_t$ uncorrelated with $y_n$, and there is no reason to suppose that such $y_t$ affects $HY^q$.

An important part of the variation in $\eta_{HY^q}$, shown in Table 29, appears to be related to $Af^q$, that is to the distribution among quality categories of households with an aged or a female head. For all of the 50 metro areas, $Af^q$ is less than 100. In other words, such households tend to concentrate where quality of housing is low. For the 50 metro areas mean $Af^q$ is 88, and its range is from 78 to 98 (see Table 29).

The expectation is that the higher $Af^q$ the higher tends to be $\eta_{HY^q}$. The correlation is as follows:

$$X_{\eta_{HY^q}} = -9.77 + 5.98\, x_{Af^q} \qquad r^2 = .207. \tag{7.1}$$

Thus $Af^q$ explains 21 per cent of the variation[13] in $\eta_{HY^q}$ among 50 metro areas. In addition, $Af^q$ is associated with a very marked increase in $\eta_{HY^q}$, and with $Af^q$ equal to 100, that is no difference among quality subsets in the distribution by Af, then $\eta_{HY^q}$ tends to be 2.19.

Variation in employment level, represented by the variable Le, accounts for some of the variation among metro areas in $\eta_{HY^q}$. The correlation is as follows:

$$X_{\eta_{HY^q}} = 3.63 - 1.58\, x_{Le} \qquad r^2 = .151. \tag{7.2}$$

The tendency observed is that anticipated. When Le is high, negative $y_t$ seems likely to be more important among those with low than high $y_n$. And such distribution of the negative $Y_t$ for a metro area tends to lower $\eta_{HY^q}$. And conversely when Le is low, the positive $Y_t$ of the metro area tends to concentrate among those with low $y_n$ and thus to increase $\eta_{HY^q}$.

---

13. Some of the unexplained variation in $\eta_{HY^q}$ may be the result of the gap between the set of households represented by $H^q$ and the set represented by $Y^q$ and $Af^q$. The first represents one-unit structures and the second and third represent all households with owner-occupancy. For some metro areas the gap is large and differs by type of household. Owner households with an aged or a female head more frequently than other households sublet to another household a portion of the structure occupied. For the U.S. metro stratum, 22 per cent of the owner households in one-unit structures and 33 per cent of those in other structures had an aged or a female head.

With Le added to the variables of equation (7.2) the following correlation is observed:

$$X_{\eta_{HY}q} = -7.17 + 5.51\, x_{Af^q} - 1.50\, x_{Le} \qquad R^2 = .328. \qquad (7.3)$$

Thus the addition of Le increases the coefficient of determination from 0.207 to 0.328,[14] but the partial regression coefficients of $Af^q$ and Le are very similar to the simple coefficients of equations (7.1) and (7.2).

Where $Af^q$ equals 100, that is, no difference in the distribution of household types among quality subsets, and with Le equal to the average of the 50 metro areas, $\eta_{HY}q$ tends to be 2.16.

Owner-Occupants within Metro Areas Stratified by Race.—Estimates of $\eta_{HY}q$ with households stratified by race are shown in Table 30 for seven metro areas. For these the mean coefficient is 1.87 for white and 2.02 for non-white households: thus, difference by race is minor. In addition, the coefficients are very similar to those shown in Table 29 for the 50 metro areas. Thus stratifying households by race does not tend to lower $\eta_{HY}q$, as it does $\eta_{hy}$ (see chapter v).

Considerable variation occurs among places in the coefficients. Among metro areas the coefficients for the two races have a slight positive correlation. This seems likely to reflect the positive correlation among places for the two races in the variable $Af^q$. In addition, the two races are quite similar in the mean $Af^q$. However, the two races differ appreciably in the distribution of lodgers among quality categories, symbolized by $Lo^q$. Its mean for white households in the seven metro areas is 102 and for the non-white households it is 108. Its range for white households is from 100 to 103, and for non-white households from 98 to 116. If the presence of lodgers implies that the housing variable overstates the housing of the persons for whom income is reported, then the higher $Lo^q$, the higher is likely to be $\eta_{HY}q$.

The variables $Af^q$ and $Lo^q$ account for much of the variation in these coefficients. For the set of 14 coefficients, the correlation is as follows:

$$X_{\eta_{HY}q} = -23.85 + 4.90\, x_{Af^q} + 8.03\, x_{Lo^q} \qquad R^2 = .776. \qquad (7.4)$$

---

14. A surprising thing about $\eta_{HY}q$ is the large part of its variation explained by $Af^q$ and Le. At the outset these two variables seemed likely to be only crude proxies for variation among metro areas in the distribution of household types in general and for the abnormality of employment opportunity.

Thus two variables, each representing the distribution of household types likely to have high housing-income ratios, explain 78 per cent[15] of the variation in $\eta_{HY}q$, and the partial regression coefficient of $Af^q$ is quite similar to that shown by equation (7.3) for the 50 metro areas. In addition, the residuals of equation (7.4) are random with respect to race.

The variable Le also explains an appreciable amount of the variation in $\eta_{HY}q$ for the two races. The higher is Le the lower tends to be $\eta_{HY}q$. The $r^2$ of these variables is .37. However, the addition of Le to the variables of equation (7.4) adds nothing to the explanation of variation in $\eta_{HY}q$. If Le has a functional relationship to $\eta_{HY}q$ for households stratified by race, it seems likely that $Lo^q$ tends to serve as its proxy. For the seven metro areas for the non-white households, $Lo^q$ and Le are negatively correlated. The $r^2$ is .94.[16] This may well signify that where Le is low, that is where employment opportunity in the metro area in general is high, that the in-migration of non-white workers is stimulated,[17] that many of them are lodgers, and that their living arrangements are such as to increase $Lo^q$.

Equation (7.4) indicates with $Af^q$ and $Lo^q$ equal to 100 (that is, no difference by quality category in the importance of household types thus represented) that $\eta_{HY}q$ tends to be 2.01. And equation (7.3) for the 50 metro areas indicates with $Af^q$ equal to 100 and Le equal to the average of the metro areas represented that $\eta_{HY}q$ tends to be 2.16. In general, these estimates give reason to expect that the elasticity of housing with respect to $y_n$ is the same for white and non-white households.

Better Data by Quality of Housing.—Quality of housing, as an instrumental variable, seems to be quite useful in revealing housing-income relationships. At the outset, I was very skeptical as to its potential because for some metro areas a very high percentage of owner-occupants

---

15. The variable $Lo^q$ explains 65 per cent of the variation. The high percentage of the variation explained, for the sets of households represented, may in part be due to the absence of a gap between the households represented by the housing, the income, and the household type. Such a gap exists for households represented by the estimates shown in Tables 28 and 29, but not for those represented in Table 30, which come from a special tabulation.

16. With four degrees of freedom this estimate is significant at the .01 probability level.

17. Various migration studies have shown that the extent of in-migration is closely related to job opportunities.

are in the top category.[18] However, for all metro areas average income varies markedly among the quality subsets, and sample size is usually such that $y_t$ uncorrelated with $y_n$ seemed likely to have a zero mean. The fact that variation in $\eta_{HY}q$ is systematic, in spite of the high concentration in many places at the top quality, testifies to the stability among places in the elasticity of housing with respect to $y_n$. However, it is hoped that a range of specifications of housing quality can be developed, suitable for a census, that will differentiate households more fully by quality of housing. The quality specifications of the Census of Housing of 1950 provide meager information on the distribution of quality of housing of owner-occupants of large metro areas.

## Correlations among Tracts Within Metro Areas, 1950

The census of population provides data by census tracts within metro areas, including value of one-unit structures in owner-occupancy, contract rent of tenant units, and income of families and unrelated individuals. In delineating the census tracts, the U.S. Bureau of the Census attempted to distinguish areas "fairly homogeneous in population characteristics." Economic characteristics, such as quality of housing and occupation of the labor force, presumably were among those considered.[19]

In the preliminary stages of the analysis presented in this monograph, considerable use was made of data by census tracts. In fact, tendencies indicated by them provided the evidence that initially convinced me[20] that much of the variation of y represents the variation of $y_t$ so that $\eta_{hy}$ is likely to understate greatly $\eta_{hy_n}$. This certainty stimulated a search for various procedures that would eliminate the effect of $y_t$ on estimates of income elasticity of housing or at least test the effect of variation in its importance. Thus the initial tendencies observed using data by tracts are largely responsible for this monograph. However, as the volume of evidence grew, the contribution of data by tracts diminished in importance.

18. For the metro areas represented in Table 29, the range is from 61 to 96 per cent.

19. It is of some interest to note that the standard deviation of value of owner-occupied one-unit structures tends to be less within tracts than by income interval of the primary units of households, at least for the Chicago metro area. From this it seems reasonable to infer that census tracts differentiate households by normal income to a greater extent than does the income reported by households.

20. See M. G. Reid, "Value of Dwelling in Relation to Income," _Journal of the American Statistical Association_, June, 1954.

Data by quality of dwelling units, described above, not only involved less computation but were found to be more suitable than data by tracts because of the information available in household types by quality of dwelling unit. Little information on the mixture of households types[21] is reported by tracts. In addition, the average income reported by tracts is far from ideal for the purpose of discovering the relation of housing to $y_n$.

The income reported by census tracts pertains to all families and unrelated individuals, irrespective of household status or tenure of dwelling unit. Within tracts it seems probable that owners tend to have a higher income than tenants and than unrelated individuals who are not heads of households. Many of these are lodgers and the bearing of their importance on housing-income relationships observed is of special interest. The housing and income variables are such that the greater the importance of lodgers the higher tends to be the value or rent of dwelling units and the lower tends to be the average income of families and unrelated individuals in the tract, that is the income represented by the estimates made.

The analysis of the housing data by tracts presented here is confined to owner units.[22] The housing variable is median value of the one-unit owner-occupied structures. It is symbolized by $H^a$. The income variable is the median income of families and unrelated individuals irrespective of tenure and household status. It is symbolized by $Y^a$. Thus there is a gap between the population represented by $H^a$ and $Y^a$. It is referred to as the gap between the housing and income variables. Because income of primary units of households with owner-occupancy tends to be somewhat higher than that of primary units of households with tenant

---

21. Information is provided on the age distribution of the population and some of the variation in the coefficients shown in Table 31 appears to be associated with age distribution. For example, there appears to be some tendency for the coefficient of income elasticity of housing among tracts to be relatively high where population 65 years of age or more concentrates in tracts with relatively high income. This relationship is more fully considered in chap. xiii which examines intertract housing-income relations as indicated by the Census of Housing of 1960.

22. A superficial examination was made of contract rent. The heterogeneity of the housing variables related to additional services in contract rent and rent control introduced complexities, so it seemed best to use resources available for extracting evidence bearing on owner-occupants. Some estimates of intertract housing-income relations for tenants of 1960 are shown in chap. xiii.

occupancy and much higher than income of unrelated individuals not primary heads of households, it seems certain that the gap is negative, so that $Y^a$ tend to understate $Y^a$ of households represented by $H^a$. The importance of families and unrelated individuals that are represented by $Y^a$ but not by $H^a$ gives some notion of the extent of the gap. However, nothing is known of the difference in the average income between those represented and not represented by $H^a$. This seems likely to result in $Y^a$ having a random error compared to a measure of Y of the population represented by $H^a$.

Because of this gap between $H^a$ and $Y^a$, the estimates shown represent tracts where the gap is likely to be small: that is, tracts high in the importance of owner-occupancy and low in the importance of unrelated individuals.[23] In addition, a standard statistical technique is used for estimating relationships where the functional variable, that is $Y^a$, is likely to have a random error. This is the use of both regressions, referred to as regressions I and II,[24] with the coefficients of income elasticity thus estimated being referred to as coefficients of income elasticity I and II. In the review of evidence where y of consumer units, Y of places, and $Y^q$ of quality categories are the explanatory variables, the possible contribution of evidence using the regression II has been ignored. In other words, in chapters v and vi and the preceding section of this chapter, the coefficients of income elasticity of housing described represent those of regression I, without this fact noted. Only where the coefficients indicated by the two regressions are compared does the notation indicate the type of regression. For the intertract estimates income elasticities I and II are symbolized as $\eta I_{HY^a}$ and $\eta II_{HY^a}$, respectively.

For regression I, $Y^a$ is the explanatory variable. If the gap between $H^a$ and $Y^a$ tend to be random then $\eta I_{HY^a}$ will tend to be lowered by the gap. For regression II, $H^a$ is the explanatory variable and reciprocal of $\eta_{YH^a}$ provides an estimate of $\eta II_{HY^a}$. This will not be affected by the random error in $Y^a$ and $H^a$ seems unlikely to have any random error of its own. Thus $\eta II_{HY^a}$ seems likely to provide the more reliable estimate than $\eta I_{HY^a}$ of the intertract elasticity of housing with respect to $Y_n$. Both types of coefficient may of course provide unreliable estimates of $\eta_{HY_n}$

23. For eligibility criteria used, see Table 31, fn. a.

24. These are discussed in chap. ii.

if the distribution of $Af^a$ or $Lo^a$ is systematically related to $H^a$ or if the intertract regressions tend to be affected by cyclical change.

Intertract coefficients of income elasticity of housing are shown in Table 31 for seven metro areas. For these mean $\eta I_{HY^a}$ is 1.55 and and $\eta II_{HY^a}$ is 2.29. The difference between these two types of coefficients provides some evidence as to the downward bias in $\eta I_{HY^a}$ because of a random gap between $H^a$ and $Y^a$.

A considerable range is shown in $\eta II_{HY^a}$, from 1.61 to 3.50. I suspect that this is largely the result of the correlation of $Af^a$ and $Lo^a$ with $H^a$. If these variables are positively correlated with $H^a$, they will result in $\eta II_{HY^a}$ overstating $\eta_{HY_n}$. On the other hand, if they are negatively correlated, they will tend to have the opposite effect. Information in the 1950 census bearing on these correlations is very meager, and its usefulness in explaining the variation just noted seems likely to be limited.[25]

The striking thing about the intertract coefficients shown in Table 31 is their similarity to the coefficients $\eta_{HY^q}$ shown in Tables 28 and 29[26] and 30. One is of course left with the question as to whether families live in tracts where average quality of housing is low because of low preference for housing compared to other consumer goods or because of low $y_n$.

## Correlations among Areas within Cities, 1933

The housing survey of 1933 reports, by area of city, mean value of owner-occupied dwellings and contract rent of tenant units and the income of primary unit of households. These variables are symbolized by $H^a$, $H_r{}^a$ and $Y^a$, respectively.[27] For these, there is no gap between the housing and the income variables, and estimates for both tenures are feasible. However, the period represents the depths of the Great Depression when average income of places tended to have a large negative transitory component. (Information about its distribution among areas is not provided.)

For the set of 14 cities mean $\eta_{HY^a}$ is 0.90 and mean $\eta_{H_rY^a}$ is 0.77 (see Table 32). This may well signify a heavier concentration of $y_t$ at low levels of $H_r{}^a$ than low levels of $H^a$. The mean $\eta_{HY^a}$ is much, much

25. This relationship is examined in chap. xiii, where intertract housing-income relations for 1960 are described.

26. Among metro areas the two sets of coefficients are not correlated. This lack of correlation seems likely to occur because of the quite different relationships of the household types to $H^q$ and to $H^a$.

27. The areas are larger than census tracts and less homogeneous in economic status of the households represented.

Table 31

Coefficients of Correlation of Average Housing with respect to the Average Income among Census Tracts, Seven Metro Areas, 1950[a]

| Metro areas[b] | Number tracts | Elasticity of housing with respect to income: independent variable[c] ($\eta_{HY^a}$) | | Coefficient of determination of average value and income |
|---|---|---|---|---|
| | | Income | Value of unit | $r^2$ |
| | (1) | (2) | (3) | (4) |
| 1. Chicago[d] | 88 | 1.76 | 2.81 | .629 |
| 2. Cleveland | 42 | 1.32 | 1.61 | .820 |
| 3. Detroit[e] | | | | |
| a) | 49 | 1.86 | 2.18 | .853 |
| b) | 49 | 1.71 | 1.86 | .919 |
| 4. Los Angeles | 29 | 1.82 | 3.50 | .520 |
| 5. Minneapolis-St. Paul | 15 | 1.54 | 1.83 | .842 |
| 6. New York[e] | | | | |
| a) | 37 | 0.83 | 2.35 | .353 |
| b) | 38 | 1.23 | 1.96 | .628 |
| 7. Philadelphia | 62 | 1.57 | 2.14 | .734 |
| 8. Mean of intertract coefficients[f] | . . . | 1.55 | 2.29 | . . . |

Source: U.S. Census of Population: 1950, Vol. III.

a. In selecting tracts for this estimate the following are criteria used.

1) Median income and value are included in the reports of the U.S. Bureau of the Census. (This criterion excludes tracts very low in number of owner-occupied units.)
2) Not more than 10 unrelated individuals per 100 families. (It seems probable that the lower the ratio of individuals to families the more likely is the income reported to represent primary units of owner households.)
3) At least 66 per cent of the dwelling units owner-occupied. (The higher the percentage of dwelling units owner-occupied the more likely are the incomes reported to represent those in dwellings for which value is reported.)
4) No more than 1 per cent of the population non-white. (This criterion is used because average income of non-whites tends to be appreciably lower than that of whites, and within a census tract non-whites are not so well represented in the owner set as are the whites; consequently, the higher the percentage of non-whites the greater the likelihood that income reported underestimates that of households in dwellings for which value is reported.)
5) No tracts where median value of dwellings is $20,000 or more. (This is the open-ended class.)
6) No tracts where median income is $6,000 or more. (This criterion is used because many tracts with median income of $6,000 or more had a median value of dwelling of $20,000 or more.)
7) No tracts with median value of dwelling under $2,000. (This criterion is used because of the likelihood of a downward bias caused by non-normal distribution of values within the lowest value interval. Few of this type met the other criteria specified above.)

None of these criteria would have been used in selecting tracts for this estimate if the U.S. Bureau of the Census had reported median value and median

lower than the corresponding coefficient of interclass correlation within place, that is $\eta_{HY}q$ and $\eta_{HY}a$ for 1950, shown in Tables 28 - 31. This is consistent with the expectation that the negative $y_t$ of 1933 was important and that it concentrated heavily in areas where $H^a$ was low.

In spite of the fact that $\eta_{HY}a$ and $\eta_{H_rY}a$ are probably lowered by a negative correlation between $H^a$ and $H_r^a$ and $Y_t^a$, they are very much higher than $\eta_{hy}$ and $\eta_{h_ry}$. The means of these for the 14 cities is 0.262 and 0.344, respectively (see Table 23). The marked difference for both tenures between these two sets of coefficients is consistent with other tendencies described above: namely, that coefficients observed, where y is the explanatory variable, tend to have a marked downward bias because of $y_t$ and that interclass coefficients of income elasticity, unaffected by such $y_t$, tend to be much higher. Interclass coefficients representing subsets within places do, however, tend to be biased downward by $Y_t^a$ of subsets, uncorrelated with $Y_n^a$, or by a positive correlation between negative $Y_t$ and $Y_n$ of subsets such as is likely to occur during the depression trough.

---

Footnotes to Table 31 (continued)

value and median income for those in owner-occupied one-unit structures.

The criteria used did not exclude the possibility of a considerable gap between the average income reported and the income of owner-occupants. The sets varied greatly in the likelihood of the gap. Some attempt was made to hold it constant by stratifying the tracts by the importance of unrelated individuals and of tenant occupancy. This was done for Detroit and New York.

These criteria, especially item (3), tend to exclude tracts in the central city of the metro area. Thus the tracts tend to be fairly homogeneous with respect to land crowding and transportation costs to the central city. The possible effect of this condition is considered in chapter viii.

Estimates shown represent variables expressed in log form, each tract having a weight of one.

b. No metro area in the South, for which data by census tract are reported, provides as many as 10 census tracts meeting the specifications described in footnote a.

c. See chapter ii for discussion of the use and interpretation of these two repressions.

d. The observations for Chicago were examined to test the effect of variation among tracts in the ratio of unrelated individuals to families, the percentage of owner-occupancy, and the percentage of males 21 years of age or more to that 65 years of age or more. Holding these conditions constant increased $\eta_{HY}a$ from 1.76 to 1.84, and increased the coefficient of determination only from 0.63 to 0.66. For none of the additional variables is regression coefficient twice its standard error. However, the percentage of owner-occupants comes close to meeting this test. Furthermore, it explains 12 per cent of the variation in $Y^a$.

e. See fn. a for comment on this stratification.

f. The means shown here are weighted by the number of census tracts represented.

The interclass within-place coefficients of income elasticity of housing of 1933 and 1950 have an important characteristic in common. They both vary widely among places. Distribution of household types and of $Y_t$ represented by Le explains an appreciable part of the variation in $\eta_{HY}q$ observed for 1950. Such conditions may also account for the variation of $\eta_{HY}a$ among cities observed in 1933. Among the 50 metro areas $\eta_{HY}q$ ranges from 1.33 to 2.57. Among the 14 cities of the survey of 1933 $\eta_{HY}a$ ranges from 0.61 to 1.35. Thus the lowest coefficient of 1950 approximates the highest coefficient of 1933, and it seems not improbable that the worst unemployment of a metro area in 1949 did not exceed that of the city with the least unemployment of 1933. This continuity creates some presumption that the same basic conditions account for the variation of the two sets of coefficients for owner-occupants, that is those of Table 29 and Table 32.

For the tenants the coefficients of $\eta_{H_rY}a$ of 1933 shown in Table 32 are only slightly less than those of $\eta_{H_rY}q$ shown in Table 28. Thus the difference between 1933 and 1950 is much less for tenants than for owners. This is not inconsistent with the interpretation relevant to owners presented above: $\eta_{H_rY}q$ shown in Table 28 seems likely to be depressed by conditions related to rent control.

Thus the tendencies observed are not inconsistent with the hypothesis that the relationship of housing to normal income was the same in 1933 as in 1950.

## Income Elasticity of Housing with h as the Explanatory Variable

The findings of this chapter add to the evidence that $y_t$ uncorrelated with $y_n$ tends to be important and that it lowers appreciably the estimates of $\eta_{hy}$. Under this condition regression II, where housing of consumer units (h) is the explanatory variable, may come closer than regression I, where income (y) is the explanatory variable, to describing h with respect to $y_n$. Such estimate of income elasticity of housing is symbolized by $\eta II_{hy}$. It will overstate $\eta_{hy_n}$ if the variation in h tends to be increased by conditions other than $y_n$ with which it tends to be positively correlated. Random error in reporting housing and variation among consumer units in preference for housing compared to other consumer products represent two such conditions. To the extent that such conditions are present $\eta II_{hy}$ will tend to overstate $\eta_{hy_n}$. The question to be considered here is the probable magnitude of this overstatement.[28]

For the metro areas of the United States $\eta II_{hy}$ is 1.99, whereas $\eta_{HY}q$ for the same universe of households is 2.05.[29] This similarly implies either that the upward bias in $\eta II_{hy}$ is insignificant or offset by some condition correlated with h, or that $\eta_{HY}q$ is also biased upward.

An extensive examination has been made of variation in $\eta II_{hy}$ for a set of 30 metro areas. This indicates that some of the upward bias in $\eta II_{hy}$ due to error in reporting h and to variation among consumers in

Table 32

Coefficients of Correlation of Average Housing with respect to Average Income among Areas, by Tenure within 14 Cities, 1933[a]

| City | Value of dwelling unit with respect to income[b] | | Contract rent of dwelling unit with respect to income | | Number of areas |
|---|---|---|---|---|---|
| | $\eta_{HY}a$ (1) | $r^2$ (2) | $\eta_{H_rY}a$ (3) | $r^2$ (4) | (5) |
| 1. Atlanta | 1.053 | 0.99 | 0.693 | 0.93 | 14 |
| 2. Birmingham | 0.904 | .66 | .963 | .83 | 13 |
| 3. Cleveland | 0.682 | .96 | .710 | .99 | 15 |
| 4. Dallas | 0.886 | .97 | .684 | .92 | 10 |
| 5. Indianapolis | 0.900 | .96 | .719 | .98 | 6 |
| 6. Minneapolis | 0.831 | .93 | .741 | .89 | 12 |
| 7. Oklahoma City | 0.940 | .80 | .721 | .82 | 8 |
| 8. Providence[b] | .... | ... | .728 | .90 | 10 |
| 9. Richmond | 1.219 | .92 | .924 | .96 | 7 |
| 10. Salt Lake City | 0.783 | .85 | .859 | .90 | 9 |
| 11. San Diego | 1.354 | .83 | .580 | .82 | 8 |
| 12. Seattle[c] | 0.613 | .66 | .780 | .47 | 11 |
| 13. Wheeling | 0.881 | .95 | .908 | .80 | 9 |
| 14. Wichita | 0.980 | 0.90 | .766 | 0.79 | 8 |
| 15. Mean of cities[d] | 0.903 | ... | 0.769 | ... | .. |

Source: Financial Survey of Urban Housing, Tables 65 and 66.

a. Value of owner-occupied structures only is reported by areas. However, information is provided on the distribution of various types of owner-occupied structures, and estimates were made of the value of the unit occupied by owner households. The adjustment thus made is important only for San Diego and Seattle. The areas were weighted by the number of households and variables were expressed in log form.

b. Providence is omitted because of errors in the income data by area—their aggregate differs appreciably from that reported for the city.

c. Posting errors seem to exist in the area data. Revisions were made on the basis of certain clues. The adjusted data are used.

d. Weighted by number of areas.

28. See chap. ii for discussion of the use of both regressions.

29. See Table 28.

preference for housing tends to be offset by a negative correlation between h and af. The examination indicates that $\eta II_{hy}$ tends to be around 2.50 where the distribution of af with respect to h is held constant and where employment level (Le) equals the average of the set of metro areas represented.[30] This is 16 per cent above $\eta_{HY}q$ observed under similar constraints (see eq. [7.3]). Thus the upward bias of $\eta II_{hy}$, as an estimate of $\eta_{hy_n}$ appears to have much, much less than the downward bias of $\eta_{hy}$ because of the correlation between y and $y_t$.

### Variation among Groups in $H^q$ with $Y^q$ Held Constant

This section presents evidence bearing on the hypothesis that with income held constant consumer units who are members of a group where high Y will tend to have higher consumption than those who are members of a group where Y is low. It was noted in chapters ii and v that phenomena giving rise to this generalization might be wholly the result of $y_t$ uncorrelated with $y_n$. If this is a correct interpretation and if $Y^q$ tends to represent $Y_n$, then where $Y^q$ is held constant $H^q$ will not be positively correlated with average $Y_n$ of groups compared.

The hypothesis is tested first by making comparisons among groups of consumer units differing in various respects. Housing-income regressions of groups are compared, first with y as the explanatory variable and then with $Y^q$ as the explanatory variable. The tendencies observed are interpreted in the light of difference in household type and other conditions that affect housing-income ratios.

The first test makes a comparison among groups differing in average income, that is Y. Housing-income repressions of such groups are compared. Other comparisons demonstrate the effect of variation between groups in Af and perhaps also in cyclical change represented.

A series of comparisons is shown in Figures 15-18. In each figure the housing-income regressions of the group with the higher average income are represented by a solid line and those of the group with the lower income by a broken line. A light line is used where y and a heavy line

30. The findings from this examination were important in the initial stages of this monograph. As the volume of evidence grew, they became less and less important. This brief summary is included because, where data are available for only a small set of households, $\eta II_{hy}$ may provide important insights as to basic relations. The 30 metro areas represented in this analysis are among those listed in Tables 22 and 29.

where $Y^q$ is the income variable. On the income-axis of each figure is shown the position of the median income of the households represented. The variables and their symbols appearing in the section are:

| Variable | Symbol |
|---|---|
| Value of dwelling of the owner households | h |
| Income of the primary units of households | y |
| Average value of dwelling units by quality category | $H^q$ |
| Average income of primary units of households by quality category | $Y^q$ |
| Average income of an entire group | Y |
| Importance of households with an aged or a female head for an entire group or some subset | Af |
| Importance of households with lodgers for an entire group or some subset | Lo |
| Percentage of the male labor force with less than 26 weeks of work during 1949 in metro areas represented | Le |

Groups Different in Y and Similar in Af.—Housing with respect to y of places differing in Y is illustrated in Figure 15. The places represented are the rural non-farm stratum[31] of New England and of the East South Central divisions. They differ markedly in Y[32] but are alike in Af. For the New England stratum, Y is \$155 per \$100 of Y of the East South Central stratum.

Where y is held constant, h has a marked positive correlation with Y. On the other hand, where $Y^q$ is held constant $H^q$ is not correlated with Y. The tendencies observed are affected by the correlation of $Af^q$ and $Y^q$. There appears to be a greater negative correlation between $Af^q$ and $Y^q$ for the East South Central than the New England Stratum. As a result East South Central stratum where $Y^q$ is low $H^q$ is relatively high, and where $Y^q$ is high $H^q$ is relatively low.

---

31. Rural non-farm areas are especially suited to this comparison because they seem likely to be at least affected by the gap between owner-occupants represented by the housing and by the income variable. In addition, the divisions are also alike in that average income of all consumer units with owner-occupancy is very similar to that of owner units in one-unit structures, the subsets of dwellings represented by the housing variable $H^q$. See Table 28, fn. a for further comment on this characteristic of the variables.

32. The variable $Af^q$ of these strata is shown in Table 28, column 4.

Groups Similar in Y but different in Af.—Figure 16 illustrates tendencies for two sets of households with much the same average income but differing in Af. For both types of regression, that is with y and with $Y^q$ as explanatory variables, housing with income held constant is higher for the place where Y is low than where it is high. This provides a

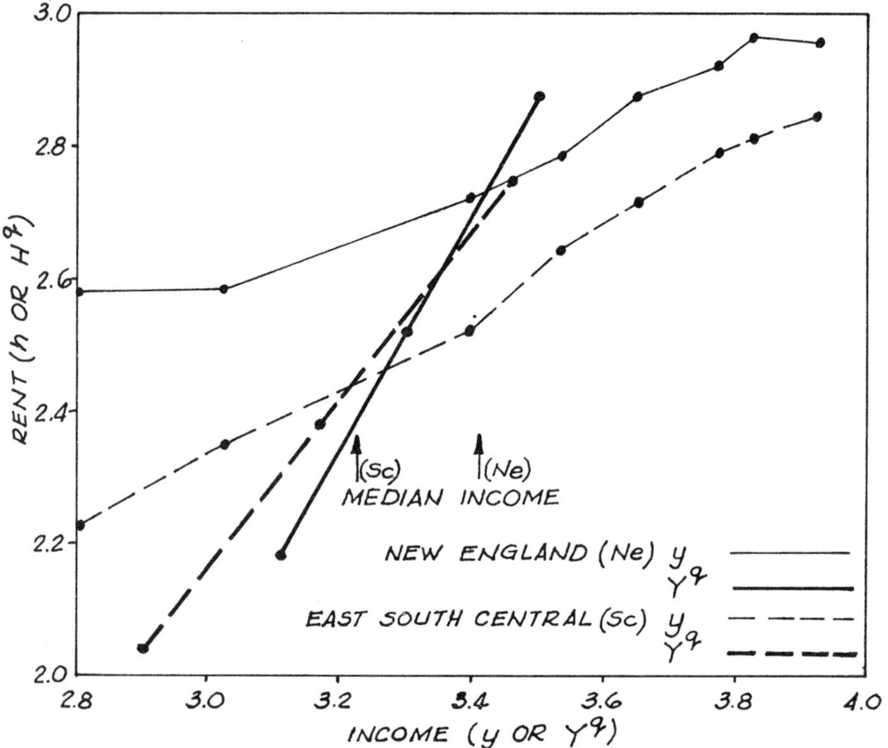


Fig. 15.—Housing with respect to income, two income variables, y and $Y^q$,[a] owner-occupants of two rural non-farm strata very different in average income (Y)[b] but similar in household types (Af), New England and East South Central divisions, 1950. (Variables in log form.)

Source of data: Census of Housing: 1950, Vol. II, chaps. 2 and 7, Table D-7.

a. Where $Y^q$ is the income variable, the regressions shown are interpolations made using equations shown in Table 28. The lowest and the highest income of the quality subsets represented here.

b. Median incomes of the two places are indicated by the arrows, Ne referring to the New England and Sc to the East South Central division.

very striking demonstration of the important effect on level of housing-income regressions of variations in Af.

White households of Houston and Los Angeles are represented in this comparison. Y of Houston is 5 per cent higher than Y of Los Angeles. This higher Y for Houston may well be the result of Af being low. Households with an aged or a female head constitute 14 per cent of the

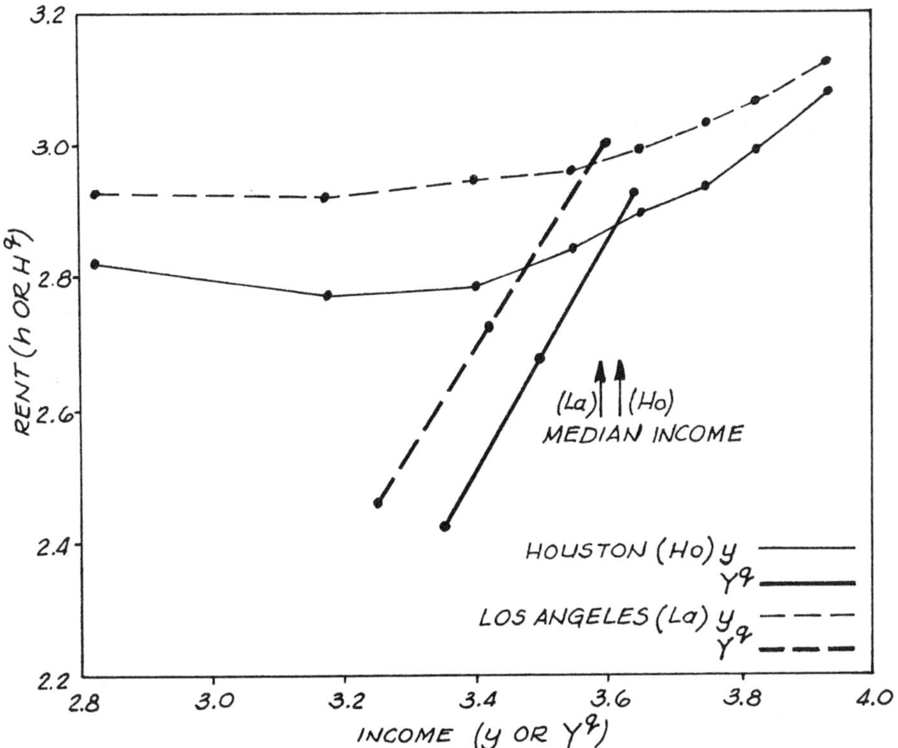


Fig. 16.—Housing with respect to income, two income variables, y and $Y^q$, owner-occupants of white households of two metro areas similar in average income (Y) but very different in household types (Af), Houston and Los Angeles, 1950.[a] (Variables in log form.)

a. The data are similar to those represented in Fig. 15, except that all observations for owner-occupants represent the same set of households. (Where data are from unpublished tabulations, the average income for the quality subsets represent owner households in one-unit structures.) The median incomes of the two groups are indicated by arrows with Ho symbolizing Houston and La, Los Angeles households.

households for Houston and 24 per cent for Los Angeles; in other words Af is 116 for Houston and 130 for Los Angeles. The higher Y of Houston than Los Angeles may also represent, in part, difference in cyclical change. It seems not unlikely that Y of Houston has a greater positive or a lesser negative $Y_t$ than average income of Los Angeles. The variable Le is 12.3 for Houston and 15.9 for Los Angeles. Thus a variety of con-

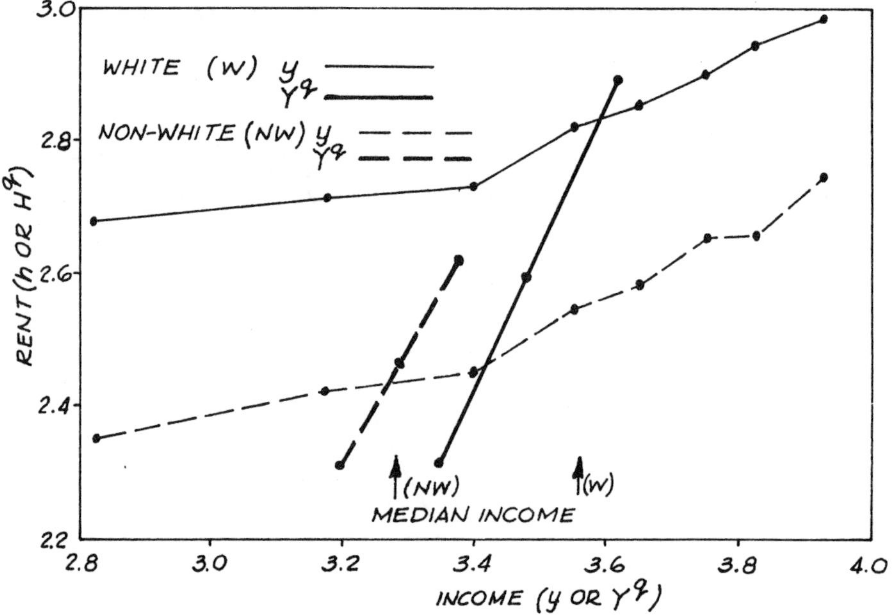


Fig. 17.—Housing with respect to income, two income variables, y and $Y^q$, owner-occupants of two races very different in average income (Y) and in household types (Af), Birmingham, 1950. (Variables in log form.)

Source of data: Unpublished tabulation of the U.S. Bureau of the Census, 1950.

a. See Fig. 16 for information bearing on the variables shown.

ditions may account for the fact that Houston, with average income 5 per cent above that of Los Angeles, has average housing 20 per cent below.

Groups Different in Race, in Y and in Af.—White and non-white households of Birmingham are represented by the comparisons shown in Figure 17. Y for white households is $195 per $100 for non-white households. And where y is held constant h is much, much higher for white than non-white households, reflecting the very great difference in Y between the races of this metro area.

On the other hand, where $Y^q$ is held constant $H^q$ appears relatively high for the non-white compared to the white households. This seems likely to represent the difference by race for this metro area in the im-

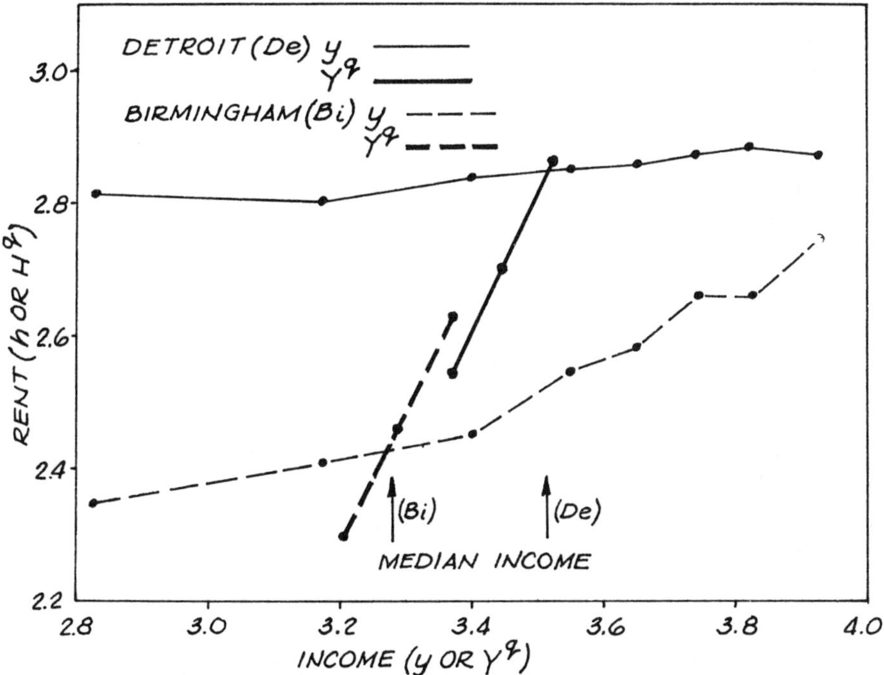


Fig. 18.—Housing with respect to income, two income variables, y and $Y^q$, owner-occupants of two metro areas, similar in race and very different in average income (Y) and in household types (Af), 1950. (Variables in log form.)

Source of data: Unpublished tabulation of the U.S. Bureau of the Census.

a. See information in Fig. 16 bearing on the variables shown.

portance of households with an aged or a female head: Af is 140 for the non-white and 122 for the white households, and the higher Af the higher tends to be the housing-income ratios. However, the difference in the position of housing-income regressions of the non-white and the white households shown in Figure 17, where $Y^q$ is the explanatory variable, is quite similar to the difference in position of the corresponding regressions for Houston and Los Angeles, shown in Figure 16, where race is held constant. Their similarity seems likely to have a common cause: for each, the housing-income regression at the lower position on the $Y^a$ axis is that for the group with a higher Af.

Groups Similar in Race but Different in Y and in Af.—Figure 18 compares non-white households of Birmingham and Detroit. The median income of the Detroit group is $172 per $100 of the Birmingham group. And where y is held constant, h is much, much higher for Detroit than for Birmingham. However, where $Y^q$ is held constant, $H^q$ of Birmingham is higher than $H^q$ of Detroit.

Difference in Af between Birmingham and Detroit seems likely to account for this difference in $H^q$ where $Y^q$ is held constant. For Birmingham, Af is 140 and for Detroit it is 122. However, difference in the position of the housing-income regressions of these two places similar in race, shown in Figure 18, where $H^q$ is the explanatory variable, has much in common with difference in positions of corresponding regressions shown in Figures 16 and 17. These similarities seem likely to be a function of difference between the groups compared in Af: the housing-income regression at the lower position on the $Y^q$ axis for each of these three comparisons is that for the group with the higher Af.

Looking at these regressions in terms of variation in $Y^q$ related to Af and to other conditions is the subject of a later section.

Concluding Comment.—These comparisons among groups support the hypothesis that, with y held constant, the difference in h observed is in large measure a function of $y_t$. They also imply that for households similar in type, little difference is likely to be observed in h where $y_n$ is held constant.

### Variation among Groups in $Y^q$ with $H^q$ Held Constant

Interpretations presented above have implied that the relative level of interclass regressions of housing with respect to average income of various groups can best be interpreted in terms of variation in mixture of household types and of income components that affect average income but have little or no effect on housing. In testing this inference, $Y^q$ is estimated for sets of white and non-white households of seven metro areas where $H^q$ is held constant. The estimating equation is

$$\log Y^q = a + b \log H^q. \quad (7.5)$$

$Y^q$ is estimated for the two races and the seven metro areas where $H^q$ equals the mean $H^q$ of the 14 groups. The estimated $Y^q$ is symbolized by $\hat{Y}$. It is shown in Table 33 together with the coefficients of regression for each set of observations and associated variables Af and Lo.

For the seven metro areas for white households, $\hat{Y}$ ranges from \$2,973 to \$3,767, and for non-white households H ranges from \$2,198 to \$3,132. Much of the variation in $\hat{Y}$ of the 14 sets of observations, of the two groups combined, is explained by Af.

$$x_{\hat{Y}} = 8.36 - 2.33\, x_{Af} \qquad r^2 = .816. \quad (7.6)$$

Thus Af explains 82 per cent of the variation in $\hat{Y}$.

Some of the remaining variation is explained by the importance of households with lodgers and by the employment level, symbolized by Lo and Le. The correlation is as follows:

$$x_{\hat{Y}} = 8.99 - 2.16\, x_{Af} - .399\, x_{Lo} - .143\, x_{Le} \qquad R^2 = .854. \quad (7.7)$$

All variables have the signs expected; in other words, the greater the importance of households with an aged or a female head or with lodgers and the higher the percentage of the male labor force with less than 26 weeks of employment the lower tends to be $\hat{Y}$. The residuals of equation (7.7) are random with respect to race.

This evidence supports the conclusion that households in dwelling units of the same value will tend to have the same income, irrespective of race, where household types are similar and employment conditions are normal. And, conversely, it implies that, with normal income and household type the same, the value of owner-occupied dwelling units is similar by race.

## Summary and Conclusions

The evidence presented in this chapter pertains to housing-income relations within places. Environmental conditions such as climate, price of housing, and community standard of housing tend to be held constant. The variables describe subsets of households within places differentiated using an instrumental variable which is correlated with normal income but not with $y_t$ uncorrelated with $y_n$. Thus the main variables are average housing and average income of subsets, and $y_t$ uncorrelated with $y_n$

Table 33

Estimated Income with Average Housing Held Constant and Related Characteristics, Households by Quality of Dwelling Unit and Race, Seven Metro Areas, 1950[a]

| Metro areas and race | Estimated income[b] | Coefficients of correlation[c] of $Y^q$ with respect to $H^q$ | | | Importance of households with | | Medians for households | |
|---|---|---|---|---|---|---|---|---|
| | | Constant | $\eta_{YH^q}$ | $r^2$ | Aged or female head (Af) | Lodgers (Lo) | Income | Rental value of dwelling |
| | (1) | (2) | (3) | (4) | (5) | (6) | (7) | (8) |
| 1. Birmingham | | | | | | | | |
| a) White | $3,705 | 2.311 | 0.448 | 0.974 | 122 | 104 | $3,690 | $695 |
| b) Non-white | 2,757 | 2.165 | .454 | .885 | 140 | 110 | 1,896 | 280 |
| 2. Chicago | | | | | | | | |
| a) White | 3,461 | 2.148 | .496 | .986 | 124 | 107 | 4,681 | 1,204 |
| b) Non-white | 2,945 | 2,304 | .415 | .961 | 132 | 128 | 3,008 | 707 |
| 3. Detroit | | | | | | | | |
| a) White | 3,767 | 2.191 | .493 | .971 | 117 | 107 | 4,431 | 904 |
| b) Non-white | 3,132 | 2.365 | .403 | .925 | 122 | 144 | 3,232 | 714 |
| 4. Houston | | | | | | | | |
| a) White | 3,690 | 2.044 | .543 | .950 | 116 | 106 | 4,133 | 805 |
| b) Non-white | 2,606 | 1.934 | .528 | .953 | 134 | 111 | 2,011 | 383 |
| 5. Los Angeles | | | | | | | | |
| a) White | 2,973 | 1.743 | .616 | .960 | 130 | 107 | 3,952 | 1,006 |
| b) Non-white | 2,444 | 1.521 | .665 | .998 | 131 | 123 | 2,838 | 816 |
| 6. New Orleans | | | | | | | | |
| a) White | 2,988 | 1.923 | .553 | .996 | 124 | 104 | 3,766 | 1,015 |
| b) Non-white | 2,398 | 2.025 | .483 | .923 | 142 | 111 | 1,748 | 369 |
| 7. St. Louis | | | | | | | | |
| a) White | 3,246 | 2.020 | .531 | .984 | 127 | 105 | 3,886 | 912 |
| b) Non-white | $2,198 | 2.233 | 0.423 | 0.991 | 142 | 119 | $2,134 | $365 |

Source: See Table 30.

a. See Table 28 for criteria differentiating the subsets by quality of housing.

b. This is the income estimated using equations shown in columns 2 and 3. Y shown here is that where $H^q$ equals mean $H^q$ of the 14 sets of households represented, that is the two races for the seven metro areas, each set with a weight of one.

c. Variables are expressed in log form.

tends to be zero for these subsets. The data examined include the Census of Housing of 1950 and the housing survey of 1933.

This summary reviews the evidence under three topics: (a) interclass coefficients of income elasticity of housing; (b) variation in housing observed among groups where income is held constant; and (c) instrumental variables for interclass correlations.

Interclass Coefficients of Income Elasticity of Housing within Places. —The main findings relate to owner-occupants of 1950. For them, the coefficients of elasticity of housing with respect to average income appears to be about 2.0. This is slightly higher than the interplace coefficient for owner households described in chapter vi. Thus there seems no reason to suppose that a positive correlation between average income of places and the price of housing tends to increase the interplace coefficient of income elasticity of owner housing.

The evidence in this chapter together with that of chapter vi is consistent with an elasticity of demand for housing with respect to price not above -1.0, and probably somewhat lower.

The interclass coefficients of income elasticity of owner housing of 1950 within places are about six times higher than the coefficient of income elasticity of housing observed where income of consumer units (y) is the explanatory variable. Such coefficients are described in chapter v. This difference seems likely to provide a measure of the extent to which $y_t$ tends to lower $\eta_{hy}$.

The interclass coefficients of income elasticity of owner housing within various metro areas of 1950 vary widely. The distribution of household type and of employment opportunity appears to contribute to this variation. Coefficients tend to be low in places where households with an aged or a female head concentrate in subsets with low average income and where the employment opportunity of 1949 was low. The first effect is not surprising since housing-income ratios tend to be high for households with an aged or a female head. A low coefficient of income elasticity of housing observed where employment opportunity is low and a high coefficient observed where employment opportunity is high are to be expected if cyclical change bring greater variation in $y_t$ to households of low than of high $y_n$.

Interclass coefficients of income elasticity of housing appear to be much the same for non-white as white owner households. For both races a considerable variation is observed among metro areas. This variation is explained by the correlation of household types with the average income of subsets.

The interclass coefficients of income elasticity of housing for the owners indicated by the survey of 1933 are lower than those for 1950. The coefficients observed for that survey seem likely to have been lowered by the widespread unemployment. For this survey a wide range in coefficients is observed among cities. And the highest coefficient for a city of the survey of 1933 is no lower than the lowest coefficient of a metro area of 1950. This similarity gives some reason for concluding that $\eta_{hy_n}$ was much the same in 1933 as in 1950.

Minor attention only is given to interclass coefficients of income elasticity of contract rent of 1950. The heterogeneity of the housing variable related to rent control made it seem likely that tendencies observed within many metro areas were far from normal. Some estimates for 1960 are shown in chapter xiii, Table 71.

The coefficient of income elasticity of housing observed where housing (h) is the explanatory variable is about 15 per cent higher than the coefficient of income elasticity observed for interclass regressions within places. This implies that the random component of h is much, much less than that of y.

Variation in Housing Observed among Groups with Income Held Constant.—Opinion is widespread that between consumer units with the same income those belonging to groups with or living in places of high average income will tend to have higher consumption than those belonging to groups with or living in places of low average income. This difference has been attributed to the effect on consumers' sense of need of the consumption of associates. It was noted in chapters ii and v that such tendencies are the type to expect if much of the variation in y represents variation in $y_t$. This interpretation is supported by the evidence presented in this chapter. It gives no reason to suppose that community or group standards have a direct effect on the value of housing occupied when normal income is held constant. However, the level of interclass housing-income regressions differs markedly among places and between nonwhite and white households within places. The difference appears, however, to be related to variation in the importance of household types that tend to have high value-income ratios. Thus the greater the importance of households with an aged or a female head the lower tends to be the income with average housing held constant.

Instrumental Variables for Interclass Correlations within Places.—Interclass correlations within places provide an important means of revealing the structure of demand for housing; hence, the relative merits of various instrumental variables should be appraised as well as the type of information needed in order to hold constant conditions other than normal income that are likely to influence tendencies observed.

In this chapter, two instrumental variables have been used, namely quality of housing and economic areas within cities and metro areas. In introducing these variables, it was noted that a positive correlation between them and preference for housing would not be surprising. However, the tendencies observed where average income of subsets is held constant give no reason to suppose that such a correlation is important, and evidence in chapter viii is consistent with this interpretation.

Evidence presented above does not indicate whether areas or quality of housing is the better instrumental variable. However, if I were permitted only one instrumental variable I would choose economic areas within cities or metro areas. These lend themselves to differentiation of subsets by economic status and are likely to be readily understood by lay users of data. Such tabulations to be most useful should provide estimates of average income of both owners and tenants. In addition, it would be highly desirable to have information by economic area on household type and perhaps also on employment level during the year represented by income reported.

# Chapter Eight

# DIFFERENCE IN HOUSING AND IN INCOME WITHIN PLACES

The evidence of chapters vi and vii is quite definitive. Hence, further evidence may seem to be redundant. However, long before that evidence was fully assembled, housing-income relations had been explored for sets of metro areas and cities using difference in housing and in income between two subsets of consumer units differentiated using an instrumental variable. In such estimates three instrumental variables have been used: (a) the main portions of metro areas, namely the central city and environs, (b) the occupation of the head of consumer units and (c) the years of schooling of the head of consumer units.

The main variables of this type are briefly described in chapter ii, so one example here will suffice. They are symbolized by the superscript [*]. Where the instrumental variable is the main portion of a metro area, the housing variable for owner-occupants is:

$$\log H_E - \log H_C = \log H^*, \qquad (8.1)$$

where $H_E$ and $H_C$ represent the median value of one-unit owner-occupied structures in the environs and in central city of a metro area, respectively. Variables representing difference in average income (Y) and in importance of households with an aged or a female head (Af) are similarly derived and symbolized. In the estimates shown, all variables are in log form and each place has a weight of one.

Such variables provide additional estimates of elasticity of housing with respect to income, where the income variable tends to be unaffected by $y_t$ uncorrelated with $y_n$. They have, however, a special advantage in that they tend to be unaffected by any direct relationship between housing and the instrumental variable used, such as its correlation with standard of housing. In addition, $H^*$ and $Y^*$ are less likely than H and Y of an interplace correlation to serve as proxies for the price of housing. Such interrelationships may affect the level of the regression of $H^*$ with respect to $Y^*$, but they seem unlikely to affect its slope.

## Differences between Environs and Cities

The Census of Housing of 1950 reports housing and income by tenure for metro areas and for any city within them with a population of 100,000 or more. The portion of the metro areas outside such cities is referred to here as the environs. Variables representing difference in H and in Y between these portions of metro areas are symbolized by $H^*$ and $Y^*$. The correlation of $H^*$ and $Y^*$ for 40 metro areas[1] is described in this section.

Characteristics of the Subsets.—Since the number of consumer units represented is large, $y_t$ uncorrelated with $y_n$ of consumer units is likely to have a zero mean for the two subsets. One can only guess as to the distribution of $y_t$ related to cyclical change.

Conditions other than normal income that affect market value of owner housing may well differ between cities and environs. For example, it seems not improbable that the price of housing of a given quality of structure tends to be higher in cities than in their environs. This will not affect housing-income ratios if the price elasticity of demand for housing tends to be -1.0, nor will it affect $\eta_{HY^*}$ if difference in relative price of housing between environs and central cities tends to be common to metro areas in general.

1. These were selected as follows: (a) Those with only one city of 100,000 or more population; (b) those with a considerable difference in value of owner-occupied units between the environs and the city; and (c) those representing many states. The first criterion was imposed in order to standardize in some measure conditions between environs and the city, and the second in order to maximize the range among metro areas in the housing variable of owner-occupants and thus to minimize the possible effect on tendencies observed of conditions not directly held constant. The third criterion was imposed in order to insure a wide representation of areas of the country. In applying final condition (c) the metro areas were arrayed alphabetically and the first one in a state not already represented was included. A limit of 40 metro areas was set merely because of computational costs and of the likelihood that such a set of 40 metro areas would adequately represent all metro areas. Almost all states with an eligible metro area are represented. There are nine states ineligible because they had no metro area for which data for a city are reported. In the set, 35 states are represented.

The value of housing occupied may also be a function of the cost of transportation to work. It seems likely, on the average, to be somewhat higher for those in environs than in cities, and it seems not unreasonable to expect that consumer units with higher transportation costs, because of their place of residence, will feel that they must spend less for housing in order to offset higher transportation costs. According to this expectation, where $Y^*$ is held constant, housing expenditure would tend to be lower in the environs than the city. Here is another condition that may affect the level of the regression of $H^*$ with respect to $Y^*$, without affecting its slope.

Difference in the size and composition of consumer units between the environs and the city may affect tendencies observed. In general, family size tends to be higher and age of head lower in the environs than in city. These two characteristics are of course functionally related. As with earlier estimates derived from census data, the distribution of household types is represented by the importance of households with an aged or a female head. The ratio of such importance between environs and the city is symbolized by $Af^*$.

Ratios between environs and cities are examined for both owner and tenant occupants. The correlation of the ratios for tenants is likely to be affected by the probable lag of tenant housing of 1950 behind income change and also by variation in additional services in contract rent. In general, the additional services appear to be less important in the environs than the central city, in part because tenants in one-unit structures are more important in environs than in cities. However, their relative importance for the two subsets differs appreciably among metro areas, so that it tends to reduce the correlation of $H_r^*$ and $Y^*$. Because of these conditions it seems highly probable that tendencies for owner-occupants are more reliable than those for tenants as indicators of $\eta_{hy_n}$, insofar as it pertains to housing in general.

Coefficients of Income Elasticity of Housing.—For the 40 metro areas the simple correlations of $H^*$ and $H_r^*$ with $Y^*$ are as follows:

Owners: $$x_H^* = 0.01 + 1.70\, x_Y^* \qquad r^2 = .765. \qquad (8.2)$$

Tenants: $$x_{H_r}^* = -0.03 + 1.05\, x_Y^* \qquad r^2 = .433. \qquad (8.3)$$

Two tendencies indicated by these correlations are of interest: (a)

$Y^*$ explains much more of the variation in $H^*$ for owners than in $H_r^*$ for tenants. This is not surprising since $H^*$ is undoubtedly more homogeneous than $H_r^*$. (b) The coefficient $\eta_{HY}^*$ is appreciably higher than $\eta_{H_rY}^*$. Such difference is consistent with the greater lag of tenant than owner housing behind incomes change in 1950. It may also be a function of additional services in contract rent.

When $H_{gr}^{*2}$ is substituted in equation (8.3) for $H_r$ the following correlation is observed.

$$x_{H_{gr}}^* = -0.13 + 0.87\, x_Y^* \qquad r^2 = .539 \qquad (8.4)$$

This substitution increases appreciably with $r^2$ of the relationship. This is the effect to be expected if some of the variation in $H_r^*$ represents additional services uncorrelated with $Y^*$. However, the substitution tends to lower the regression coefficient of $Y^*$. This is the effect to be expected since the elasticity of expenditure for fuel and light with respect to $y_n$ tends to be appreciably less than 1.0 (see chap. iii, eq. [3.2]).

The correlations shown in equations (8.2) and (8.3) are affected by a variety of conditions. Two only are examined here, namely the difference between environs and cities in the importance of households with an aged or a female head[3] and the importance of dwelling units built in 1945 or later. These are symbolized by $Af^*$ and $B_1^*$, respectively.

When these variables are added to those of equations (8.2) and (8.3) the following correlations are observed:

Owners: $$x_H^* = 0.028 + 1.96\, x_Y^* + 0.76\, x_{Af}^* + 0.21\, x_{B_1}^* \qquad R^2 = .785. \qquad (8.5)$$

Tenants: $$x_{H_r}^* = -0.027 + 1.19\, x_Y^* + 0.65\, x_{Af}^* + 0.48\, x_{B_1}^* \qquad R^2 = .515. \qquad (8.6)$$

Several characteristics of the relations indicated by these correlations seem of interest:

---

2. This is the median gross rent of tenant units in the environs per $100 of such rent in the central city.

3. An appreciable part of the variation in $Y^*$, especially that of owner set, is explained by $Af^*$: For the owner set 49 per cent, and for the tenant set 21 per cent.

(a) The addition of these two variables, that is $Af^*$ and $B_1^*$, increases $R^2$ slightly for owners and appreciably for tenants, and for both tenures the regression coefficients of these variables have the sign expected. The conditions causing $B_1^*$ to have a positive sign may differ by tenure. For tenants, the positive sign may represent, in part, the higher rent for new stock, because of a lesser effect of rent control. For owners, the positive sign may reflect the fact that the purchase of a dwelling unit tends to represent a long-run commitment, and, in general, dwelling units tend to be close to their peak value in early years[4] of their occupancy.

(b) The additional variables increase somewhat $\eta_{HY}^*$ and $\eta_{H_rY}^*$ They do little, however, to narrow the difference between these two coefficients.

(c) For owners the coefficients of $\eta_{HY}^*$ are very similar to the interclass coefficients described in chapters vi and vii. This gives further reason for assuming that differences in price and standard of housing between places or among sub-areas in metro areas have little effect on the coefficient of income elasticity of housing shown in chapters vi and vii.

(d) For tenants the coefficient of $\eta_{H_rY}^*$ is appreciably higher than that indicated by the interplace coefficient $\eta_{H_rY}$ described in chapter vi. It is, however, almost identical with $\eta_{H_rYq}$ of the metro stratum of the United States, shown in Table 28. A combination of conditions, with offsetting effects, may account for this identity. Further testing of this relationship using the data of the Census of Housing of 1960 will be of interest (such data were not available at the time of writing).

Variation between Subsets in $H^*$ with $Y^*$ Held Constant.—Equations (8.2) and (8.3) indicate that, with $Y^*$ equal to \$100, $H^*$ equals \$102 and $H_r^*$ equals \$92. The slightly higher housing level predicted for owners in the environs than the city, where $Y^*$ is held constant, is small. It is, however, inconsistent with the assumption that higher transportation costs in the environs to be offset by lower expenditure for housing. The relatively low level of $H_r^*$ predicted for environs rather than cities is not surprising, since additional services in contract rent tend to be less in the environs than the city.

4. Peak values seem likely to come a few years after initial occupancy when basement and attic rooms get finished, porches and terraces added, and landscaping completed.

Equations (8.5) and (8.6) indicate that, where $Y^*$, $Af^*$ and $B_1^*$ equal 100, $H^*$ equals \$107. This tendency casts further doubt on whether the additional transportation cost in the environs tends to lower the ratio of value or housing to $y_n$. The corresponding estimate for contract rent is \$94. That it is less than \$100 may reflect the effect of lower importance of additional services in contract rent in the environs than in the city.

Equation (8.4) indicates that with $Y^*$ equal to \$100 that $H_{gr}^*$ equals \$102. This provides further evidence, where $Y^*$ is held constant, that expenditure for housing tends to be much the same in the environs as in the city. Furthermore, the greater importance of new housing in the environs than in the city seems likely to have increased $H_{gr}^*$

## Differences between Subsets by Schooling and Occupation[5] of the Head of Consumer Units

The observations examined in this section represent differences in housing and income between two subsets of consumer units for the nine urban[6] areas as described by the consumption survey of 1950.

The instrumental variables are occupation and years of schooling of the head of consumer units. The subsets thus derived are referred to as the schooling and the occupational subsets. Housing is represented by expenditure, irrespective of tenure. The housing is symbolized by $H_{er}^*$. Income is symbolized by $Y^*$. These represent difference between consumer units of high and of low economic status with average housing expenditure and average income of such consumer units expressed in log form.

Characteristics of the Schooling and the Occupational Subsets.—Average housing expenditure[7] and average income and associated characteristics of consumer units of high compared to low economic status are shown in Table 34, with characteristics of consumer units of low economic status equal to 100. A considerable range in these is observed among the nine urban areas. For example, the range of $H_{er}^*$ is from

5. The Consumer Purchases Study of 1935-36 reports data for a few cities with consumer units stratified by occupation of the head. No information is provided on the distribution of household types.

6. These are the large cities, suburbs, and small cities of the North, South, and West. Similar data are reported by city, but apart from a few large cities the sample size is too small to justify estimates of this type.

7. This excludes expenditure for housing away from home.

Table 34

Characteristics of Consumer Units of High Economic Status, with Those of Low Economic Status Equal to 100, Schooling and Occupational Subsets, Nine Urban Areas, Consumption Survey, 1950[a]

| Urban areas | Housing expenditure[b] ($H_{er}$*) (1) | Disposable income[c] (Y*) (2) | Number of earners[d] (Ea*) (3) | Percentage of owner-occupancy[e] (O*) (4) | Age of head[f] (Ag*) (5) |
|---|---|---|---|---|---|
| | A. By Years of Schooling of the Head | | | | |
| 1. North | | | | | |
| a) Large cities | 133.3 | 130.8 | 115.8 | 92.2 | 78.1 |
| b) Suburbs | 140.6 | 134.3 | 110.2 | 93.8 | 79.1 |
| c) Small cities | 149.8 | 129.1 | 106.3 | 94.5 | 81.3 |
| 2. South | | | | | |
| a) Large cities | 164.2 | 149.9 | 116.4 | 109.5 | 81.8 |
| b) Suburbs | 169.3 | 142.1 | 111.8 | 100.6 | 81.5 |
| c) Small cities | 228.4 | 153.7 | 117.1 | 101.8 | 83.9 |
| 3. West | | | | | |
| a) Large cities | 137.5 | 137.3 | 128.6 | 93.3 | 76.4 |
| b) Suburbs | 190.2 | 151.2 | 169.0 | 98.0 | 75.9 |
| c) Small cities | 169.4 | 144.2 | 128.0 | 90.5 | 76.1 |
| 4. Mean of nine areas[g] | 164.7 | 141.4 | 122.6[h] | 97.1 | 79.3 |
| | B. By Occupation of the Head | | | | |
| 1. North | | | | | |
| a) Large cities | 132.2 | 148.3 | 130.7 | 121.8 | 89.9 |
| b) Suburbs | 149.9 | 155.4 | 150.0 | 105.4 | 85.7 |
| c) Small cities | 143.4 | 165.6 | 167.2 | 106.0 | 86.2 |
| 2. South | | | | | |
| a) Large cities | 149.9 | 160.2 | 127.3 | 139.4 | 91.3 |
| b) Suburbs | 152.7 | 160.2 | 142.1 | 106.5 | 88.0 |
| c) Small cities | 196.4 | 174.0 | 143.4 | 118.3 | 88.9 |
| 3. West | | | | | |
| a) Large cities | 131.4 | 162.5 | 150.0 | 125.9 | 83.3 |
| b) Suburbs | 165.2 | 161.9 | 164.8 | 115.2 | 81.5 |
| c) Small cities | 147.6 | 168.0 | 163.9 | 107.7 | 83.5 |
| 4. Mean of nine areas[g] | 152.1 | 162.5 | 148.8[h] | 116.2 | 86.5 |

Source: Vol. IV, Tables 6 and 7.

a. The ratios describe the characteristics of consumer units of the subsets of high economic status with those of the subset of low economic status equal to 100. The low status group, by years of schooling of the head, is confined to consumer units with head having eight years of schooling or less. The high status groups include all other consumer units. The low status group by occupation of the head consists of consumer units with head a semiskilled or unskilled worker or with head not gainfully employed. The high status group includes all other consumer units, namely those units with head self-employed, a salaried professional worker, or an official or a clerical worker or a skilled worker.

The variables used in deriving the coefficients shown in Tables 35 and 36 are the logs of these ratios minus 2.0.

b. Housing represents expenditure for the main dwelling unit. In other words, expenditure for housing away from home is not included. Among the urban areas the two sets of observations are quite highly correlated.

c. Among the urban areas the two sets of Y* are correlated but not so highly as the two sets of $H_{er}$*.

d. There is no correlation between the two sets of Ea*.

e. There is very little correlation between the two sets of O*.

f. There is considerable correlation between the two sets of Ag*.

g. Each urban area has a weight of one.

h. The relatively high Ea* for the subsets by occupation of the head occurs because the subset of low economic status includes those consumer units with head not gainfully employed.

138 to 190 for the schooling subsets and from 132 to 196[8] for the occupational subsets. The corresponding ranges for $Y^*$ are somewhat less.

Years of schooling and occupation of the head are likely to differ somewhat with respect to their correlation with $y_t$. Years of schooling tend to be the more stable index of economic status. Occupation at the time of a consumption survey may depend on job opportunity to some extent. The higher the occupation reported the greater is the likelihood that average income has a positive transitory component, and the lower the occupational classification the more likely is it to have a negative transitory component. The low economic group by occupation, as defined in this analysis, includes consumer units with head not gainfully employed.[9] Thus there can be no doubt that the magnitude of $Y^*$ observed, where occupation is the instrumental variable, is in part the result of negative $y_t$. However, if this and other shifting in the occupation hierarchy, representing $y_t$, is common to various places it will tend to affect the level of the housing-income regression rather than its slope.

Difference in transitory income between subsets seems likely in some measure to be held constant by $Ea^*$. The higher $Ea^*$ the greater the likelihood that positive $Y_t$ is greater or negative $Y_t$ is less for the high than the low economic status group. Hence, one would expect that the higher $Ea^*$ the lower would tend to be $H_{er}^*$ with $Y^*$ held constant. For the schooling subsets of the nine areas $Ea^*$ ranges from 106 to 169, and for the occupational subsets from 127 to 167 (see Table 34, column 3).

Because $H_{er}^*$ represents housing expenditure, it is important to take account of difference in owner-occupancy between the subsets. This is symbolized by $O^*$. The higher is $O^*$, that is the more the owner-occupancy of the subset of high economic status exceeds that of the subset of low economic status, the lower is likely to be $H_{er}^*$, with $Y^*$ held constant. Among the urban areas the range in $O^*$ is smaller where years of schooling than where occupation are the instrumental variable.

8. See Table 34, fn. a, for definition of these two broad categories. For no subset does the number of consumer units represented fall below 170 so that $y_t$ uncorrelated with $y_n$ seems likely to have a zero mean for all subsets.

9. Some examination was made of observations which exclude consumer units with head not gainfully employed. It gave no reason to suppose that such exclusion affects materially the coefficients of income elasticity of housing observed, and for comparative purposes it seems useful to have all consumer units represented.

There is no variable to represent the effect of rent control or additional services in contract rent.

The size and composition of consumer units differ between the subsets. In the estimates made, these are represented in part by $Ea^*$, and in part by difference in average age of head,[10] symbolized by $Ag^*$. $Ag^*$ is lower for the schooling than for the occupational subsets and its range is less. For the nine urban areas, its range for the schooling subsets is small, from 76 to 79, whereas for the occupational subsets it is from 82 to 91. The expectation is that the higher $Ag^*$ the higher will tend to be $H_{er}^*$, where $Y^*$ is held constant.

The likelihood of observing this effect for the nine urban areas is reduced by a positive correlation between $Ag^*$ and $O^*$, one tending to increase and the other tending to decrease $H_{er}^*$. The $r^2$ of these variables is .43 for the schooling and .17 for the occupational subsets.

The variables $Ag^*$ and $Ea^*$ are negatively correlated. For the schooling subsets $r^2$ of these variables is .44 and for the occupational subsets it is .70 (see Table 35).

The main independent variable of the estimates that follow is $Y^*$. In addition, estimates are shown with $Ea^*$, $O^*$, and $Ag^*$ held constant. The four independent variables are intercorrelated. The correlation matrix of these variables is summarized in Table 35.

Coefficients of Income Elasticity of Housing.—Figure 19 indicates that $H_{er}^*$ is closely related to $Y^*$ and that $\eta_{H_{er}Y}^*$ is high. Coefficients of correlation shown in Table 36, equations (8.6) and (8.10), indicate that $Y^*$ explains 72 per cent of the variation in $H_{er}^*$ for the schooling and 48 per cent for the occupational subsets. The coefficients of $\eta_{H_{er}Y}^*$ are 2.28 and 1.76, respectively.

Partial income elasticity of housing is shown in Table 36 with $Ea^*$, $O^*$, and $Ag^*$ held constant. For the schooling subsets, holding constant these variables has only minor effect on $\eta_{H_{er}Y}^*$. For the occupational subsets, holding constant $Ea^*$ increases $\eta_{H_{er}Y}^*$ from 1.76 to 2.32, and $R^2$ from .48 to .60.

In general these coefficients are consistent with the evidence of oth-

10. For tenants, $Ag^*$ may explain an appreciable part of the variation in $H_r^*$. It seems likely to be less useful in explaining $H_e^*$ for owner-occupants because the higher $Ag^*$ of owners the greater tends to be the gap between $H_e^*$ and housing consumption, because the mortgage is fully paid off.

er data. Thus they add to the stock of evidence that $\eta_{hy}$ tends to be around 2.0.[11]

## A Summing Up

This chapter adds one additional piece of evidence that $\eta_{hy_n}$ tends to be around 2.0. This tendency is indicated by variables that represent,

Table 35

Correlation Matrix of Differences between Subsets of Housing Expenditure and Other Characteristics, Nine Urban Areas, Consumption Survey, 1950[a]

| Variable | $H_{er}^*$ (1) | $Y^*$ (2) | $O^*$ (3) | $Ea^*$ (4) | $Ag^*$ (5) |
|---|---|---|---|---|---|
| | A. By Years of Schooling of Head | | | | |
| 1. Housing expenditure ($H_{er}^*$) | 1.000 | 0.850 | 0.499 | 0.325 | 0.374 |
| 2. Income ($Y^*$) | .... | 1.000 | 0.642 | 0.510 | 0.136 |
| 3. Percentage of owner-occupancy ($O^*$) | | .... | 1.000 | -0.049 | 0.656 |
| 4. Number of earners ($Ea^*$) | | | .... | 1.000 | -0.660 |
| 5. Age of head ($Ag^*$) | | | | .... | 1.000 |
| | B. By Occupation of the Head | | | | |
| 1. Housing expenditure ($H_{er}^*$) | 1.000 | 0.693 | -0.094 | 0.081 | 0.069 |
| 2. Income ($Y^*$) | .... | 1.000 | -0.124 | 0.538 | -0.368 |
| 3. Percentage of owner-occupancy ($O^*$) | | .... | 1.000 | -0.669 | 0.408 |
| 4. Number of earners ($Ea^*$) | | | .... | 1.000 | -0.838 |
| 5. Age of head ($Ag^*$) | | | | .... | 1.000 |

a. The variables are derived from the observations shown in Table 34.

11. The interclass correlation of average housing expenditure and average income of subsets of urban consumer units by years of schooling, indicates an income elasticity of average housing expenditure of 1.11. Such a coefficient tends to be depressed by the much greater average age of those of low than of high years of schooling. The corresponding interclass regression for the occupational subsets is 0.66. With the

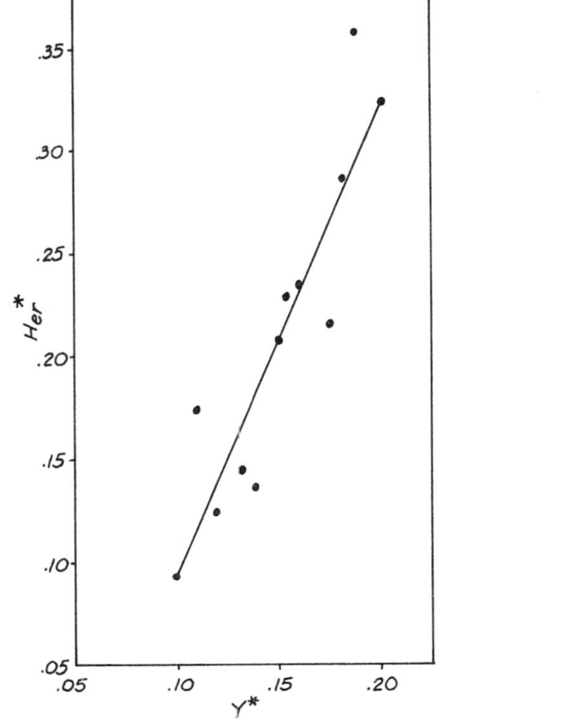


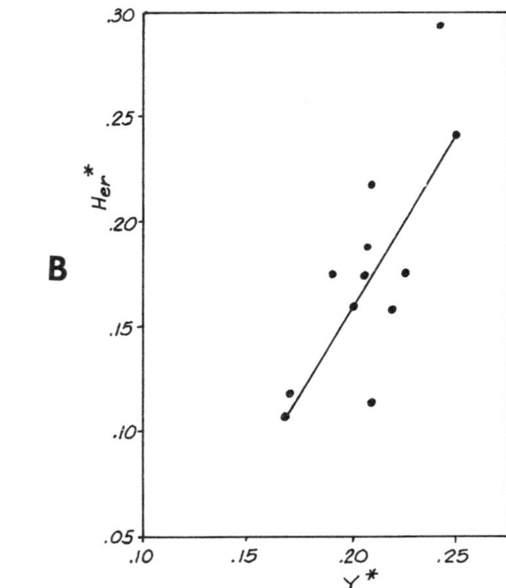

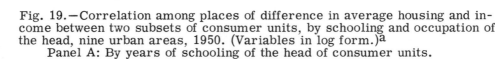

Fig. 19.—Correlation among places of difference in average housing and income between two subsets of consumer units, by schooling and occupation of the head, nine urban areas, 1950. (Variables in log form.)[a]

Panel A: By years of schooling of the head of consumer units.

Panel B: By occupation of the head of consumer units.

a. See Table 34 for information on the source and characteristics of the observations shown here. The regression coefficients are shown in Table 36.

for a set of places, difference in average housing and income of subsets differentiated with using an instrumental variable. Coefficients of income elasticity of housing thus estimated seem likely to be unaffected

Table 36

Coefficients of Correlation of Differences between Subsets of Housing Expenditure with respect to Income and Other Characteristices, Nine Urban Areas, Consumption Survey, 1950[a]

| Equation Number (1) | Constant (2) | Regression coefficients | | | | $R^2$ (7) |
|---|---|---|---|---|---|---|
| | | $Y^*$ (3) | $Ea^*$ (4) | $O^*$ (5) | $Ag^*$ (6) | |
| A. By Years of Schooling of the Head | | | | | | |
| (8.6) | -0.13 | 2.28 | ... | ... | ... | 0.72 |
| (8.7) | -.14 | 2.47 | -0.18 | ... | ... | .74 |
| (8.8) | -.19 | 2.42 | ... | -0.23 | ... | .73 |
| (8.9) | .04 | 2.18 | ... | ... | 1.19 | .79 |
| B. By Occupation of the Head | | | | | | |
| (8.10) | -.19 | 1.76 | ... | ... | ... | .48 |
| (8.11) | -.22 | 2.32 | -0.50 | ... | ... | .60 |
| (8.12) | -.19 | 1.76 | ... | 0.01 | ... | .48 |
| (8.13) | .19 | 2.08 | ... | ... | 1.13 | 0.59 |

a. Variables are derived from observations shown in Table 34.

by difference in the price of housing among places and by any correlation between standard of housing and the instrumental variable used. These conditions may of course affect the level of the housing-income regression observed among places, even though they do not affect the slope.

---

exclusion of consumer units with head not gainfully employed the coefficient is 0.92. With the further exclusion of those with head self-employed the coefficient is 1.03. None of these come close to the coefficients indicated by the correlation of the differences here described.

Thus there is no reason to suppose that years of schooling or occupation of the head are suitable instrumental variables for interclass correlations. However, they appear to be quite suitable for deriving ratios or differences for estimating the relationship of consumption, such as housing, to normal income.

# Chapter Nine

# AVERAGE TOTAL EXPENDITURE AS A PROXY FOR INCOME

Many early surveys of consumption, especially those outside the United States, did not secure information on income. For these, total consumption was used as a proxy[1] for income in investigating variation in food, housing, and other products. Such estimates have had an important place in the growth of knowledge of consumption patterns. For example, the pioneer investigation by Allen and Bowley[2] in the thirties, and the important investigation of consumption of the United Kingdom by Prais and Houthakker,[3] in the forties, both used this variable.

Prais and Houthakker argued as follows for the use of total expenditure as a proxy for income:[4]

> The use of total expenditures as the determining variable in the Engel curve can be justified on the assumption that while total expenditures may depend in a complicated way on income expectations and the like, the distribution of expenditures among the various commodities depends only on the level of total expenditures.

The first important test of the suitability of total expenditure as a proxy for income was made by the U.S. Bureau of Labor Statistics. Data

1. There appears to be some tendency to refer to average total expenditure, used in this manner, as an instrumental variable. In this monograph that term is confined to a variable used to group consumer units into subsets in order to minimize the random components of an explanatory variable such as income—in other words a variable that does not directly enter into the estimate (see chap. ii).

2. R. G. D. Allen and A. L. Bowley, *Family Expenditure* (London: P. S. King & Sons, 1935).

3. S. J. Prais and H. S. Houthakker, *The Analysis of Family Budgets* (Cambridge University Press, 1955).

4. *Ibid.*, p. 81.

from the large-scale survey of 1934-36 were examined with families classified by both income and by total expenditure.[5] Where they were classified by total expenditure, the ratio of savings to total expenditure fell with rise in total expenditure, whereas the ratio of savings to total expenditure rose markedly where families were classified by income. This difference made it seem likely, at least for American consumers, that total expenditure tends to have a very important transitory component,[6] so that the higher is current total expenditure the more families are dipping into savings or restricting current savings in order to expand current expenditure.

The permanent-income hypothesis revived an interest in the use of a measure of consumption as a proxy for normal income. The variable assumed to serve this purpose is average consumption by income interval, that is with consumers ranked by y. The nearest substitute for this is total expenditure by income interval as reported in consumption surveys. This expenditure is symbolized by c.

This chapter presents a brief consideration of coefficients of elasticity of housing expenditure with respect to c. The main topics are: (a) postulates of the permanent-income hypothesis; (b) evidence in the economic literature; and (c) other evidence of c as a proxy for $y_n$.

## Postulates of the Permanent-Income Hypothesis

One of the postulates of Friedman's permanent-income hypothesis is that consumption is uncorrelated with transitory income. If this is valid, then the transitory component of consumption for consumer units grouped by y tends to have a zero mean. A further postulate of the theory is that, with other conditions held constant, savings is a constant percentage of $y_n$. Under these conditions average consumption by income interval will provide a proxy for $y_n$ among subsets of consumer units ranked by y.

The testing of the first postulate is rendered difficult by the absence

5. See, for example, U.S. Department of Labor, Bul. 638. The independent variable was expenditure per "expenditure unit," and expenditure units represent both size and composition of families.

6. For general discussion of this method, its merits and demerits, see William Vickrey, "Resource Distribution Patterns and the Classification of Families," and "Comment," in Conference on Research in Income and Wealth, *Studies in Income and Wealth* (National Bureau of Economic Research), X, 266-329.

of a reliable measure of consumption. Total expenditure (c) is the substitute most readily available in consumption surveys. It is, however, imperfect. For example, at some levels of measured income c is likely to overstate consumption because consumer capital is being increased, and at other levels it is likely to understate consumption since consumer capital is being depleted. A positive correlation between $y_t$ and the purchase of some consumer durable goods seems not unlikely.[7] If so, c has a transitory component positively correlated with that of y. The usefulness of c as a proxy for $y_n$ is affected by the extent of this correlation. If the correlation between c and $y_t$ is confined to expenditure for products commonly classified as durable, such as automobiles and furnishings and equipment, then c minus expenditure for these might be expected to be a fairly good proxy for $y_n$. The correlation between c and $y_t$ may, however, not be confined to consumer durable goods as they are commonly defined.

Bodkin[8] and others have presented evidence indicating a more ex-

---

7. See, for example, L. Klein (ed.), Contributions of Survey Methods to Economics (New York, Columbia University Press, 1954). Klein observed relatively high expenditure-income ratios for durable goods of spending units whose incomes had increased from the preceding year. The mean ratios of expenditure on durable goods to disposable income, for specified income-change subsets for 1949, are as follows:

| Income Change (in Percentages), 1949 to 1949 | Mean Ratio of Expenditure for Durable Goods to Income |
|---|---|
| plus 25 or more | 0.114 |
| plus 5 to plus 24 | .110 |
| plus 4 to minus 4 | .076 |
| minus 5 to minus 24 | .084 |
| minus 25 or more | .077 |
| change unknown | .063 |
| not ascertained | 0.097 |

Klein in commenting on these data says: "The spread of the mean ratio between groups of positive and negative income change suggests a definite possibility of a positive income change effect on expenditure for durables. The fact that the mean ratio is smaller for the group with unchanged income than for those with increases or decreases is, however, worth noting and may suggest a somewhat more complicated relationship." Some of the income change reported in such a survey is related to short-run changes which put income up one year and down another and some of it is the result of change on the age-income cycle. Expenditure for furnishings and equipment is unusually high in the early years of household formation when income tends to be increasing with age of head.

8. See, for example, R. Bodkin, "Windfall Income and Consumption," American Economic Review, September, 1959, pp. 602-14; and Robert C. Jones, "Transitory Income and Expenditures on Consumption Categories,"

tensive correlation between transitory income and total expenditure other than that for durable goods. However, the residual expenditure thus estimated includes expenditure that may have added to the physical stock of consumer capital. For example, it includes all clothing items, among which are expensive items of considerable durability such as suits and top coats, the expense of acquiring title to a dwelling for owner-occupancy and outlays for major repairs and maintenance of owner-occupied dwelling units.[9] Furthermore, in testing whether consumption is dependent solely on $y_n$, it seems advisable to conceive of consumer capital as seen by consumers rather than as a parallel with producer capital. The concept of capital to consumers may be quite broad. It may include a stock of experience as well as physical products. Both of these are useful for sustaining later satisfactions at a level in excess of current expenditure. Thus high-cost recreation, for example, a visit to the national parks or to Europe, may well occur at a time of temporary affluence. Such a concept of consumer capital does not lend itself readily to empirical investigation. It would, for example, be difficult to get a reliable estimate of the existing stock of such consumer capital or the extent to which its increase or decrease is correlated with $y_t$.

In addition, some direct evidence has been reported which indicates that short-run income change tends to bring a reduction in expenditure for products, such as food, liquor, tobacco, and operation of the automobile. It indicates, however, no change in housing, and considerable resistance to change in consumption in general, in that assets tend to be drawn upon and debts increased during periods of unemployment.[10]

The usefulness of total expenditure as a proxy for $y_n$ is further complicated by the heterogeneity of consumer units represented. The theory postulates that other conditions are held constant, including size and composition of consumer units, job-related expense, tenure, and many other conditions often correlated with $y_t$. Some future survey may provide ob-

American Economic Review, Papers and Proceedings, May, 1960, pp. 584-92.

9. Some of these are large and are postponable; hence they have something in common with automobiles and household equipment. For discussion of their probable effect, see Margaret G. Reid, "Consumption, Savings and Windfall Gains," American Economic Review, September, 1962, pp. 728-37.

10. See Philip A. Klein, "The Pattern of Credit and Expenditure Adjustment to Unemployment," in National Bureau of Economic Research, Annual Report, 1961, p. 58. (See chap. ii for further comments.)

servations for a homogeneous set of consumer units classified by y. However, none of those considered in earlier chapters even approaches such homogeneity.

## Evidence in the Economic Literature

Friend and Kravis used data of the consumption survey of 1950 to test the use of c as a proxy for $y_n$. They compared coefficients of elasticity of housing using both y and c as explanatory variables. Their housing variable is expenditure for the main dwelling unit, symbolized in this monograph by $h_{er}$, and the group of families represented is fairly homogeneous as to number of persons and age of head. They observed a coefficient of $\eta_{h_{er}y}$ of 0.65, and of $\eta_{h_{er}c}$ of 0.86. Thus for their set of consumer units the substitution of c for y increases the coefficient by 32 per cent.[11] My corresponding estimates for all consumer units are 0.401 and 0.606—an increase of 39 per cent.[12]

Houthakker[13] also used the data of the consumption survey of 1950

11. Irwin Friend and Irving Kravis, "Consumption Patterns and Permanent Income," *American Economic Review, Papers and Proceedings*, May, 1957, p. 548. The coefficients cited relate to data expressed in log form. Only families with head 35 to 55 years of age and of three or four persons are represented.

12. The higher level of both coefficients observed by Friend and Kravis seems likely to reflect the effect of increased homogeneity with respect to age of head and tenure of dwelling unit. For evidence as to the effect of standardizing for tenure see Table 19.

13. H. S. Houthakker, "An International Comparison of Household Expenditure Patterns Commemorating the Centenary of Engel's Law," *Econometrica*, October, 1957, pp. 532-50. Houthakker examined many sets of data, most of them from European surveys. For some, the explanatory variable appears to be total expenditure, whereas for others it is average total expenditure by income interval, that is, c as defined above. Houthakker appears to have assumed that these variables are very similar since he does not explicitly state which is used. It seems highly probable that the "income" elasticity of housing plus household operation observed will be appreciably less where the explanatory variable is total expenditure of consumer units than where it is average total expenditure by income interval. It has not been feasible to examine all the sets of data utilized by Houthakker. One comparison is, however, of interest. The estimates shown for the United Kingdom use total expenditure of consumer units as the explanatory variable and those for the United States where it is average total expenditure by income interval. The coefficient of elasticity of expenditure for housing plus household operation with respect to total expenditure observed for the United Kingdom is 0.477 and that for the United States is 0.895. This difference may well be solely the result of difference in the explanatory variable used. The transitory component is probably much greater for total expenditure than

to estimate partial coefficients of elasticity of housing expenditure with respect to c, holding constant number of persons per consumer unit. His housing variable is expenditure for all housing plus that for household operation.[14] This is symbolized here by $h_o$. And his partial elasticity coefficients of $h_o$ with respect to total expenditure (c) and to number of persons (s) are symbolized by $\eta_{h_o c}$ and $\eta_{h_o s}$, respectively.

For urban consumer units in general, he observed a coefficient of $\eta_{h_o c}$ of 0.895. In addition, he made similar estimates for each of the nine urban areas and observed a wide range in coefficients. On these Houthakker comments:

> Even within the U.S. there are considerable differences in elasticities; it appears that they are largest in the suburbs (except in the South) and smallest in large cities. The reason might be that only persons who are prepared to spend a relatively large part of additional income on housing will move to the suburbs. Apart from this factor . . . the pattern is . . . fairly random. . . . It appears . . . that on the whole housing is a necessity in the technical sense, a phenomenon known as Schwabe's law.[15]

The coefficients of elasticity of housing with respect to total expenditure, observed by Friend, Kravis, and Houthakker, are much, much lower[16] than those reported in chapters vii and viii, and there is good rea-

---

for average total expenditure by income interval (symbolized by c in this monograph).

In this monograph Houthakker's housing variable is symbolized by $h_o$. For all consumer units, that is with no control as to number of persons, the coefficient $\eta_{h_o c}$ is about 14 per cent higher than $\eta_{h_{er} c}$. Several types of items included in household operation probably contribute appreciably to this difference. Household operation, for example, includes wages and tips to domestic servants, fees for day nurseries and child care, postage and stationery, flowers for the house. This category in general has a relatively high elasticity of expenditures with respect to income of consumer units.

14. In these estimates the housing variable represents expenditure for all housing, including that away from home, and in addition expenditure for fuel, light, and refrigeration and household operation. Housing expenditure as defined in chap. iv, and symbolized by $h_{er}$, is 53 per cent of this set of expenditures.

15. Ibid., p. 543.

16. In general, the elasticity of total expenditure with respect to income among consumer units is less than 1.0. Hence the use of c as a substitute for y tends to increase the estimates of income elasticity of housing. The increase is proportional to the elasticity of total expenditure with respect to measured income. The more this coefficient falls below 1.0, the more the substitution of c for y will increase the coefficient of income elasticity of housing observed.

son to believe that the income variables there used come close to representing variation in $y_n$. Furthermore the variation in $\eta h_o c$ among the nine urban areas, reported by Houthakker, is appreciable. Houthakker suspected this to be related to preference associated with suburbanization. However, it seems to be a function of the heterogeneity of the housing variable, the mixture of household type, and the transitory component of c. One systematic relationship is indicated by the partial coefficients reported by Houthakker. For example, there is a negative and very close association between $\eta h_o s$ and $\eta h_o c$: the respective ranges are from -0.182 to -0.543 and from 0.654 to 1.222 (see Table 37, columns 1 and 2). There is, of course, no reason to suppose that the negative correlation between $\eta h_o c$ and $\eta h_o s$ is direct. Instead it seems probable that s serves as a proxy for one or more conditions directly related to $h_o$.

The coefficient of $\eta h_o s$ may well be a proxy for the increase in owner-occupancy with income ($o_y$). Among the nine urban areas the coefficient $\eta h_o s$ is positively correlated with $o_y$. For example $\eta h_o s$ ranges from -0.155 for large cities in the North to -0.543 for small cities in the South, and $o_y$ for these urban areas is 168 and 122, respectively (see Table 37). The negative correlation between $\eta h_o c$ and $o_y$ is to be expected, since the higher is $o_y$ the more the gap between housing consumption and expenditure at high income exceeds that at low income. Thus, if the housing variable had represented consumption, a different tendency would have been observed.

Another characteristic of the partial coefficients of $\eta h_o c$ reported by Houthakker is of very great interest: A marked positive correlation exists between $\eta h_o c$ and $Y_{ov}$.[17] This is shown in Figure 20. This[18] seems to imply that the more y represents $y_n$ the higher tends to be the coefficient of $\eta h_o c$. Or, otherwise stated, the less the importance of $y_t$ uncorrelated with $y_n$ the higher tends to be $\eta h_o c$. The relationship shown in Figure 20 has much in common with that shown in Figure 7 A, which shows

---

17. The equation is as follows:

$$X_{\eta h_o c} = 0.043 + 8.27 X_{Y_{ov}} \qquad r^2 = .593. \tag{9.1}$$

$Y_{ov}$ seems likely to be a proxy for the variance of normal incomes. Hence the higher $Y_{ov}$ the lower tends to be the importance of $y_t$ uncorrelated with $y_n$.

18. This is significant at about the .02 probability level.

for the same areas the coefficients of $\eta_{h_{er}y}$ in relation to $Y_{ov}$: The degree of correlation is somewhat less for the relationship of Figure 20 than those of Figure 7. This comparison gives reason to suppose that coefficients of $\eta_{h_oc}$ tend to have an appreciable downward bias because

Table 37

Coefficients of Elasticity of Expenditure for Housing plus Household Operation ($h_o$) and for Housing ($h_{er}$) with respect to Average Total Expenditure and Related Characteristics, Nine Urban Areas, Consumption Survey, 1950

| Area | Partial elasticity coefficients[a] | | | $s_y$ [e] | $o_y$ [f] | $Y_{ov}$ [g] |
|---|---|---|---|---|---|---|
| | $\eta_{h_oc}$ [b] | $\eta_{h_os}$ [c] | $\eta_{h_{er}c}$ [d] | | | |
| 1. North | | | | | | |
| a. Large cities | 0.764 | -0.155 | 0.525 | 155 | 168 | 0.085 |
| b. Suburbs | 0.978 | - .236 | .697 | 129 | 134 | .099 |
| c. Small cities | 0.810 | - .237 | .523 | 148 | 141 | .096 |
| 2. South | | | | | | |
| a. Large cities | 0.789 | - .271 | .665 | 126 | 177 | .106 |
| b. Suburbs | 0.984 | - .292 | .678 | 121 | 126 | .103 |
| c. Small cities | 1.122 | - .543 | .845 | 124 | 122 | .130 |
| 3. West | | | | | | |
| a. Large cities | 0.654 | - .182 | .518 | 148 | 157 | .085 |
| b. Suburbs | 0.933 | - .401 | .638 | 128 | 129 | .093 |
| c. Small cities | 0.766 | -0.292 | 0.575 | 139 | 132 | 0.099 |

Source: H. S. Houthakker, "An International Comparison of Household Expenditure Patterns Commemorating the Centenary of Engel's Law," Econometrica, October, 1957, p. 542, and Study of Consumer Expenditures, Vols. I and II.

a. The dependent variable is expenditure for all housing including that away from home and expenditure for all household operation, symbolized by $h_o$.

b. The explanatory variable is average total expenditure for consumer units classified by y. It is symbolized by c.

c. The explanatory variable is number of persons per consumer unit with consumer units ranked by y. It is symbolized by s.

d. The dependent variable is housing expenditure for the main dwelling and the explanatory variable is c. This coefficient was estimated by dividing the $\eta_{h_{er}y}$ shown in Table 19 A by the coefficient of $\eta_{cy}$ (Number of persons is not held constant.)

e. This is an index of the increase in number of persons with income. See Table 19.

f. This is an index of the increase in owner-occupancy with income. See Table 19.

g. This is an index of the variance of average income among occupations. See Table 19.

of a transitory component in c that is positively correlated with $y_t$ and that has little or no correlation with $h_o$.

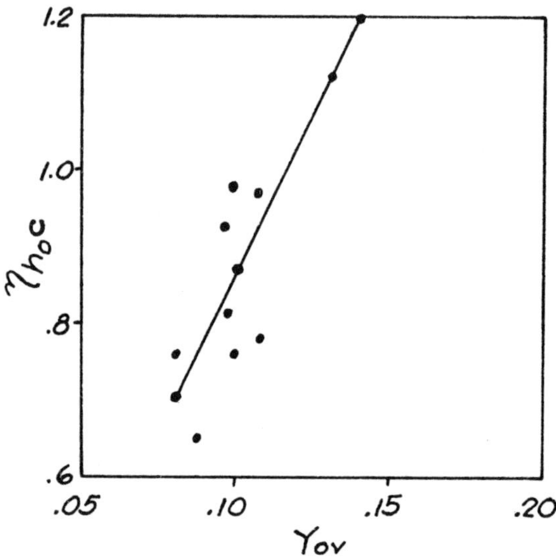


Fig. 20.—Partial coefficients of $\eta_{h_oc}$ in relation to $Y_{ov}$, a proxy for variance of normal incomes, nine urban areas, consumption survey,[a] 1950. (Estimates are shown in Table 37).

### Other Evidence of c as a Proxy for $y_n$

The preceding section provides powerful evidence that c is likely to be an unsatisfactory proxy for $y_n$. Estimates shown in this section confirm this judgment. Comparisons are made for a set of cities between $\eta_{h_{er}y}$ and $\eta_{h_{er}c}$, and between coefficients elasticity of total expenditure with respect to y and similar coefficients of total expenditure with housing excluded.

Comparison for 30 Cities between $\eta_{h_{er}y}$ and $\eta_{h_{er}c}$.—For 30 cities mean $\eta_{h_{er}y}$ is 0.401 and mean $\eta_{h_{er}c}$ is 0.534—an increase of 34 per cent.

For the 30 cities the range in $\eta_{h_{er}y}$ is from 0.133 to 0.716, whereas that of $\eta_{h_{er}c}$ is from 0.193 to 0.854 (see Tables 21 and 38). Thus the substitution of c for y increases the coefficient of income elasticity of housing observed by one-third, but it narrows only slightly the range in the coefficients observed among the 30 cities.

Among the cities, $\eta_{h_{er}c}$ is highly correlated with $\eta_{h_{er}y}$. Hence it is

Table 38

Coefficients of $\eta_{h_{er}c}$ and $\eta_{cy}$ and Related Characteristics, 30 Cities, Consumption Survey, 1950[a]

| City | $\eta_{h_{er}c}$[b] (1) | $\eta_{cy}$[c] (2) | $\eta_{c_oy}$[d] (3) |
|---|---|---|---|
| 1. Atlanta | 0.548 | 0.944 | 0.994 |
| 2. Baltimore | .424 | .564 | .609 |
| 3. Birmingham | .548 | .938 | .995 |
| 4. Boston | .386 | .694 | .773 |
| 5. Canton | .427 | .715 | .751 |
| 6. Chicago | .371 | .703 | .771 |
| 7. Cincinnati | .643 | .734 | .774 |
| 8. Cleveland | .454 | .757 | .823 |
| 9. Hartford | .604 | .664 | .697 |
| 10. Indianapolis | .429 | .678 | .730 |
| 11. Kansas City | .854 | .838 | .882 |
| 12. Los Angeles | .448 | .553 | .602 |
| 13. Louisville | .788 | .749 | .770 |
| 14. Miami | .686 | .757 | .799 |
| 15. Milwaukee | .193 | .690 | .786 |
| 16. Minneapolis-St. Paul | .400 | .813 | .893 |
| 17. New Orleans | .543 | .816 | .856 |
| 18. New Jersey, Northern Area | .530 | .698 | .748 |
| 19. New York | .624 | .692 | .736 |
| 20. Norfolk-Portsmouth | .662 | .934 | .979 |
| 21. Omaha | .427 | .766 | .838 |
| 22. Philadelphia-Camden | .587 | .812 | .860 |
| 23. Pittsburgh | .634 | .733 | .773 |
| 24. Portland, Oregon | .475 | .770 | .833 |
| 25. Providence | .448 | .623 | .666 |
| 26. St. Louis | .664 | .712 | .745 |
| 27. San Francisco-Oakland | .627 | .711 | .750 |
| 28. Scranton | .586 | .765 | .796 |
| 29. Seattle | .378 | .701 | .758 |
| 30. Youngstown | .661 | .697 | .724 |
| 31. Mean[e] | 0.535 | 0.741 | 0.790 |

a. The cities are those represented by estimates of $\eta_{h_{er}y}$ shown in Table 21. All estimates use grouped data, and variables are expressed in log form. The estimates represent regression coefficients weighted by the number of consumer units reporting.

b. The dependent variable is expenditure for housing irrespective of tenure ($h_{er}$), and the explanatory variable is average total expenditure by income interval (c). The estimates shown here are coefficients $\eta_{h_{er}y}$ shown in Table 21 divided by the coefficient $\eta_{cy}$ shown in column 2 of this table.

c. The dependent variable is total expenditure which includes outlays for gifts and contributions. The income variable is y.

d. The dependent variable is total consumption expenditure, as defined in fn. c, less $h_{er}$. The explanatory variable is y.

e. Each city has a weight of one.

not surprising that the coefficients of $\eta_{h_{er}c}$ are positively correlated with $Y_{ov}$, a proxy for the variance of $y_n$, and that they are negatively correlated with $ea_y$, a joint proxy for the importance of $y_t$, and for the rise in job-related expense with y. These two variables, $Y_{ov}$ and $ea_y$, explain 20 per cent of the variation in $\eta_{h_{er}c}$ of 29 cities.[19] The regression coefficients of $Y_{ov}$ and $ea_y$ are, however, of lower magnitude than the corresponding coefficients where $\eta_{h_{er}y}$ is the dependent variable (see Table 39, A, eq. [9.5], and Table 24, eq. [5.9]).

The distribution of owner-occupancy by income, represented by $o_y$,

Table 39

Coefficients of Correlation of $\eta_{h_{er}c}$ and $\eta_{c_oy}$ and Characteristics of the Income Distribution, 29 Cities, Consumption Survey, 1950[a]

| Equation number | Regression coefficients | | | | | |
|---|---|---|---|---|---|---|
| | $Y_{ov}$ (1) | $ag_y$ (2) | $s_y$ (3) | $ea_y$ (4) | $o_y$ (5) | $R^2$ (6) |
| | A. Dependent variable, $\eta_{h_{er}c}$ | | | | | |
| (9.2) | 2.633 | .... | .... | .... | .... | .134 |
| (9.3) | 2.603 | -0.085 | .... | .... | .... | .134 |
| (9.4) | 2.608 | .... | -0.023 | .... | .... | .134 |
| (9.5) | 1.746 | .... | .... | -0.522 | .... | .196 |
| (9.6) | 2.856 | .... | .... | .... | -0.386 | .179 |
| (9.7) | 2.300 | .... | 0.198 | -0.409 | -0.251 | .210 |
| | B. Dependent variable, $\eta_{c_oy}$ | | | | | |
| (9.10) | 2.880 | .... | .... | .... | .... | .343 |
| (9.11) | 2.846 | -0.097 | .... | .... | .... | .344 |
| (9.12) | 3.572 | .... | 0.617 | .... | .... | .410 |
| (9.13) | 2.294 | .... | .... | -0.345 | .... | .401 |
| (9.14) | 2.812 | .... | .... | .... | 0.131 | .355 |
| (9.15) | 2.508 | .... | 0.671 | -0.567 | 0.283 | .532 |

a. Variables represented by these estimates are shown in Tables 21 and 38. Findings from a similar examination of coefficients of $\eta_{h_{er}y}$ are presented in Table 24.

19. An extimate of $Y_{ov}$ is not available for one of the cities.

appears to affect $\eta_{h_{er}c}$ in much the same way as it affects $\eta_{h_{er}y}$, in that the higher is $o_y$ the lower tends to be the respective coefficients (see Table 39, eq. [9.6], and Table 24, eq. [5.10]).

Elasticity of c with respect to y.—Prais pointed out that total expenditure will be a good proxy for normal income if the distribution of total expenditure among the various consumer products depends solely on the level of total expenditure.[20] This likelihood is now to be tested further. Coefficients of income elasticity of total expenditure for 30 cities are shown in Table 38, column 2. These are symbolized by $\eta_{cy}$.[21]

The coefficients $\eta_{h_{er}y}$ and $\eta_{cy}$ are positively correlated. This relationship is shown in Figure 21, A. The $r^2$ of the variables is .421. Some of this correlation occurs because total expenditure includes $h_{er}$. An estimate has been made of income elasticity of total expenditure excluding $h_{er}$. This expenditure is symbolized by $c_o$, that is total expenditure other than that for the main dwelling unit. The relationship for the 30 cities of $\eta_{h_{er}y}$ and $\eta_{c_oy}$ is shown in Figure 21, B. The $r^2$ of this relationship is .279. This is appreciably lower than $r^2$ of the relationship shown in Figure 20, A. However, the lower correlation is highly significant. This implies that the two sets of coefficients of income elasticity, that is $\eta_{h_{er}y}$ and $\eta_{c_oy}$, are affected by a common set of conditions. Reporting error is one such condition. In addition, it seems highly probable that the coefficient of elasticity of $c_o$ with respect to such $y_t$ as is actually experienced by consumer units[22] is appreciably less than that with respect to $y_n$. Determining the correlation of expenditure for various consumer products with $y_t$ is, however, only in a very preliminary stage.

Furthermore, there is no reason to suppose that other conditions associated with the income distribution, such as size and composition of consumer units, number of earners and tenure, will affect the two coefficients in the same manner. This likelihood has been tested through an examination of the variation of $\eta_{h_{er}y}$ and of $\eta_{c_oy}$ for 29 cities. Estimates of the probable effect of conditions associated with $\eta_{h_{er}y}$ are

---

20. Loc. cit.

21. The coefficient of $\eta_{h_{er}c}$ is a product of $\eta_{h_{er}y}$ and the reciprocal of $\eta_{cy}$. Thus conditions affecting $\eta_{cy}$ will also affect $\eta_{h_{er}c}$, even though they may not affect $\eta_{h_{er}y}$.

22. That is, $y_t$ exclusive of reporting error.

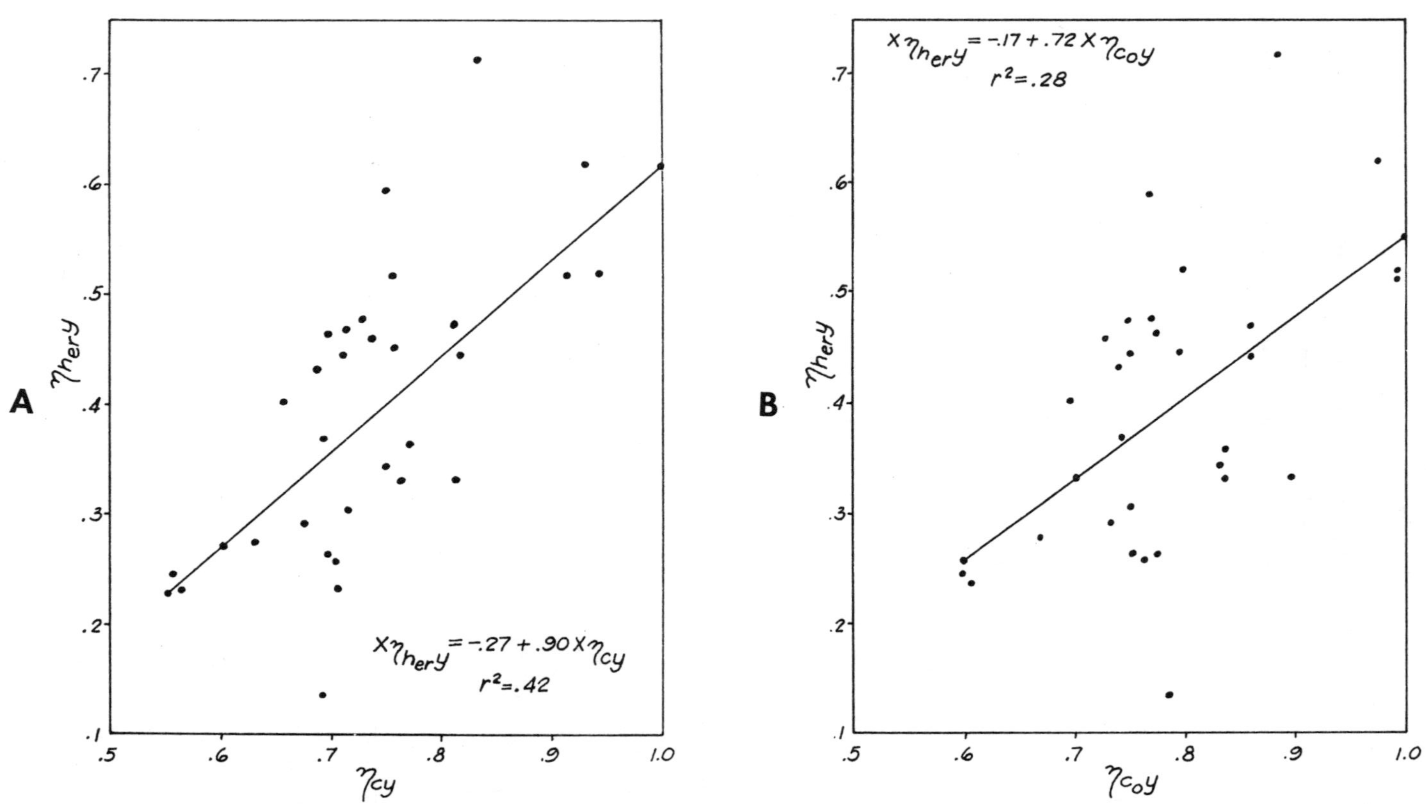


Fig. 21.—Coefficients of $\eta_{h_{er}y}$ in relation to $\eta_{cy}$ and to $\eta_{c_oy}$, 30 cities, consumption survey, 1950 (coefficients are shown in Tables 38 and 21).

Panel A: $\eta_{h_{er}y}$ with respect to $\eta_{cy}$.

Panel B: $\eta_{h_{er}y}$ with respect to $\eta_{c_oy}$.

shown in Table 24, and of those associated with $\eta_{c_o y}$ in Table 39 B.

For the cities, these coefficients are positively correlated with $Y_{ov}$ and negatively correlated with $ea_y$. The partial regression coefficients of these variables as they relate to the two sets of coefficients of income elasticity are as follows:

| Coefficients of income elasticities | Partial regression coefficients of variables representing mixture of income components | |
|---|---|---|
| | $Y_{ov}$ [23] | $ea_y$ |
| $\eta_{h_{er} y}$ [24] | 2.277 | -0.635 |
| $\eta_{c_o y}$ [25] | 2.294 | -0.345 |

The only difference indicated here is that increase in $ea_y$ tends to lower the coefficient of $\eta_{h_{er} y}$ more than $\eta_{c_o y}$. This is the tendency to expect if $ea_y$ has less positive correlation with $h_{er}$ than with such things as job-related expenditure and outlays for consumer durable goods, types of expenditure represented by $c_o$.

Other characteristics of consumer units affect the two coefficients differently. For example, variation in $s_y$, that is the increase in the number of persons with y, appears to have little effect on $\eta_{h_{er} y}$ and an appreciable effect on $\eta_{c_o y}$. The higher $s_y$ the higher tends to be $\eta_{c_o y}$. This is the effect to be expected, since consumption surveys show that the higher is s the greater tends to be the increase in food and clothing compared to other consumer products.

The variables describing the importance of $y_n$ and $y_t$ and the size and composition of consumer units and number of earners by income are at best crude measures of difference. The tendencies observed are, however, consistent in direction with expectations. They leave no reason to doubt that many conditions are likely to lower $\eta_{h_{er} c}$. But they give no

---

23. The variable $Y_{ov}$ seems likely to serve as a proxy for reporting error, in that the greater the equality of $y_n$ the more the variation in y is likely to represent reporting error. The similarity of the two regression coefficients of $Y_{ov}$ shown here may occur because reporting error is a very important part of the $y_t$ as defined by Friedman and tends to affect all coefficients of elasticity of expenditure to the same extent.

24. See Table 24, equation (5.9).

25. See Table 39 B, equation (9.13).

reason to suppose that c is a good proxy for $y_n$ if one wishes to estimate demand for housing. Whether it is suitable for estimating demand for any consumer products remains to be determined.

## Summary and Conclusions

The evidence presented in this chapter implies that the average total expenditure by income interval (c) is not a good proxy for normal income ($y_n$), at least where the variation in housing is being investigated. Such substitution may reduce somewhat the downward bias present where income of consumer units (y) is the explanatory variable. There seems, however, no reason to expect that the downward bias is entirely, or even largely, eliminated by the substitution.

This judgment rests on the evidence of the earlier chapters where the income variable seems likely to come close to representing $y_n$ and on evidence presented in this chapter, bearing on conditions associated with y that affect total expenditure appreciably but have little or no effect on housing. Among these are increase with y in the number of persons and earners per consumer unit. If these could be held constant together with the age of members and the heterogeneity of the housing variable related to owner-occupancy, it might be that average total expenditure would be found to be a good proxy for normal income.

# Chapter Ten

# YEAR-BY-YEAR CHANGE IN HOUSING

So far attention has centered on cross-section estimates. This and the chapter that follows describe intertemporal change. This chapter considers evidence of annual time series, and the next presents estimates, derived from survey data, of change between two years for sets of cities.

In this as in other chapters, attention centers on the evidence as to elasticity of housing with respect to income. An important issue is the extent to which measures of housing provided by times series represent consumption. Another is the extent to which estimates of annual income represent (a) cyclical change and hence a transitory income component or (b) a secular trend in normal income. No attempt is made to provide a definitive estimate of the income elasticity of housing with respect to normal income holding constant the other types of change, such as relative price of housing to consumer products in general and to the price of products complementary, as well as closely competitive, with housing.

This chapter reviews briefly the data available and presents some estimates of tendencies. Its main topics are (a) housing time series: their quality; (b) price series; (c) cyclical and secular change in space rent; (d) trend in residential capital; and (e) current outlays for stock.

## Housing Time Series: Their Quality

There are two main federal series. One represents services of residential housing. It reports space rent[1] and is a part of the national sta-

1. Space rent covers facilities for heating and plumbing, water heaters, lighting fixtures, kitchen cabinets, linoleum, storm windows and doors, window screens, screen doors, and window blinds and shades

tistics of income and consumption, prepared by the U.S. Department of Commerce. Official comment on this series as of 1958 states:[2] "Despite the revisions . . . the rent estimates continue to be among the least satisfactory components of the national income statistics. This condition is largely a reflection of the heterogeneity, the poor statistical quality, and serious gaps which characterize the basic data at many points. . . ." This series relies on data reported by the census of housing, on some intercensal surveys, and on interpolations using the evidence of housing-income regression of cross section surveys such as are reported in chapter v.

The second series describes non-farm residential construction and is based largely on reports of building permits as granted by cities and counties. By the late fifties the reliability of this series came to be recognized. For example, the U.S. Department of Commerce in 1958 commented[3] on it:

> . . . Despite . . . substantial revision, the basic data for estimating the value of residential construction remain unsatisfactory. The situation was pointed up most recently in connection with tabulations from the 1956 National Housing Inventory. After such allowances as are possible for differences in definition and coverage, the NHI sample-based units added by new construction . . . were found to exceed substantially the BLS series on new non-farm dwelling units. . . .[4]

A revision of the series describing new dwelling units started was introduced in 1959. Estimates using old and new methods are provided for a short overlapping period. For the non-farm sector these indicate that the old methods resulted in an underestimate of more than 10 per cent.[5] Furthermore, there seems some possibility that the need for up-

---

but excludes other furnishings, equipment, and related services—furniture, stoves and ranges, refrigerators, repairs of furniture and appliances, fuel, electricity, etc.

2. U.S. Office of Business Economics (Department of Commerce), U.S. Income and Output, Supplement to Survey of Current Business, 1958, pp. 85 and 93.

3. Ibid.

4. For further discussion of this discrepancy, see U.S. Bureau of Census, "Components of Change 1950 to 1956," 1956 National Housing Inventory, Vol. I, Part I (1958), p. 11.

5. "Introduction of the New Series of Housing Starts," Construction Review, June, 1960, pp. 4-10. Errors in the old series appear to have occurred because of some failure to report in the permit-issuing areas,

ward revision in the series is even greater[6] for some years prior to 1959-60—the overlapping period of the series.

Prior to the revision, the series purporting to represent the value of new construction was estimated primarily from applications for permission to build. These have been found to be unreliable evidence of the trend in number of units entering the stock. They may also understate the value of new units. Understatement of such value on an application to build seems not unlikely if such understatement is looked upon as a means of minimizing the real property tax to be paid. So far, the likelihood of this practice seems not to have been systematically investigated.

Several series prepared by private investigators supplement these two main housing series.[7] They have been summarized in a volume on historical statistics prepared under the sponsorship of the U.S. Bureau of the Census.[8] Among these are estimates of stock for a base year with adjustments for annual additions to and losses from the stock. Those currently available have utilized estimates of new construction based on reports of building permits. Hence they tend to have the shortcomings of these reports. In other words, they tend to understate the number of new units added to the stock and may also understate their average value. Furthermore, understatement of growth in the real value of the stock seems not unlikely because of upward bias in the construction cost index used to estimate the stock in dollars of constant purchasing power. In addition, errors of various sorts, some perhaps offsetting, seem not unlikely, for example in estimates pertaining to depreciation and the extent to which owner-occupants build and maintain the units occupied.

The most carefully developed estimate of change in residential stock is undoubtedly that by Grebler, Blank, and Winnick.[9] The estimates as-

---

and higher rate of new construction in the areas not issuing permits than in areas issuing permits. (Together, that is, with the imputation of the rate of construction in the permit-issuing areas to areas not issuing permits.)

6. Ibid., p. 7.

7. In July, 1959, full responsibility for compiling and publishing federal estimates of residential construction was placed with the U.S. Department of Commerce. Prior to that time responsibility had been shared with the Department of Labor.

8. Historical Statistics of the United States: Colonial Times to 1957 (Washington, D.C.: U.S. Government Printing Office, 1960).

9. Leo Grebler, David M. Blank, and L. Winnick, Capital Formation in Residential Real Estate (Princeton: Princeton University Press, 1956).

sembled led them to conclude that between 1900 and 1950 the average, real value of non-farm dwelling units exclusive of land fell by 33 per cent, per capita value by 11 per cent, and average value of new units added to the stock by 35 per cent.[10]

Information about the physical characteristics of the stock that are indicative of change in real value are available in the censuses beginning with that of 1940. Grebler, Blank, and Winnick observed a decrease from 1940 to 1950 of 15 per cent in average real value of non-farm dwelling units. Such a change seems highly improbable in view of the change in physical characteristics of the stock. Change in some of the important features of non-farm dwelling units is given in Table 40. Only in rooms per dwelling unit is there any indication of a decline in quality of dwelling unit, and this is small compared to the increase in quality indicated by greater frequency of preferred facilities[11] (see chapter xii for further evidence on rooms).

Table 40

Characteristics of Non-farm Dwelling Units, 1940 and 1950

| | 1940 | 1950 | 1950 with 1940 equal to 100 |
|---|---|---|---|
| Median rooms per dwelling unit | 4.74 | 4.57 | 96 |
| Percentage of units with | | | |
| private bath and flush toilet | 66.4 | 74.5 | 112 |
| running water | 83.0 | 91.5 | 110 |
| electric light | 90.9 | 94.7 | 104 |
| central heating | 50.2 | 55.3 | 110 |

Source: U.S. Census of Housing: 1940, Vol. II, Part 1, and U.S. Census of Housing: 1950, Vol. I, chapter 1.

10. Ibid., pp. 72, 130, and 426. For my appraisal of this series and the reply by the authors, see "Capital Formation in Residental Real Estate," Journal of Political Economy, April, 1958, pp. 131-54, and "Once more: Capital Formation in Residential Real Estate," ibid., December, 1959, pp. 612-27.

11. For an interesting analysis of quality change for the metro areas represented, see Beverly Duncan and Philip Hauser, Housing a Metropolis—Chicago (Glencoe, Ill.: Free Press, 1960), pp. 20-55.

Estimates of income elasticity of housing derived from series available are reviewed below. No attempt is made to deal fully with the inadequacies of the data. They may have serious defects.

## Price Series

Estimates of trends in housing consumption are complicated by price change. Hence, price indexes are essential for translating any series in current dollars into a series describing consumption. Interpretation of housing derived from the use of indexes currently available should be made with care. Indexes used to measure price change are very imperfect.

The rent component of Consumer Price Index of the U.S. Bureau of Labor Statistics seems likely to be a good index of change in contract rent of dwelling units of constant quality together with additional services represented by it.[12] Even so, it seems likely to have certain shortcomings as a measure of change in the price of housing space. It seems highly probable that prices of additional services included in rent have been increasing at a lesser rate than price of space. Such difference would cause the rent index to understate the rise in the price of space. The understatement, however, seems likely to be small—at least prior to 1940: For large cities additional services in contract rent of 1933 accounted for only 13 per cent of contract rent.

The rent index of the Consumer Price Index presumes to represent only contract rent. In a free market it seems likely, in addition, to represent the rental value of the owner-occupied units, when adjustment is made for additional services included in contract rent. However, under rent control the rent index tends greatly to understate the rise in the price of space rental value of owner units priced in a free market. In addition, it seems likely to understate somewhat the rise in payments made for tenant units. Charges for acquiring occupancy rights tend to be omitted as is expense involved in a shift of maintenance from landlords to tenants. Characteristics of rent related to these conditions have already been considered.

Construction cost indexes are the chief means that have been used to measure residential stock and new construction in constant prices.

---

12. For one appraisal of the rent index, see Margaret G. Reid, "Increase in Rent of Dwelling Units from 1940 to 1950," _Journal of American Statistical Association_, June, 1959, pp. 358-76.

The Boeckh residential index appears to be the one most widely used. This index, in common with many other construction cost indexes,[13] uses fixed weights and makes no allowance for technological changes tending to reduce cost of on-site construction.

These two indexes, that is the rent component of the Consumer Price Index and the Boeckh index, show very different rates of change. Between 1915 and 1940, increases indicated are 12 and 89 per cent, and between 1940 and 1957, 45 and 161 per cent, respectively. Since the two indexes measure different things,[14] identical change is not to be expected. They have, however, a large common component. The differences shown above are very, very large, and there seems no likelihood whatever that they are accounted for by components of the rent index not represented by the construction cost index. The nature of the construction cost index suggests that it has an upward bias, and the comparison with the rent index gives some grounds for assuming that it is large. If this is true, adjustment for price change using this index leads to a serious downward bias in the estimate of secular trend of residential capital.

Upward bias in the construction cost index may well be sufficient to offset any quality improvement that actually occurred in the stock. If so, it has been an important condition contributing to the widespread notion that capital investment in housing is solely a function of population growth and the formation of new households.

The committee to review federal statistics points out that construction is a price area of great importance and is "one that cries for improvement."[15] The committee recognizes that "construction is a partic-

13. For summary of various indexes, see Historical Statistics of the United States, op. cit., pp. 377-88.

14. A construction cost index, even if it measured accurately change in the cost of housing of constant quality, would not be affected by change in the price of land and taxes on residential property, both of those tending to affect the cost of space rent, and it would be little affected by the interest rate, which is likely to have an important bearing on space rent. However, trends in these things seem unlikely to account for much of the difference observed in the movement of the two indexes. For example, the interest rate has had ups and downs but secular change between 1915 and 1957, for example, has been small. That of twenty-year maturity bonds was 39 per cent higher in 1940 than in 1915, and 37 per cent higher in 1957 than in 1940.

15. George J. Stigler (chairman), The Price Statistics of the Federal Government: Review, Appraisal and Recommendations (New York: National Bureau of Economic Research, No. 73, General Series, 1961), p. 29.

ularly difficult field to price because the units built are constantly changing, and the quality change problem is acute." Even so, it believes that a better construction price index is feasible as well as highly desirable.[16]

## Cyclical and Secular Change in Space Rent

Annual estimates of space rent for the nation, provided by the U.S. Department of Commerce, begin with 1929. This series has three components. These are (a) space rental value of non-farm owner-occupied dwellings, (b) space rent of tenant non-farm dwellings including lodging houses, and (c) rental value of farm dwellings. No one of these series relies solely on direct evidence.

Beginning with 1930, decennial censuses provide a fairly firm basis for estimates of the (a) and (b) components.[17] These censuses have reported the value of owner-occupied and the contract rent of tenant units for the non-farm population. Data for the rural farm component have always been and are likely to remain crude: There is no market value of the stock of farm housing.[18] The main shortcoming of the series may come from the meager evidence for filling the gap between decennial censuses. The housing survey of 1933 provides evidence for one year

---

16. Ibid., p. 89.

17. The housing survey of 1933 is an important source of evidence for adjusting contract rent for additional services included. This is discussed in chap. iii. And the 1940 census and a few family surveys report the estimated rental value of owner-occupied units.

18. The distribution of space rent among the three components in 1929 and 1959 is as follows:

| | 1929 | 1959 |
|---|---|---|
| a) owner-occupied, non-farm | 52.8 | 65.4 |
| b) tenant-occupied, non-farm | 39.8 | 29.5 |
| c) farm | 7.4 | 5.1 |

The farm sector in 1929 represented 7.4 per cent of the estimated space rent, whereas in the spring of 1930 it represented 22.6 per cent of the dwelling units. This implies a very much lower space rent for the farm than the non-farm units at that time. Lower cost of farm than non-farm dwelling units and site of constant quality may have accounted for some of this difference. In 1959 the farm sector represented 5.1 per cent of the space rent and in the spring of 1960 it represented 12.0 per cent of the dwelling units. The changes seem to imply that space rent rose faster for the farm than the non-farm sector. This could represent greater increase in cost for the farm than the non-farm sector or greater improvement in quality of housing. With its shrinking, the insufficient information for a satisfactory estimate for the farm sector is becoming of lesser importance.

between the 1930 and 1940 census. It represents large cities, and the gap between these and the population in general is very great. The national survey of 1941 provides an estimate for one year between the 1940 and 1950 census. However, during much of this decade markets were abnormal, so that annual estimates have merit chiefly for indicating the effect of rent control. The gap for the thirties is more serious. Reliable estimates would describe a free market during years of marked cyclical change.

Estimates of Space Rent with Respect to Income.—Data on annual space rent have been used by several analysts to estimate increase in housing associated with increase in income. Paradiso made such an estimate in 1945. Using national aggregates in current dollars, he examined expenditure for 174 categories of consumption in relation to disposable income for the years 1929 through 1940 on the assumption that "consumer behavior will tend to conform with patterns that prevailed in the prewar years."[19] He classed the various consumption categories as "insensitive" to income, "somewhat sensitive," and "sensitive." Space rent he judged to be insensitive to income.

In 1955, Paradiso and Winston made a similar examination of the consumption expenditure using national aggregates and reported tendencies for prewar and postwar years. They report, for example, that 1 per cent change in aggregate income tends to be associated with a 0.5 per cent increase in housing for the years 1929 through 1940 and a 1.5 per cent increase for the years 1947 through 1954.[20] Thus for postwar years housing is found to be sensitive to income change.

Discontinuity in Tendency Observed.—Data for the years 1929 through 1959 are shown in Figure 22. Space rent, to be referred to as housing, is symbolized by $H^t$, and disposable income is symbolized by $Y^t$. Both are per capita estimates in constant dollars.[21] During war years $H^t$ rose very little. This tendency is not surprising because of rent control and restriction on new construction. The periods of greatest interest are the pre- and postwar years. These show very different tendencies.

Figure 22 shows two regressions, one for the prewar years of 1929

---

19. L. J. Paradiso, "Classification of Consumer Expenditures by Income Elasticity," Survey of Current Business, January, 1945, pp. 7-10.

20. L. J. Paradiso and Clement Winston, "Consumer Expenditure-Income Patterns," Survey of Current Business, September, 1955, p. 29.

21. Adjusted using the Consumer Price Index.

through 1940 and the other for postwar years 1947 through 1959. The correlations of $H^t$ with $Y^t$ for these periods are as follows:

Prewar $x_H{}^t = 1.45 + 0.15\, x_Y{}^t$ $r^2 = .66$ (10.1)

Postwar $x_H{}^t = -2.31 + 1.41\, x_Y{}^t$ $r^2 = .92$ (10.2)

Thus $\eta_{HY}{}^t$ is 0.15 for the 12 prewar years 1929 through 1940, and 1.41 for the 13 years 1947 through 1959. This is a large difference. Did it oc-

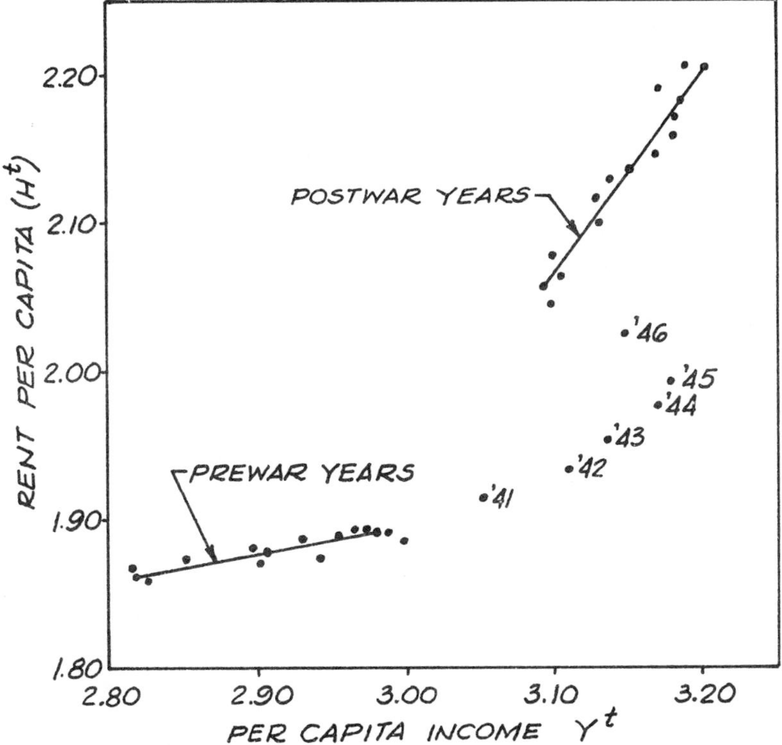


Fig. 22.—Per capita space rent ($H^t$) in relation to per capita disposable income ($Y^t$), in dollars of constant purchasing power, United States 1929 through 1959.[a] (Variables in log form; 1947-49 equals 100.)

a. For national income data used, see U.S. Income and Output, U.S. Office of Business Economics Commerce, 1958, and earlier editions, and The Survey of Current Business, July, 1960. Adjustment for price change was made using the Consumer Price Index and its rent component, as estimated by the U.S. Bureau of Labor Statistics.

cur? If so, how should it be interpreted? Or does it represent the shortcomings of the data rather than consumer behavior?

Various conditions could have contributed to the difference shown above: (a) Housing is a durable good and the lag in the contraction of residential atock accompanying a fall in real[22] income is likely to be appreciably greater than the lag in expansion accompanying a rise in normal income. Thus, even if the drop in per capita income from 1929 to 1933 was assumed to represent change in normal income, its affect on housing presumably would have been small;[23] (b) the per capita income in constant dollars was much the same in 1940 as in 1929, so that much of the variation in annual income during the thirties probably represents variation in negative transitory income insofar as housing consumption is concerned. If so, it is not surprising that the housing-income curve of this period is very flat. There is a third condition that could have resulted in the difference observed, namely a downward shift in preference for housing compared to other consumer products, greater in prewar than postwar years. A downward shift may have been occurring.[24] There seems no reason, however, to expect it to be less in postwar than prewar years. The importance of new products appearing in the market, a condition that might cause a downward shift, was certainly no less in postwar than in prewar years.

The possibility of interpolation errors because of the absence of di-

22. In dollars of constant purchasing power.

23. Some fall will occur if new construction does not keep pace with population growth or if the maintenance of the stock falls. In addition, housing consumption will fall more than the stock if an increase occurs in the vacancy rate. The housing survey of 1933 indicated such an increase with fall in national income: from 1930 to 1935 vacancies increased from 5.0 in January, 1930, to 7.8 in January, 1934 (see David L. Wickens, Residential Real Estate [New York: National Bureau of Economic Research, 1941], p. 22). This increase occurred in spite of the fact that during this period the rent index declined more sharply than the CPI. The rent index of 1934 was 67, the CPI 78, and the relative price of housing 87, with 1930 equal to 100. The marked fall in the price of housing with fall in income is consistent with both a marked income and price elasticity of demand for housing.

24. The downward trend in residential capital per capita observed by Grebler, Blank, and Winnick when real income was rising and, under the assumption that rise in relative price of housing has no effect on consumption, seemed to imply a marked downward shift in consumer preference for housing. See, for example, op. cit., chap. 8, and Louis Winnick, "Housing: Has there been a downward shift in Consumer Preferences," Quarterly Journal of Economics, February, 1955, pp. 85-98.

rect evidence makes the curve of the prewar period suspect. Surveys are one source of information for interpolation, and the time-series curve, shown in Figure 22 for the prewar years, looks very like the housing-income curve shown in Figure 1 where y is the explanatory variable and where $y_t$ is probably very important. Thus the similarity of the two curves may represent similar mixture of income components rather than interpolation errors of the annual series. For the prewar period $Y^t$, like the variable y, may have a large transitory component correlated with measured income. Under this condition cross-section relationships among consumer units tend to be a suitable basis for interpolation of an annual series. They would, however, be quite unsuitable for such interpolation during the intercensal years of the fifties. For these years there is no reason to expect that much of the variation in annual income represents that of a transitory component.

There is no question that housing-income relations of the postwar years of this series have little in common with those shown for prewar years. One must, however, consider whether conditions unique to the postwar years tend to increase $\eta_{HY}{}^t$ of equation (10.2). Wartime restrictions resulted in a large backlog of demand for consumer capital in general and for housing in particular. This may have stimulated a marked increase in $H^t$ as $Y^t$ rose during the postwar years. At the same time information on change in housing from year to year had improved so that during the fifties estimating error may have declined.

A question of considerable interest is the extent to which equation (10.2) represents long-run tendencies with respect to normal income. One test has been made. The period covered was increased[25] to include the years 1929, 1930, 1939, and 1940, years likely to have small errors of estimation[26] and only slightly affected by abnormal employment level. The following correlation is observed[27]

25. Seventeen years are included, ranging from 1929 to 1959.

26. The decennial census are a main source of direct information.

27. Robert Ferber has also examined per capita expenditure for housing in constant dollars for the years 1935 through 1953. He found the years 1942 through 1946 abnormal, and hence excluded them in estimating income elasticities. He includes the years, 1935-41 and 1947-53. Ferber concluded that income does not explain much of the difference in housing. One estimate made yielded an income elasticity of -0.31 and another an estimate of 1.31. See "Temporal Variation in Service Expenditures," Consumer Behavior, op. cit., p. 411.

$$x_H{}^t = -1.94 + 1.29\, x_Y{}^t \qquad r^2 = .98 \qquad (10.3)$$

Thus observations spanning nearly three decades show much the same regression as those of the postwar years. The inclusion of the observations of the four earlier years lowered slightly $\eta_{HY}{}^t$—from 1.41 to 1.29.[28]

So far, the effect of other conditions correlated with income have been ignored. The effect of only one additional variable has been examined—relative price.[29] This is symbolized by $P_r{}^t$. When it is added to the variables of equation (10.3) the following correlation is observed:

$$x_H{}^t = -2.19 + 1.33\, x_Y{}^t + .06\, x_{P_r}{}^t \qquad R^2 = .98 \qquad (10.4)$$

The addition of $P_r{}^t$ does not increase $R^2$ and increases only slightly the coefficient of $Y^t$, from 1.29 to 1.33.

Equation (10.4) indicates a coefficient of income elasticity of housing similar to the lower range of interclass coefficients for 1950 shown in chapter vii. In other words, it is comparable to the interclass income elasticities of housing within places where households with low normal income were experiencing somewhat more unemployment than those of high normal income. In general, it is appreciably lower than the coefficients of cross-section estimates shown in chapters vii and viii. These presumably hold price effects constant and many of them represent normal employment.

Equation (10.4) indicates no effect from $P_r{}^t$. This is not surprising. Chapter vii indicates that even as late as 1950 the rent index did not represent change in the price of housing in general, nor did the rental market reflect adjustment to income change of the forties. The relationship of equation (10.4) is dominated by the correlation of housing and income, and the relative price of housing, as indicated by $P_r{}^t$, is negatively correlated with $Y^t$.[30]

## Trend in Residential Capital

Muth used time series of estimated residential stocks and flows to

---

28. If total consumption expenditures per capita are used as a proxy representing normal income the corresponding coefficient is 1.49.

29. This is the rent index divided by the Consumer Price Index, 1947-49 equals 100.

30. The correlation coefficient of $P_r{}^t$ and $Y^t$ is -.806. The correlation of $P_r{}^t$ and $H^t$ is only slightly less.

estimate income elasticity of housing. He confined his estimate to the years 1915 and 1916 and 1919 through 1941, a total of 26 years.[31] His income variable is annual permanent income as estimated by Friedman. This is compounded of current and past income. Muth took into account the relative price of housing and the interest rate as well as income. His findings indicate the following elasticities:[32]

| | Income | Price |
|---|---|---|
| 1) Desired stock as indicated by | | |
| a) flow demand | 0.88 | -0.90 |
| b) demand for services | 0.94 | -1.47 |
| 2) Quality of new dwellings | 1.87 | -1.21 |

It may well be that, for the years selected, estimates of stock are more subject to errors than those of new construction. If so, Muth's findings are not inconsistent with the hypothesis that the income elasticity of housing tends to be between 1.50 and 2.00. The price elasticities observed are consistent with the implication of some of the cross-sections estimates, that is the similarity of the interclass coefficients of income elasticity of housing between and within places.

## Current Outlays for Stock

Current outlays for residential stock have a marked cyclical pattern, closely correlated with change in income. In other words, outlays for new stock appear to have a positive correlation with the cyclical or transitory component of average annual income of the nation in general and of cities within it. This is also a characteristic of durable goods and of savings; and housing is probably the most important of all consumer durable goods and a very important form of savings.

Durable consumer goods other than housing, such as house furnishings, refrigerators, laundry equipment, and automobiles, are similar to housing in that consumption, that is the use of products, is much more stable than current outlays to maintain stock. Year-by-byear change in these, however, is usually considered only in terms of outlays. Housing is the only durable product for which estimates of consumption are reg-

---

31. The years of World War II were excluded because of the obvious abnormality of the housing market and those of some postwar years because estimates in the series appear to be understated.

32. A. C. Harberger (ed.), *op. cit.*, p. 72.

ularly provided. While housing consumption may have little relation to transitory income, outlays or investment in new stock may have a good deal. Housing in both of these respects may be very similar to other durable consumer products.

## Concluding Comments

Gaps in direct evidence, rent control, the downward bias in the annual estimates of new stock and an upward bias in or the absence of a suitable price index of housing are hurdles for investigators who hope that time series will provide reliable estimates of the income and price elasticity of demand for housing. Investigators of demand for housing with respect to income who have used time series have followed two lines of action. Some have ignored the shortcomings of the data in the hope that they are random. Others have selected sets of years for which the shortcomings described above seem likely to be least serious.

My estimates of income elasticity of space rent, for years of high reliability of the data and fairly normal markets, indicate an income elasticity of housing consumption around 1.3. This estimate is slightly higher than those by Muth, where housing was represented by stock. He, too, used data for years for which the reliability of the data seemed relatively high.

Muth's estimate for income elasticity of demand for quality of new dwellings using time series is consistent with the cross-section evidence of chapters viii and ix. In other words his estimate using time series like the interclass correlations of cross-section data indicate an income elasticity of housing not far from 2.0.

Fragmentary evidence on physical characteristics of residential stock indicate that the upward push of real income has more than offset the downward pull of rise in price and competition with the new products becoming available. Secular improvement in the quality of housing for the nation in general appear to have occurred because real income has increased and in spite of rise in the price of housing.

# Chapter Eleven

# CHANGES BETWEEN TWO YEARS FOR SETS OF CITIES

In using time series of housing, income, and price indexes, observational errors and conditions not directly represented seem likely to affect the estimates of income elasticity of housing derived. The effect of some of these can be held constant through the use of observations representing changes between two years for a set of cities. Where such observations are used, there seems some likelihood that estimates will be little affected by secular change in consumer preferences, by bias in the price indexes because of failure to hold constant the quality of all products priced, and by price changes not adequately represented by the price indexes.

This chapter presents estimates, derived from survey data, of income and price elasticities of housing between years. The sets of observations describe change in housing and income between years for cities represented in two surveys, and change in price represented by the Consumer Price Index. The measures of change describe a terminal year with a base year equal to 100. The log of this ratio equals the difference between the two years in the respective variables expressed in log form. The variables are symbolized using lower case letters and subscripts, and superscripts indicate the years represented. The definition of variables and symbols representing them are summarized in Tables 41 and 42.

For each city represented, average housing and average income of the terminal year are adjusted for price change using the Consumer Price Index for that city. Such averages are then divided by average housing and average income of the base year to obtain ratios describing change in housing and in income, adjusted for price change. Change in relative price of housing between the base and terminal year, indicated by the Consumer Price Index, provides a measure of price change tending to affect housing consumption. Where the terminal and the base years are common to all cities represented, the income and price elasticities derived from such ratios will be unaffected by secular change common to all cities.[1]

### The Sets of Ratios

Three[2] sets of basic data are used: (a) those of the consumption surveys of 1918-19 and 1934-36, and (b) those of the Census of Housing of 1950. These are referred to as the surveys of 1918 and 1934 and the

1. Secular trends affecting housing-income ratios, common to all cities, will tend to affect the level rather than the slope of the regression of a set of ratios. Over periods of two or more decades many changes seem likely: (a) Decrease in preference for housing compared to other consumer products may have occurred because functions of dwelling units have shifted elsewhere, such as food storage to the nearby grocery store and care of the sick to the hospital. (b) Job-related expenses seem likely to have increased in importance with additional earners per consumer unit or greater distance of travel to work. This seems likely to have resulted in higher income overstating somewhat the increase in income available for housing consumption and thus to have decreased housing-income ratios of later years. (c) An increase has occurred in additional services represented by contract rent so that expenditure for tenant housing, to an increasing extent, overstates housing consumption. (d) Biases are present in the Consumer Price Index, such as those arising because of failure to hold constant the quality of durable goods, medical and various other types of services. As a result of these, there is likely to be a systematic downward bias in the relative price of housing estimated from the Consumer Price Index. (e) Change in the relative price of housing compared to that of other consumer products has varied and cross-elasticities of housing and other consumer products probably differ. Over the decades the price movements of food and automobiles have been quite different. Which of these had the greater influence in housing? There is also the question as to whether the rise in the price of domestic service is of special significance. The rise has been very great and relates directly to the cost of household operation and may have had a special bearing on housing consumption. The cross-price elasticities of housing and other consumer goods is a virgin field of inquiry.

2. These sets do not exhaust the stock of data available. The consumption survey of 1950 is omitted. Ratios of the type described in the text for 1934 and the census of 1950 were examined for a set of 21 cities. Tendencies observed were so similar to those with the terminal year represented by the census of 1950 that this survey seems to add little additional information. In addition, the number of consumer units reporting for the various cities is relatively small so that sampling variability seems not unlikely.

Among other sets of data not used are the Census of Housing of

census of 1950. Two sets of ratios[3] describing intertemporal change are examined. The terminal years are represented by the survey of 1934 and the census of 1950, with the survey of 1918 representing the base year for each[4] of these sets. They represent 26 and 30 cities, respectively. They thus provide a total of 56 observations[5] of intertemporal change between pairs of years.

The terminal year of the various sets is identified by a superscript. For example, the housing ratios of the terminal period represented by surveys of 1934 and of the census of 1950 are symbolized by $h'$ and $h^{\#}$, respectively.

The data used represent different economic conditions. For example, those of 1918 and 1950 represent quite high employment levels, whereas the survey of 1934 represents the economy close to the bottom of the Great Depression.[6] It seems likely that incomes represented by the survey of 1918, on the average, have a positive transitory component and that those represented by the survey of 1934, on the average, have a

---

1940, the 1956 National Housing Inventory, the housing survey of 1933, and surveys of a few cities made in the twenties and the later forties. The 1940 Census of Housing is omitted because only crude estimates of average rent are feasible for those households for which a reasonably good estimate of income is provided and also because rent and income are reported for only eleven places for which the rent index is available. The evidence of this monograph makes it apparent that eleven observations are a very meager set. The other surveys are omitted because few cities are included for which the Consumer Price Index is reported. A superficial examination of various sets indicated nothing inconsistent with the findings of this chapter.

3. With a single exception these sets include all cities directly represented by the CPI that are common to the surveys used. The exception is Norfolk, Va. This is an important naval base, and public housing was important in both 1918 and 1950.

4. Because of the probable bias on the rent index of 1934, no comparison is made between the data of the 1934 and the 1950 sets. For discussion of such bias see pp. 248-49.

5. No estimates are made combining these 56 observations. Because of difference in conditions represented by the surveys, it has seemed best to confine estimates to sets of ratios with a common base and terminal period.

6. Gross national product in constant dollars of 1934 was 24 per cent below that of 1929. In addition, national income originating in manufacturing and construction—workers from which were heavily represented in the 1934 survey—was down 43 per cent. The eligibility criteria did exclude many families whose members were experiencing very low employment. Even so, it seems likely that for many of the cities average income reported in the 1934 survey was below normal income of families represented.

negative transitory component. To the extent that such difference between years is common to all cities, it will not affect the estimates of income elasticity. However, random variation among the cities in the change in $y_t$ seem not unlikely, and some tests are made of its probable effect. These are described later.

The surveys of 1918 and 1934 report market-determined rents. Thus, where 1934 is the terminal period, the ratios should be useful for indicating tendencies of a free market. Since rent control appears to have been an important condition affecting interplace regressions shown in chapter vi, some effects from rent control are to be expected where the census of 1950 represents the terminal period.

The data represent different universes. In fact each set of data has certain unique characteristics. Some of these affect the mixture of the income components and the suitability of the price variables, and others affect the size and composition of consumer units.

The main topics that follow are (a) characteristics of variables; (b) survey of 1934: the terminal period; and (c) census of 1950: the terminal period. Readers concerned only with the main findings and not with problems encountered in holding other things constant may find their purpose served by the general summary and conclusions.

## Characteristics of Variables

The main dependent variable is housing of the terminal year adjusted for change in the rent index with the base year equal to 100. The two main explanatory variables are change in income, in dollars of constant purchasing power, and change in the relative price of housing compared to that of other consumer products. Supplementary variables are used in an attempt to hold constant the heterogeneity of the main variables and the size and composition of consumer units.

Information on the universe of consumer units represented, the mean and the range of the variables and the symbols used to represent them are summarized in Tables 41 and 42. The text comments on these but does not presume to summarize the evidence there presented. One word of caution seems advisable. The data do not describe the change between years for the cities in general, for example the change in average housing or income. Instead they describe difference observed between years for special sets of households that differ from place to place and between periods in their representativeness of the total population of the places. Even so, they seem likely to yield estimates of income and price elasticities of housing that are representative of the populations in general.

The superscripts symbolizing time periods represented have already been described. In addition, a system of subscripts is used to distinguish variables unique to a base or to a terminal period. Variables representing a base period, such as those from the survey of 1918, are symbolized by the subscript 1, and those of any terminal period such as those of the survey of 1934 by the subscript 2. Variables unique to 1950 are also identified by the subscript 2. The periods are identified by the superscript.

Housing Variables.—The object is to estimate change in demand for housing space as affected by income. Unfortunately, the sets of data do not represent housing space only. Instead, they pertain to housing space plus varying amounts of additional services paid for by contract rent. The survey of 1918 comes closest to describing space rent. The data used represent tenant households without heat included in rent.[7] The 1934 survey differs from it in two respects: (a) housing of owners, represented by estimated rental value of units, is included, and (b) all tenants, irrespective of services paid for in contract rent, are represented. The census set of 1950 is similar to the 1918 set in that only tenants are represented.

This diversity of housing concepts is unfortunate. However, the sets of data selected from the various surveys seem the best feasible, and some information is available bearing on services covered by contract rent. In testing their probable effect, several variables have been used, depending on the information available. These differ among the sets and are described in later sections.

Income Variables.—The income variables of this chapter are symbolized by $y'$ and $y^{\#}$. These describe change in average[8] income for consumer units represented in dollars of constant purchasing power.

Transitory income may account for some of the variation among cities in income change. Two procedures are used in an attempt to hold

7. At that time inclusion of heat in rent appears to have been quite unusual.

8. The averages of the 1918 and 1934 surveys are means and those of the census of 1950, medians. There seems no reason to suppose that this difference affects the estimates of income elasticity of housing derived for the ratios measuring change between years.

transitory income constant in its effect. One uses change in average total expenditure, in dollars of constant purchasing power, as a proxy for change in income. Where the survey of 1934 represents the terminal period, this variable is symbolized by c'. The second method introduces supplementary variables likely to represent transitory conditions, such as the average number of gainful workers per consumer unit. As in earlier chapters, the expectation is that the higher the number of earners the greater the likelihood that average income has a positive and the less the likelihood that it has a negative transitory component. A positive transitory component in the base year seems likely to increase the income elasticity of housing observed, and a positive transitory component in the terminal year to reduce it.

The information bearing on transitory income is fairly satisfactory for the 1918 and the 1934 surveys, if only because it relates specifically to the consumer units represented. On the other hand, the information for tenant households of the 1950 census is very far from satisfactory. The income variable is subject to two important types of transitory income: one is the result of abnormal employment opportunity and the other results from the gap between the period represented by contract rent and by income. This gap[9] is of considerable importance for newly formed households that tend to concentrate in rented dwelling units, and any information bearing on such transitory income represents owner as well as tenant households.

In the estimates shown, abnormal employment is represented by le, symbolizing the percentage of the male labor force with less than 26 weeks of employment during 1949. This variable represents owner as well as tenant households, and for this reason alone seems likely to be very crude, since the housing variable of 1950 represents tenants only. The variables used to represent transitory income occurring because of the gap between the housing and the income variable seem likely to be even cruder. These variables describe the mobility of the population among households and among places, the assumption being that the greater this mobility the less likely is the income variable reported to represent normal income. These variables also represent the population in general. However, they seem likely to be especially relevant to tenant

9. This type of transitory income is not present in the data of the 1918 and the 1934 surveys, because the housing and the income variables represent the same period of time.

households because of the heavy concentration in rented dwelling units of newly formed households and in-migrants.

Price Variables.—The main price variables describe change in the rent index[10] relative to the Consumer Price Index between the periods[11] represented. They are symbolized by p' and $p^{\#}$. Several supplementary price variables are used. These are now to be considered.

The 1918 survey represents early stages of the boom associated with World War I, with the rise in the rent index lagging behind that of the Consumer Price Index. On the other hand, the 1934 survey represents a depression and the rent index, from 1929 to the time of the survey, fell more than the Consumer Price Index. The census of 1950 came after several years of postwar boom with the Consumer Price Index rising markedly and the rent index rising much less, in part at least because of continuing rent control. In addition, the 1950 set includes at least three cities[12] in which public housing was important. Rents charged for such dwellings are not a function of market demand in the city in general. These conditions reduce the likelihood that the sets of data examined will reveal the long-run response of consumers to change in relative price of housing.

Each period represented and each set of variables available have unique features likely to affect the suitability of the main price variable as a measure of change in the price of housing. These are considered in turn.

Survey of 1918.—The Consumer Price Index for the years 1917 and 1918 is reported only for the month of December. Interpolation to the midyear of the survey could result in considerable error if prices changed markedly during the year. Among cities, changes in the Consumer Price

---

10. See fn. 1 of this chapter for comment on characteristics of the CPI assumed to be held constant among cities.

11. Period represented by the Census of Housing of 1950 is the same for all places. In addition, for 1950 information on the CPI was provided with sufficient frequency so that only minor interpolations were necessary. The periods represented by the surveys of 1918 and 1934 differ among the cities. The price index is assumed to represent the midpoint of the survey year. However, information on the midyear of the survey is vague, especially for the survey of 1918. In addition, interpolation error of the CPI is likely to be appreciable for this survey. See p. 248 for comment.

12. These are Atlanta, Georgia, Portland, Oregon, and Seattle, Washington. In Portland, 14 per cent of all tenant units of 1950 were public housing.

Table 41

Characteristics of Housing, Families, Prices, and Incomes, 1934 and 1918 Surveys,[a] 26 Cities[b]

| Item | Symbol for variable[c] | Variables | |
|---|---|---|---|
| | | Mean | Range |
| A. Characteristics of dwelling units in 1934 | | | |
| 1) Average rent (owners and tenants), contract rent of 1918 equals $100, adjusted for price change[d] | h' | $169 | $131 - $228 |
| 2) Percentage of units that were owner-occupied | $o_2$ | 31 | 12 - 51 |
| 3) Importance of units with heat in rent[e] | $rh_2$ | 118 | 101 - 255 |
| B. Persons in families and households in 1934 | | | |
| 1) Ratio of persons per family (1918 = 100) | s' | 75[f] | 68 - 83 |
| 2) Ratio of persons per family 16 years of age or more per person under 16 years of age—all families versus families of the type reporting in 1918[g] | $ad_2$ | 1.84 | 1.49 - 2.13 |
| 3) Importance of households with lodgers | | | |
| a) 1918[h] | $lo_1$ | 105 | 100 - 114 |
| b) 1934[i] | $lo_2$ | 117 | 102 - 132 |
| C. Earners per family | | | |
| 1) Average number of earners per family[j] | | | |
| a) 1918[k] | $ea_1$ | 1.25 | 1.14 - 1.41 |
| b) 1934[l] | $ea_2$ | 1.39 | 1.18 - 1.59 |
| 2) Ratio of earners per family in 1934 (1918 = 100)[m] | ea' | 111 | 90 - 131 |
| 3) Ratio of importance of earning by subsidiary earners[n] in 1934 (1918 = 100) | se' | 105 | 96 - 112 |
| D. Price index at the time of the survey of 1934 (survey of 1918 equals 100)[o] | | | |
| 1) CPI | . . . | 90 | 75 - 97 |
| 2) Its rent component | . . . | 95 | 66 - 124 |
| E. Rent in relation to CPI | | | |
| 1) 1934 survey (1918 survey = 100) | p' | 105 | $ 80 - $132 |
| 2) Dec., 1929 (1918 survey = 100)[p] | pa' | 124 | $103 - $145 |
| 3) 1934 survey (Dec., 1929 = 100)[p] | pb' | 85 | $ 68 - $ 98 |
| 4) Dec., 1918 (Dec., 1917 = 100)[q] | $p_1$ | 95 | $ 90 - $108 |
| F. During 1934, 1918 equals $100, adjusted for price change | | | |
| 1) Income[r] | y' | $120 | $106 - $138 |
| 2) Total expenditure[s] | c' | $132 | $120 - $155 |

Source: U.S. Department of Labor, Bulletins 357, 635, 636, 637, 639, 640, and 641.

a. The year covered by the survey differed among the cities, especially that of 1934.

b. A precise description of the drawing the sample of the 1918 survey is not provided. Some kind of randomization was doubtless used. For the survey of 1934 employer lists of employed workers were used to draw a random sample of earners in specified occupations, and various precautions were taken to minimize overrepresentation of multiearner families. The eligibility criteria of the two surveys are similar in that each presumes to represent moderate-income wage earners and lower-salaried clerical workers. The eligibility criteria are as follows:

| Item | Survey of 1918-19 | Survey of 1934-36 |
|---|---|---|
| 1) Members of the economic family | | |
| a. Head | Male. | None. |
| b. Spouse | Present. | None. |
| c. Children | At least one child not a boarder or lodger. | None. |
| d. Number of persons | None other than that implicit in other requirements. | At least two persons eating at least two meals a day prepared at home for at least 11 months. |
| e. Unrelated dependents | None. | No family with two unrelated persons dependent on it. |
| 2) Other members of the household | No family included with boarders nor with as many as three lodgers. | No family with more than the equivalent of two boarders and/or lodgers. |
| 3) Occupation | The sample to represent proportionally wage earners and low- and medium-salaried families of the locality. Self-employed head excluded. | Chief earner either a wage earner or a lower salaried clerical worker, except foremen and domestic servants. |
| 4) Income | | |
| a. Source | Charity families excluded. Earnings of members who contribute all to the family fund to make up 75 per cent of total income. | No family receiving relief or on work relief during the year included. At least 75 per cent of total income to be from earning of the members. Those with considerable income in kind excluded. |
| b. Amount | None beyond that implicit in other requirements. | Family income to be at least $500. If a chief earner was found to be in a clerical occupation, the family was excluded if his annual income was $2,000 or his monthly income $200 or more. |
| 5) Employment | None except employment of the husband. | One member within the economic family to have worked approximately 3-1/2 days of 8 hours in each of 36 weeks. |
| 6) Payment for dwelling | None. | Those with housing in lieu of rent excluded as well as those who received three or more months of free rent. |
| 7) Residence | Must have kept house in the locality at least one year. | Must have resided in the area at least nine months. |

| Item | Survey of 1918-19 | Survey of 1934-36 |
|---|---|---|
| 8) Other | Slum or non-English-speaking families not in the United States at least five years excluded. | Minor requirement. |

Criterion (1) resulted in families of 1934 having fewer members, a higher ratio of adults to children, and more unrelated dependents than families of 1918. Criterion (2) tended to make the importance of boarders and lodgers greater in the 1934 than the 1918 set. However, data describing the importance of such household members are very crude. Criteria (3) and (4) are essentially the same for the two surveys. Criterion (5) relating to employment level is much more specific for 1934 than for the 1918 survey. This was undoubtedly occasioned by the unemployment existing at the time of the 1934 survey. In spite of the more precise criteria of the 1934 than the 1918 survey, designed to exclude the underemployed, the degree of underemployment seems likely to have been greater among those reporting in the survey of 1934 than of 1918. Criterion (6) was also doubtless a function of cyclical change in that landlords during the thirties tended to give free rent for one or more months in order to check the fall in the monthly rate occurring because tenants would move if rent concessions were not received. Criterion (7) is essentially the same for the two surveys. Criterion (8) tended to exclude low-income families in 1918. It thus reduces the likelihood that the data for 1918 are representative of the income and consumption of wage earners and clerical families in general. Since this analysis is concerned with ratios of change, the exclusion of families in slum housing in the 1918 set is immaterial to this analysis.

A subset of families within 26 cities included in the 1918 survey was selected for this analysis: From the 1918 survey only tenants without heat provided by contract rent are included. This selection reduced the heterogeneity of the housing variable for 1918 and provided a suitable base for estimating change in demand for space. Furthermore, except for the city of New York, a very small percentage of tenants reporting in the 1918 survey had heat provided in rent.

The survey of 1918 excludes the owner-occupied units because information is not provided on what is represented by housing expenditure, nor is any information given as to inclusion of income in kind from housing. The owner units are, however, included in the 1934 set. This combination of tenures of the survey of 1934 is made because the published data permit no more than crude estimates of the income of tenants, and, in addition, information on the owner housing and income in kind from housing permit a reasonably good measure of total housing and income of tenures combined. For example, estimates of market rent of owner dwellings are reported. Furthermore, chapter vi indicates that rent-income ratios of tenants and owners differ only slightly where normal income is the same. Thus there seems no reason to expect that the combination of tenures in the 1934 set will affect the estimate of h' with respect to y'.

No distinction as to race is made in the data of the 1918 survey. However, certain eligibility requirements (see above) as to income and quality of housing make it seem likely that few non-white families were included in the 1918 survey. The 1934 subset is confined to white families, exclusive of Mexicans. This selection was made because of the manner in which the published data are presented. It also seems likely to have increased the homogeneity between periods in the strata of the economy represented.

The estimates represent the main portion of the families reporting in the 26 cities; for the 1918 survey, 74 per cent, and for the 1934 survey, 86 per cent are represented.

c. Ratios of 1934 to 1918 are designated by the superscript [']. Estimates pertaining to the 1918 and 1934 surveys are designated by subscripts 1 and 2 respectively.

d. This is average contract rent of tenants and estimated rental value of owner-occupied units. (Expenditure for housing away from home not represented.) For the 1918 survey the data come from <u>Bul</u>. 357, Table D, and for the 1934 survey from <u>Bul</u>. 635, and others, Table 10. <u>See</u> fn. o for discussion of the rent index used to adjust for price change.

e. This is the number of all units per 100 without heat in rent.

f. This implies a drop of 25 per cent in average number of persons per family. A considerable part of this drop represents a difference between the surveys in eligibility criteria as to family type. The corresponding ratio for the family types similar in the two surveys in .90. Some of the drop may also have occurred because many families with young children were ineligible because of their relief status in 1934. Direct evidence on the high representation of families with children among those relief status is provided by the Consumer Purchases Study of 1935-36. See, for example, U.S. Bureau of Labor Statistics Bul., Vol. I, Nos. 642-47.

g. These data are from Bul. 635, and others, Tables 2 and 22. An assumption is made here that if the eligibility criteria as to family type in the 1934 survey had been identical with those of the 1918 survey that the ratio of adults to children in 1934 approximates the ratio in the 1918 set. The data seem likely to afford only a rough approximation. However, information on the ratio of adults to children is not reported for the 1918 set.

h. This is an estimate of the number of all households per 100 without lodgers. The survey of 1918 reports only the number of families reporting net income from lodgers (Table A). Insofar as families often consider that lodgers pay only their share of the rent of the dwelling, the estimate shown seems likely to understate the importance of lodgers in the households of 1918 survey. One other condition makes it seem likely that this is a very crude variable, namely the inclusion in this estimate of all families reporting in the 1918 survey, whereas the estimates for housing and income pertain to tenants without heat included in rent.

i. Information on lodgers represented here describes the number of persons in households that are not in the economic family (Table 2). The higher level reported for the 1934 than the 1918 survey may relate in part to the type of information on which the respective estimates are based. It may also reflect difference related to household types, since families with young children seem less likely to have lodgers than those consisting only of adults. It may also be the result of a trend to greater economic independence of older children in the parental dwelling, or it may represent a depression phenomenon.

j. In neither survey was account taken of the length of time the persons were employed during the report year.

k. This count relates to all families rather than to the selected subset (the data are from Bul. 357, Table A). In addition, the estimate of earners, apart from the head, who for each family was an earner, is the percentage of families with income from earnings of the wife or children or dependents. It will understate the number of earners to the extent that some families had two or more children or dependents who were earners.

l. This is the mean earner per family as reported in Bul. 635, and others, Table 2. It describes the earners of the families represented by the data examined. Hence it should be subject to less error than the corresponding estimate for 1918. The higher number of earners per family shown here is in part the result of difference in information as to number of earners (see fn. k). It is also in part the result of the greater importance of adults in the families of the 1934 than 1918 because of the eligibility criteria.

m. This is the ratio of $ea_2$ to $ea_1$. This ratio was used only after tests indicated that it explains much the same proportion of the variation in h' with y' held constant as $ea_1$ and $ea_2$.

n. This is the total earnings per $100 of earnings by the principal earner. The estimate for 1918 comes from Bul. 357, Table A, and that of 1934 from Table 2 of the respective bulletins.

o. Estimates of price change are from the city indexes reported in U.S. Bureau of Labor Statistics, Bul. 699, 1941. In estimating the price change relevant to this monograph, an attempt was made to relate it to the change between the years covered by the income and consumption data of the respective sets. For both of these surveys, the year of the survey differed among cities. For the approximate periods covered in the 1918 survey, see Monthly Labor Review, May, 1919, p. 1374; June, 1919, p. 1651, and July, 1919, p. 75. For those of the 1934 survey, see Appendix C of the various bulletins.

p. See pp. 248-49 for discussion of the rationale of these measures.

Index apart from rent were quite similar. However, marked difference occurred in change in the rent index, indicating quite different inflationary pressures on housing. In one city, an increase of 44 per cent occurred between December, 1917, and December, 1918, the year that includes the midpoint of the year represented by the survey of most cities. Uniform distribution of rent increase throughout the year seems unlikely.

A supplementary price variable has been used. It represents change between December, 1917, and December, 1918, and is symbolized by $p_1$. If the rent change tended to concentrate before the midyear of the survey, the level of the rent index assumed to represent the period of the 1918 survey is understated. Under this condition there would be an upward bias in p' and $p^{\#}$ and a downward bias in h' and $h^{\#}$ as estimated. On the other hand, if the rent change had concentrated after the midyear of the survey, the rent index assumed to represent the period of the 1918 survey is too high and consequently there is a downward bias in p' and $p^{\#}$ and an upward bias in h' and $h^{\#}$. Estimates shown later indicate that there was some tendency for the rent change of 1918 to occur after the midyear of the survey so that the rent index of 1918, as estimated, tends to overstate the change in housing between the base and terminal years.

Survey of 1934.—Suspicion as to the suitability of the rent index of 1934 as a measure of rent change experienced by families represented in this survey stems (a) from the chaotic condition of the rental market because of severe depression and (b) from the eligibility criteria of the survey. The fall in the demand for housing brought on by marked decline in income appears to have been accompanied by intense competition among landlords. Rent concessions, that is free rent for one or more months granted in lieu of a decrease in monthly rate, were not uncom-

---

Footnotes to Table 41 (continued)

q. Change in consumer prices occurring around the time of the 1918 survey. For comments on this variable, see text, p. 248.

r. This is money income plus income in kind from equity in owner-occupied dwellings. (The latter is zero for the 1918 subset, it being confined to tenant units.) For the 1934 survey it represents the estimated rental value of owner unit less current expenditures. It is 2.9 per cent of total income.

s. This includes income in kind from the equity of owners in the dwelling occupied. In addition, it includes outlays for personal insurance. These are included in total expenditures of 1918. In addition, principal payments on the owner dwelling in 1934 is included. I suspect that these are included in total expenditure of all families in 1918. If so, this inclusion may have affected the estimate of total expenditure of tenants for 1918. This was estimated using a ratio of total expenditure to income for the entire set of families.

mon. In considering the implication of this practice, the first question is whether the index adequately reflected the rental market of wage earners and lower-salaried clerical workers in general. On this issue definitive evidence is not available.[13] But even if the rent index of various cities treats rent concessions as a decline in average rent, it seems likely, at least for some cities, that the rent index overstates the decline in the rent of families reporting in the survey of 1934. This is to be expected because rent concessions within a city tended to be positively correlated with the degree of unemployment experienced by tenant occupants. Under this condition, the rent index is unlikely to represent the families of the survey, since eligibility criteria excluded those below a certain norm of employment as well as those above a certain norm of rent concessions (see Table 41, fn. b).

In view of this likelihood, the rent index of a pre-depression year may provide a better index than that of 1934 of the variation in rent change among cities affecting housing of families reporting in the survey of 1934. Consequently, the measure of rent change for the entire period between the surveys, symbolized by p', is supplemented by two measures of rent change, namely relative price of housing in December, 1929, with the index at the time of survey of 1918 equal to 100, and that

---

13. The information collected appears to describe rent charge rather than the rate applying to months when rent was paid. (For method of collection of rent information, see U.S. Bureau of Labor Statistics, Bul. 699, 1941, pp. 19-20.) One cannot, however, be certain as to the sample of landlords. In collecting rent charges during the period under consideration, two sources were drawn on: (a) real estate agencies and (b) landlords renting their own properties. In many cities rents were collected solely from source (a). Rent concessions by real estate agencies may have been more or less important than those by other landlords. If they were more important, the rent index of 1934 would have a downward bias as a measure of change in rent of families presumably represented by the index. No test of possible bias of this type seems feasible. In describing the representation of rents from source (b) the Bureau of Labor Statistics states: "In certain cities where a large proportion of the dwellings rented to low- and moderate-income families are rented by their owners direct, rents are also obtained from individual owners" (Bul. 699, p. 20). The depression brought a change in rental practice. Some competition for tenants took the form of unpaid rent bills. This would not lower the rent index, nor would it lower housing expenditure reported by families. If landlords renting their own property resorted to unpaid rent as a form of holding tenants more commonly than did real estate agencies, this too would contribute to the downward bias in the rent index in cities where the rent index represented only practices of rental agencies. Since the forties rental information for the index has come from tenants in a sample of dwelling units.

Table 42

Characteristics of Tenant Housing, Income, and Related Variables, Census of Housing of 1950 the Terminal Period, 30 Cities[a]

| Item | Symbol for variable[b] | Variables | |
|---|---|---|---|
| | | Mean | Range |
| A. Characteristics of tenant units, Census of Housing, 1950[c] | | | |
| 1) Average contract rent, rent of 1918 equals $100, adjusted for price change[d] | $h^{\#}$ | $189 | $122 - $251 |
| 2) Importance of tenant units built in 1945 or later[e] | $ne_2$ | 106 | 100 - 123 |
| 3) Percentage of tenant units with services included in rent[f] | | | |
| a) Heat | $rh_2$ | 38 | 6 - 74 |
| b) Light or cooking fuel | $rlc_2$ | 22 | 5 - 56 |
| c) Furnishings | $rf_2$ | 22 | 1 - 51 |
| B. Persons in families and households in 1950 | | | |
| 1) Ratio of persons per household[g] in 1950 (1918 = 100) | $s^{\#}$ | 62 | 46 - 70 |
| 2) Importance of households with an aged[h] or female head | $af_2$ | 141 | 130 - 154 |
| 3) Importance of households with lodgers[i] | $lo_2$ | 109 | 104 - 118 |
| C. Population mobility | | | |
| 1) Importance of change in dwelling unit[j] | $cd_2$ | 116 | 106 - 127 |
| 2) Importance of recent in-migrants[k] | $ip_2$ | 105 | 102 - 111 |
| D. Percentage of the male labor force with less than 26 weeks employment in 1949[l] | $le_2$ | 14 | 11 - 19 |
| E. Relative price of housing | | | |
| 1) March, 1950 (1918 survey = 100)[m] | $p^{\#}$ | 81 | 69 - 95 |
| 2) March - June, 1941 (1918 = 100) | $pa^{\#}$ | 112 | 100 - 121 |
| 3) March, 1950 (March - June, 1941 = 100) | $pb^{\#}$ | 72 | 67 - 80 |
| F. Average income of 1949, income of 1918 equals $100, adjusted for price change[n] | $y^{\#}$ | $120 | $ 85 - $151 |

Source: U.S. Census of Housing: 1950, Vol. II; U.S. Census of Population: 1950, Vol. II, and Construction (publication of the U.S. Department of Labor), January, 1951.

a. With one exception the data pertain to cities, that is the data for Portland, Me., pertain to the metro area. These are used since data on income and household type are not shown for the city. Unless otherwise specified, the data pertain to all tenant households irrespective of number of persons and employment status of members. (For information on the source of the data of the 1918 survey and its eligibility criteria, see Table 41, fn. b.)

b. The superscript [#] is used to designate estimates where data of the Census of Housing of 1950 represent the terminal period, and those of the survey of 1918, the base period. The subscript 2 symbolizes a variable describing a condition at the time of the 1950 census, representing a terminal period.

c. The estimate of housing of the 1950 census is the median monthly contract rent multiplied by 12. The median is used because of the lesser computation involved. Furthermore experience with the relation of the mean to the median gives no reason to suppose that means, estimated from distributions available, would yield more reliable averages than the medians. The use of the medians rather than the means does tend to lower the estimates. But, such lowering may not affect the estimates of income elasticity of housing.

d. It should be noted that all references to the index of 1918 pertain to the time of the survey (see Table 41, fn. o).

e. This is the number of all tenant dwelling units per 100 of those built prior to 1945 or later.

f. See Construction. The data are from rent surveys in December, 1949, and January and February, 1951.

g. This ratio compares the average persons per household of the 1950 census set and the average persons per family of the 1918 survey set. The 1950 census does not report the persons per family within households. It does, however, report the frequency of households with persons not related to the head (see fn. i, below). These are in the household, but not in the family. However, the composition of the households of the 1950 census and the 1918 survey is so different that this difference in concept by itself is immaterial. The relatively low number of persons for the 1950 census seems in large part the result of the exclusion from the 1918 survey of all families with less than three persons. The 1950 census on the other hand includes all households and many of these have only one person.

h. Sixty-five years of age or more.

i. This is the number of all households per 100 without a non-relative present.

j. The population one year of age or more in the same county in 1949 as in 1950 per 100 in the same dwelling in 1949 as in 1950 (Census of Population: 1950, state reports, Table 34).

k. The 1950 population one year of age or more per 100 in the same county in 1949 as in 1950 (ibid.).

l. The percentage of the male labor force of 1950 working less than 26 weeks during 1949. The data pertain to the metro areas (ibid., Table 72). For discussion of this variable, see chapters vi and vii.

m. For information on the time of the 1918 survey, see Table 41, fn. o.

n. This is an estimate of median disposable income of 1949 adjusted for price change, with mean income of 1918 equal to 100. The income reported in the census of housing represents income before taxes. An estimate has been made of disposable income using the relationships reported in the 1950 consumption survey. The equation used to estimate disposable income for the census set describes tendencies among 48 cities as reported in the consumption study of 1950. The correlation is as follows:

$$x_Y = 0.079 + 0.962\, x_{Y_r} + 0.063\, x_S \qquad R^2 = .999$$

where Y is mean disposable income, $Y_r$ is mean total money income and S is average persons per family or consumer unit with variables expressed in log form. (Money income of the 1918 and 1934 surveys relate to income before taxes. However, income tax is so low in these years that the income can be assumed to represent disposable income.)

Both median income and median rent probably understate the respective means. If the degree of understatement of these is much the same in the various cities, the use of the medians rather than the means is immaterial to this analysis, since in this monograph the chief interest lies in the regression coefficients of $h^{\#}$ in relation to $y^{\#}$ and $p^{\#}$. However, the variation in the degree of inequality of economic status among cities and other conditions may have reduced the degree of correlation among the cities between the means and medians of income and rent. If the

at the time of the 1934 survey with December, 1929, equal to 100. These are symbolized by pa' and pb', respectively. In every city pa' exceeds 100 and in every city pb' is less than 100. These relative prices varied widely among cities. Tendencies described later give no reason to suppose that the rent index of 1934 represents the housing market of the families reporting in that survey.

Census of 1950.—There is no doubt that the rent index of 1950 had some downward bias as a measure of relative rent. This occurred because of its failure to reflect the extent to which new units during the late forties entered into occupancy at rent above that of units of equivalent quality, the rent of which was depressed by rent control. This characteristic of the rent index is commonly referred to as the new unit bias.[14] This characteristic of the price index is considered further in a later section.

Size and Composition of Consumer Units.—Population change and the difference in the universe represented by the sets of data seem likely to affect tendencies observed. In general, there tends to be a positive correlation between population growth and the importance of young families. These tend to have lower housing-income ratios than families with an aged head. The later tend to be important in cities with a declining population.

Considerable difference occurred among the surveys in the universe represented. For example, all families of the 1918 survey included a husband and wife and at least one child, whereas the 1934 survey represented families of a husband and wife, with or without another person present. Thus, like the 1918 survey, it excluded one-person households

14. See "Correction for the New Unit Bias in the Rent Component of the CPI," Monthly Labor Review, 1951, p. 442.

Footnotes to Table 42 (continued)

difference between the median and the mean tends to be the same for rent as for income, a tendency not unlikely if both are a function of the inequality of normal income, then the difference among cities between the mean and the median is immaterial. If such correspondence did not occur, then one should expect a random component in $y^{\#}$ that would tend to lower $\eta_{hy^{\#}}$. No attempt has been made to test this possibility.

It should, however, be noted that mean income and mean rent estimated from the distributions reported for the 1950 census seem unlikely to be any more satisfactory than the medians. The means would be much influenced by grouping errors and methods of estimating the mean income of the interval of $10,000 or more.

and those with a female head. It did not, however, exclude families with no children. On the other hand, the 1950 census sampled all households.

Estimates presented later take into account the number of persons in households or other consumer units and age and sex of household heads. These characteristics are of course correlated with the number of earners and probably with transitory income. The precise variables used are described later.

Sampling Variability.—The variables should not be assumed to be free from sampling variability. Each set of observations includes some cities where the average represents less than 100 families.[15]. Errors of many kinds plague users of all consumption and income data. There seems, however, no reason to suppose that sample size contributes appreciably to tendencies observed.

## Survey of 1934: the Terminal Period

Change from 1918 to 1934 is estimated for 26 cities. The variable h' ranges from \$131 to \$228. It is positively correlated with y' and c', the two measures of income change. Many other conditions are, however, associated with its variation. Coefficients of multiple correlation of h' with variables y' and c' and associated variables are summarized in Table 43. Some of the simpler correlations are presented in the text. In addition, Table 44 presents the correlation matrix of the variables.

Association between h' and y' and c'.—The variables y' and c' explain a significant portion of the variation in h'. The correlations are as follows:

$$x_h' = -0.204 + 1.167\, x_y' \qquad r^2 = .45. \qquad (11.1)$$

$$x_h' = 0.072 + 1.013\, x_c' \qquad r^2 = .36. \qquad (11.2)$$

The income elasticity of housing indicated is much the same for these

---

15. Among the cities of the 1918 set, the number of families included ranged from 66 to 392, and of the 1934 set from 146 to 897. In spite of these differences, in all estimates shown each city has a weight of one. This practice is followed in part to minimize computation costs and in part to avoid the possibility that characteristics peculiar to cities with a large number reporting would unduly influence the estimate. The number of households represented by the samples of the census of housing is much, much larger than those represented by the samples of the consumption surveys.

Table 43

Coefficients of Correlation Describing Change in Housing with respect to Change in Income and Other Variables, Survey 1934 Representing the Terminal Period, 26 Cities (Housing [h'] and Income [y'] and Total Consumption Expenditures [c'] Adjusted for Price Change)

| Item | h' in relation to Sets of Explanatory Variables | | | | | | | |
|---|---|---|---|---|---|---|---|---|
| | y' plus others | | | | c' plus others | | | |
| Equation number | (11.7) | (11.9) | (11.11) | (11.13) | (11.8) | (11.10) | (11.12) | (11.14) |
| $R^2$ | .51 | .52 | .59 | .71 | .48 | .52 | .54 | .80 |
| Constant | 0.372 | 0.339 | -0.417 | 0.606 | 0.368 | 0.099 | -0.461 | 0.471 |
| Independent variables | Regression Coefficients and Standard Errors | | | | | | | |
| A. y' or c' | 1.197<br>(.259) | 1.219<br>(.284) | 1.461<br>(.313) | 1.805<br>(.337) | 1.145<br>(.268) | 1.228<br>(.288) | 1.339<br>(.316) | 2.039<br>(.294) |
| B. Price | | | | | | | | |
| 1) Pa' | -0.324<br>(.193) | -0.319<br>(.212) | -0.304<br>(.213) | -0.447<br>(.205) | -0.406<br>(.202) | -0.420<br>(.215) | -0.429<br>(.228) | -0.724<br>(.183) |
| b) Pb' | 0.0200<br>(.1654) | 0.0483<br>(.1860) | 0.0270<br>(.1839) | -0.0213<br>(.2084) | 0.143<br>(.175) | 0.226<br>(.193) | 0.222<br>(.199) | 0.212<br>(.182) |
| C. Housing | | | | | | | | |
| 1) Percentage owner-occupants ($o_2$) | .....<br>..... | 0.000092<br>(.000834) | -0.000041<br>(.000868) | -0.00047<br>(.00080) | .....<br>..... | -0.00059<br>(.00083) | -0.00051<br>(.00090) | -0.000040<br>(.000658) |
| 2) Importance of heat in rent ($rh_2$) | .....<br>..... | -0.0454<br>(.1133) | -0.00284<br>(.11393) | -0.0304<br>(.1054) | .....<br>..... | -0.0536<br>(.1139) | -0.0254<br>(.1207) | -0.0824<br>(.0894) |
| 3) Mean January temperature (jt) | .....<br>..... | 0.00986<br>(.05484) | 0.0220<br>(.0637) | 0.0875<br>(.0633) | .....<br>..... | 0.0349<br>(.0556) | 0.0506<br>(.0684) | 0.175<br>(.057) |
| D. Family | | | | | | | | |
| 1) Family size (s') | .....<br>..... | .....<br>..... | 0.128<br>(.472) | 0.344<br>(.432) | .....<br>..... | .....<br>..... | 0.167<br>(.500) | 0.590<br>(.367) |
| 2) Ratio of adults to children ($ad_2$) | .....<br>..... | .....<br>..... | -0.305<br>(.224) | -0.234<br>(.203) | .....<br>..... | .....<br>..... | -0.151<br>(.228) | -0.0129<br>(.1662) |
| E. Mixture of income components | | | | | | | | |
| 1) Average earners in 1934 compared to 1918 (ea') | .....<br>..... | .....<br>..... | .....<br>..... | -0.215<br>(.382) | .....<br>..... | .....<br>..... | .....<br>..... | -0.424<br>(.310) |
| 2) Importance supplementary earnings (se') | .....<br>..... | .....<br>..... | .....<br>..... | -0.669<br>(.972) | .....<br>..... | .....<br>..... | .....<br>..... | -0.891<br>(.811) |

a. See Table 41 for information about the variables. All variables are expressed in log form except $o_2$.

two variables, namely 1.17 and 1.01. In addition the $r^2$ of the two relationships are quite similar.[16]

Relative Price of Housing.—Change in the relative price of housing between the surveys of 1918 and 1934, symbolized by p', explains little of the variation in h'. When this variable is added to those of equations (11.1) and (11.2) the following correlations are observed:

$$x_h' = +0.043 + 1.174\, x_y' - 0.129\, x_p' \qquad R^2 = .47. \qquad (11.3)$$

$$x_h' = +0.281 + 1.006\, x_c' - 0.0973\, x_p' \qquad R^2 = .38. \qquad (11.4)$$

Thus p' has a negative relationship to h', as is to be expected. However, the regression coefficients are low. In addition, p' explains little of the variation in h'.

It was postulated above that the rent index of 1934 might not represent the change of rent for families reporting in the survey of 1934. In the equations shown below, rent change from 1918 to 1929, symbolized

Table 44

Correlation Matrix of Variables, Survey of 1934 Representing the Terminal Period, 26 Cities[a]

| | c' (2) | p' (3) | pa' (4) | pb' (5) | $o_2$ (6) | $rh_2$ (7) | jt (8) | s' (9) | $ad_2$ (10) | ea' (11) | se' (12) |
|---|---|---|---|---|---|---|---|---|---|---|---|
| 1. y' | .907 | .028 | .068 | -.028 | .082 | .163 | -.055 | -.253 | .470 | .280 | .455 |
| 2. c' | . . . | -.036 | .170 | -.196 | -.024 | .203 | -.132 | -.212 | .370 | .418 | .469 |
| 3. p' | | . . . | .633 | .739 | -.227 | .252 | .037 | .073 | .110 | -.231 | -.076 |
| 4. pa' | | | . . . | -.051 | -.031 | .115 | .183 | .007 | .134 | -.059 | -.155 |
| 5. pb' | | | | . . . | -.270 | .226 | -.115 | .092 | .001 | -.266 | .013 |
| 6. $o_2$ | | | | | . . . | -.347 | .120 | .199 | -.067 | -.026 | .004 |
| 7. $rh_2$ | | | | | | . . . | -.227 | -.057 | .303 | -.057 | -.091 |
| 8. jt | | | | | | | . . . | -.416 | -.034 | .271 | .300 |
| 9. s' | | | | | | | | . . . | -.460 | -.141 | -.221 |
| 10. $ad_2$ | | | | | | | | | . . . | .137 | .221 |
| 11. ea' | | | | | | | | | | . . . | .842 |

a. See Table 41 for information about the variables.

16. An important difference between these two measures is indicated by estimating h' where y' and c' equal 100, that is a situation where y and c, in dollars of constant purchasing power, are the same for 1918 and 1934. Under that condition h' is \$131 where y', and \$125 where c', is the explanatory variable. Some but not all of this difference probably represents a greater average negative transitory component of y than of c for the 1934 period. For the 26 cities mean y' is \$120 and mean c' is \$132. This indicates that families represented by the 1934 survey were saving less or dissaving more than those represented by the 1918 survey.

by pa', is substituted for p'. The following correlations are observed:

$$x_h' = 0.415 + 1.197\, x_y' - 0.325\, x_{pa}' \qquad R^2 = .51. \qquad (11.5)$$

$$x_h' = 0.737 + 1.103\, x_c' - 0.408\, x_{pa}' \qquad R^2 = .46. \qquad (11.6)$$

The substitution of pa' and p'[17] has little effect on $\eta_{hy}'$ or $\eta_{hc}'$. It does, however, increase the $R^2$ of the respective relationships. In addition, the regression coefficients of pa' are appreciably higher than those of p'.

When the relative price of housing in 1934 compared to 1929, symbolized by pb', is also taken into account, $R^2$ is increased little, and little change occurs in the estimates of $\eta_{hy}'$, $\eta_{hc}'$, or $\eta_{hpa}'$ (see Table 43, equations [11.7] and [11.8]). In addition, the higher pb' the higher tends to be h'. In other words, the greater the decrease in the relative price of housing from 1929 to 1934 the lower tends to be h'.

Owner-Occupancy and Other Characteristics of Housing.—The 1918 set is restricted to tenant households without heat included in rent, whereas the 1934 set includes all households of the survey. Some of these were owner-occupants and some were tenants whose rent included heat. In addition, there may have been considerable variation among cities in the increase between 1918 and 1934 in services other than heat included in rent, for example, light, cooking fuel, hot water, and related things. Some of these conditions may have contributed to the variation in h', and some may be systematically related to y', c', or relative price.

To test the possible effect of the inclusion of owner-occupants[18] in the 1934 set, a variable representing the percentage of owner-occupancy is included. This is symbolized by $o_2$. Insofar as estimated rental value of owner-occupied units represents less additional services than the contract rent of tenants, the higher $o_2$ the lower is likely to be h', under the

---

17. No further estimates are shown where price is represented by p'. However, the effect of the substitution of p' for pa' and pb' has been tested in a combination of variables explaining 70 per cent of the variation h'. In such combination the regression coefficient of p' is negative but not significant. In addition $R^2$ of the variables tends to be lowered by such substitution. In none of the combinations explored was the regression coefficient of p' more than twice its standard error, whereas several of the coefficients of regression of pa' had such a standard error. (Standard errors are shown in Table 43.)

18. The housing of owner-occupants of the survey of 1934 is represented by estimated rental value of dwelling units occupied rather than current housing expenditure.

assumption that housing with normal income held constant does not differ by tenure.

The 1934 survey provides only one piece of information bearing on other services included in rent. This is the number of tenants with heat included in rent. The importance of such tenants in the entire set of households is represented by $rh_2$. The expectation is that the higher $rh_2$ the higher tends to be h', other things being held constant. One other condition is taken into account, namely, the mean January temperature, symbolized by jt. This is taken into account on the assumption that the lower jt, that is the colder the winter, the more the provision of heat in the rent tends to increase h'.

The addition of the three variables, namely $o_2$, $rh_2$ and jt add little to the explanation of the variation in h'. The correlations are shown in Table 43, equations (11.9) and (11.10). The inclusion of these supplementary housing variables influences little the regression coefficients of y' or c' or pa'. It seems likely, at least for $rh_2$, that intercorrelation with other variables obscured its effect.[19].

Family Type.—In general, the number of persons per family is lower[20] and the ratio of adults to children higher for the survey of 1934

---

19. Equations (11.13) and (11.14) indicate that the higher $rh_2$, that is the higher the percentage of families with heat included in rent of the terminal period, the lower tend to be h'. This seems highly improbable. In addition, they indicate that the higher jt the higher ends to be h'. The regression coefficient of this variable is significant, and there seems no reason to suppose that jt is related to h' except through its relation with heat in rent. It may well be that both $rh_2$ and jt are correlated with a condition associated with h' that has not been taken into account.

It may be the bias in the relative prices of 1918, represented by $p_1$. The variables jt and $rh_2$ are both positively correlated with $p_1$. In addition, $p_1$ is positively related to the residuals of equation (11.14). The possible existence of a bias in relative price of 1918 was not suspected until $h^{\#}$ was being examined. Its bearing on the variation in h' was not considered of sufficient importance to warrant rerunning the correlations. (For further comment on $p_1$, see pages 267-68 below.)

20. Husband-wife families only are represented in the surveys of 1918 and 1934. All families of the survey of 1918 had at least one child, whereas 45 per cent of the families represented in the survey of 1934 had no children (see U.S. Bureau of Labor Statistics, Bul. 638, pp. 18-19). Data are available for the survey of 1934 for families similar in type to those of the 1918 survey are reported (see Tables 22 and 23 of the respective bulletins). However, for this subset of families no information is provided on the imputed rent of owner-occupants, and it seemed best to maximize the homogeneity of the housing variable and to use supplementary variables in an attempt to hold constant the difference between cities in family types represented.

than of 1918. These differences are symbolized by s' and $ad_2$.

The addition of these two variables, describing family type, to those representing income, price, and characteristics of housing adds somewhat to the explanation of h' (see Table 43, equations [11.11] and [11.12]). Furthermore, their inclusion increased the regression coefficients of y' and c'. The regression coefficient of s' is positive, whereas a negative sign seems more reasonable. However, its standard error is very high. On the other hand, the regression coefficient of $ad_2$ is negative. This is the sign to be expected, in that a relatively high ratio of adults to children in the terminal year indicates a stage on the family cycle when income tends to be relatively high and housing-income ratios tend to be low. However, for this too the standard error is relatively high. The significance of each of these family type variables may come more through its relation to the mixture of income components than through a direct relationship to h' as such.

Number of Earners.—Information is available for the surveys of 1918 and 1934 on the average number of earners per family,[21] irrespective of the duration of employment, and also on the importance of earnings of supplementary earners compared to those of the chief earner. Measures of such difference between the years are symbolized by ea' and se', respectively.[22] The expectation is that the higher the correlation of y' or c' with ea' or se' the more the housing-income ratios tend to be a function of transitory income. A positive correlation exists, and it is higher where difference in employment level is represented by se' than by ea'. The correlations of y' and c' with se' are significant at the .02 level (see Table 44).

---

21. The number of usual earners per family probably differs among cities. Hence, the average number of earners per family tends to be only a crude estimate of the mixture of income components among cities in a given year. However, the ratio of earners between years represented by ea' seems likely to be little influenced by normal variation among cities in the usual number of earners per family. In general, the average number of earners per family tends to be higher for the 1934 than the 1918 set. For the 26 cities, the means for the two surveys are 1.39 and 1.25, respectively. This increase appears to have been in large measure the result of the greater importance of adults in the 1934 than the 1918 survey, a difference related to eligibility requirements.

22. These two variables are positively correlated. Expressed in log form, their $r^2$ is .71. The variable se' is also positively correlated with $ad_2$. In other words the greater the increase in the importance of adults to children, the greater the importance of the earnings of supplementary earners.

The addition of ea' and se' to the independent variables already considered increases greatly the explanation of variation in h' (see Table 43, equations [11.13] and [11.14]). With income represented by y', $R^2$ is .71 and c', it is .80. Their inclusion also increased greatly the estimate of $\eta_{hy}'$ from 1.46 to 1.81, and of $\eta_{hc}'$ from 1.34 to 2.04. In addition, $\eta_{hpa}'$ is increased. The coefficients of ea' and se' both have a negative sign. This is the sign expected. However, for neither of these variables is the regression coefficient twice its standard error. It should, however, be noted that h' seems unlikely to have a direct relationship to these variables. They represent the mixture of income components, that in turn affect housing-income ratios. Their significance is indicated by the increase in the partial regression coefficient of y' and of c'.

A Summing Up.—This section examines, for 26 cities, change in housing between the periods and families represented by the surveys of 1918 and 1934, with housing and income adjusted for price change. These variables are symbolized by h' and y', respectively. In addition, change in total expenditure, adjusted for price change, is used as a proxy for normal income. It is symbolized by c'. The housing of the base period is contract rent of tenant units without heat included in rent and that of 1934 is housing of all consumer units with that of owner-occupied units represented by estimated rental value and of tenant units by contract rent.

Change in relative price of housing is represented by the Consumer Price Index. For the entire period it is symbolized by p', and for the years 1918 to 1929 by pa'. The variable pa' appears to be a better index than p' of difference among cities in change in price of housing affecting families reporting in the 1934 survey. Eligibility criteria may account for this. Those of the 1934 survey excluded families above a certain level in rent concessions. Thus it seems likely that rent concessions were less important for families reporting in the survey than for those represented by the Consumer Price Index.

The tendencies observed imply a price elasticity of housing between -0.5 and -0.7. Standard errors of regression coefficients indicate considerable reliability. However, the usefulness of the rent index leaves much to be desired.

The evidence also implies an elasticity of housing with respect to normal income around 2.0. (This is the coefficient observed where c' represents change in normal income and change in number of earners as well as rent is held constant. See Table 43, equation [11.14]). It is of considerable interest that the coefficient is only slightly lower where income change is represented by y' than where it is represented by c'. Furthermore, variables representing employment level affect the partial regression coefficients of these two variables in much the same way. This common effect may come from job-related expense. Or it may also represent the correlation of expenditure with transitory income. It does, however, suggest that variation among cities in changes in average money income and in average total expenditure are about equal as proxies for variation of change in normal incomes for this type of intertemporal estimate.

In general, the variables taken into account, other than those directly or indirectly representing income and price, are of minor importance. This can be inferred from the fact that the partial regression coefficient of none of them is significant, as judged by its standard error. Estimate of these conditions is not, however, the main purpose of this monograph.

A high percentage of the total variation of h' is explained. And the income elasticity of housing consumption observed is quite consistent with the cross-section estimates of chapters vii and viii. For these it seems reasonable to assume that price difference does not affect tendencies observed.

### Census of Housing of 1950: the Terminal Period

Change from 1918 to the period represented by the census of housing has been examined for a set of 30 cities. The variable $h^{\#}$, representing change in contract rent, ranges from \$122 to \$251. The variable $y^{\#}$, representing change in money income,[23] ranges from \$85[24] to \$155.

---

23. Money income alone represents economic status. Only when the housing data are a part of a general consumption study is it feasible to use total expenditure as a proxy for normal income. For description of the income for census set see Table 42 fn. n.

24. A lower average income in a few cities for primary units of households of the census of housing than for the 1918 survey is a result of several things. One is the exclusion from the 1918 survey of all families in slum housing. Because of this the average income reported for some cities greatly overstated the income of all families. In addition, the 1918 survey excluded all broken families and those with an unemployed head. Furthermore, the income of the census of housing is represented by the median, whereas that of the 1918 survey is represented by the mean (see Tables 41 and 42 for further description of the income variables).

Both are expressed in dollars of constant purchasing power.

The correlation of these two variables is as follows:

$$x_h^{\#} = 1.221 + 0.511\, x_y^{\#} \qquad r^2 = .15. \qquad (11.15)$$

Thus change in income explains much less of the change in housing where 1950 rather than 1934 is the terminal period (see equation [11.1]).

Many conditions other than $y^{\#}$ are associated with the variation in $h^{\#}$. In fact, $y^{\#}$ explains only 15 per cent of its variation. Variables representing population mobility are first examined, then, in turn, employment levels, household type, relative price of housing, and additional services included in rent.[25] The number of observations is insufficient to permit an estimate of the joint effect of all conditions considered and at the same time to have a fair number of degrees of freedom. Equations are, however, shown with some variables to represent each of the main conditions. Their selection represents hunches as to those likely to be most important, and some hunches may not have been good. A good deal of correlation exists among the explanatory variables (see Table 45).

Population Mobility.—Two types of population mobility are considered in this section. The first is the recent shift among dwellings of the population within a county, and the second is the volume of recent inmigrants.

The shifting of population among dwellings tends to affect the validity of income reported by the Census of Housing of 1950 as a measure of normal income of households. The eligibility criteria of the 1918 survey[26] excluded a similar effect from that survey. It was confined to families that had kept house for at least one year. Thus newly formed households were excluded. On the other hand, the 1950 census excluded no households. The income of the previous year, that is the income of 1949, of newly formed households seems likely to understate normal income, that is the income affecting housing occupied at the time of the census. This tendency is to be expected if a considerable proportion of the chief earners of such households had had an increase in income between 1949 and the spring of 1950. Since many of these were newly formed households with a young head, such an increase would not be surprising. Some such heads that were full-time earners in the spring of 1950 were at

25. See Table 42 for range in the variables.

26. The survey of 1934 is very similar.

least partial dependents in parental households during much of 1949.

Direct information is not provided on the importance of this subset. Information is, however, provided on the importance of the population in the same county in 1950 as in 1949, but in a different house. Various conditions lead to a change of house occupied. One is the formation of new households. Thus variation among cities in the importance of the population changing the house occupied, without changing the county of residence, should provide a proxy for the importance of new households apart from in-migrants. This measure of the regrouping of the households is symbolized by $cd_2$.[27] This is the number of persons one year of age or more in the same county in 1950 as in 1949 per 100 such persons making no change in the house occupied. Such a measure pertains to the population in general, that is to population in owner as well as tenant households and in quasi-households and institutions. (Most of the population is in private households.) In addition, a very high percentage of the newly formed households rent rather than own the unit occupied.

When $cd_2$ is added to the variables of equation (11.15) the following correlation is observed:

$$x_h^{\#} = -3.736 + 0.841\, x_y^{\#} + 2.075\, x_{cd_2} \qquad R^2 = .35. \qquad (11.16)$$

Thus, taking into account $cd_2$ increases the coefficient of determination from 0.15 to 0.35, and increases $\eta_{hy}^{\#}$ from 0.51 to 0.84. In addition, the regression coefficient of $cd_2$ is positive, which is the sign to be expected if it represents the importance of newly formed households. It may be that $cd_2$ is related to the imperfections of the housing market because of rent control. It seems not unlikely that newly formed households were paying a relatively high rent in the spring of 1950 because of rent control.

The demand of in-migrants as well as local residents affects the housing market. In the absence of any lag of rents behind change in demand, it seems reasonable to expect that the greater the recent in-migration the higher tends to be the rent of dwellings in general. This alone might make rent-income ratios high in cities experiencing a marked in-migration, especially under conditions of abnormally low supplies of building materials. Another condition seems likely to lead to high rent-income ratios in the cities experiencing high in-migration. This is the

27. Translated this means "changing dwelling-unit."

abnormally low income of in-migrants, either because unemployment had induced migration or migration had interrupted employment. This effect is absent in the 1918 survey because only families resident in the community for the entire year of the survey are included.

The Census of Population of 1950 provides information on the importance of the population of 1950 living in a different county in 1949. This variable is represented by $ip_2$.[28] When this variable is added to those of equation (11.11), the following correlation is observed:

$$x_h^{\#} = -9.01 + \underset{(.219)}{0.797}\, x_y^{\#} + \underset{(.925)}{0.556}\, x_{cd_2} + \underset{(1.87)}{4.20}\, x_{ip_2} \qquad R^2 = .46 \tag{11.17}$$

Thus taking into account the importance of the recent in-migrants ($ip_2$) increases $R^2$ from .35 to .46. In addition, the regression coefficient of $ip_2$ is more than twice its standard error. The marked positive relationship between $h^{\#}$ and $ip_2$ shown in equation (11.17), may well represent the increase in demand for housing in the community accompanying increase in population. It may also represent the importance of the new construction that tended to enter the market at rent levels above those depressed by rent control.

The effect of the inclusion of $ip_2$ on two of the regression coefficients of equation (11.16) is of interest. A slight lowering of the coefficient of $y^{\#}$ occurs—from 0.841 to 0.797. In addition, a very marked decrease in the coefficient of $cd_2$ occurs—from 2.017 to 0.556. The variables $cd_2$ and $ip_2$, are highly correlated—the $r^2$ of their relationship is .55. In addition they are both positively correlated with the importance of units built in 1945 or later represented by $ne_2$ (see Table 45).

Employment Level.—The importance of holding constant change in employment level is demonstrated in estimates shown for h'. The information available in the 1918 survey and the 1950 census bearing on relative employment levels of the various cities is not comparable. Hence a variable akin to ea' or se' is not feasible. Instead two variables are used, one for 1918 and one for 1950.

The information relative to the employment level in 1918 is described above. Two variables representing the situation depicted in that survey are described there, namely the average number of earners,

28. The total population one year of age or more per 100 living in the same county in 1949 as in 1950.

symbolized by $ea_1$, and total earnings per \$100 of earnings by the head, symbolized by $se_1$. The higher is $ea_1$ and $se_1$ the greater the likelihood that the incomes of 1918 have a positive transitory component. Such a component tend to lower $y^\#$ but not $h^\#$. Thus one would expect that the higher $ea_1$ or $se_1$ the higher would tend to be $\eta_{hy}{}^\#$. The two variables $ea_1$ and $se_1$ are highly correlated. In the analysis that follows, the relative employment level among cities of the 1918 set is represented by $ea_1$.[29]

The employment level of 1949 is represented by the percentage of the male labor force with less than 26 weeks of work. Estimates of chapters vi and vii gave reason to believe that this tends to be a proxy for average transitory income of places. It is symbolized by $le_2$. The expectation is that the higher $le_2$ the greater the likelihood that average income of 1949 had a negative transitory component, hence the higher $le_2$ the higher is likely to be $h^\#$.

When two variables representing employment level are added to the variables of equation (11.17), the following correlation is observed:

$$x_h{}^\# = \underset{}{-10.131} + \underset{(.217)}{1.082}\, x_y{}^\# + \underset{(.882)}{1.637}\, x_{cd_2} \qquad (11.18)$$

$$+ \underset{(1.710)}{3.221}\, x_{ip_2} + \underset{(.405)}{1.064}\, x_{ea_1} + \underset{(.00566)}{0.0139}\, x_{le_2} \qquad R^2 = .65.$$

The regression coefficients of the two indexes of employment have the signs expected and each is twice its standard error. Furthermore, their addition to the variables of equation (11.17) increases $R^2$ from .46 to .65. Their inclusion also has an important effect on the coefficient of $y^\#$. It is increased from 0.797 to 1.082. This is the type of effect to expect if the employment indexes are correlated with transitory incomes and if housing is unresponsive to such income.

Household Type.—The universe of households represented is very different in the 1918 survey and the 1950 census. Fortunately, the 1950 census provides extensive information on characteristics of households, including the frequency of tenant households by age and sex of head and presence of non-relatives. Variation in these among cities has been examined.

---

29. Equations with $se_1$ as well as $ea_1$ represented, did not in any way affect the coefficient of $\eta_{hy}{}^\#$ observed.

There is a general tendency for rent-income ratios to be high for households with an aged or a female head—types of households for the most part excluded from the 1918 survey.[30] Their importance varies among the 30 cities of the 1950 set—from 130 to 154. It is symbolized by $af_2$. The expectation is that the higher $af_2$ the higher tends to be $h^{\#}$ held constant.

The greater the importance of lodgers in tenant households the more the housing occupied overstates the housing of those whose income is reported. Under this condition it would not be surprising to find a positive relationship between $h^{\#}$ and the importance of lodgers in tenant households of the spring of 1950. Their importance has been measured in terms of the number of all households per 100 without non-relatives present.[31] This is symbolized by $lo_2$.

When this variable and $af_2$ are added to the variables of equation (11.8), the following correlation is observed:

$$x_h^{\#} = -16.135 + \underset{(0.233)}{1.376}\, x_y^{\#} + \underset{(0.373)}{1.036}\, x_{ea_1} \qquad (11.19)$$

$$+ \underset{(0.00666)}{.0230}\, x_{le_2} + \underset{(0.826)}{1.333}\, x_{cd_2} + \underset{(1.743)}{3.165}\, x_{ip_2} + \underset{(0.00294)}{0.00268}\, x_{af_2}$$

$$+ \underset{(1.144)}{2.919}\, x_{lo_2} \qquad R^2 = .73.$$

Both variables representing household type, namely $af_2$ and $lo_2$, have the signs expected. The greater percentage of households with an aged or a female head and the importance of households with lodgers the higher tends to be $h^{\#}$. The regression coefficient of $af_2$ is about equal to its standard error. On the other hand, the regression coefficient of $lo_2$ is more than twice its standard error. The addition of these two variables raises $R^2$ from .65 to .73 and also raises the regression coefficient of $y^{\#}$ from 1.082 to 1.376.

Price of Housing.—Price is an important condition. Change in

30. The universe of the 1918 survey included no families with an unemployed head or a female head, and all had at least one child. The 1950 census, on the other hand, included all households.

31. Only 3 per cent of the total population in private households were reported to be lodgers in the spring of 1950. There is, however, considerable variation among cities.

the relative price of housing from 1918 to 1950 is represented by $p^{\#}$. The simple correlation of $h^{\#}$ and $p^{\#}$ is negative. However, the $r^2$ of these variables is low, being only .084. When $y^{\#}$ is held constant, $p^{\#}$ appears to have considerable effect on $h^{\#}$. The correlation of these variables is as follows:

$$x_h^{\#} = 2.624 + \underset{(0.212)}{0.536}\, x_y^{\#} - \underset{(0.388)}{0.769}\, x_p^{\#} \qquad R^2 = .26. \qquad (11.20)$$

Thus two variables explain about one-quarter of the variation in $h^{\#}$. Holding constant $p^{\#}$ has little influence on the regression coefficient of $y^{\#}$. Equation (11.20) does, however, indicate that relative price of housing tends to have a marked effect on housing consumption. The observed elasticity of demand for housing with respect to price indicated by equation (11.20) is -0.769. In addition, the regression coefficient of $p^{\#}$ is about twice its standard error.

Rent control and lag in the rise of rent following decontrol may affect tendencies indicated by equation (11.20). An estimate has been made by the U.S. Bureau of Labor Statistics as to the extent of the new-unit bias in the rent index. The rent index was adjusted using this estimate, and the housing and relative price of housing similarly adjusted are symbolized by $h_n^{\#}$ and $p_n^{\#}$, respectively. With these variables used the following correlation is observed.

$$x_{h_n}^{\#} = 2.521 + 0.573\, x_y^{\#} - 0.744\, x_{p_n}^{\#} \qquad R^2 = .31. \quad (11.21)$$

A comparison of equations (11.20) and (11.21) indicates little effect from this adjustment. It may well be that the inability of consumers to improve their housing at the same price as they are currently reported to be paying tends to affect the coefficient of $p^{\#}$ in equation (11.20).

Importance of New Construction and Other Conditions Associated with $p^{\#}$.—Peculiarities of the housing market of 1950 and their possible interaction with $p^{\#}$ were explored, taking into account the importance of new units not under rent control. This importance is probably closely related to the importance of tenant units built in 1945 or later. This variable is symbolized by $ne_2$. Insofar as rent control tended to depress the rents reported in 1950, the higher $ne_2$ the higher is likely to be $h^{\#}$ and, other things being equal, the higher $ne_2$ the more $p^{\#}$ understates the increase in the relative price of housing. However, the new units seem likely to have added to the quality of the stock and may have been in part a response to increased income.

One other condition that may affect the usefulness of $p^{\#}$ as a measure of change in the relative price of housing has been considered: the possible interpolation bias in estimating the price index of 1918. This is represented by $p_1$.[32]

When $ne_2$ and $p_1$ are added to the variables of equation (11.20), the following correlation is observed:

$$x_h^{\#} = -4.056 + \underset{(0.205)}{0.869}\, x_y^{\#} - \underset{(0.350)}{0.861}\, x_p^{\#} \qquad (11.22)$$

$$+ \underset{(0.624)}{1.900}\, x_{ne_2} + \underset{(0.675)}{1.184}\, x_{p_1} \qquad R^2 = .52.$$

Thus the inclusion of $ne_2$ and $p_1$ increases $R^2$ from .26 to .52. In addition, it increases[33] slightly the regression coefficient of $p^{\#}$. In this equation it is slightly more than twice its standard error. The regression coefficient of $ne_2$ is positive, and it is close to three times its standard error. The marked effect indicated is to be expected if $ne_2$ represents both the new unit bias and some improvement in quality. If it represents an improvement in quality, then it may be serving in some measure as a proxy for income. In addition, the regression coefficient of $p_1$ is positive. This is the sign to be expected if the rent index of the 1918 survey is systomatically underestimated in cities with marked increase in rent during

32. See p. 248 for discussion of this variable.

33. One other exploration of the possible effect of rent control was made using price variables to represent two segments of the period represented. These are the relative price of housing in December, 1941, with that of the 1918 survey equal to 100, and the other the relative price in March, 1950, with that of December, 1941, equal to 100. The dual measures of change in relative price are symbolized by $pa^{\#}$ and $pb^{\#}$, respectively. These were substituted for $p^{\#}$ of equation (11.22) and the following correlation was observed:

$$x_h^{\#} = -2.243 + \underset{(.211)}{.876}\, x_y^{\#} - \underset{(.386)}{.847}\, x_{pa}^{\#} \qquad (11.23)$$

$$- \underset{(.651)}{.993}\, x_{pb}^{\#} + \underset{(.702)}{1.191}\, x_{ne_2} + \underset{(.667)}{1.947}\, x_{p_1} \qquad R^2 = .52$$

Thus the substitution of $pa^{\#}$ and $pb^{\#}$ for $p^{\#}$ of equation (11.23) has little effect on $R^2$. It does, however, affect appreciably the regression coefficients of $ne_2$ and $p_1$.

1918. However, the regression coefficient is not quite twice its standard error.

Plus Other Conditions.—So far the association of the so-called price variables with $h^{\#}$ has been examined with only importance of new construction and $y^{\#}$ held constant. Where the set of variables of equation (11.22) and the additional variables of equation (11.19) are combined, the following relationship is observed:

$$x_h^{\#} = -14.491 + \underset{(0.238)}{1.332\, x_y^{\#}} + \underset{(0.401)}{1.077\, x_{ea_1}} \tag{11.24}$$

$$+ \underset{(.0072)}{.0195\, x_{le_2}} + \underset{(1.246)}{0.978\, x_{cd_2}} + \underset{(1.772)}{2.453\, ip_2} - \underset{(0.00306)}{0.00156\, x_{af_2}}$$

$$+ \underset{(1.144)}{2.772\, x_{lo_2}} - \underset{(0.342)}{0.485\, x_p^{\#}} + \underset{(0.993)}{0.454\, x_{ne_2}} + \underset{(0.610)}{0.505\, x_{p_1}}$$

$$R^2 = .77.$$

This set of ten independent variables explains 77 per cent of the variation in $h^{\#}$. The partial regression coefficient of $y^{\#}$ of equation (11.19) is

Table 45

Coefficients of Correlation between Variables of Two Equations, Census of Housing of 1950, Representing the Terminal Period, 30 Cities[a]

| Variables of equation (11.19) | Variables of equation (11.22) | | | | |
|---|---|---|---|---|---|
| | $p^{\#}$ (1) | $ne_2$ (2) | $p_1$ (3) | $y^{\#}$ (4) | $h^{\#}$ (5) |
| 1. $h^{\#}$ | -.290 | .218 | .219 | .384 | 1.000 |
| 2. $y^{\#}$ | .115 | -.309 | -.317 | 1.000 | .384 |
| 3. $ea_1$ | .091 | -.126 | -.151 | .195 | .314 |
| 4. $le_2$ | -.178 | .118 | .316 | -.529 | .172 |
| 5. $cd_2$ | -.187 | .778 | .372 | -.476 | .217 |
| 6. $ip_2$ | -.258 | .550 | .411 | -.305 | .408 |
| 7. $af_2$ | -.342 | .001 | .253 | -.058 | .324 |
| 8. $lo_2$ | .044 | .216 | .048 | -.314 | -.005 |

a. See Table 42 for information about the variables. All variables are expressed in log form.

little affected by the addition of variables representing price and associated conditions. Thus the partial coefficients of $\eta_{hy}^{\#}$ of equations (11.19) and (11.24) are very similar. They are 1.38 and 1.33. On the other hand, the coefficients of $p^{\#}$ in equations (11.22) and (11.24) are quite different —being -0.869 and -0.485, respectively. The intercorrelation of variables accounting for this increase has by no means been fully explored. Many of the correlations represented by equations (11.19) and (11.22) are highly significant. Table 45 shows these correlations. It indicates a high correlation between variables representing population mobility, that is $ip_2$ and $cd_2$, and $p^{\#}$, $ne_2$, and $p_1$.

Additional Services Represented by Contract Rent.—Estimates for 1918 represent families without heat included in rent, whereas the Census of Housing represents all households. In 1950 a high percentage of the tenant households had heat and other services included in rent. These together with differences in universe represented may have contributed to variation in $h^{\#}$. The range among cities in percentage of households with additional services in rent around the time of the 1950 census is shown in Table 42. The relation of $h^{\#}$ to percentage of rental units with heating fuel, with furnishings, and with light or a cooking fuel has been examined. These are symbolized by $rh_2$, $rf_2$, and $rlc_2$, respectively. One further variable is included, namely the mean January temperature, symbolized by jt. The assumption is that the lower such temperature the more the provision of heating fuel would tend to increase $h^{\#}$.

Of the three housing variables,[34] $rf_2$ ranks first in its correlation with $h^{\#}$. The $r^2$ of these two variables is .29. In general, the higher the percentage of tenant units having specified services represented in contract rent of 1950 the higher tends to be $h^{\#}$. Two variables representing services explain 38 per cent of the variation in $h^{\#}$. The correlation is as follows:

$$x_h^{\#} = 2.172 + 0.00117\, X_{rh_2} + 0.00234\, X_{rf_2} \qquad R^2 = .38. \qquad (11.25)$$

The correlation of $h^{\#}$ with the set of four variables representing other services in rent of the 1950 census is as follows:

34. These variables are used in arithmetic form.

$$x_h^{\#} = 1.965 + \underset{(0.000772)}{0.00139\, X_{rh_2}} + \underset{(0.00143)}{0.00108\, X_{rlc_2}} \qquad (11.26)$$

$$+ \underset{(0.00107)}{0.00155\, X_{rf_2}} + \underset{(0.114)}{0.125\, x_{jt}} \qquad R^2 = .42.$$

Thus, the addition of $rlc_2$ and jt to the variables of equation (11.25) increases the $R^2$ of the variables only slightly. And the standard errors of all variables representing additional services in contract rent are high.

Furthermore, the addition of the variables $rh_2$ and $rf_2$ to the variables of equation (11.24) adds nothing to the explanation of $h^{\#}$. Their inclusion[35] reduces the regression coefficient of $y^{\#}$ from 1.33 to 1.22, and that of $p^{\#}$ from -0.485 to -0.403.

A Summing Up.—This section examines, for 30 cities, change in average contract rent and income between the periods and the universes represented by the survey of 1918 and the Census of 1950, with rent and income adjusted for price change. Variables representing these changes are symbolized by $h^{\#}$ and $y^{\#}$, respectively, and change in relative price of housing is symbolized by $p^{\#}$.

Among the cities a wide variation is observed in $h^{\#}$. Little of the variation is explained by $y^{\#}$ alone, and the simple coefficient of $\eta_{hy}{}^{\#}$ is 0.511. However, when mobility of population, employment levels represented, and household type are held constant a partial coefficient of $\eta_{hy}{}^{\#}$ of 1.38 is observed (see equation [11.19]). There seems good reason to suppose that this coefficient tends to be biased downward by transitory income of the tenant households of 1950. Three conditions seem likely to contribute to this: (a) a gap between the period represented by the housing and the income variable for 1950 that tends to be especially important for newly formed households who are heavily represented among tenants; (b) migration that tends to interrupt employment; and (c) cyclical change in employment opportunity. Some information bearing on these is available. However, it is not specific to the tenant households represented by $h^{\#}$. Because of lack of information bearing on $y_t$ and the peculiarities of the universe represented, the estimates where 1934 represents the terminal period are probably more reliable than where 1950 represents the terminal period. The relative price of housing, symbolized by $p^{\#}$, by itself explains little of the variation in $h^{\#}$. However, when

35. This equation is not shown.

$y^{\#}$ is held constant a partial coefficient of $\eta_{hp}{}^{\#}$ around -0.8 is observed (see equation [11.20]).

## Summary and Conclusions

This chapter presents evidence for two sets of cities on change in between two years in average housing, income, and relative price of housing. The surveys of 1934 and the census of 1950 represent the terminal periods and the survey of 1918 the base period. The respective sets include 26 and 30 cities.

The findings can be simply stated: (a) an elasticity of housing with respect to normal income between 1.3 and 2.0 is indicated; (b) an elasticity of housing with respect to price close to -1.0 is indicated; and (c) a great many conditions associated with change in housing, income, and price are likely to affect the simple correlations.

The income elasticity of housing indicated is much higher where 1934 than where 1950 is the terminal year. The estimates where 1934 is the terminal year represent housing in a free market. The relatively low coefficients where 1950 is the terminal year may represent the effect of rent control. Because of rent control and the greater reliability of information for 1934 than for 1950 with respect to $y_t$, the estimates of income elasticity of housing between the years seems likely to be more reliable where 1934 than where 1950 represents the terminal period.

In general, the intertemporal estimates indicate an appreciable price elasticity of demand for housing. In other words, they indicate that increase in the price of housing relative to the price of other consumer products has a marked tendency to lower housing consumption. For none of the estimates is the price variable entirely satisfactory. Nevertheless, the tendencies observed for the two sets of intertemporal comparisons are quite consistent. In addition the tendencies observed are consistent with Muth's estimate described in chapter x and also with the evidence of chapters vi and vii. Those chapters indicate much the same income elasticity of market value among places where price of housing seems likely to be positively correlated with income, as among areas within cities where market price is unlikely to be correlated with income. This similarity of income elasticity of housing under these two different conditions implies a price elasticity of around -1.0.[36]

36. Duesenberry and Kistin used survey data to estimate the price elasticity of housing and some other products. See James Duesenberry

All the estimates of intertemporal change have one thing in common: The variables representing additional services paid for in contract rent explain little of the variation among cities in change in housing observed. A common secular change among cities in their importance might account for this. Or the variables may have been very crude.

The analysis presented in this chapter appears to represent the first

---

and Helen Kistin, "The Role of Demand in the Economic Structure," in W. Leontief et al., Studies in the Structure of the American Economy (New York: Oxford University Press, 1953), p. 453. A brief comment on their method and findings is of interest.

They used data of surveys of 1918, the late twenties, and 1934. A large proportion of their observations represented change from 1918 to 1934. The housing variable represented change in housing expenditure without regard to the mixture of tenures. They estimated price elasticity of housing under the assumption that their measure of change in housing was standardized for income change, that CPI represented the families reporting in the surveys, and that gap between housing consumption and expenditure for owners and other conditions, such as level, were either unimportant or randomly related to price change observed.

They observed a price elasticity of housing close to zero, which implies that housing consumption is little affected by relative price of housing. The reliability of estimate is, however, very low, as indicated by a coefficient of correlation among places of change in housing and in price close to zero. An examination of ratios with 1934 representing the terminal and 1918 the base period was made, using much the same data and procedures as those of Duesenberry and Kistin. A price elasticity of housing close to zero was observed.

Several conditions appear to have contributed to the low coefficient of price elasticity of housing. One has already been discussed in some detail in this chapter: namely the failure of the rent index to represent the change in rent of the families represented by the 1934 survey —a failure probably attributrable to the eligibility requirements of that survey. Duesenberry and Kistin expressed some skepticism as to the accuracy of the rent index and noted that the deletion of the rent component from the Consumer Price Index improved the fit of the relative price of food and of clothing to the consumption of these products. As a consequence they postulated that the relative price of housing might be an irrelevant variable with respect to the consumption of food and clothing. However, they did not postulate that the rent index of 1934 might have been irrelevant to the explanation of consumption of housing observed in the 1934 survey.

Another condition influencing their findings is the method for holding constant change in real income. They selected the range in the income distribution where total expenditure, in dollars of constant purchasing power, was approximitely the same for the two years. Under certain conditions this would result in holding constant real normal income between years. An essential condition is that total expenditure represent normal income and that the allocation of total expenditure among consumer products is not a function of short-run change or other conditions, such as family size, which are correlated with measured income of families. The analysis of chap. ix demonstrates that this assumption is not valid. Hence, it is not surprising that the procedure used by

use of survey data to provide intertemporal estimates of elasticity of consumption with respect to income. It demonstrates that for housing such estimates may be useful supplements to time series. They may well be useful for the investigation of other consumer products. They have certain advantages over time series in that estimates of income and price elasticity are largely free from trend effects common to all cities, such as any change in preference because of the appearance of new goods on the market, the increasing importance of the population in large cities, change in services included in the rent, bias in price indexes, and the phase of the business cycle represented. They have the further advantage of being direct observations; hence they are free from effects of interpolation errors and shortcomings of secondary sources of information used, conditions that may reduce the reliability of time series.

The analysis of this monograph demonstrates that tendencies observed between years for a set of cities may give a biased estimate of income and price elasticities unless several conditions are taken into account. Cyclical change is one of these. Attention needs to be given to information best representing change in normalcy of employment opportunity. In addition, more complete information on type of consumer unit and of other services included in rent would be useful.

---

Duesenberry and Kistin for holding constant real income was not wholly effective.

An examination was made of change in housing expenditure between 1918 and 1934, holding constant real income with much the same procedure as that of Duesenberry and Kistin. This measure of housing change is symbolized by $h^d$. Among the 26 cities $h^d$ and p' are positively correlated. $r^2$ of the relationship equals .049. Holding constant the position in the income distribution represented by $h^d$, as well as o', ea', $rh_2$, and jt, a partial regression coefficient of pa' with respect to $h^d$ is observed to be -0.630. Its standard error is .287. The $R^2$ of the multiple correlation is .57. This is not inconsistent with the regression coefficients of pa' of equations (11.13) and (11.14). They are -0.447 and -0.724, respectively. Their standard errors are .205 and .183 (see Table 43, eqs. [11.13] and 11.14]).

The position in the income distribution represented by $h^d$ seems likely to have served as a proxy for that change in real income not held constant by the procedure used by Duesenberry and Kistin.

The estimate of price elasticity observed by Duesenberry and Kistin appears to have been biased downward by (a) failure to hold constant change in real normal income, (b) the failure of the rent index of 1934 to represent rent change experienced by those reporting in the 1934 survey, (c) the use of housing expenditure to represent change in housing without holding constant the importance of owner-occupancy, and (d) ignoring the effect of variation among cities in extent of cyclical change.

So far, the collection and tabulation of survey data would have been done without much thought of their usefulness for intertemporal estimates of demand of the type shown here. For this purpose greater comparability of definitions between years and collection of comparable types of information in various surveys are needed. In addition, the data should be tabulated to minimize heterogeneity between years in universe represented. For example, data by tenure should be reported, with tenant households and lodger households as separate categories. The usefulness of survey data for intertemporal estimates is contingent on the availability of price indexes for a fairly large set of cities or other areas. And later surveys might well include all cities for which a price index is available. Because of the many conditions affecting tendencies observed, observations for a large set of cities are needed.

# Chapter Twelve

# ROOMS AND THEIR OCCUPANCY

So far attention has centered on variation in the market value or rent of dwelling units or change in housing as represented by dwelling units in terms of dollars of constant purchasing power. This chapter examines variation in rooms per dwelling unit and in rooms per person with special attention to their relationship to income. It is thus concerned with physical characteristics of the dwelling units and their occupancy, characteristics that are responsive to both price and income. To most households an additional room is looked upon with favor. Low income and high cost of its acquisition and maintenance are important limiting conditions. The higher the income and the lower the cost of housing compared to other products the more rooms per dwelling per person seems likely; and, conversely, the lower the income or the higher the cost of acquiring or maintaining space the fewer the number of rooms per dwelling unit and per person seems likely. Ample space is only one of the characteristics of high-quality housing. Hence, where there is much space per person there seem likely to be other preferred characteristics. However, households will substitute space at low price combined with shabbiness for preferred facilities and newness. Hence, rooms per person are only a crude proxy for the quality of housing in general.

Extensive information is available in the 1950 census on rooms per dwelling unit and their relationship to income and to household size. Some of it is examined in this chapter together with information bearing on cost. The main topics are: (a) conditions affecting rooms and their occupancy; (b) variation in rooms and their occupancy; (c) rooms and their occupancy by income of households; (d) rooms and their occupancy among census tracts within a metro area; (e) variation among places in change from 1940 to 1950; (f) variation among places in rooms and their occupancy; (g) differences between environs versus central cities; and (h) an estimate of change from 1940 to 1950.

This chapter follows the pattern of earlier analyses. First, variables describing rooms and their occupancy and conditions related thereto are reviewed and some tendencies by conditions other than income are described. Then rooms and their occupancy are examined in relation to income of households. Next variation among subsets of households both within and among places and between environs and central cities is examined. And finally an estimate of intertemporal change is presented for a set of cities. Each type of regression contributes to an understanding of conditions causing variation in rooms per dwelling and their occupancy.

## The Variables

This chapter introduces variables related to rooms and their occupancy. The main variables of this chapter and their symbols are:

| The variable | The symbol |
|---|---|
| Average rooms per dwelling unit | $r_o$ |
| Average rooms per person (a measure of room crowding) | $r_p$ |
| Percentage of households with 1.01 or more persons per room (a second measure of room crowding) | $r_c$ |
| Number of persons per household | s |
| Importance of households with an aged or a female head | af |
| Importance of households with an aged head[1] | $a_h$ |
| Income of the primary unit of the household | y |

Other less frequently used variables are described later. The symbols here shown are those used in general discussion, where variation in rooms and their occupancy with respect to y is examined. Where interplace or other interclass correlations are specifically referred to, the symbols are shown in upper-case letters.

1. Signifying head of consumer unit is 65 years of age or more.

## Conditions Affecting Rooms and Their Occupancy

This section considers some general conditions affecting rooms of dwelling units and who is likely to occupy them.

Rooms[2] in Dwelling Units.—Number of rooms in dwelling units is similar to value of dwelling units in that it tends to be affected by (a) normal income and (b) relative cost of and preference for housing compared to other products. However, one important difference between market value of dwelling units and $r_o$ must be reckoned with. Values are volatile. They rise and fall with market conditions, and dwellings are durable entities, largely immobile. The market of second-hand automobiles is not confined to the area of initial sale. They can readily be shipped to other cities and even to a foreign market. But second-hand houses have a local market whose demand may change greatly between the time of construction and later decades when the dwellings are still in use.

Although structures are immobile, rooms within them may change. Many one-unit structures have rooms added to those of the initial structure. In addition, where conversion occurs a unit is subdivided into two or more units each with less floor space and usually fewer rooms than the original unit. Merging of units also occurs. Adding rooms to or con-

---

2. The Census of Housing of 1950 describes its count of rooms as follows: "All rooms such as kitchens, bedrooms, dining rooms, living rooms, permanently enclosed sunporches of substantial size, finished basement or attic rooms, and recreation rooms, which are used or are suitable for use as living quarters, where counted in determining the number of rooms in the dwelling unit" op. cit., "Introduction," p. 2).

Some judgment is involved as to whether a sun porch is a room and whether certain space in the dwelling unit is suitable for living quarters. Thus space not counted as a room may constitute living space from the standpoint of occupants. For example, an unfinished attic or basement may be looked upon by families as playroom for children. The extra space in a dwelling unit not represented by the room count seems likely to be more important in one-unit than in multi-unit structures and thus, in general, to be more important for owner and tenants units.

Such judgment as to room count plus variation among dwelling units in average room size result in room count being a very imperfect measure of space available to a household. Even so, it is the best measure of space and privacy available for the population in general. A start has been made in measuring floor space of one-family units being added to the stock (see Construction Review, monthly publication of U.S. Department of Commerce). Such information supplements rather than duplicates that on number of rooms, although number of rooms is likely to be positively correlated with floor space. Number of rooms has more bearing on the privacy a dwelling unit affords persons sharing it than does floor space as such.

verting and merging units of the existing stock are all methods of adapting an existing stock to change in demand. They all involve costs which undoubtedly play a part in determining the number of persons per household—for example whether a group of persons decides to live together as one household in a dwelling unit or to subdivide it in order to provide for two or more households. It would thus not be surprising if the existing stock, in some measure, determines s, in that the grouping of the population into households in some measure is an adaptation to the stock that evades the cost of changing the stock.

The rate of new construction is a measure of the extent to which the stock of any year is a function of recent decisions to build. It was relatively high during the early fifties. Yet the 1956 National Housing Inventory reported only 20 per cent of the national stock of units at that time as built in 1950 or later. This suggests a construction rate of about 3 per cent of the stock per year in a period of high-level construction. This rate is likely to bring only a gradual change in average rooms per unit.

Change in $r_o$ through conversions is likely to modify the stock less than new construction. In the 1956 stock there were 13 such units added between 1950 and 1956 for every 100 from new construction. Much of the conversion represents an adaptation of structures initially built for households of higher income. It is a part of the process of utilizing the stock through various stages of depreciation and obsolescence.

The imprint of the past will of course be related to the extent of current growth. Where population is stationary or declining, the imprint of earlier conditions, some of them long since past, is sure to be very important. The more the stock of dwelling units is growing the less the effect on it of the income, prices, and consumer preferences of an earlier generation.

Attention to change seems important even when cross-section data of cities are being examined. For example, correlation between Y and $R_o$ or $R_p$ seems likely to be affected by the direction and degree of population change.

Occupancy of Rooms.—The census of housing reports $r_o$, $r_p$, and $r_c$. Thus room occupancy can be measured in two ways, and the variables $r_p$ and $r_c$[3] both summarize the effect of the interrelation of $r_o$ and s.

3. It seems highly probable that inequality of the income distribution affects $r_c$ more than $r_p$.

Conditions likely to cause $r_o$ to change or differ with growth of cities, and much has already been said about such conditions, are likely to cause variation in s, such as the stage in the family cycle, birth rate, and the doubling up of potential households, all of which appear to be related to normal income. In addition, s may, in part, be a function of $r_o$. In other words, household size is in part an adaptation to an existing stock. Both households and the stock can be adapted. Presumably, the psychological cost to persons from the doubling up of potential households is weighed against the monetary and other costs involved in converting the existing stock. Because these interrelationships seem likely to be present, the variation among places in s, as well as in $r_o$, has been examined.

There seems little doubt that some of the improvement in the quality of housing of the nation in general has taken the form of undoubling of potential households with rise in real income. This together with the decline in the birth rate has tended to reduce s. Such declines tend to increase $r_p$, even though $r_o$ remains unchanged. In fact $r_p$ will rise so long as $r_o$ does not decline as much as s.

Things other than increase in real income have undoubtedly contributed to the decline in s. Mobility of the population is one. It has tended to increase the distance between the place of residence of parents and their adult offspring and this reduces the likelihood of parents, as they grow older, sharing the household of a son or daughter. Social security programs may also have reduced household size. This will have been their effect if they have increased the likelihood of aged persons maintaining a separate household. Such households tend to be low in s.

## Variation in Rooms and Their Occupancy

Rooms and their occupancy are affected by a great many conditions. As in earlier chapters attention centers on the effect of normal income. ($y_n$). However, incomes observed are correlated with many things likely to affect rooms and their occupancy. Some general tendencies are first reviewed. The review provides a general frame of reference for later estimates where income effects are tested. This section describes four tendencies: (a) secular change, (b) difference by type of urbanization, (c) difference by stage in the family cycle, and (d) difference by number of persons per household.

Secular Change in Rooms and Their Occupancy.—Observations describing secular change are meager. The Census of Housing of 1940 is the first to report both s and $r_o$. This information together with similar information for 1950 and 1956 indicates that $r_o$, for the nation in general, shows some tendency to increase,[4] and s a considerable tendency to decrease. The net effect has been an increase in $r_p$, from 1.46 in 1940 to 1.62 in 1956, an increase of 11 per cent in 16 years (see Table 46).

The decade of the forties saw a slight decline in $r_o$. This may well represent the effect of restrictions on housing construction. Because of them, the units constructed during the middle and the late forties may have been smaller than would have been built under normal market conditions. However, by 1956 average rooms per dwelling unit exceeded the average of 1940.

A somewhat different trend is observed when tenure is held constant. For example, for owner-occupants $r_o$ fell from 1940 to 1956. This difference between all and owner households may be compounded of a variety of conditions. The increase in the proportion of owner-occupancy is one. The increasing percentage of the owner-occupants is likely to represent those with low normal income. If normal income, with household type held constant, is an important determinant of $r_o$, then increase in importance of owner-occupancy, other things held constant, will tend to lower $r_o$ of owners. Such a change would not necessarily increase $r_o$ of tenants. No increase for them is to be expected if the net shift from tenant to owner-occupancy concentrated among tenants of relatively high normal income—that is, high among tenants. Under this condition the normal in-

4. The data shown in Table 46 represent the stock occupied in successive periods, none earlier than 1940. They are too meager either to support or challenge Winnick's conclusion that the "average dwelling unit has been shrinking for many decades" (see L. Winnick, American Housing and Its Use [New York: John Wiley & Sons, 1957], p. 9). The data supporting this conclusion represent the rooms per unit built in earlier periods that survived in the stock of 1950. The earlier the year of construction of units in the stock of 1950, the higher the number of rooms per unit. Insofar as size and survival rates are positively correlated, as seems not improbable, such data should be viewed with suspicion in reaching a judgment as to secular trend in new construction. Winnick does note that "from the early 1950's on some movement back to larger dwelling units has appeared." It may well be that no break has occurred in the upward secular trend in dwelling rooms per dwelling unit where the secular trend in income has been upward and explicit building restrictions absent. The Great Depression and the restrictions of a war economy may have brought deviations for such an upward trend. It seems unlikely, however, that reliable evidence will be forthcoming for the total stock on rooms per dwelling built prior to 1940.

come of both owners and tenants would tend to be lowered. Data shown in Table 46 indicate a fall from 1940 to 1956 in $r_o$ of both tenures, but a greater percentage fall for owners than tenants.[5]

Table 46

Median Persons and Rooms, All Households and by Tenure, United States, 1940, 1950, and 1956

| Year | Median per occupied dwelling unit | | Rooms per person[a] | Per cent of owner-occupancy |
|---|---|---|---|---|
| | Persons | Rooms | | |
| (1) | (2) | (3) | (4) | (5) |
| 1940 | 3.28 | 4.78 | 1.46 | 43.6 |
| 1950 | 3.05 | 4.69 | 1.54 | 55.0 |
| 1956 | 3.00 | 4.87 | 1.62 | 60.4 |
| | Owner-Occupants | | | |
| 1940 | 3.34 | 5.58 | 1.67 | . . . |
| 1950 | 3.19 | 5.35 | 1.68 | . . . |
| 1956 | 3.14 | 5.34 | 1.70 | . . . |
| | Tenants | | | |
| 1940 | 3.24 | 4.10 | 1.27 | . . . |
| 1950 | 2.89 | 3.83 | 1.33 | . . . |
| 1956 | 2.79 | 3.99 | 1.43 | . . . |

Source: U.S. Census of Housing: 1950, Vol. I, Part 1, Tables 9 and 10; U.S. Census of Housing: 1940, Vol. II, Part 1, Tables 8 and 9; 1956 National Housing Inventory, Vol. III, Part 1, Tables 1, 4, and 7.

a. This is median number of rooms per persons divided by median number of persons.

5. This differential change by tenure is in part a regional phenomenon. For example, between 1940 and 1950 the importance of owner-occupants increased more in the South than in the West or North. In other words, it increased most in the region of lowest average income. The percentage of owner-occupants by region is as follows:

| Region | 1940 | 1950 | 1950 with 1940 = 100 |
|---|---|---|---|
| North | 50 | 55 | 110 |
| South | 42 | 54 | 129 |
| West | 51 | 58 | 114 |

Between 1940 and 1956 $r_o$ fell more for owners than tenants. Yet, for each period represented, $r_o$ is higher for owners than tenants. Fewer persons per household among tenants than owners may contribute to this. Evidence presented later leads one to expect that the lower is s the higher tends to be $r_p$.[6] Yet for each period $r_p$ is lower for tenants than for owners. It may well be that lower income of tenants than owners accounts for this difference.

Most of the estimates shown later pertain to households stratified by tenure. However, comparison is made between tenures with average income, household type, and place held constant.

By Type of Urbanization.—For the tenures combined, little difference by type of urbanization occurs in $r_o$ or in $r_p$, in spite of considerable difference in average income (see Table 47). There is, however, some tendency for room crowding, represented by $r_c$, to be higher for rural non-farm than metro areas.[7] This occurs in spite of the fact that households with an aged or a female head tend to be more important for the rural non-farm than the metro stratum, and $r_c$ for such households tends to be low.

Characteristics of strata by type of urbanization have not been examined further. Observations are too few to permit a test of the effect of income with household type held constant. Difference in $r_o$ and $r_p$ by urbanization seems likely to be affected by cost of housing, and measures of cost by type of urbanization are not available. The data shown in Table 47 give no reason, however, to expect that secular change in $r_o$ or $r_p$, for the nation in general, has been affected by the distribution of household types by type of urbanization.

By Age and Sex of Household Head.—Average rooms per dwelling unit and their occupancy by age of and sex of household head for the metro stratum[8] of the United States are shown in Table 48. Three tendencies by age of head are important: (a) In the early stages of the family history s and $r_o$ tend to increase at about the same rate, so that little change oc-

6. This may be related to certain overhead characteristics of the dwelling units, such as the need for a kitchen irrespective of number of persons.

7. I suspect that this represents the effect of marked inequality of normal income for this strata of the population. The variation among states in average family income of rural non-farm strata of the population is relatively high.

8. The urban and rural non-farm strata show similar tendencies.

Table 47

Number of Persons and Rooms per Dwelling Unit and Related Characteristics by Degree of Urbanization and Tenure, 1950[a]

| | Income (Y) | Persons per household (S) | Rooms per dwelling unit ($R_o$) | Rooms per persons ($R_p$) | Percentage with 1.01 persons per room ($R_c$) | Percentage of household heads | | Units built in 1945 or later |
|---|---|---|---|---|---|---|---|---|
| | | | | | | Aged or female | Aged | |
| | (1) | (2) | (3) | (4) | (5) | (6) | (7) | (8) |
| Metro stratum | $3,413 | 3.00 | 4.62 | 1.54 | 13.2 | 25.1 | 13.3 | 12.1 |
| a) Owner-occupants | 3,784 | 3.26 | 5.40 | 1.66 | 8.8 | 24.3 | 15.9 | 17.2 |
| b) Tenants | 3,044 | 2.74 | 3.74 | 1.37 | 17.7 | 26.0 | 10.7 | 7.0 |
| Urban stratum | 2,771 | 2.85 | 4.59 | 1.61 | 14.1 | 29.3 | 17.6 | 12.1 |
| a) Owner-occupants | 3,000 | 2.95 | 5.23 | 1.77 | 10.0 | 31.8 | 22.0 | 14.5 |
| b) Tenants | 2,535 | 2.74 | 3.66 | 1.34 | 19.2 | 26.1 | 11.9 | 9.1 |
| Rural non-farm stratum | 2,152 | 2.98 | 4.49 | 1.51 | 19.4 | 28.0 | 19.6 | 18.2 |
| a) Owner-occupants | 2,259 | 2.88 | 4.98 | 1.73 | 14.5 | 31.8 | 23.7 | 21.5 |
| b) Tenants | $2,006 | 3.11 | 3.87 | 1.24 | 26.7 | 22.4 | 13.9 | 13.2 |

Source: U.S. Census of Housing: 1950, Vol. II, chapter 1.

a. The estimates shown represent households in all types of structures. All averages are medians.

Table 48

Number of Persons and Rooms per Household by Age and Sex and Age of Head, Metro Stratum of the United States, by Tenure, 1950[a]

| Household type by age and sex of head | Owner-occupants | | | Tenants | | | | |
|---|---|---|---|---|---|---|---|---|
| | Median persons | Percentage of households with 5 or more[b] | | Medians | | Percentage of households with 5 or more | | Rooms per persons ($R_P$) |
| | | Persons | Rooms | Persons | Rooms | Persons | Rooms | |
| | (1) | (2) | (3) | (4) | (5) | (6) | (7) | (8) |
| A. Male head, wife present, no non-relatives | | | | | | | | |
| 1) Under 35 years | 3.7 | 22.8 | 60.2 | 3.1 | 3.58 | 13.6 | 22.2 | 1.15 |
| 2) 35 - 45 | 4.0 | 34.0 | 77.6 | 3.6 | 3.98 | 25.7 | 26.1 | 1.10 |
| 3) 45 - 55 | 3.4 | 24.7 | 81.3 | 3.0 | 4.14 | 19.4 | 41.1 | 1.38 |
| 4) 55 - 65 | 2.7 | 17.0 | 80.6 | 2.5 | 4.20 | 12.7 | 42.9 | 1.68 |
| 5) 65 years or more | 2.4 | 11.9 | 76.8 | 2.3 | 4.02 | 8.2 | 37.9 | 1.75 |
| B. Other male head | | | | | | | | |
| 1) Under 45 years | 3.9 | 40.0 | 76.1 | 2.3 | 3.36 | 18.4 | 27.2 | 1.46 |
| 2) 45 - 65 | 3.2 | 25.8 | 78.1 | 1.9 | 3.44 | 12.5 | 30.5 | 1.81 |
| 3) 65 years or more | 2.6 | 15.0 | 75.2 | 1.5 | 3.24 | 5.3 | 27.8 | 2.16 |
| C. Female head | | | | | | | | |
| 1) Under 45 years | 2.9 | 19.0 | 67.1 | 2.1 | 3.18 | 11.0 | 17.8 | 1.51 |
| 2) 45 - 65 | 2.3 | 14.1 | 74.0 | 1.8 | 3.54 | 8.2 | 26.7 | 1.97 |
| 3) 65 years or more | 2.0 | 8.7 | 73.4 | 1.4 | 3.42 | 3.8 | 25.5 | 2.44 |

Source: U.S. Census of Housing: 1950, Vol. II, chapter 1, Table B.

a. The estimates shown represent households in all types of structure.

b. This measure of persons and rooms is used because the data available do not permit an estimate of median rooms per dwelling units by household type for the owner-occupants. The percentages do, however, give some indication of the low relationship between rooms and persons.

curs in $r_p$. (b) The peak in $r_o$ tends to occur when the household head is around 55 years. This is the peak on the age-income cycle. It occurs later than the peak of s, so that for a while $r_p$ falls slightly with increase in age of head. This may represent a lag in the increase of $r_o$ behind s. Or it may represent the tendency for $r_p$ to rise as the ratio of adults to children in the household increases—a common tendency after the head passes 50 years of age. (c) Among households with head 55 years of age or more, there is only a slight tendency for $r_o$ to decline with increased age of head, even though s declines greatly. The increase in size between young and middle-aged heads is accompanied by corresponding increase in $r_o$, but fall in s between middle-aged and aged head brings little change in $r_o$. Consequently, $r_p$ is very high for households with an aged head. It is especially high for those with an aged female head. Aged female more than aged male heads represent the final stage in the life cycle of families. These tendencies reflect a willingness of aged heads to devote a higher percentage of their resources to housing, perhaps, in part, because of a desire to retain familiar surroundings. It should be noted, however, that the space occupied by the aged is relatively low cost because of the obsolescence of the dwelling units. The higher the age of the household head, the higher seems likely to be the age of the dwelling unit occupied.

There thus seems good reason to expect that room occupancy of any set of households will be much affected by its mixture of types. Where young heads are important, $r_c$ will tend to be high and $r_p$ low, and where aged heads are important $r_c$ will be low and $r_p$ high.[9] Thus, to estimate the relation of $r_c$ and $r_p$ to normal income, the mixture of household types must be held constant.

The importance of households with an aged or a female head, symbolized by af, has been used extensively in earlier chapters to hold constant the effect of variation in mixture. It is so used in this chapter. A variable representing the importance of households with an aged head is also used. It is symbolized by $a_h$.[10] The expectation is that $a_h$, to a great-

9. Increased mobility of the aged population, for example change of city of residence with retirement, may modify tendencies by age of head as indicated by the 1950 census.

10. These two variables ignore variation among places in the relative importance of young- and middle-aged heads. One analysis presented later gives direct representation to the importance of younger heads. It is described later.

er extent than af, will serve as a proxy for earlier conditions affecting the current stock of dwelling units. It also seems likely that households with a female head under 65 years of age, represented by af but not by $a_h$, are more likely than other households to have lodgers present.

By Number of Persons Per Household.—The higher is s the higher tends to be $r_o$. However, with household types ignored the variation in $r_o$ with s is small, so that the higher is s the lower tends to be $r_p$. These tendencies are common to both tenures. They are illustrated in Table 49 using data for the metro stratum of the United States for 1950.

As household size rises from 1 to 10 persons, $r_o$ for owners rises from 4.5 to 6.5, and for tenants from 2.4 to 5.1. This increase in s is accompanied by a fall in $r_p$, for owners, from 4.50 to 0.59 and, for tenants, from 2.38 to 0.47. These tendencies indicate less correlation between $r_o$ and s for owner than tenant households. Lesser mobility of owner than tenant households would contribute to this. In other words, throughout the household-size cycle owners less than tenants change the number of rooms in the dwelling unit occupied.

For every household size $r_p$ is higher for owners than tenants. This difference is not surprising since owners have higher average income than tenants.

The percentage of households with 1.01 or more persons per room, symbolized by $r_c$, rises with s. It is especially high for households of five or more persons. It seems not unlikely that the tendency observed is affected by the negative correlation between s and normal income, when age and sex of household head are held constant (see chap. iv).

The tendencies illustrated in Tables 48 and 49 make it obvious that any estimate of rooms and their occupancy with respect to normal income should give attention to age and sex of head as well as to number of persons per household. They show that $r_p$ and $r_c$ are closely correlated with number of persons per household, especially as number of persons is correlated with age of household head.

## Rooms and Their Occupancy by Income of Households

The higher is measured income of consumer units (y), the higher tends to be $r_o$ and s. The increase in $r_o$ with y is small, and for some portion of the income distribution the rise in s outstrips the rise in $r_o$, so that the higher is y the lower tends to be $r_p$. This tendency is com-

Table 49

Number of Rooms per Household and Related Characteristics by Persons per Household, Metro Stratum of the United States, by Tenure, 1950

| Number of persons per household | Owner-occupants | | | Tenants | | |
|---|---|---|---|---|---|---|
| | Mean rooms per dwelling unit[a] (1) | Rooms per person (2) | Percentage of households with 1.01 persons per room (3) | Mean rooms per dwelling unit[a] (4) | Rooms per person (5) | Percentage of households with 1.01 persons per room (6) |
| 1 | 4.50 | 4.50 | 0.0 | 2.38 | 2.38 | 0.0 |
| 2 | 5.07 | 2.54 | 0.8 | 3.34 | 1.67 | 4.6 |
| 3 | 5.29 | 1.76 | 1.6 | 3.89 | 1.30 | 10.5 |
| 4 | 5.54 | 1.39 | 4.2 | 4.23 | 1.06 | 25.2 |
| 5 | 5.83 | 1.17 | 15.9 | 4.56 | 0.91 | 48.3 |
| 6 | 6.02 | 1.00 | 33.1 | 4.79 | 0.80 | 68.9 |
| 7 | 6.17 | 0.88 | 59.7 | 4.89 | 0.70 | 86.9 |
| 8 | 6.26 | 0.78 | 73.2 | 4.92 | 0.62 | 92.7 |
| 9 | 6.36 | 0.71 | 84.7 | 4.98 | 0.55 | 94.7 |
| 10 or more | 6.46 | 0.59 | 88.5 | 5.12 | 0.47 | 97.0 |

Source: U.S. Census of Housing: 1950, Vol. II, chapter 1, Table B-5.

a. The assumption was made that dwelling units with 10 or more rooms had a mean of 11 rooms.

mon to the two tenures and is illustrated in Table 50 by data for the metro stratum of the United States.

The small increase in $r_o$ with y is not surprising. This is the tendency to expect because of the great importance of $y_t$. The even smaller increase in $r_p$ with y occurs because s is positively correlated with y, which is largely a function of the age of head. Hence $r_p$ in relation to y reflects conditions associated with age of head.

Stratification of households by age of head would tend to increase the linearity of the regression of $r_p$ with respect to y and to increase the tendency for $r_p$ to rise with y. However, elasticity of $r_p$ with respect to y would tend to be low because of $y_t$.

Tendencies such as those shown in Table 50 led Winnick[11] to conclude that "the lowest income groups tend to enjoy surprisingly favorable PPR[12] ratios; overcrowding is most frequent in the groups that lie between the bottom and the middle of the income structure." He sounded a note of warning with respect to this interpretation: "Quite clearly, at the lowest income levels, income is not representative of consumer expenditures or living standards." Nevertheless, he concluded that "the relation between density and income is not as strong or as straightforward as is often believed."[13] However, the tendencies observed when age of head and $y_t$ are held constant indicate that the relationship between density of room occupancy and normal income is very strong and very straightforward and that room crowding is a very important characteristic of housing where $y_n$ is low. Such a tendency is now to be described.

### Room Occupancy among Census Tracts within a Metro Area

Chapter vii indicates that average income of households by census tract ($Y^a$) will under certain circumstances be a good proxy for normal income. A necessary condition is that employment level is normal. The metro area of Chicago during 1949 appears to have been fairly normal[14]

---

11. *Op. cit.*, p. 8.

12. This symbolizes persons per room. It is positively correlated with $r_c$ and negatively correlated with $r_p$.

13. *Ibid.*, p. 25.

14. The percentage of the male labor force with less than 26 weeks of work during 1949 of this area was close to the average of all metro areas.

Table 50

Number of Rooms per Household and Related Characteristics, by Income of Primary Unit of Households and Tenure, Metro Stratum of the United States, 1950

| Income in 1949 | Owner-occupants | | | | Tenants | | | |
|---|---|---|---|---|---|---|---|---|
| | Median | | Rooms per person | Percentage with 1.01 persons per room | Median | | Rooms per person | Percentage with 1.01 persons per room |
| | Persons (1) | Rooms (2) | (3) | (4) | Persons (5) | Rooms (6) | (7) | (8) |
| Under $1,000 | 2.4 | 5.08 | 2.12 | 6.3 | 2.0 | 3.18 | 1.59 | 15.7 |
| $1,000 - $2,000 | 2.5 | 4.96 | 1.98 | 11.1 | 2.4 | 3.29 | 1.37 | 22.4 |
| 2,000 - 3,000 | 3.1 | 5.05 | 1.63 | 12.0 | 2.8 | 3.60 | 1.29 | 21.8 |
| 3,000 - 4,000 | 3.4 | 5.17 | 1.52 | 10.4 | 3.0 | 3.86 | 1.29 | 18.8 |
| 4,000 - 5,000 | 3.5 | 5.34 | 1.53 | 8.8 | 3.0 | 4.01 | 1.34 | 15.4 |
| 5,000 - 6,000 | 3.5 | 5.54 | 1.58 | 7.3 | 2.9 | 4.10 | 1.41 | 12.7 |
| 6,000 - 7,500 | 3.5 | 5.71 | 1.63 | 6.9 | 2.9 | 4.24 | 1.46 | 11.5 |
| 7,500 - 10,000 | 3.8 | 5.98 | 1.58 | 7.2 | 3.1 | 4.44 | 1.43 | 12.0 |
| $10,000 or more | 3.7 | 6.82 | 1.84 | 4.3 | 2.8 | 4.60 | 1.64 | 8.3 |

Source: U.S. Census of Housing: 1950, Vol. II, chapter 1, Table B-7.

in this respect. Accordingly, room occupancy with respect to $Y^a$ has been examined for this metro area.

Information on percentage of households with 1.01 or more persons per room is reported by census tract.[15] This measure of room crowding is symbolized by $R_c{}^a$. For the set of 88 tracts, represented by the data of Tables 51, 52, and 53, $R_c{}^a$ ranges from 5 to 28 per cent. $Y^a$ explains 55 per cent of this variation, $S^a$ explains 36 per cent. Together they explain 71 per cent. The higher $Y^a$ the lower tends to be $R_c{}^a$ and the higher $S^a$ the higher tends to be $R_c{}^a$. The partial income elasticity of $R_c{}^a$ ($\eta_{R_cY}{}^a$) is -2.74 and the partial elasticity of $R_c{}^a$ with respect to $S^a$ ($\eta_{R_cS}{}^a$) is 4.33.

Table 51

Characteristics of Housing and Related Characteristics, among 88 Census Tracts, Chicago Metro Area, 1950[a]

| | Symbol | Variables | |
|---|---|---|---|
| | | Mean | Range |
| 1. Median | | | |
| a) income of families and unrelated individuals | $Y^a$ | \$4,445 | \$3,225 - \$ 6,385 |
| b) value of owner-occupied dwellings in one-unit structures | $H^a$ | \$12,145 | \$5,981 - \$18,974 |
| 2. Population per household | $S^a$ | 3.61 | 3.26 - 3.94 |
| 3. Percentage of households with 1.01 persons per room | $R_c{}^a$ | 10.2 | 4.8 - 28.1 |
| 4. Number of unrelated individuals per 100 families | $U^a$ | 7 | 0 - 10 |
| 5. Percentage of dwelling units | | | |
| a) built in 1940 or later | $B^a$ | 39 | 0 - 95 |
| b) with owner-occupancy | $O^a$ | 79 | 66 - 96 |
| 6. Percentage of adult males 60 years of age or more per 100 21 years of age or more | $A_m{}^a$ | 7.2 | 3.7 - 15.9 |

Source: U.S. Census of Population: 1950, Vol. III, chapter 10.

a. See Table 31, fn. a, for description of the set of census tracts represented here.

These coefficients are affected by holding constant several additional variables representing conditions that seem likely to account for some of the variation in $R_c{}^a$. Among those whose effect was tested are: (a) the

15. Average rooms per dwelling unit are not reported by census tracts for 1950.

importance of adult males 60 years of age or more, (b) the number of unrelated individuals per 100 families, (c) the percentage of the dwelling units built in 1940 or later, and (d) the percentage of owner-occupancy. For the most part, partial regression coefficients of the variables representing these conditions are twice their standard error. However, their addition has only a minor effect on the regression coefficient of $Y^a$ and $S^a$; the $R^2$ of the relationship is increased only from .71 to .76 (see Table 52).

Table 52

Coefficients of Correlation, Percentage of Households with 1.01 or More Persons per Room ($R_c{}^a$) with Respect to Several Sets of Related Conditions among 88 Census Tracts, Chicago Metro Area, 1950[a]

| | (1) | (2) | (3) | (4) | (5) | (6) |
|---|---|---|---|---|---|---|
| 1. $R^2$ | .527 | .708 | .716 | .731 | .745 | .760 |
| 2. Constant | 12.831 | 8.553 | 9.444 | 8.702 | 8.632 | 7.424 |
| 3. Median income ($Y^a$) | -3.254 | -2.743 | -2.828 (.275) | -2.640 (.283) | -2.656 (.278) | -2.307 (.313) |
| 4. Number of persons per household ($S^a$) | . . . . . | 4.333 | 3.441 (.819) | 3.487 (.802) | 3.385 (.788) | 3.919 (.806) |
| 5. Percentage of adult males 60 years of age or more[b] ($A_m{}^a$) | | . . . . . | -0.007 (.004) | -0.011 (.005) | -0.005 (.005) | -0.007 (.005) |
| 6. Number of unrelated with individuals period families ($U^a$) | | | . . . . . | 0.013 (.006) | 0.014 (.006) | 0.013 (.006) |
| 7. Percentage of units built in 1940 or later ($B^a$) | | | | . . . . . | 0.073 (.035) | 0.090 (.035) |
| 8. Percentage of units owner-occupied[b] ($O^a$) | | | | | . . . . . | -0.004 (.002) |

Source: U.S. Census of Population: 1950, Bul. P-D 10.

a. See Table 31 for description of tracts represented.

b. These variables are expressed in arithmetic form. All others are in log form.

The following tendencies seem of some interest: (a) The higher the percentage of adult males that are 60 years of age or more, the lower tends to be $R_c{}^a$. This is the effect to be expected by ratios shown in Table 48. (b) The higher the number of unrelated individuals per family in a tract, the higher tends to be $R_c{}^a$. This is the effect to be expected if, for this set of tracts, the unrelated individuals for the most part are lodgers. Their negative correlation with $Y^a$ makes this seem likely (see Table 53). (c) With $Y^a$ and $S^a$ held constant, the higher the percentage of dwelling units built in 1940 or later, the higher tends to be $R_c{}^a$. Several conditions could contribute to this tendency. One is that newly constructed units of this period tend to be occupied by households in a stage when family size tend to be at its peak and when income has not yet reached its peak on the age-income cycle of the head. Another is that restrictions on building during much of the forties resulted in $R_o{}^a$ being low.[16] And

Table 53

Correlation Matrix of Variables Representing Room Occupancy ($R_c{}^a$) and Related Conditions, among 88 Census Tracts, Chicago Metro Area 1950[a]

| Variables | Variables | | | | | |
|---|---|---|---|---|---|---|
| | $Y^a$ (1) | $S^a$ (2) | $A_m{}^a$ (3) | $U^a$ (4) | $B^a$ (5) | $O^a$ (6) |
| 1. $R_c{}^a$ | -.726 | .599 | -.387 | .052 | .356 | -.058 |
| 2. $Y^a$ | ... | -.258 | .036 | -.239 | -.009 | .353 |
| 3. $S^a$ | | ... | -.678 | -.344 | .518 | .460 |
| 4. $A_m{}^a$ | | | ... | .574 | -.726 | -.582 |
| 5. $U^a$ | | | | ... | -.445 | -.471 |
| 6. $B^a$ | | | | | ... | .541 |

a. See Tables 51 and 52 for description of these variables.

still another is that much of the construction of this period was occupied by households who chose new construction, in a period of increased cost, for larger and shabbier dwelling units surviving from the earlier stock.

The high intertract income elasticity of $R_c{}^a$ is consistent with the high $\eta_{HY}{}^a$ described in chapter vii. It stands in marked contrast to the low income elasticity of $r_c$ with respect to y that is observed. Figure 23 illustrates the striking difference in the tendencies indicated by the two types of regression from the metro area of Chicago. Where y is the ex-

16. For the metro area of Chicago the median number of rooms per owner-occupied unit of 1950 is less for units built during the forties than earlier, being 5.09 and 5.45 rooms, respectively.

planatory variable, $r_c$ first rises, then flattens and later shows some tendency to fall, then reverses itself and rises somewhat, and at the extreme upper tail of the income distribution shows some tendency to decline (see Table 50). On the other hand, among census tracts $R_c^a$ falls

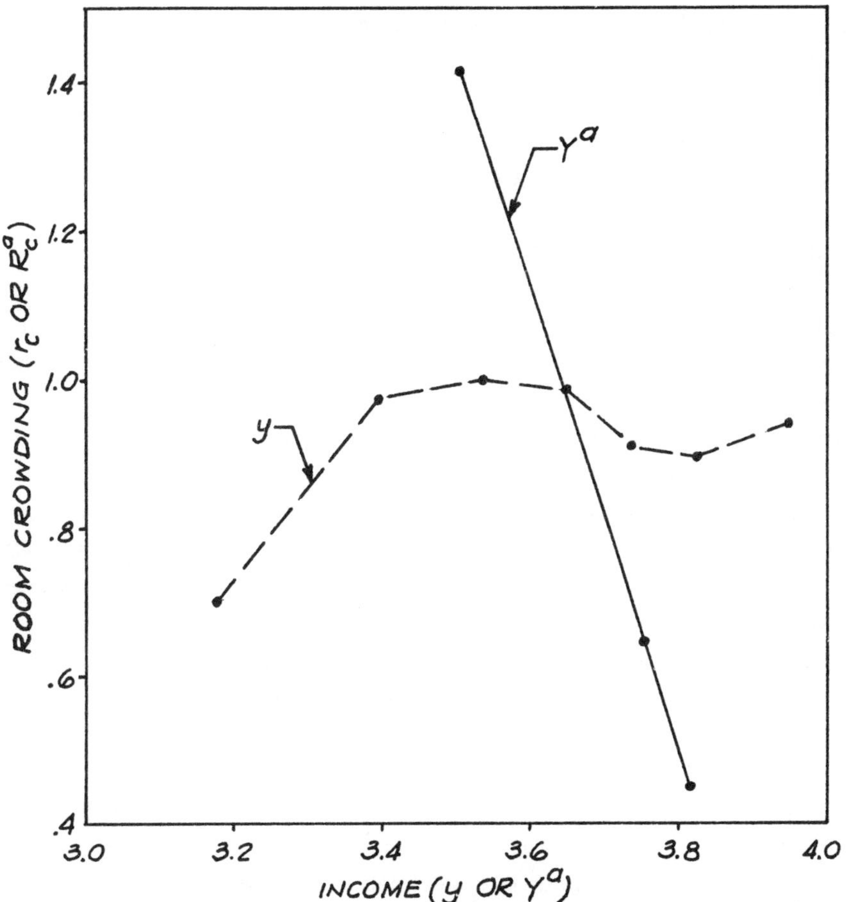


Fig. 23.—Percentage of households with 1.01 or more persons per room with respect to income of households (y) or average income among census tracts ($Y^a$), Chicago metro area, 1950.[a] (Variables in log form.)

Source of data: U.S. Bureau of the Census, Census of Housing: 1950, Vol. II, chap. 38, Table A-7, and Census of Population: 1950, Vol. III, chap. 10.

a. The regression representing tendencies among census tracts is estimated from coefficients shown in Table 52, column 1. It is an interpolation of the observations. Only the range of $Y^a$ among the tracts is represented.

very, very markedly with rise in $Y^a$. Probably nowhere in this monograph is the failure of y to represent $y_n$ better illustrated than in Figure 23. The low point of $r_c$ where y is low and the wobbles of the curve of $r_c$ with respect to y represent the variation in the mixture of household types at various points of the income distribution, and the general flatness of the middle income range reflects the importance of $y_t$.

### Variation among Places in Change from 1940 to 1950

If the stock of dwelling units were highly responsive to current demand, variation in $R_o$ among places should be explained by Y, the relative cost of the dwelling unit and the cost of its maintenance compared to other consumer products. However, housing stock being durable, the income horizon affecting consumer decisions seems likely to be relatively long and the production period involves several months. So in large measure the stock represents decisions of earlier periods, and these bear the imprint of past incomes and costs at the time when units entered the stock or were later modified. The history of a stock of dwelling units would not affect intercity correlations if the lag were similar in all places. Such uniformity did not occur: Cities differ in rates of growth and in secular change in average income of consumer units and the price of housing of a given quality. Hence, the stock of any one period differs in the mixture of construction costs and of income of consumer units at the time the units entered the stock. In addition, the mixture of household types differs appreciably among cities, since this is much affected by the migration associated with the rise and decline of city size. These conditions make it seem likely that important variation occurred in 1950 among cities in the lag of $r_o$ behind change in demand and in cost.

This section is primarily concerned with variation among cities in change from 1940 to 1950 and with tendencies likely to be observed because of it. Change is illustrated using data for a set of 57 cities that seem likely to be quite representative of general tendencies affecting urban places.[17]

Change in $R_o$ of Cities between 1940 and 1950.—It has already been noted that between 1940 and 1950 a slight decline occurred in $r_o$ for dwelling units in general. That average summarizes marked difference in the

---

17. See Table 57 for a description of this set.

change of various places. In general the higher was $R_o$ in 1940, the less is the increase of $R_o$ from 1940 to 1950.[18] Where the 57 cities are ranked by $R_o$ of 1940,[19] the following tendencies are observed:

| $R_o$ In 1940 | $R_o$ For sets of cities[20] 1940 | 1950 | $R_o$ In 1950 (1940 equals 100) |
|---|---|---|---|
| Under 4.00 | 3.73 | 3.95 | 106 |
| 4.00 to 5.00 | 4.53 | 4.49 | 99 |
| 5.00 or more | 5.58 | 5.34 | 96 |

Thus in cities in which 1940 dwelling units averaged less than 4.0 rooms, over the decade $R_o$ increased by 6 per cent, and in those where they averaged 5.0 rooms or more it decreased by 4 per cent.[21]

Since the housing stock is durable and immobile and housing decisions tend to have a long horizon, there seems no reason to suppose that these changes in $R_o$ fully reflect changes in demand and in cost. These will of course have a very different effect on the new than the existing stock. Units entering the stock will respond to current situations, such as income and relative cost or price. These will also affect withdrawals from and conversions and mergers of existing stock. Where the effect of rise in relative costs outstrips rise in real income, one should expect to find conversions of considerable importance and $R_o$ of new units to be below the average of the existing stock.

The impact of difference among cities in secular trend of income and of cost of housing should be most clearly seen in the dwelling units entering the stock. The possible effect of such difference is illustrated

18. This estimate pertains to the entire urban housing stock. A similar estimate by tenure would be influenced by the net shift of dwelling units from tenant to owner occupancy during the forties. For example, a marked decline occurred between 1940 and 1950 in the average number of rooms per tenant units. Much of this decrease appears to represent the shift of units relatively high in $r_o$ from tenant to owner occupancy. For discussion of this shift see Reid, "Increase in Rent of Dwelling Units from 1940 to 1950," op. cit.

19. The number of cities represented in these sets is 11, 32, and 14, respectively.

20. These are means of the medians of cities.

21. Because of these differences in rates of change the variation of $R_o$ among places tended to decline: The variance of the log of $R_o$ of the 57 cities fell from .0631 for 1940 to .0488 for 1959—a decline of 23 per cent. This narrowing could have been stimulated by market restrictions or it could reflect increased equality of average income among places.

using data for the two cities,[22] in the set of 57 cities referred to above, that represent the extremes of change in $R_o$ between 1940 and 1950: the one with the greatest increase in $R_o$ and the other with the greatest decrease. For specified types of units in the stock, $R_o$ is given in Table 54. Thus the city with the highest increase in $R_o$ between 1940 and 1950 shows the following tendencies: In the 1950 stock $R_o$ of units built in 1945 or later is 36 per cent above $R_o$ of the 1940 stock, and that of units built from 1940 to 1945 is very similar. Furthermore, $R_o$ of the units in the

Table 54

Average Rooms per Dwelling Unit ($R_o$) in 1950, by Year of Building, in the Two Cities[a] with the Greatest Change from 1940 to 1950

| Stock represented | Increase in $R_o$ | | Decrease in $R_o$ | |
|---|---|---|---|---|
| 1940 stock[b] | 3.43 | 100 | 4.58 | 100 |
| 1950 stock[c] built in | | | | |
| 1945 or later | 4.67 | 136 | 4.21 | 92 |
| 1940 - 1945 | 4.62 | 135 | 3.91 | 85 |
| Prior to 1940 | 3.48 | 101 | 4.34 | 95 |

Source: *U.S. Census of Housing: 1940*, Vol. II, Part 1, Table 79, and *U.S. Census of Housing: 1950*, Vol. II, chapters 90 and 156, Table B-5.

a. The cities are Wichita, Kansas and Memphis, Tennessee. See fn. 22 for discussion of this selection.

b. All dwelling units in the stock are represented.

c. Occupied units only are represented. This information is not available for the entire stock. However, the vacancy rate was low in 1950.

1950 stock remaining from 1940 is slightly higher than $R_o$ of the 1940 stock. This implies some disappearance of units of 1940 low in $R_o$ and/or rooms having been added to the units of the 1940 stock.

The reverse of these tendencies is observed for the city experiencing the greatest decrease in $R_o$: In the 1950 stock $R_o$ of units built in

22. The cities are Wichita, Kansas and Memphis, Tennessee. A similar comparison could be made for a very large set of cities. The labor involved in computing median rooms for the stock of 1950 by year built made this unfeasible. However, other evidence makes it seem not unlikely that these two cities represent the play of forces bringing change in the existing stock and influencing the character of the new stock.

1945 or later is lower by 8 per cent than $R_0$ of the 1940 stock, and that of units built in 1940 to 1945 is even lower. In addition $R_0$ of the stock remaining from 1940 is lower by 5 per cent than $R_0$ of the 1940 stock. A relatively high conversion rate during the forties could have caused the second drop. In general, these changes[23] are the type to expect if the effect in rise in normal income had been offset by rise in the price of housing or by an increase in the effect of other conditions tending to limit rooms per dwelling.

Change in Average Income of Cities between 1940 and 1950.—There is considerable evidence of increased equality of income among regions. The U.S. Department of Commerce makes available estimates of per capita income by states beginning with 1929.[24] These show states low in average income in 1929 gaining at a greater rate than those high in 1929. Change in income among cities shows a similar pattern. The 1940 and 1950 censuses report, for large cities, wage and salary income of the experienced labor force. The lower such income for 1939, the greater its percentage increase between 1939 and 1949. For the set of cities[25] described above, the changes indicated by the data are given in Table 55. Thus, during the decade of the forties, average wage and salary income rose by 195 per cent in cities with average wage and salary income of 1939 below $800, and by 144 per cent in cities where it was $1,100 or more. Some of this difference in increase in income may represent cyclical change and some may represent change in the average age of worker. However, variation among places in increase in income is positively correlated with change in $R_0$ of cities described above. For the four categories of cities shown above, that is with cities ranked by average income of 1939, average rooms per dwelling units in 1950 (with those of 1940 equal to 100) are as follows: 1.04, 1.01, 0.97, and 0.96. Thus $R_0$ in-

---

23. Other conditions include (a) the progressive income tax, the incidence of which tends to be relatively high in 1949 in places that experienced relatively low increase in money income during the forties and (b) a rise in occupational expenses so that increase in money income tends to overstate the increase available for consumption apart from job-related expenditure.

24. See Office of Business Economics (Department of Commerce), U.S. Income and Output, Supplement to the Survey of Current Business, 1958, pp. 156-57.

25. Fifty-two places are represented. They are fairly evenly distributed among the income categories shown. Five cities in the set of 57 are excluded because of lack of income data for 1939.

creased by 4 per cent in cities where incomes were the lowest in 1939 and rose by a relatively high rate, and decreased by 4 per cent in cities where the income of 1939 was highest and increased at a relatively low rate.

Table 55

Median Wage and Salary Income of Males during 1949 of Cities Ranked by Median Wage and Salary Income of Males during 1939

| Median wage and salary income of 1939 | Mean of average wage and salary income of males[a] | | 1949 with 1939 equal to $100[b] |
|---|---|---|---|
| | 1939 | 1949 | |
| Under $800 | $ 698 | $2,062 | $295 |
| $800 to $1,000 | 887 | 2,433 | 274 |
| $1,000 to $1,100 | 1,046 | 2,673 | 256 |
| $1,100 or more | $1,165 | $2,838 | $244 |

a. The incomes represented are wage and salary income of all experienced male labor force. All averages are medians. They were computed from distributions shown in the U.S. Census of Population: 1940, Vol. III, Table 15, and U.S. Census of Population: 1950, Vol. II, Table 94. Some change shown between years may represent transitory income related to current employment opportunity, either in 1939 or 1949. But its effect seems likely to be rather small. The correlation of the two sets of income is very high, and there is no reason to suppose that the average transitory income of places in 1939 and 1949 were correlated. The $r^2$ of the average wage and salary income of 1939 and 1949 described by these data is probably around .8.

b. Change in average income represents two things: (a) experience of a population stationary as to place of residence but changing in age distribution, and in employment and income opportunities within their environment, and (b) population mobility. Population mobility may raise or lower average income of a place. It seems likely to have been one of the important factors tending to increase the equality of income among places. The measures of change shown tend to understate the extent to which low- compared to high-income places have experienced increases in disposable income.

Change in Cost of Residential Construction of Cities between 1939 and 1949.—There has been an upward trend in the cost of residential construction, and according to the Boeckh index its increase during the forties differed somewhat among cities. During the forties it rose more in places where it was low in 1939 than where it was high. Cities, grouped by level of the index in 1939, show changes in cost as given in Table 56.

Such change in cost seems likely to have checked increase in $R_o$ more in places where cost had formerly been low than where it had been high. However, its effect is merged with other kinds of change. It is, for example, positively correlated with the change in income, in population, and in importance of new units added to the stock. Where income rose, the greatest rise in the cost appears to have been insufficient to offset the upward push on $R_o$ from increase in Y.

Table 56

Change in the Residential Construction Cost Index, 1939 to 1949, 47 Cities[a] by Intercity Residential Construction Cost Index of 1939

| Intercity cost index as of 1939[a] | Index of 1949 with that of 1939 equal to 100 |
|---|---|
| Low | 214 |
| Moderate | 204 |
| High | 194 |

Source: Information as to construction cost indexes was made available by E. W. Boeckh & Associates.

a. The 47 cities are uniformly distributed among these categories.

A Concluding Comment.—The evidence of change between 1940 and 1950 presented above was assembled only after an examination of tendencies described in the section that follows. The estimates presented below leave no doubt that the stock of 1950 in part represented a lag of change in $R_o$ behind change in demand and probably also behind change in cost, and that the lag varied among places.

## Variation among Places in Rooms and Their Occupancy

Variation among places in rooms and their occupancy is examined below for owners and tenants of the central city and environs of 57 metro areas.[26] Four sets of observations are thus examined describing tendencies among places for two contiguous populations homogeneous as

26. To minimize computational cost the main analysis was restricted to the metro areas represented in the estimates shown in chapter 8 pertaining to difference between environs and the central city. To these metro areas were added those represented by the CPI for which data are reported for one and only one central city. These criteria provided a set of 57 metro areas.

to tenure and for the two tenures standardized as to type of environment. These will be referred to as the four sets of places. They are symbolized by $C_o$, $C_t$, $E_o$, and $E_t$, referring to owners and tenants of the central city and environs, respectively.

This section describes tendencies among these sets of places. Its main topics are: (a) variables representing interplace difference, (b) variation among places in $R_o$, (c) variation among places in $R_p$, (d) variation among places in $R_c$, (e) variation among places in S, and (f) variation of residuals.

Variables Representing Interplace Difference.—The main variables explaining $R_o$, $R_p$, and $R_c$ are average income, employment opportunity, and mixture of household types. With few exceptions[27] the variables are expressed in log form. Their mean and range for the $C_o$ set, that is owner-occupants of central cities, are summarized in Table 57. Those of the other three sets have a similar range. In fact, the four sets have many features in common, including similar correlation among the variables. (The correlation matrix is shown in Table 58 for each of the four sets of places.)

Variation in four characteristics of rooms and their occupancy is examined: average number of rooms per occupied dwelling unit ($R_o$), average number of rooms per person ($R_p$), the percentage of households with 1.01 persons per room ($R_c$), and average number of persons per household (S). The variable $R_o$ represents a physical characteristic of the stock and seems likely to be much affected by income and cost at the time of construction and hence is the characteristic most affected by lag of the stock behind change in demand and in price. The variations in $R_p$ and $R_c$ seem likely to have been affected by the physical characteristics of the stock as well as by the age distribution of the population.

The correlation between the two measures of room occupancy, namely $R_p$ and $R_c$, is high.

| Sets of Places | $r^2$ |
|---|---|
| $C_o$ | .815 |
| $C_t$ | .887 |
| $E_o$ | .815 |
| $E_t$ | .933 |

27. See Table 58, fn. a, for information on exceptions.

Table 57

Rooms per Dwelling Unit, Their Occupancy, and Related Characteristics, Owner-Occupants,[a] among 57[b] Cities, 1950[c]

| Variable | Symbol of the variable | Mean | Range |
|---|---|---|---|
| A. Rooms and their utilization | | | |
| 1) Median rooms | $R_o$ | 5.60 | 4.7 - 6.9 |
| 2) Percentage of households with 1.01 persons per room | $R_c$ | 7.9 | 2.7 - 21.9 |
| 3) Number of rooms per person | $R_p$ | 1.68 | 1.39 - 2.06 |
| B. Income of 1949 | | | |
| 1) Median money income | Y | $3,750 | $2,774 - $4,607 |
| 2) Percentage of the male labor force with less than 26 weeks of work | Le | 13.5 | 9.6 - 20.0 |
| C. Households | | | |
| 1) Median persons | S | 3.33 | 2.81 - 3.81 |
| 2) Importance of households with | | | |
| a) an aged or a female head | Af | 135 | 119 - 152 |
| b) an aged head | $A_h$ | 119 | 106 - 131 |
| c) lodgers | Lo | 107 | 104 - 113 |
| D. Percentage of dwelling units built | | | |
| 1) 1945 or later | $B_1$ | 14 | 1 - 39 |
| 2) 1940 through 1944 | $B_2$ | 9 | 0 - 28 |
| E. Other characteristics of the city | | | |
| 1) Importance of persons | | | |
| a) Changing dwelling unit but not county—1949 - 1930 | Cd | 117 | 106 - 129 |
| b) Changing county 1949 - 1950 | Ip | 106 | 102 - 117 |
| 2) Population per square mile | De | 7,360 | 2,861 - 17,779 |
| 3) Area of the city, square miles | Ar | 48 | 7 - 199 |
| 4) Population of metropolitan area in 1950 per 100 in 1940 | Po'' | 130 | 85 - 192 |

Source: U.S. Census of Housing: 1950, Vol. II, and U.S. Census of Population: 1950, Vol. II.

a. Those in one-unit structures only.

b. These are the central cities of the 40 metropolitan areas represented in Table 29 and those of additional metropolitan areas represented in Table 23 that have only one central city, for which data are reported. Because of it, several large metro areas represented by estimates of Table 29 are excluded, e.g. New York, Chicago, Boston, Philadelphia, Minneapolis-St. Paul, Los Angeles, and San Francisco. Nevertheless large metropolitan areas are represented by this set by Birmingham, Cleveland, Detroit, Houston, Milwaukee, Pittsburgh, St. Louis, San Diego, and Seattle.

Table 58

Correlation Matrix of Variables Representing Rooms, Their Occupancy, and Related Characteristics, among Central City and Environs of 57 Metro Areas, by Tenure, 1950[a]

| Variables | Rc (1) | Rp (2) | Y (3) | Le (4) | S (5) | Af (6) | Ah (7) | Lo (8) | $B_1$ (9) | $B_2$ (10) | De (11) | Ar[b] (12) | Cd (13) | Ip (14) |
|---|---|---|---|---|---|---|---|---|---|---|---|---|---|---|
| **Panel A: Owners in Central Cities ($C_o$ Set)** | | | | | | | | | | | | | | |
| 1. $R_o$ | -.683 | .718 | .321 | -.046 | .554 | .547 | .619 | .396 | -.673 | -.595 | .407 | -.361 | -.778 | -.621 |
| 2. $R_c$ | .... | -.903 | -.458 | .083 | .119 | -.462 | -.539 | -.274 | .466 | .349 | -.288 | .258 | .390 | .215 |
| 3. $R_p$ | | .... | .231 | .018 | -.180 | .605 | .633 | .338 | -.495 | -.422 | .248 | -.339 | -.365 | -.186 |
| 4. Y | | | .... | -.505 | .167 | -.157 | -.001 | .157 | -.133 | .051 | .256 | .134 | -.264 | -.154 |
| 5. Le | | | | .... | -.087 | .280 | .178 | -.221 | .132 | .054 | -.219 | -.105 | .134 | .102 |
| 6. S | | | | | .... | .053 | .117 | .164 | -.370 | -.337 | .284 | -.102 | -.658 | -.656 |
| 7. Af | | | | | | .... | .923 | .342 | -.661 | -.570 | .320 | -.450 | -.540 | -.306 |
| 8. $A_h$ | | | | | | | .... | .220 | -.738 | -.639 | .340 | -.405 | -.632 | -.441 |
| 9. Lo | | | | | | | | .... | -.258 | -.136 | .467 | -.312 | -.201 | -.069 |
| 10. $B_1$ | | | | | | | | | .... | .709 | -.488 | .361 | .779 | .642 |
| 11. $B_2$ | | | | | | | | | | .... | -.284 | .288 | .682 | .594 |
| 12. De | | | | | | | | | | | .... | -.373 | -.410 | -.338 |
| 13. Ar | | | | | | | | | | | | .... | .300 | .090 |
| 14. Cd | | | | | | | | | | | | | .... | .806 |
| **Panel B: Tenants in Central Cities ($C_t$ Set)** | | | | | | | | | | | | | | |
| 1. $R_o$ | -.609 | .702 | .396 | -.049 | .553 | -.286 | .065 | -.107 | -.425 | -.315 | .318 | -.289 | -.680 | -.610 |
| 2. $R_c$ | .... | -.942 | -.623 | .065 | .258 | -.167 | -.501 | .372 | .277 | .180 | -.182 | .249 | .424 | .270 |
| 3. $R_p$ | | .... | .599 | -.132 | -.201 | .139 | .450 | -.249 | -.320 | -.296 | .228 | -.260 | -.452 | -.321 |
| 4. Y | | | .... | -.522 | -.141 | -.230 | .212 | -.244 | -.216 | -.150 | .306 | -.021 | -.337 | -.277 |
| 5. Le | | | | .... | .092 | .210 | .135 | -.214 | .203 | .174 | -.219 | -.105 | .134 | .102 |
| 6. S | | | | | .... | -.571 | -.437 | .136 | -.196 | -.065 | .157 | -.087 | -.393 | -.455 |
| 7. Af | | | | | | .... | .708 | -.138 | -.111 | -.116 | -.210 | -.038 | -.001 | .155 |
| 8. $A_h$ | | | | | | | .... | -.554 | -.399 | -.320 | -.021 | -.079 | -.375 | -.212 |
| 9. Lo | | | | | | | | .... | .252 | -.023 | .149 | .011 | .267 | .221 |
| 10. $B_1$ | | | | | | | | | .... | .327 | -.379 | .222 | .720 | .654 |
| 11. $B_2$ | | | | | | | | | | .... | -.185 | .220 | .502 | .460 |
| 12. De | | | | | | | | | | | .... | -.373 | -.410 | -.338 |
| 13. Ar | | | | | | | | | | | | .... | .300 | .090 |
| 14. Cd | | | | | | | | | | | | | .... | .806 |

Table 58 (continued)

| Variables | Rc (1) | Rp (2) | Y (3) | Le (4) | S (5) | Af (6) | Ah (7) | Lo (8) | $B_1$ (9) | $B_2$ (10) | De (11) | Ar[b] (12) | Cd (13) | Ip (14) |
|---|---|---|---|---|---|---|---|---|---|---|---|---|---|---|
| Panel C: Owners in Environs ($E_o$ Set) | | | | | | | | | | | | | | |
| 1. $R_o$ | -.881 | .856 | .580 | -.137 | .177 | .179 | .242 | .469 | -.653 | -.402 | .620 | .506 | -.564 | -.486 |
| 2. $R_c$ | .... | -.903 | -.640 | .189 | .107 | -.220 | -.332 | -.482 | .605 | .335 | -.510 | -.531 | .476 | .404 |
| 3. $R_p$ | | .... | .475 | -.085 | -.342 | .369 | .462 | .515 | -.587 | -.365 | .418 | .424 | -.418 | -.342 |
| 4. Y | | | .... | -.564 | .179 | -.416 | -.255 | .355 | -.290 | -.145 | .551 | .608 | -.237 | -.185 |
| 5. Le | | | | .... | -.117 | .377 | .254 | .026 | .241 | -.132 | -.234 | -.219 | .209 | .152 |
| 6. S | | | | | .... | -.398 | -.463 | -.117 | -.083 | -.010 | .325 | .130 | -.235 | -.262 |
| 7. Af | | | | | | .... | .945 | .020 | -.401 | -.373 | -.043 | -.169 | -.241 | -.202 |
| 8. $A_h$ | | | | | | | .... | -.008 | -.481 | -.392 | -.001 | -.125 | -.279 | -.273 |
| 9. Lo | | | | | | | | .... | -.150 | -.108 | .302 | .408 | -.038 | .075 |
| 10. $B_1$ | | | | | | | | | .... | .272 | -.490 | -.286 | .765 | .669 |
| 11. $B_2$ | | | | | | | | | | .... | -.181 | -.044 | .307 | .115 |
| 12. De | | | | | | | | | | | .... | .425 | -.408 | -.443 |
| 13. De' | | | | | | | | | | | | .... | -.270 | -.179 |
| 14. Cd | | | | | | | | | | | | | .... | .462 |
| Panel D: Tenants in Environs ($E_t$ Set) | | | | | | | | | | | | | | |
| 1. $R_o$ | -.840 | .816 | .546 | -.219 | .082 | -.019 | .046 | -.022 | -.589 | -.133 | .453 | .411 | -.598 | -.546 |
| 2. $R_c$ | .... | -.966 | -.592 | .131 | .391 | -.312 | -.344 | -.200 | .601 | .256 | -.510 | -.433 | .530 | .448 |
| 3. $R_p$ | | .... | .566 | -.130 | -.484 | .344 | .333 | .279 | -.560 | -.295 | .508 | .484 | -.479 | -.375 |
| 4. Y | | | .... | -.480 | -.163 | -.316 | -.095 | -.047 | -.300 | .011 | .465 | .481 | -.349 | -.226 |
| 5. Le | | | | .... | -.095 | .252 | .089 | .027 | .131 | .025 | -.234 | -.219 | .209 | .152 |
| 6. S | | | | | .... | -.568 | -.546 | -.488 | .077 | .341 | -.172 | -.233 | -.092 | -.173 |
| 7. Af | | | | | | .... | .622 | .456 | -.152 | -.292 | .114 | -.030 | -.052 | .005 |
| 8. $A_h$ | | | | | | | .... | .122 | -.282 | -.443 | -.012 | -.089 | -.111 | -.191 |
| 9. Lo | | | | | | | | .... | .005 | -.071 | .154 | .326 | .114 | .054 |
| 10. $B_1$ | | | | | | | | | .... | .341 | -.377 | -.244 | .625 | .663 |
| 11. $B_2$ | | | | | | | | | | .... | -.236 | -.049 | .222 | .083 |
| 12. De | | | | | | | | | | | .... | .425 | -.408 | -.443 |
| 13. De' | | | | | | | | | | | | .... | -.270 | -.179 |
| 14. Cd | | | | | | | | | | | | | .... | .462 |

Source: See Table 57.

a. Information as to places represented and definitions of variables are given in Table 57. All variables are expressed in log form except $B_1$ and $B_2$, representing units constructed during the forties.

b. For the environs the variable of this column is the density of the population per square mile of the environs whereas the variable of column 11 is the density of the central city.

This occurs in spite of the fact that $R_c$ represents the upper tail of the distribution of degree of room crowding and $R_p$ represents an average.

Y is the main independent variable. And the regression coefficients of Y describe the coefficients of income elasticity of rooms and their occupancy. Such coefficients are symbolized by $\eta_{R_oY}$, $\eta_{R_pY}$, and $\eta_{R_cY}$.

The percentage of the male labor force with less than 26 weeks of employment during 1949, symbolized by Le, is used to represent variation among places in the transitory component of income related to employment opportunity. The expectation is that holding Le constant will tend to increase the regression coefficient of Y if its sign tends to be positive and to decrease it if its sign tends to be negative. Information on Le is available only for the entire metro area. Nevertheless, it is negatively and significantly correlated with Y of each of the four sets of observations. This is the tendency to expect if Le is a proxy for transitory income related to cyclical change and uncorrelated with $Y_n$ of cities. The $r^2$ of Y and Le is as follows:

| | $r^2$ |
|---|---|
| $C_o$ | .255 |
| $C_t$ | .271 |
| $E_o$ | .318 |
| $E_t$ | .230 |

These correlations are all highly significant.

The preceding section indicates that household size has a very important bearing on variation of $R_c$. It is, however, highly correlated with other characteristics of households such as age and sex of head. Tests have been made as to the bearing of various household characteristics on $R_o$, $R_p$, and $R_c$. Four variables are used to represent household type: average persons per household, and the importance of households with an aged or a female head, with an aged head, and with lodgers. These variables are symbolized by S, Af, $A_h$, and Lo, respectively. The variables S and Af are looked upon as the main variables representing household type.

The variables Af and $A_h$ are closely and positively correlated. This is not surprising since Af represents households with an aged or a female head and $A_h$ those with an aged head.[28] Both Af and $A_h$ are nega-

28. In other words, households with a female head under 65 years

tively correlated with Y, and for three of the four sets of places their correlation with S is negative and highly significant.

An upward trend in the price of housing of constant quality has been occurring, and, other things being equal, the higher the price of housing the lower is $R_o$. Hence, variables to represent the period of construction seem likely to explain some of the variation in $R_o$.[29] The importance of units constructed during the forties is represented by two variables, namely those constructed during 1945 or later and during 1940 through 1944. The variables are symbolized by $B_1$ and $B_2$. For the four sets, $B_1$ and $B_2$ are negatively and significantly correlated with Y. Thus there was a tendency for the units constructed during the late forties to concentrate in cities and environs of metro areas where average income of 1949 was low. Such concentration is appreciably greater for tenants than owners.

The importance of new units constructed during the forties is positively and significantly correlated with population growth of metro areas during the forties. This growth is symbolized by Po''.[30] This variable is positively correlated with $B_1$. The coefficients of determination are as follows:

| Set | $r^2$ |
|---|---|
| $C_o$ | .482 |
| $C_t$ | .591 |
| $E_o$ | .523 |
| $E_t$ | .309 |

Thus if population growth of the decade was affecting tendencies observed among places in 1950 it seems likely to have had a similar effect for each of the four sets.

Population growth seems likely to be associated with a variety of con-

---

of age are not represented.

29. Tendencies among census tracts of Chicago, described in the preceding section, give some reason to expect, with average income held constant, that the greater the importance of dwelling units constructed during the forties the higher tends to be $R_c{}^a$. This tendency is to be expected if construction costs have been rising and within tracts newness is in some measure a substitute for extra rooms in shabbier units of earlier construction.

30. This is the population in 1950 with that of the metro area with the same name in 1940 equal to 100. No adjustment has been made for the change between 1940 and 1950 in the boundaries of the respective metro areas.

ditions likely to affect $R_o$, $R_p$, and $R_c$. Other things being equal, the higher Po'', the greater seems likely to be the pressure to convert existing stock in order to provide additional units, the greater the frequency of lodgers in private households (Lo) and the less the undoubling of potential households. These conditions all seem likely to decrease $R_o$ and $R_p$ and to raise $R_c$.

Population growth also tends to stimulate new construction. It seems probable, however, that a lag occurs. If so, the more recent the in-migration, the more intense tends to be the pressure of demand on the existing stock. In-migration just prior to the time of the census of 1950 is represented by the importance of the population of 1950, one year of age or more, residing in another county during 1949. This is symbolized by Ip.[31]

Ip is positively correlated with Po''. It is also highly correlated with $B_1$. For the four sets of observations the correlation of Ip and $B_1$ is as follows:

| | $r^2$ |
|---|---|
| $C_o$ | .412 |
| $C_t$ | .428 |
| $E_o$ | .448 |
| $E_t$ | .440 |

This correlation implies that in-migration from 1949 to 1950 is positively and closely correlated with $B_1$ as well as with in-migration of the forties in general.

One additional characteristic of the population is taken into account, namely, the importance of population changing dwelling unit occupied without changing county of residence. This variable is symbolized by Cd. The evidence of chapter xi gives some reason to expect that this variable tends to be a crude proxy for variation among places in the formation of new households and that because of this it may serve as a proxy for negative $Y_t$ of cities.[32] Under this condition, one would expect to find it negatively correlated with Y. Such correlation is observed. For each of the four

31. This is shorthand for recent in-migrant population. This information is available for both the central city and the environs.

32. The income of the preceding year seems likely to understate the income that determines the dwelling unit occupied by newly formed households.

sets it is significant at the .01 probability level. Furthermore, the correlation is appreciably higher for tenants than owners. This is the difference to expect, since new households tend to be more heavily represented among tenants than owners (see Table 58).

The importance of those changing the dwelling unit occupied may affect the tendencies observed in yet other ways. It will be negatively correlated with S if it serves as a proxy for the undoubling of households, perhaps because of a termination of the lag between in-migration and the availability of a dwelling unit making feasible a reduction of lodgers in private households and the population of quasi-households, such as hotels and lodging houses. The likelihood of this is implied by a marked positive correlation for both the central cities and the environs between Cd and Po''. The $r^2$ of these relationships, for the 57 central cities and environs, is .60 and .53, respectively.

Direct information on the cost of housing of similar quality is one of the big gaps in the set of variables used. It would not be surprising if Ip serves as a proxy for temporarily high cost of housing. There seems, however, no reason to expect it to be positively correlated with normal costs. In fact, insofar as cost of living is one of the conditions affecting migration, there seems some reason to expect a negative correlation between Ip and cost of housing.

Two variables representing central cities are used in the hope that they will serve as proxies for cost. These are the density of the population per square mile and the area of the city. These are symbolized by De and Ar, respectively. Some positive correlation between them and cost is to be expected if only because they tend to be positively correlated with the price of land. For the environs, two variables have been used in the hope of picking up some of the effect of difference in cost among places. These are the density of the population of the environs and of the central city, symbolized by De and De'. It seems possible that these variables representing environment may be positively correlated with cost. If so, the higher De and Ar the lower is likely to be $R_o$ and $R_p$ and the higher is likely to be $R_c$. The availability of Univac made their inclusion feasible, and the findings, though inconclusive, seem of sufficient interest to deserve presentation.

No variable directly represents lag of housing behind change in income and price. However, population change and importance of units constructed during the forties may serve as proxies for such lag.

$R_o$, $R_p$, and $R_c$ vary widely among places. In examining this variation, attention is given first to the probable effect of Y. Then the effect of household types is examined. Next variables representing the importance of new units are introduced. These are the complete set of variables that describe the households represented by the housing, income, and household type variables. The other variables representing population change and environment are common to both tenures.

The regression coefficients together with their standard errors and coefficient of determination are shown in Tables 59-61. The standard errors are shown in brackets below the regression coefficients. In reviewing coefficients they are referred to as significant if they are at least twice their standard error.

Variation among Places in $R_o$.—A wide range occurs among cities in $R_o$ for the four sets of places and the $R_o$ estimates shown explain from 66 to 76 per cent of their variation. The coefficient of correlation of $R_o$ with various sets of explanatory variables is shown in Table 59.

$R_o$ with respect to Y.—

1. Y explains from 10 to 34 per cent of the variation in $R_o$. The simple income coefficients and $r^2$ of the variables for the four sets of places are as follows:

| Set | $\eta_{R_oY}$ | $r^2$ |
|---|---|---|
| $C_o$ | 0.302 | .103 |
| $C_t$ | 0.379 | .157 |
| $E_o$ | 0.361 | .336 |
| $E_t$ | 0.398 | .298 |

The higher $r^2$ for the environs than central cities may well reflect the likelihood that the more recent the construction, the more $R_o$ tends to be a function of Y. The coefficients of $\eta_{R_oY}$ are quite similar, although those of owners tend to be lower than those of tenants. This may reflect the effect of the lesser mobility of owners than tenants.

2. The difference by tenure shown above seems to be associated with some basic difference. It persists in the mean of the 12 partial coefficients shown in Table 59. These are:

| Owners | | Tenants | |
|---|---|---|---|
| $C_o$ | 0.312 | $C_t$ | 0.529 |
| $E_o$ | 0.419 | $E_t$ | 0.487 |

However, the difference by tenure is very much greater in the central city than the environs.

3. The inclusion of Le tends to increase $\eta_{R_oY}$.[33] For the four sets of places its mean coefficient is thereby increased from 0.360 to 0.435. Again the variable Le shows an effect that implies that it serves as a proxy for $Y_t$.

4. The further addition of S or Af or $A_h$ has little effect on $\eta_{R_oY}$.[34] However, holding S and Af as well as Le constant has a considerable tendency to increase $\eta_{R_oY}$. For the four sets the increase in the mean is from 0.435 to 0.525.[35]

5. All coefficients of $\eta_{R_oY}$ are highly significant, implying that Y is a very important determinant of $R_o$. A coefficient between 0.3 and 0.5 is indicated. The question remains as to whether holding constant cost of housing and lag of housing would modify this coefficient.

$R_o$ with respect to Household Size and Type.—The variables representing household size and type explain an appreciable portion of the variation in $R_o$:

1. In general the higher is S the higher tends to be $R_o$. It seems to have a much more consistent relation to $R_o$ than does either Af or $A_h$. With Y and Le held constant, the range of the partial regression coefficients of the household type variables and related characteristics for the four sets of places are as follows:[36]

| | Partial regression coefficients | $R^2$ |
|---|---|---|
| S | 0.152 to 0.852<br>(0.206) (0.126) | .336 - .565 |
| Af | -0.597 to 1.135<br>(0.322) (0.192) | .241 - .570 |
| $A_h$ | -0.424 to 1.386<br>(0.672) (0.226) | .197 - .487 |

33. See Table 59, columns 1 and 2.
34. See Table 59, columns 3, 4, and 5.
35. See Table 59, columns 2 and 8.
36. See Table 59, columns 3, 4, and 5.

Table 59

Coefficients of Correlation, Number of Rooms per Dwelling Unit ($R_O$) with respect to Income and Sets of Other Variables among Central City and Environs of 57 Metro Areas by Tenure, 1950

| | (1) | (2) | (3) | (4) | (5) | (6) | (7) | (8) | (9) | (10) | (11) | (12) | (13) |
|---|---|---|---|---|---|---|---|---|---|---|---|---|---|
| | A. Owners, Central Cities ($C_O$) | | | | | | | | | | | | |
| $R^2$ | .103 | .121 | .379 | .469 | .487 | .678 | .709 | .680 | .687 | .733 | .745 | .757 | .759 |
| Constant | -.334 | -.698 | -.793 | -3.054 | -3.235 | -3.092 | -4.444 | -2.984 | -3.598 | -3.125 | -1.643 | -1.592 | -1.443 |
| Regression coefficients | | | | | | | | | | | | | |
| Y | .302 (.120) | .377 (.139) | .296 (.120) | .389 (.109) | .307 (.108) | .243 (.087) | .241 (.084) | .315 (.087) | .311 (.087) | .332 (.084) | .284 (.090) | .320 (.094) | .327 (.095) |
| Le | . . . . | .087 (.082) | .088 (.070) | .005 (.060) | .005 (.065) | .013 (.052) | .039 (.051) | .0018 (.052) | .018 (.054) | .089 (.057) | .099 (.058) | .091 (.058) | .082 (.060) |
| S | | . . . . | .730 (.155) | . . . . | . . . . | .633 (.114) | .604 (.110) | .663 (.113) | .649 (.114) | .474 (.124) | .283 (.179) | .299 (.179) | .322 (.185) |
| Af | | | . . . . | 1.135 (.192) | . . . . | . . . . | . . . . | 1.060 (.151) | .986 (.167) | .463 (.254) | .310 (.288) | .309 (.288) | .311 (.290) |
| $A_h$ | | | | . . . . | 1.386 (.226) | 1.263 (.182) | 1.157 (.180) | . . . . | . . . . | . . . . | . . . . | . . . . | . . . . |
| Lo | | | | | . . . . | . . . . | .769 (.332) | . . . . | .382 (.368) | .676 (.361) | .830 (.375) | .845 (.398) | .820 (.404) |
| $B_1$ | | | | | | | . . . . | . . . . | . . . . | -.00064 (.00060) | -.00030 (.00065) | -.00035 (.00067) | -.0004 (.0007) |
| $B_2$ | | | | | | | | | | -.0019 (.00087) | -.0015 (.00091) | -.0014 (.00091) | -.0017 (.0011) |
| Cd | | | | | | | | | | . . . . . | -.451 (.387) | -.322 (.396) | -.324 (.399) |
| Ip | | | | | | | | | | | -.143 (.436) | -.327 (.453) | -.440 (.497) |
| De | | | | | | | | | | | . . . . . | -.020 (.020) | -.024 (.022) |
| Ar | | | | | | | | | | | | -.016 (.012) | -.017 (.012) |
| Po'' | | | | | | | | | | | | . . . . . | .0598 (.104) |

Table 59 (continued)

| | (1) | (2) | (3) | (4) | (5) | (6) | (7) | (8) | (9) | (10) | (11) | (12) | (13) |
|---|---|---|---|---|---|---|---|---|---|---|---|---|---|
| | B. Tenants, Central Cities ($C_t$) | | | | | | | | | | | | |
| $R^2$ | .157 | .191 | .565 | .241 | .197 | .613 | .625 | .610 | .611 | .658 | .682 | .695 | .695 |
| Constant | -.751 | -1.307 | -1.908 | .073 | -.569 | -4.346 | -6.592 | -3.781 | -4.096 | -3.438 | -1.333 | .977 | -.931 |
| Regression coefficients | | | | | | | | | | | | | |
| Y | .379 | .488 | .563 | .452 | .519 | .479 | .521 | .629 | .642 | .583 | .482 | .492 | .492 |
| | (.119) | (.137) | (.102) | (.136) | (.147) | (.103) | (.107) | (.101) | (.114) | (.111) | (.123) | (.124) | (.125) |
| Le | . . . . | .163 | .151 | .185 | .184 | .082 | .114 | .121 | .130 | .193 | .183 | .163 | .161 |
| | | (.108) | (.080) | (.106) | (.114) | (.081) | (.084) | (.077) | (.085) | (.096) | (.085) | (.088) | (.091) |
| S | | . . . . | .852 | . . . . | . . . . | 1.005 | 1.023 | 1.094 | 1.093 | .885 | .671 | .658 | .661 |
| | | | (.126) | | | (.134) | (.134) | (.156) | (.157) | (.174) | (.210) | (.215) | (.219) |
| Af | | | . . . . | -.597 | . . . . | . . . . | . . . . | .737 | .747 | .360 | .135 | .128 | .130 |
| | | | | (.322) | | | | (.300) | (.306) | (.330) | (.348) | (.363) | (.368) |
| $A_h$ | | | | . . . . | -.424 | 1.338 | 1.691 | . . . . | . . . . | . . . . | . . . . | . . . . | . . . . |
| | | | | | (.672) | (.527) | (.591) | | | | | | |
| Lo | | | | | . . . . | . . . . | .657 | . . . . | .119 | .319 | .470 | .531 | .522 |
| | | | | | | | (.513) | | (.467) | (.470) | (.472) | (.512) | (.529) |
| $B_1$ | | | | | | | . . . . | . . . . | . . . . | -.0018 | -.00049 | -.00043 | -.00052 |
| | | | | | | | | | | (.0011) | (.0014) | (.0014) | (.0017) |
| $B_2$ | | | | | | | | | | -.0016) | -.00076 | -.00047 | -.00055 |
| | | | | | | | | | | (.00094) | (.0011) | (.0011) | (.0014) |
| Cd | | | | | | | | | | . . . . . | -.827 | -.710 | -.714 |
| | | | | | | | | | | | (.467) | (.497) | (.504) |
| Ip | | | | | | | | | | | .106 | -.186 | -.211 |
| | | | | | | | | | | | (.654) | (.691) | (.755) |
| De | | | | | | | | | | | . . . . . | -.022 | -.023 |
| | | | | | | | | | | | | (.030) | (.032) |
| Ar | | | | | | | | | | | | -.024 | -.024 |
| | | | | | | | | | | | | (.018) | (.018) |
| Po'' | | | | | | | | | | | | . . . . . | .016 |
| | | | | | | | | | | | | | (.182) |

Table 59 (continued)

| | (1) | (2) | (3) | (4) | (5) | (6) | (7) | (8) | (9) | (10) | (11) | (12) | (13) |
|---|---|---|---|---|---|---|---|---|---|---|---|---|---|
| | C. Owners, Environs ($E_o$) | | | | | | | | | | | | |
| $R^2$ | .336 | .389 | .395 | .570 | .530 | .604 | .673 | .634 | .676 | .747 | .771 | .773 | .780 |
| Constant | -.570 | -1.110 | -1.162 | -3.155 | -3.066 | -3.959 | -7.932 | -3.805 | -6.760 | -4.757 | -3.747 | -3.482 | -4.144 |
| Regression coefficients | | | | | | | | | | | | | |
| Y | .361 (.068) | .458 (.080) | .450 (.081) | .546 (.070) | .498 (.072) | .481 (.067) | .374 (.069) | .538 (.066) | .452 (.071) | .331 (.075) | .324 (.073) | .293 (.089) | .286 (.089) |
| Le | .... | .173 (.080) | .174 (.081) | .111 (.069) | .134 (.072) | .124 (.066) | .062 (.064) | .100 (.065) | .055 (.064) | .111 (.061) | .104 (.060) | .098 (.062) | .097 (.062) |
| S | | .... | .152 (.206) | .... | .... | .586 (.187) | .699 (.175) | .523 (.174) | .590 (.167) | .344 (.165) | .221 (.170) | .188 (.180) | .198 (.179) |
| Af | | | .... | .862 (.182) | .... | .... | .... | 1.062 (.182) | 1.024 (.174) | .386 (.239) | .385 (.233) | .364 (.239) | .431 (.244) |
| $A_h$ | | | | .... | .903 (.227) | 1.225 (.234) | 1.252 (.215) | .... | .... | .... | .... | .... | .... |
| Lo | | | | | .... | .... | 2.131 (.649) | .... | 1.661 (.648) | 1.599 (.586) | 1.911 (.589) | 1.800 (.624) | 2.007 (.645) |
| $B_1$ | | | | | | | .... | .... | .... | -.0013 (.00036) | -.00040 (.00055) | -.00038 (.00056) | -.00017 (.00058) |
| $B_2$ | | | | | | | | | | -.00057 (.00054) | -.00052 (.00053) | -.00057 (.00055) | -.00005 (.00070) |
| Cd | | | | | | | | | | ..... | -.344 (.219) | -.328 (.225) | -.223 (.241) |
| Ip | | | | | | | | | | | -.424 (.233) | -.394 (.241) | -.316 (.249) |
| De | | | | | | | | | | | ..... | .0083 (.013) | .0044 (.014) |
| De' | | | | | | | | | | | | .0066 (.022) | .0110 (.022) |
| Po'' | | | | | | | | | | | | ..... | -.129 (.108) |

Table 59 (continued)

| | (1) | (2) | (3) | (4) | (5) | (6) | (7) | (8) | (9) | (10) | (11) | (12) | (13) |
|---|---|---|---|---|---|---|---|---|---|---|---|---|---|
| | D. Tenants, Environs ($E_t$) | | | | | | | | | | | | |
| $R^2$ | .298 | .301 | .336 | .325 | .310 | .397 | .431 | .473 | .475 | .623 | .642 | .656 | .659 |
| Constant | -.792 | -.905 | -1.213 | -1.782 | -1.825 | -4.404 | -8.797 | -4.481 | -5.245 | -4.848 | -2.869 | -2.263 | -3.416 |
| Regression coefficients | | | | | | | | | | | | | |
| Y | .398 (.082) | .418 (.095) | .456 (.096) | .449 (.096) | .423 (.095) | .507 (.095) | .547 (.096) | .619 (.097) | .622 (.098) | .501 (.092) | .450 (.098) | .424 (.108) | .425 (.109) |
| Le | .... | .040 (.093) | .071 (.093) | .025 (.093) | .036 (.093) | .088 (.090) | .110 (.089) | .077 (.084) | .080 (.085) | .097 (.074) | .096 (.074) | .093 (.074) | .096 (.075) |
| S | | .... | .293 (.174) | .... | .... | .565 (.205) | .795 (.241) | .796 (.208) | .824 (.221) | .789 (.202) | .625 (.226) | .650 (.228) | .706 (.247) |
| Af | | | .... | .377 (.270) | .... | .... | .... | 1.177 (.320) | 1.150 (.329) | .677 (.305) | .567 (.314) | .642 (.322) | .683 (.331) |
| $A_h$ | | | | .... | .445 (.523) | 1.404 (.608) | 1.674 (.616) | .... | .... | .... | .... | .... | .... |
| Lo | | | | | .... | .... | 1.767 (1.013) | .... | .392 (.963) | .912 (.846) | .851 (.848) | .420 (.921) | .766 (1.087) |
| $B_1$ | | | | | | | .... | .... | .... | -.0017 (.00044) | -.00097 (.00064) | -.00094 (.00064) | -.00098 (.00065) |
| $B_2$ | | | | | | | | | | -.00082 (.00044) | -.00060 (.00046) | -.00064 (.00047) | -.00043 (.00059) |
| Cd | | | | | | | | | | ..... | -.306 (.272) | -.260 (.278) | -.117 (.364) |
| Ip | | | | | | | | | | | -.371 (.325) | -.393 (.342) | -.263 (.406) |
| De | | | | | | | | | | | ..... | -.0068 (.018) | -.0098 (.019) |
| De' | | | | | | | | | | | | .040 (.030) | .041 (.030) |
| Po'' | | | | | | | | | | | | ..... | -.106 (.174) |

a. See Tables 57 and 58 for information on the definition of these variables and their form.

The low coefficients are not significant, whereas the high coefficients are all highly significant. However, there is so much correlation with other variables that a possible functional relationship remains in doubt.

2. With the addition of variables representing new units and population changes, the partial coefficients of S and Af both fall, the fall being less for S than for Af. The mean partial coefficients and their standard errors of Af and S for the four sets of places shown in Table 59, columns 11, 12, and 13 are 0.367 (.302) and 0.457 (.202), respectively. The regression coefficient of Af is not significant, whereas that of S is. (These two variables are highly correlated.) The regression coefficients indicate an elasticity of $R_o$ with respect to S of around 0.5. (It seems of interest to note that this marked change in the regression coefficients of Af and S referred to is brought about by the inclusion of variables representing secular change, and hence it may be related to the way in which the age distribution of the population is related to the lag of housing behind change in demand and change in cost.)

$R_o$ with respect to Importance of New Units and to Population Change.—

1. With Y, Le, S, Af, and Lo held constant, the partial regression coefficients of $B_1$ and $B_2$ are all negative (see Table 59, column 10). The secular change in cost of construction would lead one to expect this. In addition, three of the eight coefficients are significant.

2. However, when variables representing population change and density also are held constant, none of the partial coefficients of $B_1$ and $B_2$ is significant. They do, however, remain negative. The effect of the population change and density on the coefficients of $B_1$ and $B_2$ is the type to expect if these in some measure serve as proxies for lag and secular change in the cost of housing. (They are also highly correlated with the importance of households with young head and young children.)

$R_o$ with respect to Other Conditions.—Variables representing population change and density explain about 14 per cent of the variation in $R_o$ not explained by the other variables. They are more frequently negative than positive. In other words, the importance of change of dwelling unit, of in-migrants, and density of land use tend to be negatively correlated with $R_o$. However, with Y and many other conditions held constant, none of the partial regression coefficients is significant. Among the places, increase in population tends to be negatively correlated with $R_o$; hence these negative signs may represent the lag in housing. This possibility is considered in the examination of the residuals later presented.

Variation among Places in $R_p$.—A wide variation occurs among places in $R_p$. For the four sets of places the estimates shown explain 58 to 81 per cent of this variation. The coefficients of $R_p$ with respect to various sets of variables are shown in Table 60.

$R_p$ with respect to Y.—

1. The simple regression coefficients of $R_p$ with respect to Y and $r^2$ of relationship for the four sets of places are as follows:

| Set | $\eta R_p Y$ | $r^2$ |
|---|---|---|
| $C_o$ | 0.186 | .053 |
| $C_t$ | 0.496 | .358 |
| $E_o$ | 0.311 | .225 |
| $E_t$ | 0.478 | .321 |

This indicates an appreciable difference by tenure: Y alone explains a much lower percentage of the variation in $R_p$ for owners than tenants, and $\eta R_p Y$ is appreciably lower for owners than tenants.

2. This difference persists even where several other conditions are held constant. The mean partial[37] $\eta R_p Y$ shown in Table 60 is as follows:

| | | | |
|---|---|---|---|
| $C_o$ | 0.278 | $C_t$ | 0.575 |
| $E_o$ | 0.421 | $E_t$ | 0.556 |

Thus $\eta R_p Y$ tends to be higher for tenants than for owners and higher for households in the environs than the central cities.

3. The coefficient $\eta R_p Y$ is increased appreciably by holding Le constant. The mean coefficient for the four sets of places increases from 0.368 to 0.457. For each set of places the effect is that to be expected if Le is a proxy for $Y_t$ and is uncorrelated with $Y_n$ (see Table 60, column 2).

4. Holding constant Af increases $\eta R_p Y$ by about 16 per cent. This effect seems likely to be a joint product of many conditions, including difference among regions in migration.

5. Taking into account the importance of new units and population

37. Means of the 12 partial coefficients shown in Table 60, columns 2 through 13.

Table 60

Coefficients of Correlation, the Number of Rooms per Person ($R_P$) with respect to Income and Sets of Other Variables, among Central City and Environs of 57 Metro Areas, by Tenure, 1950[a]

| | (1) | (2) | (3) | (4) | (5) | (6) | (7) | (8) | (9) | (10) | (11) | (12) | (13) |
|---|---|---|---|---|---|---|---|---|---|---|---|---|---|
| | A. Owners, Central Cities ($C_o$) | | | | | | | | | | | | |
| $R^2$ | .053 | .078 | .127 | .475 | .454 | .543 | .590 | .550 | .561 | .628 | .642 | .657 | .660 |
| Constant | -.440 | -.798 | -.763 | -2.944 | -2.994 | -3.078 | -4.494 | -2.980 | -3.646 | -3.124 | -1.775 | -1.742 | -1.604 |
| Regression coefficients | | | | | | | | | | | | | |
| Y | .186 (.106) | .259 (.122) | .289 (.121) | .270 (.093) | .199 (.095) | .236 (.089) | .233 (.085) | .308 (.088) | .303 (.088) | .322 (.084) | .281 (.092) | .316 (.095) | .322 (.097) |
| Le | .... | .086 (.072) | .085 (.071) | .002 (.056) | .015 (.057) | .011 (.053) | .037 (.051) | -.0019 (.053) | .015 (.055) | .090 (.058) | .098 (.059) | .091 (.059) | .082 (.061) |
| S | | .... | -.271 (.157) | .... | .... | -.368 (.116) | -.399 (.111) | -.338 (.114) | -.354 (.114) | -.537 (.125) | -.710 (.181) | -.693 (.182) | -.672 (.187) |
| Af | | | .... | 1.034 (.163) | .... | .... | .... | 1.072 (.153) | .992 (.169) | .442 (.255) | .311 (.292) | .311 (.292) | .313 (.294) |
| $A_h$ | | | | .... | 1.200 (.198) | 1.271 (.184) | 1.160 (.183) | .... | .... | .... | .... | .... | .... |
| Lo | | | | | .... | .... | .805 (.336) | .... | .414 (.372) | .717 (.363) | .857 (.379) | .879 (.403) | .855 (.409) |
| $B_1$ | | | | | | | .... | .... | .... | -.00075 (.00061) | -.00043 (.00066) | -.00050 (.00067) | -.00058 (.00070) |
| $B_2$ | | | | | | | | | | -.0018 (.00088) | -.0014 (.00092) | -.0014 (.00092) | -.0017 (.0011) |
| Cd | | | | | | | | | | ..... | -.388 (.391) | -.264 (.401) | -.265 (.404) |
| Ip | | | | | | | | | | | -.163 (.441) | -.340 (.458) | -.445 (.504) |
| De | | | | | | | | | | | ..... | -.020 (.020) | -.024 (.020) |
| Ar | | | | | | | | | | | | -.015 (.012) | -.016 (.012) |
| Po'' | | | | | | | | | | | | ..... | .055 (.106) |

Table 60 (continued)

| | (1) | (2) | (3) | (4) | (5) | (6) | (7) | (8) | (9) | (10) | (11) | (12) | (13) |
|---|---|---|---|---|---|---|---|---|---|---|---|---|---|
| | B. Tenants, Central Cities ($C_t$) | | | | | | | | | | | | |
| $R^2$ | .358 | .403 | .418 | .472 | .482 | .482 | .498 | .475 | .476 | .532 | .561 | .581 | .581 |
| Constant | -1.570 | -2.120 | -2.016 | -3.532 | -4.425 | -4.443 | -6.679 | -3.842 | -4.149 | -3.536 | -1.510 | -1.135 | -1.074 |
| Regression coefficients | | | | | | | | | | | | | |
| Y | .496 (.090) | .604 (.102) | .591 (.102) | .641 (.098) | .507 (.101) | .507 (.103) | .549 (.108) | .655 (.102) | .667 (.114) | .612 (.112) | .516 (.124) | .527 (.126) | .527 (.127) |
| Le | . . . . | .161 (.080) | .163 (.080) | .139 (.077) | .096 (.079) | .095 (.081) | .127 (.084) | .134 (.078) | .143 (.085) | .202 (.087) | .193 (.087) | .173 (.089) | .170 (.093) |
| S | | . . . . | -.148 (.126) | . . . . | . . . . | .0046 (.135) | .023 (.135) | .088 (.156) | .087 (.157) | -.109 (.176) | -.314 (.214) | -.331 (.218) | -.327 (.222) |
| Af | | | . . . . | .610 (.232) | . . . . | . . . . | . . . . | .718 (.306) | .727 (.206) | .364 (.334) | .149 (.354) | .134 (.368) | .137 (.373) |
| Hf | | | | . . . . | 1.324 (.467) | 1.332 (.527) | 1.682 (.592) | . . . . | . . . . | . . . . | . . . . | . . . . | . . . . |
| Lo | | | | | . . . . | . . . . | .654 (.514) | . . . . | .116 (.469) | .307 (.476) | .452 (.480) | .531 (.520) | .519 (.537) |
| $B_1$ | | | | | | | . . . . | . . . . | . . . . | -.0017 (.0011) | -.00045 (.0014) | -.00042 (.0014) | -.00053 (.0017) |
| $B_2$ | | | | | | | | | | -.0015 (.0010) | -.00067 (.0011) | -.00037 (.0011) | -.00046 (.0014) |
| Cd | | | | | | | | | | . . . . . | -.787 (.475) | -.677 (.504) | -.681 (.511) |
| Ip | | | | | | | | | | | .091 (.665) | -.211 (.702) | -.245 (.766) |
| De | | | | | | | | | | | . . . . . | -.0248 (.0304) | -.0260 (.0330) |
| Ar | | | | | | | | | | | | -.0252 (.0179) | -.0252 (.0181) |
| Po'' | | | | | | | | | | | | . . . . . | .0214 (.184) |

Table 60 (continued)

| | (1) | (2) | (3) | (4) | (5) | (6) | (7) | (8) | (9) | (10) | (11) | (12) | (13) |
|---|---|---|---|---|---|---|---|---|---|---|---|---|---|
| | C. Owners, Environs ($E_o$) | | | | | | | | | | | | |
| $R^2$ | .225 | .274 | .459 | .624 | .609 | .647 | .712 | .676 | .716 | .780 | .804 | .804 | .812 |
| Constant | -.915 | -1.464 | -1.172 | -4.452 | -4.638 | -3.967 | -8.041 | -3.829 | -6.878 | -4.915 | -3.864 | -3.717 | -4.438 |
| Rgression coefficients | | | | | | | | | | | | | |
| Y | .311<br>(.078) | .410<br>(.092) | .458<br>(.081) | .539<br>(.069) | .475<br>(.069) | .489<br>(.066) | .380<br>(.068) | .547<br>(.065) | .458<br>(.070) | .342<br>(.073) | .334<br>(.071) | .316<br>(.087) | .309<br>(.087) |
| Le | . . . . | .176<br>(.092) | .169<br>(.080) | .085<br>(.068) | .112<br>(.069) | .119<br>(.066) | .056<br>(.063) | .095<br>(.064) | .049<br>(.063) | .108<br>(.060) | .100<br>(.058) | .096<br>(.061) | .096<br>(.060) |
| S | | . . . . | -.872<br>(.205) | . . . . | . . . . | -.440<br>(.187) | -.324<br>(.173) | -.500<br>(.172) | -.431<br>(.165) | -.672<br>(.162) | -.801<br>(.166) | -.816<br>(.176) | -.805<br>(.174) |
| Af | | | . . . . | 1.259<br>(.180) | . . . . | . . . . | . . . . | 1.068<br>(.181) | 1.029<br>(.171) | .406<br>(.235) | .402<br>(.227) | .392<br>(.234) | .464<br>(.238) |
| $A_h$ | | | | . . . . | 1.466<br>(.218) | 1.224<br>(.233) | 1.252<br>(.212) | . . . . | . . . . | . . . . | . . . . | . . . . | . . . . |
| Lo | | | | | . . . . | . . . . | 2.186<br>(.642) | . . . . | 1.714<br>(.639) | 1.642<br>(.576) | 1.976<br>(.574) | 1.913<br>(.611) | 2.138<br>(.629) |
| $B_1$ | | | | | | | . . . . | . . . . | . . . . | -.0013<br>(.00035) | -.00038<br>(.00053) | -.00037<br>(.00054) | -.00015<br>(.00057) |
| $B_2$ | | | | | | | | | | -.00044<br>(.00053) | -.00041<br>(.00052) | -.00044<br>(.00054) | -.00012<br>(.00068) |
| Cd | | | | | | | | | | . . . . . | -.337<br>(.213) | -.326<br>(.220) | -.212<br>(.234) |
| Ip | | | | | | | | | | | -.466<br>(.228) | -.453<br>(.236) | -.368<br>(.243) |
| De | | | | | | | | | | | . . . . . | .0035<br>(.0131) | -.00068<br>(.0131) |
| De' | | | | | | | | | | | | .0054<br>(.0215) | .0102<br>(.0216) |
| Po'' | | | | | | | | | | | | . . . . . | -.140<br>(.105) |

Table 60 (continued)

| | (1) | (2) | (3) | (4) | (5) | (6) | (7) | (8) | (9) | (10) | (11) | (12) | (13) |
|---|---|---|---|---|---|---|---|---|---|---|---|---|---|
| | D. Tenants, Environs ($E_t$) | | | | | | | | | | | | |
| $R^2$ | .321 | .347 | .485 | .634 | .492 | .527 | .563 | .635 | .638 | .737 | .748 | .756 | .759 |
| Constant | -1.549 | -1.978 | -1.270 | -5.434 | -6.193 | -4.039 | -9.572 | -5.212 | -6.411 | -6.016 | -4.293 | -3.737 | -5.064 |
| Regression coefficients | | | | | | | | | | | | | |
| Y | .478 (.094) | .553 (.106) | .465 (.098) | .674 (.082) | .574 (.094) | .513 (.097) | .561 (.097) | .660 (.093) | .665 (.094) | .549 (.089) | .503 (.095) | .476 (.105) | .476 (.106) |
| Le | .... | .153 (.104) | .081 (.095) | .091 (.079) | .135 (.093) | .097 (.092) | .122 (.090) | .087 (.081) | .093 (.082) | .108 (.072) | .107 (.072) | .105 (.072) | .108 (.072) |
| S | | .... | -.672 (.178) | .... | .... | -.414 (.211) | -.138 (.244) | -.065 (.201) | -.022 (.212) | -.057 (.195) | -.202 (.220) | -.181 (.222) | -.117 (.240) |
| Af | | | .... | 1.486 (.230) | .... | .... | .... | 1.420 (.308) | 1.377 (.316) | .928 (.294) | .826 (.304) | .888 (.313) | .934 (.322) |
| $A_h$ | | | | .... | 2.038 (.524) | 1.335 (.624) | 1.659 (.625) | .... | .... | .... | .... | .... | .... |
| Lo | | | | | .... | .... | 2.120 (1.027) | .... | .616 (.925) | 1.104 (.817) | 1.062 (.822) | .666 (.896) | 1.064 (1.056) |
| $B_1$ | | | | | | | .... | .... | .... | -.0016 (.00043) | -.00099 (.00062) | -.00096 (.00063) | -.0010 (.00063) |
| $B_2$ | | | | | | | | | | -.00075 (.00043) | -.00056 (.00045) | -.00058 (.00046) | -.00034 (.00057) |
| Cd | | | | | | | | | | ..... | -.292 (.264) | -.247 (.270) | -.0829 (.354) |
| Ip | | | | | | | | | | | -.298 (.316) | -.306 (.333) | -.155 (.394) |
| De | | | | | | | | | | | ..... | -.0041 (.017) | -.0075 (.018) |
| De' | | | | | | | | | | | | -.035 (.029) | -.037 (.029) |
| Po'' | | | | | | | | | | | | ..... | -.122 (.169) |

a. See Tables 57 and 58 for information on the definition of these variables and their form.

change modifies $\eta_{R_pY}$ only slightly.

6. With few exceptions all coefficients of $\eta_{R_pY}$ are highly significant. Several of them are six times their standard error. For owners the coefficients appear to be around 0.3 and for tenants around 0.5.

$R_p$ with respect to Household Size and Type.—

1. The higher Af and $A_h$ the higher tends to be $R_p$, and the higher is S the lower tends to be $R_p$.[38]

2. Partial regression coefficients of the three variables representing household type, with Y and Le held constant, are shown below. The means of the partial regression coefficients for the four sets of places, together with their mean standard errors, and $R^2$ of the relationships are:

| Household size and type | Regression coefficient | $R^2$ |
|---|---|---|
| S | -0.491 (0.167) | .372 |
| Af | 1.097 (0.201) | .551 |
| $A_h$ | 1.507 (0.352) | .509 |

These three coefficients are significant.

3. Where variables representing new units and population change are added, the magnitude of the regression coefficients of Af and S are modified appreciably. In general, the negative magnitude of S[39] increases and the positive magnitude of Af falls.

4. The regression coefficients observed for Lo, in general, are positive. For the owners eight of the ten coefficients shown are significant, and for the tenants only one in ten is significant. For the owners the positive sign may imply that the presence of lodgers tends to occur at the stage in the family cycle when the number of family members is low. Such a tendency undoubtedly represents some situations. Some households sublet space to lodgers after the peak of family size is past. Subletting may in fact be a means of avoiding change of dwelling unit following a decline in income. For tenants, Lo for some equations has a negative and for others a positive sign. Few of these regression coefficients of Lo are significant. Lo may be correlated with other conditions that obscure its relationship to $R_p$. It has, for example, a positive correlation with Af,

38. See Table 60, columns 3, 4, and 5.

39. This may to some extent occur because of a spurious correlation between S and $R_p$: $R_p$ is the product of $R_o$ and the reciprocal of S.

which in turn has a marked negative correlation with $R_p$.

<u>$R_p$ with respect to Importance of New Units.</u>[40]—With Y, household type, and other sets of variables held constant, the partial regression coefficients of $R_p$ with respect to $B_1$ and $B_2$ are all negative. There are 32 such coefficients and only two of them are significant. Both of these pertain to owner units, one is the coefficient of $B_1$ and the other of $B_2$. This evidence[41] implies that the importance of new units has little direct relationship to $R_p$.

<u>$R_p$ with respect to Other Conditions.</u>—Partial regression coefficients of $R_p$ with respect to population change and area characteristics tend to have negative signs. This sign is observed for 38 of the 44 coefficients shown. A positive correlation of these with cost of housing may account for the consistency of the signs. However, they add little to the explanation of variation in $R_p$.

<u>Variation among Places in $R_c$.</u>—Wide variation among places occurs in the frequency of households with high density of room use, represented by the percentage having more than 1.01 persons per room ($R_c$). For the four sets of places the variables examined explain 65 to 80 per cent of its variation. The coefficients of correlation of $R_c$ with various sets of independent variables are shown in Table 61.

<u>$R_c$ with respect to Y.</u>—

1. Y explains from 21 to 41 per cent of the variation in $R_c$ for the four sets of places. The simple regression coefficients and the $r^2$ of the variables for the sets are as follows:

| Set | $\eta R_c Y$ | $r^2$ |
|---|---|---|
| $C_o$ | -1.99 | .210 |
| $C_t$ | -1.71 | .388 |
| $E_o$ | -1.86 | .410 |
| $E_t$ | -1.49 | .351 |

Within the central city and the environs the regression coefficients have a greater negative magnitude for owners than for tenants.

40. That is dwelling units constructed during the forties.

41. Some coefficients describe tendencies with population and area characteristics also held constant. See equations of Table 60, columns 10-13.

Table 61

Coefficients of Correlation, the Percentage of Households with 1.01 Persons or More per Room ($R_c$) with respect to Income and Sets of Other Variables among Central City and Environs of 57 Metro Areas, by Tenure, 1950[a]

| | (1) | (2) | (3) | (4) | (5) | (6) | (7) | (8) | (9) | (10) | (11) | (12) | (13) |
|---|---|---|---|---|---|---|---|---|---|---|---|---|---|
| | A. Owners, Central Cities ($C_o$) | | | | | | | | | | | | |
| $R^2$ | .210 | .239 | .278 | .504 | .504 | .573 | .591 | .563 | .565 | .630 | .647 | .658 | .662 |
| Constant | 7.977 | 10.122 | 9.952 | 19.621 | 20.095 | 20.493 | 25.302 | 19.791 | 21.333 | 18.196 | 10.088 | 9.319 | 8.301 |
| Regression coefficients | | | | | | | | | | | | | |
| Y | -1.994 (.522) | -2.433 (.599) | -2.578 (.595) | -2.482 (.488) | -2.158 (.491) | -2.335 (.464) | -2.327 (.458) | -2.662 (.468) | -2.650 (.472) | -2.721 (.455) | -2.466 (.494) | -2.509 (.515) | -2.656 (.522) |
| Le | . . . . | -.512 (.354) | -.511 (.348) | -.141 (.296) | -.191 (.294) | -.168 (.276) | -.260 (.279) | -.124 (.281) | -.164 (.295) | -.570 (.311) | -.626 (.315) | -.593 (.318) | -.532 (.331) |
| S | | . . . . | 1.313 (.774) | . . . . | . . . . | 1.756 (.606) | 1.861 (.602) | 1.614 (.610) | 1.649 (.619) | 2.648 (.676) | 3.692 (.973) | 3.645 (.983) | 3.491 (1.011) |
| Af | | | . . . . | -4.577 (.860) | . . . . | . . . . | . . . . | -4.760 (.818) | -4.574 (.911) | -1.526 (1.378) | -.701 (1.568) | -.670 (1.580) | -.690 (1.589) |
| $A_h$ | | | | . . . . | -5.448 (1.023) | -5.790 (.966) | -5.413 (.987) | . . . . | . . . . | . . . . | . . . . | . . . . | . . . . |
| Lo | | | | | . . . . | . . . . | -2.733 (1.815) | . . . . | -.958 (2.004) | -2.578 (1.963) | -3.421 (2.039) | -3.214 (2.184) | -3.044 (2.209) |
| $B_1$ | | | | | | | . . . . | . . . . | . . . . | .0049 (.0033) | .0030 (.0035) | .0029 (.0037) | .0035 (.0038) |
| $B_2$ | | | | | | | | | | .0085 (.0047) | .0064 (.0050) | .0062 (.0050) | .0084 (.0059) |
| Cd | | | | | | | | | | . . . . . | 2.432 (2.102) | 1.876 (2.170) | 1.888 (2.182) |
| Ip | | | | | | | | | | | .833 (2.370) | 1.633 (2.484) | 2.409 (2.722) |
| De | | | | | | | | | | | . . . . . | .051 (.109) | .085 (.119) |
| Ar | | | | | | | | | | | | .077 (.066) | .079 (.067) |
| Po'' | | | | | | | | | | | | . . . . . | -.408 (.570) |

Table 61 (continued)

| | (1) | (2) | (3) | (4) | (5) | (6) | (7) | (8) | (9) | (10) | (11) | (12) | (13) |
|---|---|---|---|---|---|---|---|---|---|---|---|---|---|
| | B. Tenants, Central Cities ($C_t$) | | | | | | | | | | | | |
| $R^2$ | .388 | .480 | .512 | .562 | .571 | .574 | .574 | .562 | .566 | .587 | .630 | .652 | .652 |
| Constant | 7.108 | 9.727 | 9.224 | 14.834 | 17.953 | 17.138 | 18.836 | 14.903 | 12.388 | 11.475 | 3.758 | 2.461 | 2.303 |
| Regression coefficients | | | | | | | | | | | | | |
| Y | -1.711 (.290) | -2.222 (.316) | -2.159 (.311) | -2.356 (.296) | -1.878 (.307) | -1.886 (.310) | -1.918 (.328) | -2.359 (.308) | -2.260 (.344) | -2.156 (.350) | -1.770 (.379) | -1.811 (.380) | -1.811 (.384) |
| Le | . . . . | -.769 (.248) | -.779 (.243) | -.689 (.231) | -.533 (.238) | -.555 (.243) | -.580 (.257) | -.688 (.235) | -.619 (.258) | -.751 (.271) | -.715 (.263) | -.647 (.270) | -.641 (.280) |
| S | | . . . . | .713 (.384) | . . . . | . . . . | .217 (.405) | .203 (.411) | -.019 (.473) | -.025 (.476) | .399 (.548) | 1.209 (.650) | 1.272 (.659) | 1.263 (.671) |
| Af | | | . . . . | -2.209 (.700) | . . . . | . . . . | . . . . | -2.233 (.913) | -2.155 (.925) | -1.404 (1.040) | -.510 (1.077) | -.448 (1.112) | -.455 (1.127) |
| $A_h$ | | | | . . . . | -4.724 (1.409) | -4.343 (1.586) | -4.610 (1.807) | . . . . | . . . . | . . . . | . . . . | . . . . | . . . . |
| Lo | | | | | . . . . | . . . . | -.497 (1.569) | . . . . | .948 (1.413) | .399 (1.484) | -.168 (1.460) | -.463 (1.569) | -.429 (1.621) |
| $B_1$ | | | | | | | . . . . | . . . . | . . . . | .0045 (.0035) | -.00038 (.0042) | -.00045 (.0043) | -.00016 (.0053) |
| $B_2$ | | | | | | | | | | .0017 (.0030) | -.0013 (.0033) | -.0023 (.0033) | -.0021 (.0043) |
| Cd | | | | | | | | | | . . . . . | 3.291 (1.444) | 2.923 (1.522) | 2.936 (1.544) |
| Ip | | | | | | | | | | | -.746 (2.023) | .290 (2.119) | .377 (2.313) |
| De | | | | | | | | | | | . . . . | .088 (.092) | .092 (.098) |
| Ar | | | | | | | | | | | | .087 (.054) | .087 (.054) |
| Po'' | | | | | | | | | | | | . . . . . | -.056 (.556) |

Table 61 (continued)

| | (1) | (2) | (3) | (4) | (5) | (6) | (7) | (8) | (9) | (10) | (11) | (12) | (13) |
|---|---|---|---|---|---|---|---|---|---|---|---|---|---|
| | C. Owners, Environs ($E_o$) | | | | | | | | | | | | |
| $R^2$ | .410 | .453 | .502 | .707 | .691 | .691 | .730 | .708 | .729 | .772 | .796 | .798 | .803 |
| Constant | 7.647 | 9.938 | 9.270 | 21.255 | 21.835 | 21.742 | 35.751 | 20.783 | 30.465 | 24.032 | 19.170 | 19.087 | 21.707 |
| Regression coefficients | | | | | | | | | | | | | |
| Y | -1.863 (.302) | -2.277 (.355) | -2.385 (.345) | -2.766 (.272) | -2.521 (.272) | -2.523 (.275) | -2.148 (.294) | -2.772 (.274) | -2.488 (.303) | -2.151 (.332) | -2.122 (.322) | -2.097 (.395) | -2.070 (.395) |
| Le | . . . . | -.735 (.355) | -.719 (.342) | -.390 (.267) | -.495 (.271) | -.496 (.275) | -.276 (.272) | -.398 (.270) | -.250 (.272) | -.502 (.273) | -.474 (.264) | -.462 (.274) | -.460 (.273) |
| S | | . . . . | 1.990 (.875) | . . . . | . . . . | .061 (.774) | -.338 (.746) | .379 (.726) | .158 (.716) | .955 (.735) | 1.543 (.750) | 1.474 (.796) | 1.433 (.795) |
| Af | | | . . . . | -4.771 (.704) | . . . . | . . . . | . . . . | -4.625 (.761) | -4.501 (.744) | -2.505 (1.063) | -2.508 (1.028) | -2.527 (1.055) | -2.791 (1.082) |
| $A_h$ | | | | . . . . | -5.494 (.860) | -5.461 (.967) | -5.557 (.913) | . . . . | . . . . | . . . . | . . . . | . . . . | . . . . |
| Lo | | | | | . . . . | . . . . | -7.515 (2.758) | . . . . | -5.445 (2.774) | -5.054 (2.606) | -6.527 (2.598) | -6.448 (2.759) | -7.267 (2.859) |
| $B_1$ | | | | | | | . . . . | . . . . | . . . . | .0048 (.0016) | .00044 (.0024) | .00054 (.0025) | -.00028 (.0026) |
| $B_2$ | | | | | | | | | | -.000072 (.0024) | -.00033 (.0024) | -.00017 (.0025) | -.0022 (.0031) |
| Cd | | | | | | | | | | . . . . . | 1.708 (.965) | 1.656 (.995) | 1.243 (1.066) |
| Ip | | | | | | | | | | | 1.976 (1.030) | 2.031 (1.066) | 1.722 (1.103) |
| De | | | | | | | | | | | . . . . . | .0223 (.059) | .0376 (.0605) |
| De' | | | | | | | | | | | | -.0431 (.097) | -.0605 (.098) |
| Po'' | | | | | | | | | | | | . . . . . | .509 (.477) |

Table 61 (continued)

| | (1) | (2) | (3) | (4) | (5) | (6) | (7) | (8) | (9) | (10) | (11) | (12) | (13) |
|---|---|---|---|---|---|---|---|---|---|---|---|---|---|
| | D. Tenants, Environs ($E_t$) | | | | | | | | | | | | |
| $R^2$ | .351 | .382 | .454 | .641 | .536 | .539 | .573 | .648 | .648 | .754 | .771 | .775 | .777 |
| Constant | 6.456 | 7.838 | 6.314 | 17.625 | 20.823 | 19.250 | 34.379 | 19.711 | 20.694 | 19.198 | 12.698 | 11.817 | 15.181 |
| Regression coefficients | | | | | | | | | | | | | |
| Y | -1.490 (.273) | -1.730 (.307) | -1.541 (.300) | -2.075 (.243) | -1.798 (.269) | -1.747 (.286) | -1.886 (.286) | -2.206 (.273) | -2.210 (.276) | -1.835 (.256) | -1.679 (.271) | -1.666 (.302) | -1.668 (.304) |
| Le | .... | -.492 (.301) | -.337 (.292) | -.317 (.234) | -.436 (.263) | -.404 (.271) | -.478 (.266) | -.357 (.236) | -.363 (.240) | -.404 (.207) | -.397 (.204) | -.393 (.207) | -.401 (.208) |
| S | | .... | 1.448 (.547) | .... | .... | .344 (.620) | -.448 (.720) | -.615 (.587) | -.651 (.623) | -.488 (.561) | .043 (.625) | -.0051 (.636) | -.168 (.689) |
| Af | | | .... | -4.208 (.681) | .... | .... | .... | -4.826 (.901) | -4.791 (.929) | -3.399 (.848) | -3.063 (.865) | -3.230 (.899) | -3.347 (.923) |
| $A_h$ | | | | .... | -6.278 (1.492) | -5.693 (1.834) | -6.623 (1.842) | .... | .... | .... | .... | .... | .... |
| Lo | | | | | .... | .... | -6.088 (3.028) | .... | -.506 (2.716) | -1.921 (2.355) | -1.669 (2.338) | -1.014 (2.568) | -2.054 (3.029) |
| $B_1$ | | | | | | | .... | .... | .... | .0051 (.0012) | .0028 (.0018) | .0027 (.0018) | .0028 (.0018) |
| $B_2$ | | | | | | | | | | .0020 (.0012) | .0013 (.0013) | .0014 (.0013) | .00083 (.0016) |
| Cd | | | | | | | | | | ..... | .884 (.751) | .832 (.774) | .415 (1.015) |
| Ip | | | | | | | | | | | 1.337 (.897) | 1.457 (.954) | 1.075 (1.131) |
| De | | | | | | | | | | | ..... | .025 (.050) | .034 (.052) |
| De' | | | | | | | | | | | | -.067 (.082) | -.071 (.083) |
| Po'' | | | | | | | | | | | | ..... | .310 (.485) |

a. See Tables 57 and 58 for information on the definition of these variables and their form.

2. This difference by tenure persists even where the effect of many conditions is held constant. The mean of the 12 partial coefficients shown in Table 61 are

| | | | |
|---|---|---|---|
| $C_o$ | -2.51 | $C_t$ | -2.05 |
| $E_o$ | -2.36 | $E_t$ | -1.84 |

Greater mobility of tenant than owner households among dwelling units may contribute to this. In addition, tenant dwelling units are more subject to adaptation through conversions and mergers than the one-unit structures of the owners represented by the $C_o$ and $E_o$ sets.

3. The inclusion of Le tends to lower $\eta_{R_cY}$. This is the effect to expect if Le is a proxy for $Y_t$ uncorrelated with $Y_n$. The percentage decrease is much the same for owners as for tenants, namely around 20 per cent. (For the four sets of places the mean coefficient falls from -1.77 to -2.17.)

4. The further inclusion of Af decreases $\eta_{R_cY}$ by 12 per cent, that is from -2.17 to -2.42 (see Table 61, column 4).

5. For the other variables examined, no systematic interaction with $\eta_{R_cY}$ has been noted.

6. All the coefficients of $\eta_{R_cY}$ are highly significant, being three to four times their standard error. Thus Y explains much of the variation in $R_c$, among places; and higher income tends to be accompanied by a marked decline in $R_c$.

7. For the $C_o$ and the $E_o$ sets, there is some tendency for $\eta_{R_cY}$ to be higher than $\eta_{R_cY}$ for owner-occupants among census tracts of Chicago. With Le and S held constant, the mean $\eta_{R_cY}$ of the $C_o$ and $E_o$ sets is -2.48[42] whereas $\eta_{R_cY}{}^{a}$ with $S^a$ held constant, is -2.74.[43] The direction of the difference is the type to expect if Y tends to be positively correlated with the cost of housing, and the greater this correlation the less $R_c$ falls with increase in Y. However, if the cost of construction is positively correlated with Y of cities, the two partial coefficients of $R_c$ shown above, that is $R_c$ with respect to average income of places and to average income of tracts within Chicago, imply that the effect of a positive correlation between Y of cities and cost tends to be small. Its effect may of course be, in part, offset by a lag of housing behind change

42. See Table 61, column 3.

43. See Table 52, column 2.

in income and cost. If such a lag occurs and if income and cost have been tending to become more equal among cities, then it seems highly probable that the lag tended to increase[44] the coefficients of income elasticity of room crowding among places and to increase its similarity with that among census tracts.

$R_c$ with respect to Household Size and Type.—

1. Variables representing household size and type explain much of the variation in $R_c$ among places. The higher are Af and $A_h$ the lower tends to be $R_c$; and the higher is S the higher tends to be $R_c$.

2. Partial regression coefficients are shown for these three variables with Y and Le held constant. Means of these partials,[45] for the four sets of places, together with mean standard errors and $R^2$'s of the variables, are as follows:

| Household Size or Type Variables | Regression Coefficients and Standard Errors | $R^2$ |
|---|---|---|
| S | 1.37 (0.65) | .437 |
| Af | -3.94 (0.94) | .604 |
| $A_h$ | -5.49 (1.20) | .576 |

Judged in terms of standard errors and $R^2$, conditions associated with age and sex of head,[46] symbolized by Af and $A_h$, explain more of the variation in $R_c$ than those associated with S. However, each measure of household size and type appears to contribute to the explanation of $R_c$.

3. The variable Af comes close to representing a stage through which most persons pass during their lifetime. The variable S summarizes such lifetime experiences and, in addition, represents the negative correlation between S and $Y_n$. Both Af and S are represented in several estimates. The combination of these two variables adds to the explanation of variation in $R_c$, but in many of the equations the coefficients observed do not seem reasonable. For some the sign of S is negative and for others the coefficient of Af is not significant. The addition of variables representing the importance of new units and population change modifies greatly the relative magnitude of the coefficients of these variables. As S gains in significance, Af loses. Among the sets the interaction be-

44. That is, it reduces its negative magnitude.

45. See Table 61, columns 3, 4, and 5.

46. Together with the variables Y and Le.

tween these two variables is very marked and the changes are highly correlated. To get a satisfactory estimate of the relation of S to $R_o$ and $R_c$, it may be necessary to have households stratified by age and sex of head.

4. For the owners the partial regression coefficients of Lo, that is the importance of households with lodgers present, tend to be negative. This implies, with income and other characteristics of household type held constant, that owner households with lodgers tend to be low in room crowding. A similar tendency is observed where room use is represented by $R_p$.

$R_c$ with respect to Importance of New Units.—

1. The simple correlations indicate that the greater the importance of construction during the forties, the higher tend to be $R_c$. For each of the four sets of places such correlation is much more marked for the late than early forties, symbolized by $B_1$ and $B_2$, respectively. For the four sets of places the mean $r^2$ of $R_c$ with $B_1$ and $B_2$ is .255 and .083, respectively (see Table 58).

2. The partial regression coefficients of these variables, with Y, Le, S, Af, and Lo held constant, is positive for seven of the eight coefficients. However, only two of the eight coefficients are significant (see Table 61, column 10).

3. When population change and area characteristics are introduced into the relationship, only 21 of the 32 coefficients are positive and only three are significant. Thus the importance of new units does not appear to explain much of the variation of $R_c$ among cities.

$R_c$ with respect to Other Conditions.—Variables representing population change and area characteristics explain little of the variation in $R_c$, and their partial regression coefficients, in general, are not significant. The findings are nevertheless suggestive. (The coefficients are shown in Table 61, columns 11, 12, and 13.)

The variable Ip, representing importance of recent in-migrants, tends to be positive. This is the sign to be expected, since the higher is Ip the greater the likelihood that Y understates $Y_n$, because of the break in employment likely to accompany migration. In addition, the greater the importance of recent in-migrants, the greater the likelihood of a lag of housing behind change in demand. The second of these conditions is likely to result in $R_c$ being temporarily high.

Each of the partial regression coefficients of De, representing density of land use, is positive. There are 12 such coefficients. The consistent positive sign gives some reason to suppose that De, in some measure, serves as a proxy for cost of land and that the higher the cost of land the greater is likely to be the frequency of $R_c$.

Each of the four partial regression coefficients of Ar, for the $C_o$ and $C_t$ sets, is positive. This is the sign to be expected if the area of the central city combined with its density is positively correlated with the cost of land.

Population change from 1940 to 1950 is represented by Po''. Its regression coefficient is negative for the $C_o$ and $C_t$ sets and positive for the $E_o$ and $E_t$ sets. Evidence shown later suggests that this difference between the central city and the environs is caused by the greater lag of housing behind income change for central cities than environs. (New units were less important in central cities than in their environs.)

Variation among Places in S.—Variation in S has been examined because of the probability that rooms per dwelling unit in the stock tends to affect it. This effect will be present if the stock, shaped by demand and supply of earlier years, tends to affect the number of persons per household, presumably through its bearing on the doubling up of potential households.

A wide variation in S occurs among places, and the variables examined explain 46 to 77 per cent of this variation (see Table 62). Number of rooms alone explains a large part of it. However, more definitive evidence as to its effect comes from estimates that hold constant income, household type, importance of new construction, population change, and density of land use.

Of the entire set of variables examined, four seem of considerable importance. These are Y, Af, Cd, and $R_o$. For the four sets of places their partial coefficients[47] and standard errors are given in Table 63. Judged in terms of its standard error, the variable Af ranks first in importance in explaining variation in S among places. Its coefficient is negative for each of the four sets and from three to six times its standard error.

The variable Y has the sign expected and three of its four coefficients

47. For the $E_t$ set the partial regression coefficients of four other variables are significant, namely Lo, $B_1$, Ip, and Po''. However, for none of the other sets are any of the partial regression coefficients of these variables significant (see Table 62).

Table 62

Coefficients of Correlation of Number of Persons per Household (S) with respect to Income and Sets of Other Variables among Central City and Environs of 57 Metro Areas, by Tenure, 1950[a]

| | (1) | (2) | (3) | (4) | (5) | (6) | (7) | (8) | (9) |
|---|---|---|---|---|---|---|---|---|---|
| | A. Owners, Central Cities ($C_o$) | | | | | | | | |
| $R^2$ | .028 | .028 | .313 | .419 | .419 | .455 | .678 | .683 | .699 |
| Constant | .124 | .130 | .411 | 1.728 | 1.720 | 1.806 | 4.300 | 4.330 | 3.822 |
| Regression coefficients | | | | | | | | | |
| Y | .111 (.089) | .110 (.104) | -.041 (.094) | -.122 (.091) | -.122 (.092) | -.095 (.096) | -.133 (.076) | -.152 (.082) | -.163 (.081) |
| Le | | -.0015 (.061) | -.036 (.052) | -.0075 (.050) | -.0073 (.052) | .042 (.059) | .059 (.047) | .059 (.047) | .073 (.047) |
| $R_o$ | | | .402 (.086) | .601 (.103) | .600 (.105) | .482 (.127) | .178 (.113) | .195 (.117) | .200 (.115) |
| Af | | | | -.568 (.185) | -.569 (.192) | -.823 (.237) | -.798 (.201) | -.794 (.204) | -.765 (.201) |
| Lo | | | | | .0046 (.358) | .205 (.376) | .564 (.302) | .494 (.329) | .507 (.324) |
| $B_1$ | | | | | | -.0091 (.00060) | .00023 (.00052) | .00030 (.00054) | .00047 (.00054) |
| $B_2$ | | | | | | -.00041 (.00092) | .00051 (.00074) | .00049 (.00075) | .00116 (.00086) |
| Cd | | | | | | | -1.062 (.270) | -1.087 (.278) | -1.022 (.277) |
| Ip | | | | | | | -.378 (.342) | -.301 (.365) | -.044 (.396) |
| De | | | | | | | | .0123 (.0161) | .022 (.017) |
| Ar | | | | | | | | .0051 (.0099) | .0058 (.0098) |
| Po'' | | | | | | | | | -.124 (.080) |

Table 62 (continued)

| | (1) | (2) | (3) | (4) | (5) | (6) | (7) | (8) | (9) |
|---|---|---|---|---|---|---|---|---|---|
| | B. Tenants, Central Cities ($C_t$) | | | | | | | | |
| $R^2$ | .020 | .020 | .473 | .698 | .698 | .712 | .761 | .769 | .773 |
| Constant | .753 | .705 | 1.414 | 3.492 | 3.558 | 3.299 | 5.113 | 4.885 | 4.559 |
| Regression coefficients | | | | | | | | | |
| Y | -.098 (.093) | -.088 (.110) | -.353 (.090) | -.363 (.069) | -.366 (.077) | -.343 (.078) | -.349 (.072) | -.329 (.076) | -.323 (.077) |
| Le | | .014 (.086) | -.075 (.065) | -.024 (.050) | -.026 (.055) | .0058 (.060) | .00079 (.056) | .016 (.058) | .026 (.059) |
| $R_o$ | | | .542 (.080) | .445 (.063) | .445 (.064) | .392 (.077) | .265 (.083) | .262 (.086) | .259 (.086) |
| Af | | | | -.954 (.153) | -.956 (.156) | -1.021 (.167) | -.995 (.164) | -1.038 (.169) | -1.036 (.170) |
| Lo | | | | | -.025 (.298) | .131 (.314) | .293 (.297) | .421 (.321) | .468 (.327) |
| $B_1$ | | | | | | -.0011 (.00074) | .00044 (.00086) | .00014 (.00089) | .00061 (.0011) |
| $B_2$ | | | | | | .00012 (.00064) | .00094 (.00066) | .00089 (.00067) | .00130 (.00085) |
| Cd | | | | | | | -.605 (.290) | -.711 (.302) | -.680 (.306) |
| Ip | | | | | | | -.424 (.407) | -.303 (.434) | -.157 (.473) |
| De | | | | | | | | -.017 (.018) | -.011 (.020) |
| Ar | | | | | | | | .0068 (.0113) | .0064 (.0114) |
| Po'' | | | | | | | | | -.0904 (.113) |

Table 62 (continued)

| | (1) | (2) | (3) | (4) | (5) | (6) | (7) | (8) | (9) |
|---|---|---|---|---|---|---|---|---|---|
| | C. Owners, Environs ($E_o$) | | | | | | | | |
| $R^2$ | .032 | .032 | .032 | .286 | .342 | .375 | .414 | .453 | .456 |
| Constant | .312 | .336 | .411 | 2.139 | 4.095 | 4.142 | 4.273 | 4.367 | 4.613 |
| Regression coefficients | | | | | | | | | |
| Y | .059 (.043) | .054 (.053) | .023 (.067) | -.140 (.071) | -.113 (.070) | -.124 (.071) | -.100 (.072) | -.138 (.079) | -.138 (.079) |
| Le | | -.0076 (.053) | -.019 (.056) | -.011 (.049) | .011 (.049) | .028 (.052) | .029 (.052) | .020 (.052) | .019 (.052) |
| $R_o$ | | | .067 (.091) | .284 (.094) | .333 (.094) | .237 (.113) | .157 (.121) | .126 (.121) | .136 (.123) |
| Af | | | | -.628 (.149) | -.630 (.144) | -.775 (.170) | -.702 (.174) | -.688 (.172) | -.711 (.180) |
| Lo | | | | | -1.042 (.496) | -.861 (.507) | -.487 (.544) | -.599 (.548) | -.688 (.582) |
| $B_1$ | | | | | | -.00044 (.00033) | .00013 (.00046) | .00017 (.00046) | .00006 (.00048) |
| $B_2$ | | | | | | -.00045 (.00045) | -.00042 (.00045) | -.00046 (.00045) | -.00064 (.00057) |
| Cd | | | | | | | -.235 (.186) | -.207 (.186) | -.239 (.198) |
| Ip | | | | | | | -.296 (.199) | -.222 (.200) | -.243 (.206) |
| De | | | | | | | | .019 (.011) | .020 (.011) |
| De' | | | | | | | | .0039 (.018) | .0022 (.018) |
| Po'' | | | | | | | | | .045 (.090) |

Table 62 (continued)

| | (1) | (2) | (3) | (4) | (5) | (6) | (7) | (8) | (9) |
|---|---|---|---|---|---|---|---|---|---|
| | D. Tenants, Environs ($E_t$) | | | | | | | | |
| $R^2$ | .027 | .066 | .112 | .584 | .621 | .671 | .709 | .716 | .755 |
| Constant | .752 | 1.052 | 1.207 | 3.883 | 5.834 | 5.782 | 6.689 | 6.326 | 8.119 |
| Regression coefficients | | | | | | | | | |
| Y | -.079<br>(.064) | -.131<br>(.072) | -.202<br>(.083) | -.336<br>(.060) | -.321<br>(.058) | -.322<br>(.055) | -.310<br>(.054) | -.303<br>(.060) | -.271<br>(.058) |
| Le | | -.106<br>(.071) | -.113<br>(.070) | -.072<br>(.049) | -.077<br>(.047) | -.089<br>(.044) | -.076<br>(.044) | -.074<br>(.043) | -.072<br>(.041) |
| $R_o$ | | | .171<br>(.102) | .275<br>(.072) | .260<br>(.070) | .302<br>(.077) | .223<br>(.081) | .235<br>(.083) | .222<br>(.078) |
| Af | | | | -1.110<br>(.145) | -.941<br>(.158) | -.798<br>(.161) | -.781<br>(.156) | -.812<br>(.162) | -.802<br>(.152) |
| Lo | | | | | -1.160<br>(.518) | -1.293<br>(.496) | -1.151<br>(.483) | -.956<br>(.537) | -1.621<br>(.562) |
| $B_1$ | | | | | | .00018<br>(.00031) | .00073<br>(.00038) | .00071<br>(.00038) | .00072<br>(.00036) |
| $B_2$ | | | | | | .00070<br>(.00026) | .00079<br>(.00026) | .00080<br>(.00026) | .00022<br>(.00033) |
| Cd | | | | | | | -.295<br>(.159) | -.301<br>(.163) | -.580<br>(.185) |
| Ip | | | | | | | -.316<br>(.191) | -.282<br>(.205) | -.534<br>(.214) |
| De | | | | | | | | .0047<br>(.0107) | .011<br>(.010) |
| De' | | | | | | | | -.018<br>(.018) | -.019<br>(.017) |
| Po'' | | | | | | | | | .243<br>(.091) |

a. See Tables 57 and 58 for information on the definitions of these variables and their form.

are significant and the other is marginal. Thus the higher Y, the lower tends to be S, or, conversely, the lower Y, the higher tends to be S. This is consistent with the evidence of chapter iv which indicated that, among occupational groups during the early fifties, the higher the income the lower tends to be the birth rate, and that among places the higher the average income of the male labor force the greater the likelihood of the doubling up of potential households.

Table 63

Variation in S with respect to Y, Af, Cd, and $R_o$, Mean Partial Regression Coefficients

| | Y | Af | Cd | $R_o$ |
|---|---|---|---|---|
| $C_o$ | -0.163<br>(.081) | -0.765<br>(.201) | -1.022<br>(.277) | 0.200<br>(.115) |
| $C_t$ | -0.323<br>(.077) | -1.036<br>(.170) | -0.680<br>(.306) | 0.259<br>(.086) |
| $E_o$ | -0.138<br>(.079) | -0.711<br>(.180) | -0.239<br>(.198) | 0.136<br>(.123) |
| $E_t$ | -0.271<br>(.058) | -0.802<br>(.152) | -0.580<br>(.185) | 0.222<br>(.078) |

Source: See Table 62, column 9.

For each of the four sets the coefficient of Cd has a negative sign and for three of the four coefficients it is significant, being three to five times its standard error. It may well be that Cd is highly correlated with the undoubling of households which leads to a high proportion of one-person households. (This undoubling is in part a postwar phenomenon.)

$R_o$ appears also to have had a role in household membership. For each of the sets of places its sign is positive indicating that the higher $R_o$ the higher tends to be S. Two of the four coefficients are significant and one is marginal. In addition, the significance of the coefficients is much more marked for tenants than owners.

Some of the correlation observed between S and $R_o$ may represent lag of housing behind income change. The residuals examined in the section that follows makes this seem likely.

Variations of Residuals.—Residuals of $R_o$, $R_p$, and $R_c$ have been examined for the four sets of places for those equations with the greatest number of variables included (see Tables 59-61, column 13). Presumably, normal income is held constant as well as much of the mixture of household types, conditions associated with construction of new units during the forties, population change, both recent and that of the forties, and city area and density of population.

The residuals of the four sets are positively correlated. This implies the presence of some condition or conditions common to the tenures and to contiguous locations that are not represented by the variables included. This correlation is higher for the $C_o$ and $C_t$ and for the $E_o$ and $E_t$ than it is for the $C_o$ and $E_o$ and for the $C_t$ and $E_t$ sets. This difference indicates that similarity of location is more important than similarity of tenure.

Two conditions common to the four sets of places are first considered: (a) the probable lag of $R_o$ behind income change, and (b) interplace difference in the cost of residential construction. This more intensive examination of residuals is confined to the $C_o$ and the $C_t$ sets.

Lag of Housing behind Change in Income.—It was noted above that a considerable change occurred during the forties in the regional distribution of income, with the income rising more in places of low than of high income in 1940. If change in rooms per dwelling unit tends to lag behind income change, then one would expect to observe the residuals of $R_o$ to be positively correlated with average $R_o$ of the stock of 1940. The explanatory variable to be considered is $R_o$[48] of the stock of 1940 for owners and tenants,[49] respectively. It is symbolized by $R_o$-t. Its relation to

48. If income of households were reported by tenure for 1940, it would also be a means of testing the extent of the lag of room per dwelling unit behind change in market conditions. Such information is not available. A cursory examination of the change in wage and salary income of the experienced male labor force gave no reason to suppose that it is especially suitable as a means of testing for the presence of a lag in housing of the owner or the tenant stock of 1950. This is not surprising. Owner-occupancy varies in importance among places and so also does the difference in average income by tenure. Furthermore change in the importance of owner occupancy between 1940 and 1950 differed greatly among cities. All of these conditions tend to make any measure of income change for the population in general, no matter how perfect, a very poor estimate of income change by tenure.

49. The shift of dwelling units between the tenures during the forties may have reduced the usefulness of these variables as evidence of lag in the adaptation of the stock to change in income. Some of the change between 1940 and 1950 in $R_o$ represents a net shift in the dwelling units from tenant- to owner-occupancy. The cities differ a good deal in the extent of this shift.

the residuals of $R_o$, $R_c$, and $R_p$ of the $C_o$ and $C_t$ sets is examined. The residuals of these variables are symbolized by the superscript z. The correlations are highly significant. They are summarized in Table 64 for the $C_o$ and $C_t$ sets.

Table 64

Coefficients of Correlation of Residuals[a] of $R_o$, $R_c$, and $R_p$ of Estimates for 1950 with Respect to Average Room per Dwelling Unit in the Stock of 1940,[b] by Tenure, 56 Cities[c]

| Dependent variable | Constant | Coefficient of $R_o^{-t}$ | $r^2$ |
|---|---|---|---|
| 1. $R_o^z$ | | | |
| a) Owners ($C_o$) | -0.234 | 0.314 | .273 |
| b) Tenants ($C_t$) | -0.117 | 0.197 | .234 |
| 2. $R_c^z$ | | | |
| a) Owners ($C_o$) | 1.309 | -1.758 | .286 |
| b) Tenants ($C_t$) | 0.348 | -0.590 | .223 |
| 3. $R_p^z$ | | | |
| a) Owners ($C_o$) | -0.237 | 0.319 | .275 |
| b) Tenants ($C_t$) | -0.119 | 0.202 | .242 |

a. The residuals analyzed are symbolized by the superscript z. They are estimated from equations shown in Tables 59, 60, and 61, column 13.

b. Data come from the U.S. Census of Housing: 1940, Vol. II, Part I, Table 79. The averages represent all types of structures for each of the tenures. They are symbolized by $R_o^{-t}$. Only one-unit structures are represented by the ($C_o$) set.

c. One city is omitted because information on rooms per dwelling unit by tenure is not reported for 1940.

The higher is $R_o$-t, the higher tends to be $R_o$z. This implies that $R_o$ tends to understate demand for rooms more in cities where $R_o$-t is low than where it is high. In addition, the higher $R_o$-t, the lower tends to be $R_c$z. This indicates that some of the variation in $R_c$ among cities is a function of lag of housing behind change in income. Where $R_o$-t is low, $R_c$ of 1950 tends to be high in part because change in the stock of rooms had not yet caught up with the change in demand. Conversely, the higher is $R_o$-t the higher tends to be $R_p$z.

The coefficients of determination ($r^2$) and of regression, shown in

Table 64, imply that the lag was greater for the owners in one-unit structures than for tenants.

Interplace Difference in the Cost of Housing.—The expectation is that the higher the cost of housing, the lower tends to be $R_o$ and $R_p$ and the higher tends to be $R_c$. Several variables used in equations summarized in Tables 59-61 seem likely to have served as crude proxies for cost: these include Y, and Ar and De representing area and density of cities. The question to be considered in this section is whether the residuals observed also reflect in part difference in construction cost among cities.

This possibility has been tested using as the explanatory variable the Boeckh intercity construction cost index described above. This index is available for 28[50] cities in the set of 57. It is symbolized by $P_c$. The higher is $P_c$, the lower tends to be $R_o z$ and $R_p z$. The correlations are shown in Table 65 for the 28 cities.

If the residuals reflect the full extent of difference in construction costs among cities, then the coefficients shown imply that the elasticity of rooms per dwelling unit with respect to cost of construction tend to be around -0.24. However, it seems not improbable that such an estimate understates the downward pull of high cost of construction on $R_o$.[51]

50. Information on the Boeckh intercity index of residential construction cost ($P_c$) is available for 43 cities for which information is reported on central city of a metro area. For owner-occupants of these, Y and $P_c$ index explain 28 per cent of the variation in $R_o$. However, the partial coefficient of Y is negative and that of the cost variable is positive, and the effect of $P_c$ is dominant. Thus the signs of the regression coefficients are the opposite from those expected. For these places the correlation is as follows:

$$x_{R_o} = -.547 - .210\, x_Y + .885\, x_{P_c} \qquad R^2 = .280 \qquad (12.1)$$

where $R_o$ is the median number of rooms of owner units in one-unit structures, Y is median income of the primary unit of households in such structures, and $P_c$ is the intercity index of cost of residential construction. These coefficients seem likely to be much influenced by various types of lag. There seems no reason to suppose that the estimates shown in Tables 57-62 would have been modified appreciably by the inclusion of metro areas in this set that are not in the set of 57 metro areas.

51. For discussion of estimation of functional relationships from residuals, see Rudolf J. Freud and others, "Residual Analysis," Journal of the American Statistical Association, March, 1961, pp. 98-104; and Arthur S. Goldberger and D. B. Jochems, "Note on Stepwise Least Squares," ibid., pp. 105-10.

Other Conditions Associated with the Residuals.—The residuals of the equations shown in Table 65, that is with $R_o$-t and $P_c$ held constant, are not correlated between the tenures. This lack of correlation reduces the likelihood that residuals reflect the effect of such things as importance of non-whites or of household types not adequately represented by the variables used. Nevertheless, residuals for the 28 cities were exam-

Table 65

Coefficients of Correlation of Residuals[a] of $R_o$ and $R_p$ of Estimates for 1950 with respect to Average Rooms per Dwelling Unit in the Stock of 1940[b] and an Intercity Cost[c] Index of 1950, by Tenure, 28 Cities[d]

| Dependent variable | Constant (1) | Regression coefficients of $R_o$-t (2) | $P_c$ (3) | $R^2$ (4) |
|---|---|---|---|---|
| 1. $R_o^z$ | | | | |
| a) Owners ($C_o$) | | | | |
| 1) | -0.197 | 0.265 | . . . | .204[e] |
| 2) | .342 | .315 | -0.246 | .283[f] |
| b) Tenants ($C_t$) | | | | |
| 1) | -.089 | .147 | . . . | .173[e] |
| 2) | .447 | .183 | -.238 | .215[g] |
| 2. $R_p^z$ | | | | |
| a) Owners ($C_o$) | | | | |
| 1) | -.194 | .262 | . . . | .197[e] |
| 2) | .367 | .314 | -.257 | .282[f] |
| b) Tenants ($C_t$) | | | | |
| 1) | -.095 | .158 | . . . | .197[e] |
| 2) | 0.386 | 0.184 | -0.212 | .223[g] |

a. For description of these see Table 64, fn. a.

b. See Table 64, fn. b.

c. This is an interplace residential construction cost index, brick structures, as of June, 1949, provided by E. W. Boeckh and Associates.

d. These are the 28 places in the respective sets for which information on construction cost was made available.

e. These coefficients are appreciably lower than those shown for these variables of the set of 56 places. This seems likely to be due chiefly to the failure of this subset to represent conditions for the entire set of 57 cities.

f. These coefficients are significant at the .01 probability level.

g. These coefficients are significant at the .02 probability level.

ined with respect to variables representing these. No systematic tendencies were observed.

A Summing Up.—This section has examined the variation in rooms per dwelling unit ($R_o$) and their occupancy for owners and tenants of central cities and environs of a large set of metro areas as of 1950. The possible effect of many variables has been considered, including average income, employment level, mixture of household types, importance of new units constructed during the forties, population change, lag of housing behind change in demand, and interplace difference in the cost of housing.

On some tendencies there seems little doubt: (1) The higher the income (Y), the higher tends to be $R_o$ and rooms per person ($R_p$) and the lower tends to be percentage of households with 1.01 or more persons per room ($R_c$). Furthermore, the effect of Y on these is very marked. The interplace coefficient of income elasticity of $R_o$ appears to be between 0.3 and 0.5, of $R_p$ between 0.3 and 0.5, and $R_c$ around -2.5.

2) $R_p$ and $R_c$ are much affected by the proportion of households with an aged or a female head. The higher this percentage, the higher tends to be $R_p$ and the lower tends to be $R_c$.

3) With income and household type held constant, high cost of housing tends to lower $R_o$ and $R_p$ and to increase $R_c$. These effects are indicated by the signs of partial coefficients of variables representing conditions correlated with price of housing, such as city density and area, and the importance of new units constructed during the forties, a time of relatively high cost; and by the relation of the residuals to an intercity index of construction cost. The estimates imply a price elasticity of demand for rooms per dwelling unit at least as low as -0.25 (Table 65).

4) An appreciable lag existed in 1950 of change in $R_o$ behind change in income and construction cost. The tendencies observed indicate a considerable backlog of demand in places where income had risen most. On the other hand, for some cities the increase in demand associated with rise in income appears to have been more than offset by the increase in the cost of housing. In them there appears to have been some tendency in 1950 to consume the existing stock of housing and for $R_o$ of the stock in general to decline.

5) There appears to be some tendency for household membership to be a function of the stock. Where $R_o$ tends to be high because of historical conditions, it will be a factor tending to increase S. If fewer per-

sons per household is a preferred condition, then rise in real income will tend to be accompanied by a reduction in S. Undoubling of potential households is one of the important ways of improving the quality of housing from the standpoint of many consumer units.

6) The direction of the effect indicated by most of the estimates shown seems likely to have quite high reliability. The reliability of several coefficients might have been increased by holding constant difference among cities in current construction cost. It would have been further improved by holding constant the income and the cost of housing at the time the units entered the stock.

## Differences between Environs and Central Cities

Correlations among metro areas of the differences between central cities and environs in $R_o$, $R_p$, Y, and related conditions tend to be unaffected by conditions common to the central city and its environs, such as the current cost of construction. If cities and their environs tend to have much the same current cost of construction, one important condition that seems likely to affect intercity correlations is held constant. In addition, secular lag in income and cost seems likely to have common tendencies for environs and central cities. The mixture of periods of construction represented by the stock of environs and central cities undoubtedly differs among metro areas. There seems no reason, however, to suppose that such difference is correlated with difference in income between environs and central cities, when household type is held constant.

The variables of this section are of the type described in chapter viii. In other words, they represent differences for a set of metro areas between two subsets of households, namely those living in the two main portions of metro areas. The variables are symbolized by the superscript [*]. The dependent variables examined are $R_o^*$ and $R_p^*$, and $Y^*$ is the main explanatory variable. Three variables are used to represent the mixture of household size and types, namely number of persons per household ($S^*$) and the importance of households with an aged or a female head ($Af^*$) and of households with a male head under 35 years of age with wife but no non-relative present ($A_y^*$).[52] The mixture of year of construction of the dwelling units is represented only by the importance of

52. This is the number of all households per 100 households exclusive of those with male head under 35 years of age with wife but no non-relative present.

units built during the decade of the forties. It is symbolized by $B^*$. Coefficients of correlation of $R_o^*$ and $R_p^*$ with respect to several sets of variables are summarized in Tables 66 and 67. Tendencies indicated there are briefly reviewed.

Variation in $R_o^*$.—

1. For both owners and tenants an appreciable part of the variation in $R_o^*$ is explained by $Y^*$. Its partial regression coefficient is increased somewhat by holding constant the mixture of household types and the importance of new units. An income elasticity of $R_o^*$ with respect to $Y^*$ of 0.3-0.4 is indicated.

2. $R_o^*$ is positively correlated with $S^*$, and this correlation is much more marked for tenants than for owners. This difference is consistent with the longer horizon of owner than tenant households in choosing a unit for occupancy.

3. For both tenures, with $Y^*$ and $Af^*$ held constant, the higher is $A_y^*$ and $B^*$ the lower tends to be $R_o^*$. The similarity of signs may come from different causes. The negative sign of $A_y^*$ may represent the normal tendency for $R_o$ to be low early in the family cycle, when children are young. The negative sign of $B^*$ may represent the effect of secular rise in cost with income held constant.

4. With no difference between the environs and the central city in $Y^*$, $S^*$, $Af^*$, and $A_y^*$ and $B^*$, there is very little difference in $R_o^*$. In other words it tends to be close to zero (see constant term, Table 66, line 2).

Variation in $R_p^*$.—

1. Much of the variation in $R_p^*$ is explained by $Y^*$. In addition, its partial regression coefficient is increased appreciably by holding $Af^*$ constant. The tendencies are much the same for the two tenures. With $A_y^*$ and $B^*$ also held constant the partial coefficient of $\eta_{R_p Y^*}$ tends to be between 0.4 and 0.5.

2. In general the higher $Af^*$, the higher tends to be $R_p^*$ and the higher $A_y^*$ the lower tends to be $R_p^*$. These are the tendencies expected because of the phase in the family cycle represented. The magnitude of these coefficients may of course also be affected somewhat by the secular lag. For example, it seems not unreasonable to expect, with Y held constant, that households with an aged head will concentrate in the older dwelling units surviving from the stock constructed during years of lower cost (and now relatively shabby), whereas there is a tendency

Table 66

Coefficients of Correlation of Difference in $R_o$ and in Y and Associated Conditions between the Central City and Environs, by Tenure, 57 Metro Areas, 1950[a]

| | Coefficients of determination and of regression | | | | | | | | | |
|---|---|---|---|---|---|---|---|---|---|---|
| | A. Owners | | | | | B. Tenants | | | | |
| | (1) | (2) | (3) | (4) | (5) | (1) | (2) | (3) | (4) | (5) |
| 1. $R^2$ | .421 | .423 | .456 | .515 | .552 | .264 | .583 | .587 | .595 | .616 |
| 2. Constant | -.031 | -.031 | -.021 | -.014 | -.011 | .025 | -.006 | -.004 | -.001 | .001 |
| 3. $Y^*$ | .238 | .236 | .308 | .300 | .297 | .323 | .344 | .372 | .384 | .404 |
| 4. $S^*$ | . . . | -.041 | .018 | .070 | .136 | . . . | .462 | .517 | .541 | .603 |
| 5. $Af^*$ | | . . . | .206 | .068 | .046 | | . . . | .123 | .035 | .051 |
| 6. $A_y^*$ | | | . . . | -.259 | -.200 | | | . . . | -.123 | -.093 |
| 7. $B^*$ | | | | . . . | -.045 | | | | . . . | -.076 |

Source: See Table 57.

a. The variables represent differences between the central cities and the environs with variables in log form. The superscript [*] is used to indicate this type of observation, as it is in chapter viii. The variables represent differences in:

$R_o^*$ number of rooms per occupied dwelling unit

$Y^*$ income of the primary units of the households

$S^*$ number of persons per household

$Af^*$ the importance of households with an aged or a female head

$A_y^*$ importance of households with male head less than 35 years of age with wife present and no non-relative

$B^*$ the importance of the dwelling units built in the 1950 stock during the forties or later.

See Tables 57 - 65 for further information bearing on these variables.

Table 67

Coefficients of Correlation of Differences between Environs and Central Cities, of $R_P$ and Y together with Other Differences, by Tenure, 57 Metro Areas, 1950[a]

| | A. Owners | | | | B. Tenants | | | |
|---|---|---|---|---|---|---|---|---|
| | (1) | (2) | (3) | (4) | (5) | (6) | (7) | (8) |
| 1. $R^2$ | 0.223 | 0.402 | 0.499 | 0.533 | 0.271 | 0.482 | 0.520 | 0.560 |
| 2. Constant | - .029 | .005 | .019 | .019 | - .039 | - .006 | - .001 | - .006 |
| 3. $Y^*$ | .278 | .506 | .468 | .436 | .342 | .477 | .488 | .488 |
| 4. $Af^*$ | . . . . | .682 | .503 | .278 | . . . . | .663 | .420 | .338 |
| 5. $A_y^*$ | . . . . | . . . . | .511 | - .347 | . . . . | . . . . | - .261 | - .199 |
| 6. $B^*$ | . . . . | . . . . | . . . . | - .098 | . . . . | . . . . | . . . . | - .109 |

Source: See Table 66.

a. The dependent variable of the estimates shown is the difference between environs and central cities in rooms per person, with variables expressed in log form. This difference is symbolized by $R_p^*$. See Table 66, footnotes, for description of the explanatory variables.

for households with a younger head, represented by $A_y^*$, to concentrate in dwelling units recently constructed under conditions of relatively high cost or in dwelling units that have not yet attained their maximum number of rooms.

3. With no difference between environs and the central city in income, in mixture of household types, and importance of new units, $R_p^*$ of the environs tends to be 104 for owners and 99 for tenants with $R_p$ of central city equal to 100. In other words, for owner-occupants rooms per person tend to be somewhat higher in the environs than in the central city, whereas for tenants no difference is observed.

Income Elasticity of Rooms and Their Occupancy within and between Metro Areas.—$\eta_{R_oY}^*$ and $\eta_{R_pY}^*$ describe tendencies within metro areas. $\eta_{R_oY}$ and $\eta_{R_pY}$ describe tendencies among metro areas. The latter are likely to be affected by several conditions unlikely to affect tendencies within metro areas such as construction cost and migration. Even so, the two sets of coefficients have much in common: $\eta_{R_oY}^*$ tends to be between 0.3 and 0.4 and $\eta_{R_oY}$ is between 0.3 and 0.5; and $\eta_{R_pY}^*$ tends to be between 0.4 and 0.5 and $\eta_{R_pY}$ is between 0.3 and 0.5.

This similarity is consistent with different sets of conditions: Both sets of observations could come close to representing housing with respect to normal income. This might imply (a) that secular lag and cost of construction have only a slight correlation with income of households as reported in the census of 1950, or, (b) that conditions held constant in estimating $\eta_{R_oY}^*$ and $\eta_{R_pY}^*$, such as the cost of construction, the price of land, and some of the secular change, tend to have offsetting effects on the interplace tendencies represented by $\eta_{R_oY}$ and $\eta_{R_pY}$. Condition (b) seems to me to be the more likely. The Northeast region is relatively high in $R_o$ and is the region that historically has ranked at the top of the income distribution. During the decade of the forties its income position among the regions fell. In addition, the age of distribution of the dwelling units of the Northeast makes it seem likely that this region was lagging most with respect to the decline in units high in $R_o$, with change in birth rate, and other conditions affecting demand for rooms.

## An Estimate of Change from 1940 to 1950

Changes between 1940 and 1950 in $R_o$ and in income and construction costs are described above in the section entitled "Variation among places in change from 1940 to 1950." The evidence presented there indicates a positive correlation between change in income and in construction cost. This section presents estimates of change in $R_o$ with respect to change in income and other conditions. Observations for a set of 41 cities[53] are examined. The estimates represent all households, that is owners and tenants combined.[54]

Change in rooms per dwelling unit between 1940 and 1950 is symbolized by $R_o''$. Income change is represented by wage and salary income of the experienced male labor force in 1949 per $100 of such income in 1939. It is symbolized by $Y_m''$, and income elasticity of $R_o''$ with respect to $Y_m''$ is symbolized by $\eta_{R_oY_m}''$.

The income variable is supplemented by two variables representing the transitory income of the respective periods. One is Le, already described. The other is the percentage of the male labor force of 1940 working less than 12 months during 1939. This is symbolized by $Le^{-t}$. The expectation is that the higher Le, the greater the importance of the negative transitory component of income of 1949 and the higher will tend to be $\eta_{R_oY_m}''$, and the higher $Le^{-t}$ the greater the importance of the negative transitory component of 1939 and the lower will tend to be $\eta_{R_oY}''$.

Two variables are used to represent household type. These are the number of persons per dwelling unit and the percentage of the population 21 years of age or more that is 65 years of age or more. The ratios of these between years are symbolized by S'' and A'', respectively. The assumption is that A'' is positively correlated with change in the importance of households with an aged head.[55] Hence, the expectation is that A'' will tend to be positively correlated with $R_o''$, when $Y_m''$ is held constant.

Change in cost is represented by the Boeckh index of the cost of residential construction. It is symbolized by $P_c''$. The effect of units constructed during the forties is also examined. As in earlier estimates it is symbolized by B. In addition, the effect of population change is examined. It is symbolized by Po''.

---

53. These are the cities for which information is available on the construction cost index and for which information was reported by the census of 1940 on wage and salary of 1939. They include 28 in the set of 57 metro areas represented by the preceding sections.

54. This combination has been made because information as to income for 1939 is not available by tenure.

55. Information is not provided by the census of 1940 on the distribution of household types.

The correlation of $R_o''$ with respect to $Y_m''$ and other variables is summarized in Table 68. Several tendencies indicated seem of interest: (1) $Y_m''$ by itself explains very little of the variation in $R_o''$.

2) The variables Le and $Le^{-t}$ have the signs one would expect if they serve as proxies for the importance of transitory income associated with employment opportunity of 1949 and 1939, respectively. Their inclusion increases $\eta R_o Y_m''$ somewhat, and increased the $R^2$ of the variables a great deal: from .063 to .270.

3) For none of the estimates does $\eta R_o Y_m''$ exceed 0.18. Thus it is about one-half of the coefficient of $\eta R_o Y^*$ observed in the preceding section where it seems highly probable that the income variable comes close to representing normal income and where cost and the lag of housing stock behind various changes are in some measure held constant. It seems not unlikely that this difference between the two estimates of income elasticity of rooms with respect to income is the result of a random transitory component in $Y_m^*$. The change in average wage and salary income of the experienced male labor force seems likely to be a very crude measure of change in normal income of hoursholds.

4) The partial regression coefficients of $P_c''$ tend to be negative. In other words, the more cost rose, the lower $R_o''$. The tendency for $R_o''$ to be depressed by increase in $P_c''$ is intensified by taking into account the importance of new units (B). This is not surprising: increase in cost seems more likely to lower average rooms of units entering the stock more than those already in the stock.

5) The lowest coefficient of $\eta R_o P_c''$ shown in Table 68 is -0.220. This is much the same as the coefficient of price or cost elasticity estimated from the residuals of the intercity regressions. Such coefficients are shown in Table 65, and their mean is -0.238. It was noted above that such coefficients estimated from the residuals seem likely to be biased upward. In other words, such coefficients probably understate the tendency for increase in cost to depress $R_o$. However, the estimates derived from the residuals have the advantage of being relatively free from the effect of lag of $R_o$ behind market changes in demand and the cost of housing.

The censuses of housing of 1950 and 1960 should together permit intertemporal estimates of the income elasticity of housing where the income variable comes close to representing change in normal income.

Table 68

Coefficients of Correlation of Differences,[a] between 1940 and 1950, of $R_o''$ and $Y_m''$ and Other Conditions, 41 Cities[b]

| | (1) | (2) | (3) | (4) | (5) | (6) | (7) |
|---|---|---|---|---|---|---|---|
| 1. $R^2$ | .063 | .270 | .270 | .400 | .406 | .468 | .469 |
| 2. $Y_m''$ | .137 | .181 | .177 | .170 | .180 | .143 | .147 |
| 3. Le | . . . | .133 | .130 | .124 | .122 | .108 | .105 |
| 4. $Le^{-t}$ | . . . | -.146 | -.142 | -.224 | -.224 | -.153 | -.151 |
| 5. $S''$ | . . . | . . . | -.071 | .094 | .075 | .020 | .041 |
| 6. $A_m''$ | . . . | . . . | . . . | .298 | .284 | .293 | .278 |
| 7. $P_c''$ | . . . | . . . | . . . | . . . | -.076 | -.208 | -.220 |
| 8. B | . . . | . . . | . . . | . . . | . . . | .00094 | .00127 |
| 9. $Po''$ | . . . | . . . | . . . | . . . | . . . | . . . | -.065 |

Source: U.S. Census of Population: 1940, Vols. II and III; U.S. Census of Housing: 1940, Vol. I; U.S. Census of Population: 1950, Vol. II; U.S. Census of Housing: 1950, Vol. I, and E. W. Boeckh & Associates.

a. Where variables represent change over the decade the symbol has the superscript ["]. Such change is measured in terms of difference between two years with variables expressed in log form. Unless otherwise specified all variables are expressed in log form. The variables are as follows:

$R_o''$ Difference in number of rooms per dwelling unit of the entire stock

$Y_m''$ Difference in the median wage and salary income of the experienced male labor force, as estimated from distributions reported in the respective censuses

Le Percentage of the male labor force of 1950 with less than 26 weeks of work during 1949

$Le^{-t}$ Percentage of the male labor force of 1940, other than those on emergency relief, working less than 12 months during 1939

$S''$ Difference in number of persons per household

$A_m''$ Difference in the importance of adult males 65 years of age or more per 100 adult males less than 65

$P_c''$ Difference in the Boeckh index of cost of residential construction between June 1939 and June 1949

B Percentage of the stock of dwelling units of 1950 built since 1940 in 1940 or later. This variable is expressed in arithmetic form

$Po''$ Population change between 1940 and 1950 ignoring the effect of change in city boundaries

b. These are the cities for which information was available on wage-and-salary income of 1939 and the Boeckh index from 1939 to 1949. They include the 28 cities represented in Table 65 and 13 additional cities.

## Summary and Conclusions

Rooms per dwelling unit, symbolized by $r_o$, are positively correlated with normal income. The coefficient of income elasticity appears to be around 0.4. This is appreciably less than the coefficients of housing consumption with respect to normal income of around 2.0 described in chapters vii, viii, and xi. It has its counterpart in the difference between demand for calories and for total food. The difference suggests that it is useful to look upon demand for rooms as relatively inelastic, whereas the demand for quality of housing is highly elastic with respect to income.

A very slight positive correlation between rooms and income is observed among consumer units. The tendency of $r_o$ to rise with normal income tends to be obscured by the transitory component of measured income. An income elasticity of $r_o$ of 0.4 tends to be observed among cities and between environs and central cities of metro areas. For such observations average income comes close to representing normal income.

The higher the cost of housing, the lower tends to be $r_o$. The evidence presented points to a price elasticity of demand for rooms around -0.30. This too is much, much higher than the price elasticity of demand for housing consumption in general. Such difference is not surprising. It seems highly probable that demand for space, as represented by rooms, is quite inelastic, whereas demand for quality of housing is quite elastic.

Two measures of room occupancy have been examined. One is number of rooms per person, and the other is percentage of households with 1.01 or more persons per room. These are symbolized by $r_p$ and $r_c$, respectively. The higher the income and the lower the cost of housing, the higher tends to be $r_p$ and the lower tends to be $r_c$. In addition, these measures of room occupancy vary markedly with household type. Over the lifetime of families, variation in $r_o$ tends to be small, whereas family size varies a great deal. Hence $r_p$ and $r_c$ vary greatly with the stage in the family cycle: $r_p$ tends to be low and $r_c$ high at the peak of the family size when the head is around 50 years of age, whereas among households with an aged head $r_p$ tends to be high and $r_c$ low.

Variation in $r_p$ and $r_c$ is also closely related to variation in persons per households, symbolized by s. Part of this is a function of the stage in the family cycle. Some of it may be a function of the negative relation of s to normal income.

Trends in rooms and their occupancy are affected by secular change in income, costs, and preference for dwelling units of a given size. For the nation in general secular change in real income has tended to increase and secular change in cost to decrease $r_0$. In addition, secular change in preference has probably been downward. This is to be expected because of the shift of certain functions from the household to the market,[56] the decline in the birth rate, and an increased preference for the separation of the generations. Some of the increased separation of the generation is undoubtedly a function of income, rather than a change in preference.

Rooms per dwelling unit in any stock is the result of decisions made earlier. Those of many decades may be represented. Thus the stock may bear an imprint of earlier decades differing with respect to income, cost, and preference. It is modified by new construction and by conversions, mergers, and withdrawals of old stock. The importance of the imprint of the past on $r_0$ varies greatly among cities. Where income tends to lag behind increase in cost, $r_0$ appears relatively high in relation to current income and cost. On the other hand, where income tends to run ahead of increase in costs, $r_0$ seems likely to appear low in relation to current income and cost. Where $r_0$ tends to be high because of high income or low costs of earlier years, number of persons per household tends to be high. High $r_0$ in the stock as well as low income and high cost seem to favor the doubling up of potential households.

The evidence on variation in rooms and their occupancy presented in this chapter comes from several sets of observations. Some represent the same households viewed through different types of cross sections. The tendencies observed differ. The differences are consistent with the permanent-income hypothesis. They support the implications of earlier chapters. The relation of any housing characteristic, number of rooms, their occupancy, or value of rent of dwelling units with respect to normal income, is revealed when the effect of transitory income is eliminated.

---

56. Some of this shift is strictly speaking a function of cost rather than preference, being the result of technological changes that affect the relative economy of consumer production versus purchases of services and changes, such as those of retailers, restaurants, launderers, and hospitals, and also changes in the cost of the maintenance of space in a dwelling unit.

# Chapter Thirteen

# CENSUS OF HOUSING OF 1960: A POSTSCRIPT

The decade of the fifties saw much new construction of dwelling units. For example, for urban places 28 per cent of the 1960 stock was built during the fifties. At the same time a marked rise occurred in the average market value of dwelling units, reflecting both their improvement and inflation. For urban places the median value of one-unit owner-occupied structures rose 53 per cent and median contract rent of tenant-units rose 61 per cent.[1] Furthermore, between 1949 and 1959, the years represented by the incomes reported by the respective censuses, median disposable income of urban families rose 59 per cent.[2] Some of this rise was represented by inflation. Between these years the Consumer Price Index of the U.S. Bureau of Labor Statistics for all cities rose 23 per cent.[3] At the same time much of the effect of rent control of the forties disappeared. In addition, the fifties saw the introduction of many new products resulting in what, on the surface at least, appeared to be a considerable change in ways of living.

Even so, the cross-section elasticity of market value of housing with respect to $y_n$, that is normal income of consumer units, appears to be unchanged. The preview of findings presented in chapter i noted that housing with respect to $y_n$ appears to have been stable over at least four decades and that the Census of Housing of 1960 like that of 1950 indicates

1. See U.S. Census of Housing: 1960, Vol. I, States and Small Areas, chapter 1.

2. See U.S. Bureau of the Census, Current Population Reports, P-60, Nos. 7 and 35. The equation used to adjust family incomes reported for income tax is shown in Table 69, fn. a.

3. Monthly Labor Review and other releases of the U.S. Department of Labor.

an elasticity of housing with respect to $y_n$ between 1.5 and 2.0. This chapter presents the evidence for 1960 on which that conclusion is based. It draws on only a small portion of the data that will eventually be available. However, the findings seem to be quite firmly based and likely to provide a reliable estimate of $\eta_{hy_n}$ for 1960.

This chapter describes tendencies among census tracts within metro areas. At the time of writing these were the only data available for estimating for 1960 any of the main housing-income relationships described in earlier chapters. The data by census tracts for 1960 and 1950 have a common shortcoming: Income is not reported by tenure. Instead they represent all families and unrelated individuals, irrespective of tenure and household status.[4] Thus the populations represented by value or rent of the housing and the income variables tend to differ. This difference is referred to in this monograph as the gap between the housing and and the income variables. Because of this gap the estimates made in this chapter, like those of chapter vii for 1950, are confined to sets of tracts relatively homogeneous with respect to it. Criteria used in selecting sets are described later.

The main purpose of this chapter is to discover whether a change had occurred between 1950 and 1960 in the intertract coefficients of income elasticity. For this purpose tracts similar in type to those represented by the 1950 estimates are most suitable, namely tracts high in owner-occupancy. For these the gap between the housing and the income variables is relatively small. The first section of this chapter is devoted to such inquiry.

Tracts very high in owner-occupancy represent a limited part of total housing, and this chapter includes some estimates for sets of tracts relatively low in owner-occupancy. For these sets, estimates are made for both owners and tenants. In addition, some examination has been made of variation among tracts in rooms per housing unit and their occupancy and in the importance of units built during the fifties.

---

4. The 1960 census also reported for tracts the median income of families. Among tracts in general this doubtless tends to be much better index of the income of households with owner-occupancy than is the income of families and unrelated individuals. Nevertheless, all estimates shown represent the income of families and unrelated individuals. This practice is followed because comparison of tendencies between 1950 and 1960 is made, and for this it seemed best to use the same income variable.

### Income Elasticity of Housing among Tracts High in Owner-Occupancy

Elasticities of housing with respect to income among tracts high in owner-occupancy have been estimated for a set of 32 metro areas[5] representing 26 states. The main variables are median value of one-unit owner-occupied structures ($H^a$) and estimated median disposable income of families[6] and unrelated individuals ($Y^a$), irrespective of tenure or household status. One supplementary variable is used, namely the percentage of the occupied dwelling units represented by $H^a$.[7] This is symbolized by $O^a$. Data used and types of estimates made are first described and then the intertract income elasticities of housing are reviewed and commented on.

Data Used and Types of Estimates Made.—Table 69 lists the 32 metro areas for which intertract estimates have been made. It shows for each area the number of tracts represented and the range among tracts in $Y^a$, in $H^a$,[8] and in $O^a$. The tracts represented by these estimates are high in owner-occupancy and low in the importance of unrelated individuals not heads of households.

---

5. An initial set of 24 metro areas was selected from those in the library file at the time the analysis was started. For these one metro area was selected for each state if it had a minimum of ten tracts that met the eligibility criteria imposed to minimize the gap between $H^a$ and $Y^a$. Where a report was available for two or more metro areas within a state the one with the largest population was selected. The early releases providing the initial set included a disproportionate number of small metro areas. Eight metro areas were later added. In general these are larger than the metro areas of the initial set. The range in size represented is appreciable. However, the initial set of 24 metro areas indicated the same tendencies as the final set of 32. Because of the timing of the releases, none of the metro areas represented in the analysis of the 1950 data reported in chap. vii are represented by the 1960 set.

6. The marked increase in income from 1949 to 1959 made it seem advisable to adjust incomes reported for income tax. See Table 69, fn. a, for description of the method of making this estimate.

7. Where all owner-occupants are in one-unit structures, this percentage represents the importance of owner-occupancy. Owner-occupancy in structures of two or more units is important for Trenton and Worcester, two metro areas of the set of 32.

8. For about one-half of the metro areas the range in $H^a$ exceeds a ratio of one to three, but for six it is less than a ratio of one to two. The less this ratio, the greater the chance of a random factor determining the tendency observed. Even so, much of the variation in coefficients where the range in $H^a$ is low appears to be explained by systematic factors represented by $O^a$ (see text for discussion).

Table 69

Average Housing ($H^a$) and Income ($Y^a$) and Associated Conditions, Tracts High in Owner-Occupancy, 32 Metro Areas, 1960[a]

| Metro area | Number of tracts represented | Range in Median income ($Y^a$) (000's) | Range in Median value ($H^a$) (000's) | Range in Percentage of occupied dwelling units represented by $H^a$ ($O^a$) |
|---|---|---|---|---|
| Albuquerque, N.M. | 17 | \$ 3.8 - \$ 8.3 | \$ 7.9 - \$19.0 | 66 - 94 |
| Birmingham, Ala. | 22 | 2.7 - 9.3 | 5.3 - 24.8 | 75 - 93 |
| Bridgeport, Conn. | 23 | 5.9 - 9.0 | 15.4 - 32.9 | 75 - 97 |
| Charlotte, N.C. | 19 | 5.4 - 9.8 | 8.6 - 28.3 | 75 - 93 |
| Denver, Colo. | 46 | 4.6 - 8.8 | 2.4 - 24.0 | 75 - 98 |
| Des Moines, Iowa | 27 | 3.7 - 8.6 | 7.4 - 24.3 | 75 - 90 |
| Duluth-Superior, Minn.-Wis. | 13 | 4.9 - 10.3 | 8.0 - 24.6 | 69 - 96 |
| Gary-Hammond-East Chicago, Ind. | 14 | 5.7 - 8.3 | 11.0 - 21.7 | 75 - 91 |
| Indianapolis, Ind.[b] | 49 | 4.9 - 10.6 | 8.0 - 32.5 | 75 - 100 |
| Knoxville, Tenn. | 10 | 4.0 - 8.3 | 6.9 - 24.1 | 67 - 82 |
| Lexington, Ky. | 14 | 5.2 - 9.4 | 10.9 - 22.4 | 71 - 90 |
| Little Rock-North Little Rock, Ark. | 15 | 4.7 - 7.9 | 8.9 - 19.3 | 75 - 94 |
| Madison, Wis. | 11 | 6.3 - 14.0 | 13.8 - 34.8 | 73 - 97 |
| Memphis, Tenn. | 27 | 4.0 - 9.6 | 8.1 - 23.6 | 77 - 94 |
| Nashville, Tenn. | 19 | 5.3 - 10.6 | 8.9 - 29.6 | 76 - 93 |
| New Haven, Conn. | 20 | 5.3 - 10.2 | 13.1 - 30.6 | 75 - 95 |
| New Orleans, La. | 13 | 5.3 - 7.8 | 14.7 - 28.0 | 74 - 96 |
| Omaha, Neb.-Iowa | 37 | 4.8 - 10.2 | 7.1 - 32.3 | 75 - 96 |
| Orlando, Fla. | 23 | 4.7 - 7.8 | 12.3 - 22.0 | 76 - 96 |
| Phoenix, Ariz. | 28 | 5.3 - 8.8 | 10.4 - 27.0 | 75 - 94 |
| Portland, Me. | 10 | 4.7 - 6.3 | 10.2 - 16.2 | 67 - 84 |
| Richmond, Va. | 17 | 5.3 - 8.3 | 7.8 - 20.7 | 77 - 96 |
| Salt Lake City, Utah | 38 | 5.0 - 8.3 | 10.6 - 27.9 | 75 - 98 |
| Savannah, Ga. | 10 | 4.3 - 6.5 | 9.7 - 14.5 | 75 - 91 |
| Seattle, Wash.[b] | 52 | 5.2 - 10.1 | 10.0 - 31.9 | 75 - 98 |
| South Bend, Ind. | 29 | 5.0 - 8.7 | 8.0 - 19.4 | 76 - 98 |
| Stamford, Conn. | 10 | 6.1 - 10.1 | 19.6 - 33.2 | 68 - 90 |
| Trenton, N.J. | 19 | 5.0 - 7.0 | 7.3 - 30.4 | 67 - 90 |
| Tulsa, Okla.[b] | 26 | 4.7 - 9.6 | 7.0 - 22.7 | 75 - 97 |
| Wichita, Kan. | 42 | 4.8 - 8.4 | 9.3 - 19.5 | 76 - 95 |
| Wilmington, Del.-N.J. | 35 | 5.3 - 10.6 | 8.8 - 28.3 | 76 - 98 |
| Worcestor, Mass. | 19 | \$ 5.7 - \$ 6.9 | \$11.2 - \$20.0 | 70 - 86 |

Source: U.S. Census of Population and Housing: 1960. Census Tracts. Final Report PHC(1), 1961 (various chapters).

a. All variables describe characteristics of census tracts. They are as follows:

$H^a$ Median value of owner-occupied one-unit structures

$Y^a$ Estimated median disposable income of families and unrelated individuals, irrespective of tenure or household status

$O^a$ The percentage of all occupied housing units represented by $H^a$

The procedure in estimating disposable income is as follows: The census reports income received. The relationship of disposable money income to income received as reported for the 1950 urban consumption survey was used to estimate disposable income by census tract. The equation is as follows:

$$\log Y = .222 + .928 \log Y_r + .00435 S$$

where Y equals estimated average disposable income, and $Y_r$ equals average income received and S equals average persons per consumer for consumer units of 2 to 5 persons and reporting disposable income of at least \$4,000. (Average income is shown for 5 income intervals of \$4,000 or more.) Thus 20 observations are used, each having a weight of one. (For source of data, see Study of Consumer Expenditures, Vol. XVIII, Table 2.) Eligibility criteria used in selecting tracts are described on p. 352, fn. 5.

b. Because of the large number of eligible tracts, the estimate shown utilizes a sample of one-half of the eligible tracts.

Both of these criteria[9] serve to minimize the gap between $H^a$ and $Y^a$. Even so it seems highly probable that some gap remains, and that difference in it among tracts is associated with a variety of things such as the importance of owner-occupancy and of unrelated individuals represented by $Y^a$ and the age distribution of the population. In addition, the gap may vary among tracts because of variation in the ratio of average income of those represented by $H^a$ to average income of those not represented by $H^a$. However, information bearing on this ratio is not available. (Methods of dealing with the variation in the gap are described later.)

The main interest lies in the intertract coefficients of income elasticity of value, symbolized by $\eta_{HY}{}^a$. There seems to be some likelihood that at least a part of the gap between the variables is randomly related to $H^a$. Hence, income elasticities have been estimated using both regressions. These are referred to as income elasticities I and II.[10] Both types of coefficients are shown in Table 70. For income elasticity I, log $Y^a$ is the explanatory variable. This represents the usual type of interclass estimate of the effect of income on consumption. It will, however, provide a reliable estimate only if $Y^a$ represents $Y_n{}^a$ of persons represented

9. Two eligibility criteria determined the selection of tracts within metro areas: (a) At least 65 per cent of the occupied dwelling units were one-unit owner-occupied units represented by $H^a$. In other words, the number of households represented by $Y^a$ must not be more than 54 per cent greater than the number represented by $H^a$. (At the outset the hope was to use a cut-off at 75 per cent. For many of the smaller metro areas of the initial stock of data available less than ten tracts were thereby eligible. For these the criterion was lowered to 65 per cent.) (b) The number of unrelated individuals not heads of households must not be greater than 20 per 100 households. (Only a few tracts meeting criterion [a] did not also meet criterion [b].)

These eligibility criteria are less stringent than those used in selecting the tracts for the 1950 estimates shown in chap. vii. This difference in the criteria used is due to the stock of data available for 1960 at the time of writing this postscript. It was largely confined to smaller metro areas with few tracts.

One feature of the tabulations of 1960 imposed a further restriction on the tracts represented: namely the failure for all metro areas to report the value of dwelling units where the median was less than \$5,000 and for some if it was \$25,000 or more. This upper terminal cut-off is relatively low compared to that of \$20,000 for 1950. Where the cut-off of \$25,000 applies to the entire metro area, the range in $H^a$ among the tracts tends to be relatively small. (The range is shown in Table 69.) For some metro areas a cut-off of \$35,000 is used, for at least some portion of the area, resulting in a wider range.

10. See chap. ii, pp. 33-35, for discussion of these two regressions.

Table 70

Coefficients of Correlation of $H^a$ with respect to $Y^a$ and $O^a$, among Tracts High in Owner-Occupancy, 32 Metro Areas, 1960[a]

| Metro area | Simple coefficients of $H^a$ and $Y^a$ | | | $\eta_{HY.O^a}$ | $\beta_{OH^a}$ |
|---|---|---|---|---|---|
| | $\eta I_{HY^a}$ (1) | $\eta II_{HY^a}$ (2) | $r^2$ (3) | (4) | (5) |
| Albuquerque, N.M. | 1.02 | 1.08 | .94 | 1.19 | 86.9 |
| Birmingham, Ala. | 1.43 | 1.57 | .91 | 1.41 | 17.1 |
| Bridgeport, Conn. | 1.58 | 2.25 | .70 | 1.73 | 30.5 |
| Charlotte, N.C. | 1.13 | 1.29 | .88 | 1.14 | 10.2 |
| Denver, Colo. | 1.33 | 1.95 | .68 | 1.34 | 26.1 |
| Des Moines, Iowa | 1.51 | 2.22 | .68 | 1.50 | 5.7 |
| Duluth-Superior, Minn.-Wis. | 1.38 | 1.75 | .71 | 1.32 | 34.5 |
| Gary-Hammond-East Chicago, Ind. | 1.58 | 1.87 | .85 | 1.80 | 21.1 |
| Indianapolis, Ind. | 1.60 | 1.75 | .92 | 1.65 | 27.7 |
| Knoxville, Tenn. | 1.73 | 1.86 | .93 | 1.86 | 7.0 |
| Lexington, Ky. | 1.29 | 1.56 | .83 | 1.37 | 19.7 |
| Little Rock-North Little Rock, Ark. | 1.54 | 1.83 | .84 | 1.83 | 7.2 |
| Madison, Wis. | 1.08 | 1.16 | .94 | 1.15 | 45.0 |
| Memphis, Tenn. | 1.41 | 1.68 | .84 | 1.43 | 29.1 |
| Nashville, Tenn. | 1.52 | 1.61 | .95 | 1.52 | 12.8 |
| New Haven, Conn. | 1.54 | 1.79 | .86 | 1.61 | -1.3 |
| New Orleans, La. | 1.27 | 1.73 | .73 | 1.28 | 3.0 |
| Omaha, Neb.-Iowa | 1.60 | 1.90 | .84 | 1.46 | 27.6 |
| Orlando, Fla. | 0.78 | 3.07 | .25[b] | 1.29 | 5.6 |
| Phoenix, Ariz. | 1.46 | 1.93 | .76 | 1.53 | 13.9 |
| Portland, Me. | 1.14 | 2.40 | .48[c] | 1.17 | 29.3 |
| Richmond, Va. | 1.97 | 2.45 | .80 | 1.92 | 31.5 |
| Salt Lake City, Utah | 1.63 | 2.04 | .81 | 1.71 | -0.6 |
| Savannah, Ga. | 1.32 | 1.76 | .75 | 1.35 | 20.7 |
| Seattle, Wash.[b] | 1.44 | 1.76 | .82 | 1.57 | 27.0 |
| South Bend, Ind. | 1.68 | 2.19 | .77 | 1.99 | 33.1 |
| Stamford, Conn. | 1.13 | 1.30 | .87 | 1.19 | 39.7 |
| Trenton, N.J. | 2.85 | 3.45 | .83 | 2.89 | -2.6 |
| Tulsa, Okla.[b] | 1.64 | 1.83 | .90 | 1.68 | 31.9 |
| Wichita, Kan. | 1.24 | 1.71 | .72 | 1.09 | 44.7 |
| Wilmington, Del.-N.J. | 1.18 | 1.54 | .76 | 1.20 | 23.1 |
| Worcestor, Mass. | 1.79 | 2.47 | .73 | 1.99 | -1.8 |
| Mean[d] | 1.46 | 1.90 | | 1.54 | 22.0 |

Source: See Table 69.

a. Variables $H^a$ and $Y^a$ and $O^a$ are described in Table 69. In these estimates the first two are used in log form and the third in arithmetic form.

I symbolizes an estimate of income elasticity of housing where $Y^a$ is the explanatory variable, and II symbolizes one where $H^a$ is the explanatory variable. The interpretation of these estimates is discussed in the text.

$\beta$ represents a regression coefficient. (It does not represent a coefficient of elasticity.)

Unless otherwise specified these coefficients of determination are significant at the .01 probability level.

b. Significant at the .02 probability level.

c. Significant at the .05 probability.

d. Each metro area has a weight of one. The mean coefficients of income elasticity weighted by the number of tracts are almost identical.

by $H^a$. For income elasticity II, $H^a$ is the explanatory variable, and the coefficient of income elasticity II of housing is the reciprocal of the regression of log $Y^a$ with respect to log $H^a$. It will represent $\eta_{hy_n}$ if $H^a$ has no random error and if all of the gap between the housing and income variables is uncorrelated with $H^a$. The absence of any condition likely to cause a random error in $H^a$ makes it seem likely that income elasticity II will provide a more reliable estimate than income elasticity I of average housing with respect to average normal income among tracts. Of course the reliability of both types of coefficient may be reduced by conditions correlated with both the housing and the income variables, such as the importance of owner-occupancy and conditions related thereto.

It has not been feasible to investigate fully the effect of conditions correlated with the housing and the income variables even to the extent of the data available. Only the effect of $O^a$ has been examined, namely the percentage of all dwelling units represented by $H^a$. Two types of estimates have been made: (a) partial coefficients of $\eta I_{HY}{}^a$ with $O^a$ held constant, and (b) the regression coefficient of $O^a$ with respect to $H^a$, symbolized by $\beta_{OH}{}^a$. The effect of the distribution of $O^a$ with respect to $H^a$ on the coefficients of income elasticity observed will depend on the difference in average income between those represented and those not represented by $H^a$.

It seems reasonable to assume that within tracts, $Y^a$ of those represented by $H^a$ exceeds $Y^a$ of those not represented by $H^a$. Hence for any tract where $O^a$ is less than 100, $Y^a$ observed understates $Y^a$ of those represented by $H^a$. If the difference in average income between these two sets of income units represented by $Y^a$ is uniform among tracts, $O^a$ should serve as a fairly good proxy[11] of the gap in the income of those represented by $H^a$ and $Y^a$, and the partial coefficient of $\eta I_{HY}{}^a$ with $O^a$ held constant would tend to be unaffected by the gap. However, if $O^a$ represents only a small portion of this gap it will not serve this purpose. This in fact is the implication of tendencies observed (estimates are shown later). However, $\beta_{OH}{}^a$ seems to represent the distribution of the gap. If $O^a$ rises with $H^a$, the negative gap appears to concentrate where both $H^a$ and $Y^a$ are low, and both types of income elasticity tend to be low. On the other hand, if $O^a$ falls with $H^a$, the negative

11. It could never be a perfect proxy since $O^a$ does not represent the unrelated individuals who are not heads of households but who are represented by $Y^a$.

gap tends to concentrate where $H^a$ and to a lesser extent $Y^a$ are high. Under this condition income elasticity of housing I and II will both tend to be relatively high.

Estimates of $\beta_{OH}{}^a$ are shown in Table 70, column 5. A wide variation occurs among metro areas: a range from -2.6 to 86.9.[12]

Characteristics of These Intertract Income Elasticities.—For the 32 metro areas the mean $\eta I_{HY}{}^a$ is 1.46. The corresponding coefficient for 1950 is 1.55 (see Table 31). For the 32 metro areas the mean $\eta II_{HY}{}^a$ is 1.90, and the corresponding coefficient for 1950 is 2.29. In addition, the coefficients of income elasticities for the two censuses show much the same range among metro areas represented: $\eta I_{HY}{}^a$ of 1960 ranges from 0.78 to 2.85, and of 1950 from 0.82 to 1.86; and $\eta II_{HY}{}^a$ of 1960 ranges from 1.08 to 3.45,[13] and of 1950 from 1.61 to 3.50. The slightly lower means and wider ranges for the 1960 than the 1950 sets of tracts are not surprising in view of the less restrictive criteria used in selecting the sets of tracts for the 1960 than the 1950 estimates. The tendencies observed are, however, so similar that one is justified in assuming that income elasticities of housing among tracts tend to be the same in 1960 as in 1950.

Holding $O^a$ constant has only a slight tendency to increase $\eta I_{HY}{}^a$. Its mean partial coefficient for the 32 metro areas is 1.54 (see Table 70, column 4). The small effect from holding $O^a$ constant, that is an increase from 1.46 to 1.54, seems to imply that $O^a$ is a relatively poor index of variation among tracts in the gap between $Y^a$ and $H^a$.

Among the metro areas of 1960 the income elasticities of value indicated by the two regressions are positively and quite closely correlated. From this it seems reasonable to infer that they are affected by a common condition or set of conditions. Conditions represented by $\beta_{OH}{}^a$ seem likely to be of considerable importance. The less $O^a$ rises with $H^a$ the higher tends to be both $\eta I_{HY}{}^a$ and $\eta II_{HY}{}^a$. Where $\beta_{OH}{}^a$ is around zero, the mean coefficients of $\eta I_{HY}{}^a$ and of $\eta II_{HY}{}^a$ are 1.82 and 2.30 re-

---

12. The variable $O^a$ is expressed in arithmetic form, whereas $H^a$ is in log form.

13. It seems of some interest to note that with two exceptions the $r^2$ of the interclass correlations for 1960 shown in Table 70 indicate a relationship significant at the .01 probability level. Yet other evidence implies that many of the coefficients of income elasticity do not represent the relation of $H^a$ to $Y_n{}^a$.

spectively.[14] On the other hand, when $\beta_{OH}{}^{a}$ is 40 or more the respective means[15] are 1.11 and 1.32. Thus it seems highly probable that conditions associated with $O^{a}$ tend to influence greatly the coefficients of income elasticity, and where such influence is absent the income elasticity of value of dwelling tends to be around 2.0.

### Income Elasticities of Housing among Tracts Low in Owner-Occupancy

The analysis described in this section can suitably be looked upon as a short fishing expedition. It was prompted by the need for knowing something of the usefulness of the large volume of tract data on tenant housing. Data examined are for tracts where owner-occupancy ranges from about 40 to 60 per cent.[16] (The tenant-occupancy has of course a similar range.) Estimates have been made for both tenures.

The main variables are: median value of one-unit owner-occupied structures ($H^{a}$), median contract rent ($H_{r}{}^{a}$) and median income of families and unrelated individuals ($Y^{a}$), irrespective of tenure or household status. These variables have been used to estimate intertract coefficients of income elasticity of housing for eight metro areas, all of which have at least 20 tracts[17] meeting criteria used to restrict somewhat heterogeneity among tracts with respect to the gap between the housing and income variables.

Coefficients of income elasticity of housing representing regressions I and II are shown in Table 71. $Y^{a}$ seems certain to have a large random error. Hence it seems highly probable that regression II provides the more reliable evidence of the elasticity of housing with respect to normal income.

---

14. Five metro areas are represented by these means, and mean $\beta_{OH}{}^{a}$ is -0.6.

15. Three metro areas are represented by these means, and mean $\beta_{OH}{}^{a}$ is 59.0.

16. The tracts selected had the following characteristics: (a) the number of owners in one-unit structures is not less than 67 nor more than 150 per 100 tenant units, and (b) unrelated individuals not primary heads of households are not more than 20 per 100 households. (This estimate of the importance of owners and tenants ignores the owners not in one-unit structures.)

17. A minimum of ten tracts seems fairly satisfactory for estimates describing tendencies among tracts high in owner-occupancy. For tracts low in owner-occupancy it seemed advisable to have at least 20 tracts per metro area.

## Table 71

Coefficients of Correlation of $H^a$ and $H_r{}^a$ with respect to $Y^a$, among Census Tracts Low in Owner-Occupancy, Eight Metro Areas, 1960[a]

| Metro area[b] | Number of tracts (1) | $\eta I_{HY^a}$ (2) | $\eta II_{HY^a}$ (3) | $r^2$ (4) |
|---|---|---|---|---|
| | Panel A: Owners | | | |
| 1. Baltimore, Md. | 38 | 1.36 | 2.19 | .623 |
| 2. Denver, Colo. | 20 | 1.11 | 1.93 | .574 |
| 3. Indianapolis, Ind. | 36 | 0.80 | 2.05 | .392 |
| 4. Louisville, Ky. | 26 | 1.20 | 1.91 | .630 |
| 5. Memphis, Tenn. | 24 | 0.67 | 1.45 | .461 |
| 6. Milwaukee, Wis. | 45 | 1.19 | 2.24 | .531 |
| 7. New Orleans, La. | 24 | 1.00 | 1.20 | .833 |
| 8. Seattle, Wash. | 22 | 0.95 | 1.93 | .490 |
| 9. Mean for 8 areas | . . . | 1.04 | 1.86 | . . . |
| | Panel B: Tenants[c] | | | |
| 1. Baltimore, Md. | 38 | 0.60 | 1.74 | .346 |
| 2. Denver, Colo. | 38 | 1.39 | 2.18 | .638 |
| 3. Indianapolis, Ind. | 36 | 0.48 | 1.39 | .341 |
| 4. Louisville, Ky. | 36 | 0.59 | 1.39 | .425 |
| 5. Memphis, Tenn. | 24 | 0.63 | 2.36 | .269 |
| 6. Milwaukee, Wis. | 45 | 1.06 | 1.99 | .531 |
| 7. New Orleans, La.[d] | 24 | 0.63 | 0.99 | .637 |
| 8. Seattle, Wash. | 22 | 1.26 | 1.45 | .866 |
| 9. Mean for 8 areas | . . . | 0.83 | 1.68 | . . . |

Source of data: See Table 69.

a. For information on definitions of variables and types of estimates shown, see Tables 69 and 70. For the estimates shown here, income is not adjusted for tax. Estimates shown in Table 70 are so adjusted. However, the adjustment has a noticeable effect only where the range among the tracts in $Y^a$ is relatively small. For the observations used for the estimates shown here, the range in $Y^a$ is rather large.
For criteria used in the selection of tracts, see p. 352, fn. 5.

b. Four of the six metro areas represented here are among those represented by estimates shown in Tables 69 and 70. A casual review of the data of other metro areas of these tables indicated none with a minimum of 20 tracts meeting the criteria imposed to minimize the gap between $H^a$ and $Y^a$.

c. For tenants, substitute $H_r{}^a$ for $H^a$.

d. Fifty-eight per cent of the variation of $Y^a$ is explained by the percentage of non-whites in the population, and the importance of non-whites seems likely to affect the gap between $H^a$ and $Y^a$.

The intertract coefficients of elasticity of housing of regression II, shown in Table 71 are relatively high. The means for the eight metro areas are 1.86 and 1.68, for owners and tenants, respectively. These coefficients give reason to expect that for 1960 the income elasticity of housing with respect to $y_n$ differs little, if at all, by tenure. This is consistent with evidence of earlier chapters.

The mean $\eta II_{HY}{}^{a}$ for tracts low in owner-occupancy, is quite similar to the corresponding mean for tracts high in owner-occupancy: that is 1.86 compared to 1.90 (see Table 70 and 71). This similarity implies that this widening of the gap between $H^{a}$ and $Y^{a}$ tends to have only a slight effect on the distribution of the systematic factors affecting $\eta II_{HY}{}^{a}$ such as the importance of owner-occupancy.

The intertract coefficients of elasticity of housing indicated by regression I are low—that is where $Y^{a}$ is the explanatory variable. The means for the eight metro areas, shown in Table 71, are 1.04 and 0.81 for owners and tenants, respectively. This mean for owners is two-thirds of that shown in Table 70, namely 1.47. The difference between the coefficients of regression I of Tables 70 and 71 further demonstrates that the incomes reported for census tracts are likely to be unsuited for indicating demand for housing as represented by value or rent of housing units reported, unless tracts are selected to reduce to a low level the gap between $H^{a}$ and $Y^{a}$ or between $H_r{}^{a}$ and $Y^{a}$.

### Income Elasticity of Rooms and Their Occupancy among Tracts

The 1960 census of housing reports average number of rooms per dwelling unit as well as the percentage of households with 1.01 or more persons per room. These measures of housing are symbolized by $R_o{}^{a}$ and $R_c{}^{a}$, respectively. Chapter xii indicates for 1950 that $R_c{}^{a}$ has a very marked negative correlation with $Y^{a}$, indicating that the lower is $Y^{a}$ of households in a tract the greater the degree of room crowding. The Census of Housing of 1950 does not report average number of rooms per dwelling unit for tracts. However, interplace tendencies for 1950 create the presumption that $\eta R_oY^{a}$ of at least 0.4 seems likely. The 1960 census permits estimates for the relation of both $R_o{}^{a}$ and $R_c{}^{a}$ with respect to income.

The examination of the relationships presented in this section is confined to two metro areas, namely Indianapolis and Seattle. The simple and partial coefficients of $\eta_{R_o Y^a}$ and of $\eta_{R_c Y^a}$ are shown in Table 72. The partial coefficients are those where household size and type are held constant. Three variables are used to represent these, namely number of persons per household, the number of adult males per 100 adult males 21 years to 65 years of age, and the number of families and unrelated individuals per 100 families. These are symbolized by $S^a$, $A_m{}^a$, and $U^a$, respectively.

The higher is $Y^a$ the higher tend to be $R_o{}^a$. The simple coefficients of income elasticity are very similar for the two places, and their mean is 0.47. Holding constant the household size and type tends to increase them very slightly—that is to 0.50. This coefficient is at the upper range of the interplace coefficients shown in Table 57, where variables likely in some measure to serve as proxies for interplace difference in cost are held constant.

The higher is $Y^a$ the lower tends to be $R_c{}^a$. Both the simple and the partial coefficients differ between the two places. The mean simple coefficient is -2.04, and with household size and type held constant it is -2.93. The corresponding coefficient shown for Chicago for 1950 is -2.64 (see Table 52). This evidence, though meager, gives some reason to expect a high degree of stability between 1950 and 1960 in cross-section relationships of degree of room crowding with respect to normal income.

## Difference in Room Crowding among Tracts, 1950 and 1960

The degree of room crowding in 1950 and 1960, represented by $R_c{}^a$, can be compared where income and household sizes and type are in considerable measure held constant. Such a comparison provides some indication of the effect of other changes such as the cost of housing, increase in occupational expense represented by income of 1960, and change in preference for housing compared to other consumer products.

Comparison made in this section is confined to two metro areas, namely Indianapolis and Seattle. The tracts of 1960 are those described in Table 72. For each metro area a set of tracts for 1950 was selected using similar criteria. Characteristics of the two sets of tracts, one for 1950 and one for 1960, are summarized in Table 73. For both metro areas the set of 1960 is lower in $R_c{}^a$ than the set of 1950 tracts. This drop occurs in spite of the fact that household size ($S^a$) is higher and the importance of aged males ($A_m{}^a$) is lower for the 1960 than for the 1950 set

Table 72

Coefficients of Correlation of $R_o^a$ and of $R_c^a$ with respect to $Y^a$ and Other Conditions, among 49 Census Tracts of Indianapolis, and 52 Census Tracts of Seattle, 1960[a]

| Explanatory variable and other item | Indianapolis, Ind. | | | | Seattle, Wash. | | | |
|---|---|---|---|---|---|---|---|---|
| | (1) | (2) | (3) | (4) | (5) | (6) | (7) | (8) |
| | A. $R_o^a$ with respect to | | | | | | | |
| 1. $R^2$ | .307 | .307 | .327 | .331 | .618 | .622 | .802 | .862 |
| 2. $Y^a$ | 0.464 | 0.464 | 0.465 | 0.510 | 0.477 | 0.480 | 0.438 | 0.494 |
| 3. $S^a$ | .... | -0.002 | 0.332 | 0.394 | .... | -0.008 | 0.797 | 0.838 |
| 4. $A_m^a$ | .... | .... | 1.058 | 0.826 | .... | .... | 2.238 | 1.877 |
| 5. $U^a$ | .... | .... | .... | 0.461 | .... | .... | .... | 0.569 |
| | B. $R_c^a$ with respect to | | | | | | | |
| 1. $R^2$ | .288 | .541 | .572 | .574 | .260 | .794 | .822 | .850 |
| 2. $Y^a$ | -2.122 | -2.201 | -2.267 | -2.324 | -1.958 | -3.480 | 3.406 | -3.530 |
| 3. $S^a$ | .... | 2.726 | 0.863 | 0.712 | .... | 3.364 | 1.828 | 1.948 |
| 4. $A_m^a$ | .... | .... | -5.913 | -5.353 | .... | .... | -4.323 | -3.985 |
| 5. $U^a$ | .... | .... | .... | -1.119 | .... | .... | .... | -0.531 |

Source: See Table 69.

a. Variables describing census tracts are as follows:

| | |
|---|---|
| $Y^a$ | Estimated median disposable income of families and unrelated individuals |
| $S^a$ | Number of persons per household |
| $A_m{}^a$ | Number of all adult males per 100 such males 21-65 years of age |
| $U^a$ | Number of families and unrelated individuals per 100 families |
| $R_o{}^a$ | Number of rooms per housing unit |
| $R_c{}^a$ | The percentage of households with 1.01 or more persons per room |

(Note the unit of observation of the 1960 census is described as a housing unit. It differs from a dwelling unit as defined in the 1950 census in that it need not have housekeeping facilities.)

b. The constant term of the equation shown in this column is 22.614.

c. The constant term of the equation shown in this column is 22.458.

of tracts, two conditions tending to increase $R_c^a$. For both metro areas, average income of 1959 is much higher than that of 1949. With income expressed in dollars of constant purchasing power it is higher by more than 40 per cent. This higher real income of the 1960 than the 1950 set

Table 73

Average Degree of Room Crowding ($R_c^a$), Disposable Income of Families and Unrelated Individuals ($Y^a$) and Associated Conditions, Selected Census Tracts of Indianapolis and Seattle, 1950 and 1960[a]

| | 1950 | 1960 | 1960 with 1950=100 |
|---|---|---|---|
| 1. Indianapolis, Indiana | | | |
| a) Number of tracts | 24 | 49 | . . . |
| b) $R_c^a$ | 8.4 | 7.5 | 89 |
| c) $Y^a$ | \$3,844 | \$6,944 | 181 |
| d) $Y^a$ in 1959 prices | 4,828 | 6,955 | 144 |
| e) $S^a$ | 3.10 | 3.37 | 109 |
| f) $A_m^a$ | 116 | 109 | 94 |
| g) $U^a$ | 110 | 110 | 100 |
| 2. Seattle, Washington | | | |
| a) Number of tracts | 62 | 52 | . . . |
| b) $R_c^a$ | 7.6 | 5.3 | 70 |
| c) $Y^a$ | \$3,612 | \$6,539 | 181 |
| d) $Y^a$ in 1959 prices | 4,562 | 6,539 | 143 |
| e) $S^a$ | 3.01 | 3.25 | 108 |
| f) $A_m^a$ | 119 | 112 | 94 |
| g) $U^a$ | 115 | 116 | 101 |

Source: U.S. Census of Population: 1950, Vol. III, Census Tract Characteristics, chapters 25 and 51, and U.S. Censuses of Population and Housing: 1960. Census Tracts. Final Report PHC(1), Reports 64 and 142.

a. The variables are described in Table 72.

The measures of income and price pertain to 1949 and 1959, respectively. Indianapolis is not included in the cities for which a Consumer Price Index (CPI) is reported by the U.S. Bureau of Labor Statistics. The assumption has been made that the index for Chicago represents the price change of Indianapolis. For Chicago the CPI of 1959 is 125.6 with that of 1949 equal to 100. For Seattle the CPI of 1959 is 126.3 with that of 1949 equal to 100.

doubtless accounts for the fall in $R_c^a$ in spite of increase in $S^a$ and fall in $A_m^a$.

Table 72, columns 4 and 8, show for 1960 the regression coefficients of $R_c^a$ with respect to $Y^a$ and to variables representing household size and type. One question that might be asked is: What would $R_c^a$ of the 1960 set be if it was similar in size and composition of households to the 1950 set.[18] The answer is that $R_c^a$ tends to be 5.00 for Indianapolis and 3.56 for Seattle. However, $R_c^a$ observed for the 1960 set is 7.5 for Indianapolis and 5.3 for Seattle. In other words, for these sets the tendency for $R_c^a$ to be lower because of the high real income for the 1960 than the 1950 set is obscured by the tendency for $S^a$ to be higher and $A_m^a$ to be lower for the 1960 than the 1950 set.

Another question that might be asked is what is estimated $R_c^a$ of 1960 where $Y^a$ equals the mean $Y^a$ of the 1950 set, expressed in dollars of constant purchasing power. With $Y^a$ so expressed, assuming that the Consumer Price Index represents price change, and household size and type are held constant, $R_c^a$ tends to be 11.7 for Indianapolis and 12.7 for Seattle. Observed mean $R_c^a$ for these sets for 1950 is 8.4 and 7.6, respectively (see Table 73). Thus with real income presumably held constant as well as household size and type, $R_c^a$ is appreciably higher for 1960 than for 1950.

This higher estimated $R_c^a$ for 1960 than is observed for 1950, where real income and household size and type is the same, could be the result of several types of change: (a) An increase in the relative price of housing compared to other consumer products may have occurred. This together with a marked negative price elasticity of demand for housing would tend to increase $R_c^a$ where real income is held constant. (b) Occupational expenses represent a higher percentage of $Y^a$ of 1959 than of 1949, a condition to be expected if only because of the increased importance of wives in the labor force. (Hence it seems not unlikely that $Y^a$ overstates net income more for 1960 than for 1950.) (c) Some decline may have occurred in preference for housing compared to other consumer products because of the introduction of new products in the market. (This is the most speculative element among conditions likely to be causing change.)

On the other hand, the estimated $R_c^a$ of 1960, where real income and

18. The variables representing household size and composition for both the 1950 and the 1960 sets are shown in Table 73.

household size and type are comparable to those of the 1950 set, may be understated by the estimates shown above. Such understatement will occur if the Consumer Price Index tends to overstate increase in consumer prices. There is considerable evidence that such overstatement occurs because of failure, in price collection, to hold constant the quality of the products represented by the index.[19] If price increase is overstated, and if there are no offsetting conditions bearing on the cost of a given level of consumption, then income of the 1950 set, in terms of dollars of constant purchasing power, as estimated above, tends to be overstated, and estimated $R_c^a$ for 1960 in terms of the incomes and household age and type of the 1950 set tends to be understated.

Bit by bit as improved measures of price and other changes become available it will be possible to isolate the effect of these things and to estimate the extent to which change in $R_c^a$ can be ascribed to change in real income, net of occupational expense, or to change in the relative price of housing or to change in consumer preference.

## Variation in New Units among Tracts

The 1960 census of housing is especially suited to the investigation of demand for new units. The volume of such units during the fifties was high, higher than during either of the two preceding decades. The information by tracts permits an estimate of the relation of the new units to normal income as well as to the age-distribution of the population. In the estimates shown, the importance of units built during the fifties is symbolized by $B^a$. Its variation has been examined for the metro areas of Indianapolis and Seattle. This has been done for two sets of tracts, namely the set high in owner-occupancy, represented by estimates just described, and a set of tracts representing the housing of the central city, with no restriction as to the importance of owner-occupancy.

For both sets of tracts and for both metro areas, a wide range in $B^a$ occurs. However, average $B^a$ is much, much higher for the set of tracts high in owner-occupancy than for the set representing the central city.

Estimates of $B^a$ with respect to average income of tracts ($Y^a$) and the importance of aged adult males ($A_m^a$) are shown in Table 74. For

19. For discussion of such a possibility see Price Review Committee, The Price Statistics of the Federal Government (National Bureau of Economic Research, 1961), esp. pp. 173-96.

both sets of tracts and both metro areas $A_m^a$ is the dominant condition explaining $B^a$: The higher is $A_m^a$ the lower tends to be $B^a$. In addition,

Table 74

Coefficients of Correlation of $B^a$ with respect to $Y^a$ and $A_m^a$, among Sets of Census Tracts, Indianapolis and Seattle, 1960[a]

| | (1) | (2) | (3) | (4) |
|---|---|---|---|---|
| | Indianapolis, Ind. | | Seattle, Wash. | |
| | A. A Set of Tracts High in Owner-Occupancy:[b] $B^a$ with respect to | | | |
| 1. $R^2$ | .089 | .903 | .226 | .675 |
| 2. $Y^a$ | 0.987 | 0.871 | 2.810 | 1.092 |
| 3. $A_m^a$ | .... | -11.404 | .... | -11.954 |
| | B. A Set of Tracts Representative of Housing of the Central City:[c] $B^a$ with respect to | | | |
| 1. $R^2$ | .252 | .536 | .235 | .528 |
| 2. $Y^a$ | 3.879 | 3.232 | 1.776 | 0.951 |
| 3. $A_m^a$ | .... | -16.360 | .... | -8.015 |

Source: U.S. Censuses of Population and Housing: 1960 Census Tracts, Reports 64 and 142.

a. This table introduces one additional variable, namely $B^a$, representing the importance in the housing stock of 1960 of units built during 1950 or later. Other variables are described in Table 72. $B^a$ refers to housing units of a census tract. A housing unit differs from a dwelling unit as defined in the 1950 census in that it need not have housekeeping facilities.

b. See Tables 69 and 70 for information on these tracts.

c. For these sets there are 67 tracts for Indianapolis and 70 for Seattle. They were selected as follows: (1) within the central city; (2) at least 1,000 housing units in the tract; (3) the number of unrelated individuals not primary heads of households is not more than 20 per 100 households, and (4) unrelated individuals that are heads of households are not more than 30 per cent of all households. (Several tracts meeting criteria [2] and [3] included new families.) The age distribution indicated that aged adults were unimportant for many of these tracts. Hence there seemed some likelihood, in view of the definition of the housing unit, that housing in these tracts had some unusual feature, such as housing of naval personnel in Seattle or of students at a university.

$B^a$ is positively[20] correlated with $Y^a$. The importance of $A_m{}^a$ undoubtedly can be attributed to the tendency of the aged to stay in the housing units selected for occupancy several years earlier. Hence, the greater the importance of the aged in the population, the greater the importance of the dwelling units that have long been in the stock. The positive correlation between $B^a$ and $Y^a$ reflects the tendency for the demand for new units to concentrate among those of relatively high normal income, and for the demand of those of low normal income to a lesser extent to be met by new construction and a greater extent by second-hand housing initially constructed for those of higher normal income. In this respect, housing is similar to other durable goods, such as automobiles and furniture.

Places may differ a good deal in the extent to which the new units are correlated with normal income. There seems some likelihood, for example, that the greater the importance of the new units, for the tracts represented, the more likely are the tracts to represent the range of the normal income of households of the total population, and conversely the more important is the old stock the more the demand of those with low normal income is likely to be met from the old stock, and the less will their demand affect the construction of new units. This hypothesis has not been tested. One piece of evidence supports this hunch: The coefficient of $Y^a$ for tracts representative of the central city is much higher for Indianapolis than for Seattle, and Indianapolis has a somewhat larger stock of old units than Seattle.

The percentage of the housing units built prior to specified years in the two central cities is given in Table 75. It may be that there is a systematic relationship here the revealing of which would add to an understanding of the demand for new units.

### Some Tendencies Anticipated for 1960

The intertract estimates shown above indicate cross-section housing-income relations similar for 1950 and 1960. This stability makes it seem likely that those cross-section relationships observed for 1950

20. Table 53 shows the simple correlation of $Y^a$ and importance of construction during the forties among a set of the census tracts for Chicago for 1950. It is negative. No estimate was made with importance of aged males held constant. However, the negative correlation between $B^a$ and $Y^a$ shown there may reflect the effect of wartime restrictions and the priorities given for the construction of dwelling unit for war workers.

come close to representing those for 1960, when changes in conditions affecting cross-section tendencies for 1950 are taken into account. Accordingly, the following tendencies are anticipated: (a) Interplace elasticities of value of dwelling units with respect to average income very similar to those for 1950 shown in Figure 13, and corresponding elasticities of contract rent appreciably higher than those of Figure 13 because of the virtual disappearance of the effects of rent control. (b) Elasticities of value of dwelling with respect to income of households very similar to those shown in Table 22, but probably slightly lower because of the increasing importance of income tax at high incomes as measured by the census. (c) Elasticities of contract rent with respect to income of households somewhat higher than those shown in Table 22 because of the disappearance of the effect of rent control.

Table 75

Percentage of Dwelling Units of the 1960 Stock Built Prior to 1950, 1940 and 1930, Two Cities

| Percentage of units built prior to | Indianapolis | Seattle |
|---|---|---|
| 1950 | 85 | 81 |
| 1940 | 73 | 63 |
| 1930 | 70 | 59 |

Source: U.S. Census of Housing: 1960, "States and Small Areas," 1961.

Among places where y is held constant, h will be found to be positively correlated with the average income of places, especially where age of head of households is held constant. Thus tendencies similar to those shown in Figures 1 and 17 are anticipated, where y is the explanatory variable.

When housing by income of households is reported it will be possible to compare h between years where y is held constant, for sets of data where h and y are comparable concepts of housing and income, although representing markets separated by considerable inflation. Where y is the same, h of 1960 will be found to be appreciably higher than h of 1950. This difference is to be expected because y of 1960 like y of 1950 seems certain to have an important transitory component. Because of this, h observed, where y is held constant, will tend to be correlated with Y of all households, and between 1950 and 1960 this average has risen.

## A Review of Evidence

This chapter demonstrates that the intertract elasticities of value of owner units ($H^a$) with respect to average income ($Y^a$) tend to be much the same for 1960 as for 1950. It also provides evidence that the income elasticity of housing with respect to normal income ($y_n$) of 1960 tends to differ little by tenure. Thus the evidence reviewed makes it seem highly probable that in 1960 as in 1950 high quality housing tended to be a luxury item as seen by consumers. Furthermore this chapter supports the evidence presented in chapters vi through xii, for 1950 and earlier, that $\eta_{hy_n}$ tends to be between 1.5 and 2.0, and probably closer to the upper than the lower limit of this range.

The higher is the average income of a tract the higher tends to be the number of rooms per housing unit. The elasticity of rooms per housing unit with respect to average income appears to be around 0.5, a tendency similar to that observed for 1950 among places. In addition, for 1960 a very marked drop occurs in frequency of room crowing, as indicated by the percentage of households with more than 1.01 or more persons per room, with increase in average income of tracts. A similar tendency is shown for the metro area of Chicago for 1950 (see Fig. 23).

Between 1950 and 1960 the frequency of room crowding tended to decline. The decline is quite marked when household type is held constant. Increase in income seems likely to account for this. However under conditions of no increase in real income, that is income in dollars of constant purchasing power, the frequency of room crowding tends to increase between 1950 and 1960. Increase in the cost of housing compared to other consumer products may be the main conditions causing this increase.

A preliminary examination was made of the importance of housing units constructed during the fifties. The importance of aged persons in a tract seems to be the condition that explains most of this variation among tracts. This is to be expected since many of the aged are in a housing unit selected for occupancy many years before. Hence the greater the importance of the aged, the greater is likely to be the importance of housing units that have long been in the stock. This implies that demand for new construction comes largely from households with a relatively young head. It may also be that purchase of a new unit tends to come at the time when the income of the household is close to its peak on the age-income cycle of the head. When the importance of the aged is held constant, the higher is the average income of a tract the greater the importance of new units. This positive correlation implies that the demand for new units tends to concentrate among those with relatively high normal income, and that the demand for those with relatively low normal income, in considerable measure, tends to be met by second-hand dwelling units at various stages of obsolescence and depreciation. Housing in this respect is like the other consumer durables, such as the automobile and furniture.

The final publications of the 1960 census of housing will permit the exploration of many types of relationships not examined here. The similarity of the housing-income relationships observed among tracts for 1950 and 1960 make it seem likely that most of the findings of the earlier chapters apply also to 1960, when account is taken of various types of change such as the disappearance of rent control, the greater importance of the income tax at high income, changes in the distribution of owner-occupancy by age of head.

The evidence of this chapter combined with that of chapter vii demonstrates that the reporting of income by tenure would add greatly to the stock of useful tract data. For one thing they would permit estimates of income elasticity of value of owner units and of contract rent of tenant units for random samples of the two tenures for entire metro areas and for their main portions. Such estimates would have many important uses for producers and sellers of residential housing as well as for those formulating or administrating public policy related to housing. I have no reason to doubt that the effect of $Y_n^a$ on housing as of 1950 and 1960 has been estimated within very narrow limits. Income data by tenure would, however, serve other purposes than using a random sample of tracts to test the validity of the inferences drawn from estimates shown in this chapter. Many conditions other than $Y_n^a$ affect housing consumption, and the gap between the populations represented by $H^a$ and $Y^a$ interferes with using the tract data to discover their effect—for example, the effect of the age, race and occupational distribution of the population. Knowledge of these would contribute to an understanding of the development of neighborhoods and other portions of metro areas.

# Chapter Fourteen

# THE VARIABILITY OF HOUSING-INCOME RELATIONS

This monograph examines demand for housing with respect to income where many other conditions are held constant. Measures of housing include value or rent of dwelling unit and expenditure of consumers for main dwelling unit occupied. In addition, two physical characteristics of housing are examined, namely rooms per unit and rooms in relation to persons occupying them. Three main types of cross-section relationships are examined. For the first, the income of consumers, for the second, average income of subsets of consumers, and for the third, difference in income between two subsets of consumers for a set of places is the explanatory variable. Two measures of intertemporal change are examined. The first describes tendencies of annual time series, and the second describes change between two years for sets of cities represented by surveys or censuses. In the estimates shown, several sets of data are represented, ranging from the large-scale consumption survey of 1918-19 to the Census of Housing of 1960.

Chapters i through iv state the purpose and describe characteristics of variables of cross-section data. Chapters v through ix present many cross-section estimates of housing-income relations and describe conditions related to their variability. Chapters x and xi describe change through time, with and without secular change held constant. Chapter xii describes rooms and their occupancy and chapter xiii presents some evidence derived from the Census of Housing of 1960. Each of these chapters includes a brief summary of its findings. This summary brings together only the highlights of various chapters.

Discovery of the conditions accounting for the variability of tendencies observed in housing with respect to income is the prime interest.

Do tendencies observed represent variation in the willingness to pay for housing out of normal income? Or do they represent conditions that happen to be correlated with the income variable? In answering these questions the possible effect of many other conditions has been considered. Price is one. Household size and type, such as age of head, are others. Cyclical change, migration, and rent control are still others.

## Characteristics of Variables Representing Housing

Housing consumption is defined as the services of residential structures and land as valued in a market homogeneous with respect to the price of housing of a given quality. Value or estimated rental value of owner-occupied units in such a market comes close to representing housing consumption. Contract rent tends to overstate housing consumption because, for many dwelling units, it covers the cost of heat, light, and furnishings (chap. iii). Information available for holding such cost constant is not very satisfactory. This characteristic of contract rent complicates comparison between tenures.

Consumption surveys describing all consumer products frequently report only expenditure for housing. This measure tends to understate housing consumption because it does not take into account the housing represented by the equity of the owner. In general, the greater the importance of owner-occupancy the more such housing expenditure tends to understate consumption. In addition, the higher the age of the owner-occupant the greater is likely to be this understatement, since the higher the age of the owners the more likely are they to have full equity. Accordingly, current expenditures are limited to taxes and upkeep. In addition, the higher the age of the owner the greater the likelihood that housing capital is being consumed because of the low level of property maintenance. This consumption of capital is not represented by housing expenditure reported.

Much of the cross-section data examined represents more than one housing market. Hence value and rent reported may be a function of local prices as well as of housing consumption as such. For this reason the effect of price on value and rent of housing and on housing consumption is considered. The information on price of housing is rather meager so that the findings as to its effect are somewhat less satisfactory than those bearing on income. They are described in a later section of this summary.

Rent control and restrictions on new construction during the late forties appear to have rendered abnormal the rental market of 1950. Although in most cities rent control was officially over its effects appear to have been present in many cities, and furthermore it appears to have depressed rents more in places of high than of low income (chap. vi).

When the measure sought is the behavior of consumers in a free housing market then all dicta that specify rent or rent-income relations are likely to obscure the effect of market forces. The rents of public housing are not determined by the market. This monograph consideres their possible effects but provides no estimates even though in some places, represented by estimates shown, public housing in 1950 was a very important part of the tenant stock.

## Theories of Consumption

Chapter ii outlines the theories of consumption tested in this monograph. The main one is Friedman's permanent-income theory. This postulates that income has two components, a permanent component correlated and a transitory component uncorrelated with consumption. In this monograph these components are referred to as normal and transitory components, respectively. The evidence presented confirms this theory, at least for that portion of consumption represented by housing. In doing so, it demonstrates that much of the variation in housing-income relations observed occurs because of mixture of these two components in the income variable used to estimate housing-income relations.

Chapter ii also reviews the distributive and the standard-of-living theories of consumption. These generalize and rationalize tendencies first observed for the large-scale surveys of the thirties and since observed for many sets of data including those of the 1950 census of housing (see chaps. v and vii). These theories assume, where income of consumer units is the same, that consumption will be higher for the place or occupational group or race or tenure with the higher average income. The distributive theory rationalizes this tendency in terms of position in the income distribution represented by consumption compared, and the standard of living theory credits the difference to the effect of average consumption of a community or occupational or other group that served as a standard of reference affecting sense of need. The tendencies predicted by these theories are wholly consistent with the permanent-income theory. Furthermore, the evidence of this monograph indicates that where normal income is the same the housing tends to be the same, irrespective of tenure or occupation or race. This evidence does not imply that the consumption of one's associates does not affect one's sense of need. This sense may only affect consumption of housing through its relationship to income. With higher long-run expected or normal income, housing will tend to improve.

## Cross-Section Estimates of the Effect of Income

The main evidence of this monograph comes from comparisons among three sets of cross-section tendencies representing the same universe of consumers: one where income of consumers is the explanatory variable, another where average income of subsets differentiated using an instrumental variable is the explanatory variable, and still another where the explanatory variable is difference in income for a set of places between two subsets, differentiated using an instrumental variable. In such estimates housing is represented in various ways, that is by value, by contract rent, by housing expenditure, and by rooms and their occupancy. The measure of greatest interest is the coefficient of income elasticity of housing. This is the ratio of the rate of increase in housing to the rate of increase in income.

Value and Rent of Units with respect to Income.—A wide range is observed in the coefficients of elasticity of value or of rent with respect to income, from close to zero to more than 3.0. The coefficients are relatively low where income of consumers is the explanatory variable and relatively high where average income of subsets is the explanatory variable. The reason for the difference seems to lie in the importance of the transitory component of these two income variables. This component appears to be a very important part of the variation of incomes of consumer units and a minor part of the variation of average incomes of subsets, such as those of cities or of census tracts within cities. For many cross-section estimates, average incomes of such subsets seem to come fairly close to representing variation in normal income, that is the income that consumer units are counting on to finance their consumption.

The evidence assembled leaves no doubt that cross-section tendencies observed among consumer units tend to understate greatly the increase in housing with normal income. They do, however, indicate considerable difference in the degree of understatement: income elasticities of housing thus derived range from 0.1 to 0.8. The evidence assembled gives reason to believe that housing is little affected by short-run income change and that the incomes reported in consumer surveys are much influenced by such change (see chap. v). If one is interested in the behavior of consumers when their income changes from year to year, one year up and another year down, then cross-section estimates of consumers homogeneous as to occupation, education, tenure, and quality of housing occupied are probably a fairly reliable guide. Estimates of this type indicate little variation in housing among consumers differing widely in current income. Of course, under this condition consumers with low current income have high housing-income ratios and those with high current incomes have low housing-income ratios. Situations where such housing-income relations are of special interest are noted in the chapter that follows. On the other hand, if one is interested in the role of income in determining the great difference in housing occurring among areas of large cities or among occupations or races or cities or the secular change in housing with rise in real income, then variation in housing with current income of consumers provides a very unreliable guide.

Surveys report current incomes. Thus the question arises as to how, from such data, one can derive evidence as to the effect of normal income. This can be done through the use of observations that represent the average of subsets of consumer units derived through the use of an instrumental variable. A suitable instrumental variable is one correlated with the normal income of consumer units but not with its transitory component. This instrumental variable enters into the estimate only indirectly. Its sole use is to rank consumers in order to derive averages for subsets. If the instrumental variable has the characteristics just specified, then the variation in average income among subsets will tend to represent difference in normal income.

Instrumental variables most frequently used in this monograph are an area of some type, such as region, city, metro area, or census tract within a metro area. The evidence examined indicate that these are useful instrumental variables for estimating the relation of housing to normal income. The estimates imply a coefficient of elasticity of value or rent of housing with respect to normal income between 1.5 and 2.0 (chaps. vi, vii, and xiii). For the same universe of consumers the coefficients of income elasticity of housing derived through interclass correlations of subsets are five to six times higher than those derived where income of consumers is the explanatory variable.

Interclass correlations, such as those among places, may of course be affected by differences among places in climate, in market prices, and in standard of consumption common to an entire community. Some conditions, such as standard of consumption can probably never be directly measured and others such as market price of housing cannot now be satisfactorily measured because of insufficient information. These may affect tendencies observed. It seems not unreasonable to suspect, for example, among cities or between urban and rural non-farm places, that the cost of housing and the average income of households are positively correlated. Or that preference of households for housing is higher in census tracts where housing on the average is superior than in those where it is inferior. To test such possibilities estimates have been made which tend to hold constant any correlation between housing and the instrumental variable, other than that present because of their mutual relationship with average normal income of consumers represented. Such estimates use observations representing differences for a set of places in housing and in income between two subsets of households, one of high and the other of low normal income, differentiated using an instrumental variable. A systematic relationship between housing and the instrumental variable will, if present, tend to affect the level but not the slope of the regression of such differences.

Estimates of this type have been made using data of the census of 1950 with subsets of metro areas represented by households of central city and environs, and of the consumption survey of 1950 with subsets of consumer units of cities differentiated by occupation and years of schooling of the head. Estimates from both sets of observations indicate an elasticity of housing with respect to normal income close to 2.0 (chap. viii). In addition, these estimates give reason to believe that any correlation between the average income of places and market price or standard of housing of places does not affect the interplace coefficient of income elasticity of value or rent observed.

In making these estimates attempts were made, not always entirely successfully, to hold constant other conditions, notably household type and cyclical change affecting employment opportunity. Although the evidence is not definitive, the probability seems high that in 1950 and 1960 the elasticity of value and rent of housing with respect to normal income differed little among places or by tenure or race. For several decades high quality housing appears to have been an important feature distinguishing the consumption of the rich from that of the poor. Housing improves markedly as one goes up the economic hierarchy of consumers—much more than does food and clothing and probably even more than automobiles.

Rooms and Their Occupancy in Relation to Income.—Income of consumer units accounts for little of the variation in rooms per dwelling unit or in rooms per person or in the percentage of households with 1.01 or more persons per room. However, the higher the normal income the higher is the rooms per dwelling unit and the higher the rooms per person, and the lower is the percentage of households with 1.01 or more persons per room.

The income elasticity of rooms with respect to normal income, with number of persons held constant, appears to be around 0.5 (chaps. xii and xiii). This is appreciably higher than the income elasticity of demand for calories, which is perhaps the characteristic of food consumption most nearly comparable to rooms as a component of housing consumption. However, with housing as with food, increase in quality rather than sheer quantity accounts for most of the rise in consumption with normal income.

The elasticity of rooms per person with respect to normal income appears to be around 0.5 and the corresponding elasticity of room crowding, as represented by the percentage of households with 1.01 or more persons per room, for both 1950 and 1960, tends to be as low as -2.0. Thus rise in normal income tends to bring an appreciable rise in rooms per person and a marked fall in the likelihood of room crowding.

## Intertemporal Estimates of Housing-Income Relations

The intertemporal estimates have much in common with the cross-section estimates. Where much of the variation in annual income represents a transitory component with respect to the stock of housing available, as during the years from 1929 to 1940, the annual space rent with respect to annual income, in dollars of constant purchasing power, has a very flat curve, with an income elasticity of housing of 0.15. For the postwar years when employment conditions were fairly normal, real income was rising, and the demand was causing important additions to the stock, income elasticity of housing observed is around 1.4 (see chap. x).

Estimates of intertemporal change derived from census or survey data indicate income elasticity of housing with respect to normal income is between 1.5 and 2.0 (see chap. xi). The observations used for such estimates represent, for a set of cities common to two surveys, difference between years in average housing, income, and related conditions. The correlation of such differences among cities provides an estimate of income elasticity of housing, unaffected by secular trend common to the cities, such as any downward shift in preference for housing because of new products becoming available or bias in the rent index. Such trends, if they occurred, would affect the level rather than the slope of the regression of the difference between years for a set of cities.

Measures of change from 1918 to 1934 and from 1918 to 1950 for sets of cities have been examined, with housing and income expressed in terms of dollars of constant purchasing power. Where 1934 is the terminal years, the income elasticity indicated is 2.0 (see Table 43), and where 1950 is the terminal period it is 1.3. The estimate where 1934 represents the terminal period appears to be more reliable. The estimate where 1950 represents the terminal period seems likely to have been lowered by the effects of rent control and because tenant incomes of 1950 had an important transitory component that had not been held constant. Such a transitory component would not be surprising because newly formed households are quite important among tenants and for many of these the income of 1949 does not represent the income determining the dwelling unit occupied in the spring of 1950 (see chaps. ii, xi, and xii).

Thus the intertemporal estimates derived from survey data indicate that from 1918 to 1950 housing as a ratio of normal income has tended to rise and that the rise has been appreciable. Furthermore, an estimate derived from the annual time series representing 1929, 1940, and the fifties is not inconsistent with this interpretation.

## Employment and Transitory Income

Variation in employment is one of the causes of short-run income change, generally referred to as transitory income. Consumers at all levels of normal income are likely to experience it, even when employment opportunity is quite stable. Transitory income may also occur because of change in the membership of consumer units, bringing either gains or losses in the number of earners, or because of change in employment of the wife, with income falling when she decides to take time off for a baby and later rising when she returns to work, or because new technology shifts demand for workers among firms, and employees lose income while locating another job. Transitory income occurring because of such conditions is important. This is indicated by the fact that average number of full-time earners rises markedly with measured income of consumer units (chaps. ii and v). It appears to contribute greatly to the low income elasticity of housing observed where income of consumer units is the explanatory variable. Insofar as it is uncorrelated with normal income it will, however, have no effect on interclass correlations, such as those among cities or census tracts within cities. Its mean will tend to be zero for the average income of the subsets of consumers representing the observations of such interclass correlations. This tendency appears to be the main reason why the elasticity of housing with respect to average income among subsets of consumers, described in chapters vi and vii, is higher than the elasticity of housing with respect to income of consumers described in chapter v.

There is, however, another type of transitory income, namely that occurring because of abnormal employment opportunity. Within a labor market such as a city, this seems likely to be correlated with the normal income of consumers, and it also seems likely to affect most those with low normal income. Hence, where employment opportunity of a labor market is abnormally low, negative transitory income seems likely to be more important for consumers of low than of high normal income. Consequently, those of low normal income are likely to have abnormally high housing-income ratios compared to consumers of high normal income. Where employment opportunity is abnormally high, the reverse tendencies seem likely to be observed: Positive transitory income and abnormally low housing-income ratios occur among consumers of low normal income. Thus in places of abnormally low employment opportunity the elasticity of housing with respect to average income among census tracts, or other subsets with a city differentiated using an instrumental variable, tends to be abnormally low, and where employment opportunity is abnormally high the income elasticity of housing from such subsets tends to be high (see chap. vii).

The variables used to represent employment level and opportunity are far from ideal. But the tendencies observed leave no doubt that much of the variation observed in interclass coefficients of income elasticity result from transitory income related to cyclical change. Thus transitory income may affect tendencies observed among subsets even where the instrumental variable used is correlated with normal income and uncorrelated with much of the transitory component of consumer incomes. Transitory income uncorrelated with normal income of consumers can be eliminated through the use of an instrumental variable, but transitory income arising from cyclical change is not of this type and cannot be so eliminated. For relationships examined in this monograph, where an instrumental variable is used, transitory income arising from cyclical change appears to have contributed to the variation observed. Thus anyone wishing through the use of an instrumental variable to estimate the relation of housing to normal income can never safely assume that transitory income is unlikely to affect tendencies observed. Consequently, there is great need for surveys and censuses to provide information on transitory income arising from cyclical change.

## Effect of Price

Cross-section estimates and estimates of intertemporal change imply an elasticity of housing with respect to relative price of at least -1.0 (see, for example, Table 43). The evidence on elasticity of demand with respect to price is less definitive than that on income. Things contributing to this include: (a) rent control and restriction on housing construction during World War II and early postwar years, (b) failure of the rent index to represent price change of families represented by the housing data, and (c) lack of information on change in market price of owner units. However, the direct evidence as to a price elasticity of at least -1.0 is consistent with the cross-section evidence: namely that interclass income elasticity by value of housing tends to be similar between and within places. If there is a positive correlation among places between average income and the market price of housing, it will have no effect on the income elasticity of value of housing observed if the price elasticity of housing is -1.0. Thus several sets of tendencies imply that the price elasticity of housing tends to be around -1.0, some representing direct and some indirect measurement (see chaps. vi, vii, viii, and xi).

The correlation of price and income of places appears, however, to reduce somewhat the income elasticity of housing consumption, for example, that represented by rooms per person. The reduction is small, however, because the price elasticity of demand of rooms is not great; it appears to be around -0.3 (chap. xii).

## Effect of Household Type

Throughout the life cycle of families, marked changes tend to occur in annual income and in number of persons per household. These go up and then down, but only slight change occurs in the type of dwelling unit occupied. Furthermore, the correlation between housing and income appears to decrease after the peak on the age-income cycle of the head is reached. In general, there is a marked variation with age of head in value- and rent-income ratios and in number of rooms per person. Value- and rent-income ratios tend to be especially high among households with an aged female head, such a household coming closest to the final stage in the history of a household. At this time the income is very low. However, rooms per person tend to be very high. Income has fallen, persons have left the family, but little change has occurred in the dwelling unit occupied.

Where households are grouped by number of persons, value- and rent-income ratios and rooms per person tend to fall with increase in number of persons. Such tendencies are in part the result of conditions associated with the age of the head, and hence tend to represent lifetime experiences that are common to all levels of normal income or economic status. Another condition seems likely to affect these tendencies. This is the negative correlation between normal income and birth rate and the doubling up of potential households. Where age of head is held constant, the higher the normal income the lower tends to be the number of persons per household (see chaps. iv, v, and xii). And the lower the normal income, the lower tends to be value- and rent-income ratios and rooms per person. Thus, when consumer units are stratified by number of persons, tendencies associated with change in age of head are merged with those related to the negative correlation of household size and normal income.

In a definitive analysis of housing with respect to normal income, several characteristics of households may need to be taken into account: notably age and sex of head, number of persons, age of persons other than the head and the presence of lodgers. Age of head appears to be the most important of these. Among places such as cities, the various household characteristics are highly correlated, and it is difficult to isolate precisely the effect of various characteristics of households with data presently available.

Among places, the mixture of household types is likely to be affected by many conditions: These include the real income of the place and its increase in population, both long-run secular and recent whether secular or cyclical. The higher the real income of the place, the less is the doubling up of potential households. The greater the population increase, the more important are likely to be households with a young head and with three or more persons present and the higher the percentage of households with lodgers. Such lodgers appear to represent a stage in getting settled in a new place, and a way of housing a portion of a very mobile population highly responsive to cyclical change in job opportunities of various places. On the other hand, the less the population increase the higher tends to be the percentage of households with an aged head, the fewer the persons per household, and the lower the percentage of households with lodgers.

## Total Expenditure, a Proxy for Normal Income

The likelihood that income for any year might not represent ability of family to consume has led some investigators to use total expenditure by income interval as a proxy for normal income. The evidence assembled in this monograph makes it seem highly probable that it is not a satisfactory proxy for normal income at least where housing is being investigated. Several conditions account for this. One is a positive correlation between total expenditure by income level and number of persons, the ratio of adults to children, and number of earners. These conditions tend to have little effect on expenditure for housing but tend to have a marked effect on expenditure for other products. Such difference among products, some of it the result of the number of persons, some of it the result of their age, and some of it the result of short-run income related to who in the consumer unit happens to be earning, reduces the correlation between housing and total expenditure and hence tends to lower the regression of housing with respect to average total expenditure (chap. ix).

If it were possible to have a large enough sample of consumer units to hold constant size and composition of consumer units, that is number of persons, age, and sex of all members and number of earners, and if one could exclude from total expenditure all types of products likely to be positively correlated with transitory income because they relate to consumer capital or to employment of members, then the remaining average expenditure by income intervals might prove to be a suitable proxy for normal income. Such an estimate would of course be affected by the elasticity of expenditure with respect to normal income of the products excluded.

These are large "ifs." In general, the estimates presented in this monograph indicate that average housing with respect to average income among subsets of households delineated using an instrumental variable is likely to provide more reliable estimates than where average total expenditure is used as a proxy for normal income.

## Instrumental Variables of Interclass Correlations

Many of the estimates shown in this monograph are derived from interclass correlations where the observations are subsets of households delineated using an instrumental variable. A suitable instrumental variable is one correlated with normal income of consumers and uncorrelated with transitory income and with no direct relationship to housing. The instrumental variables used include areas as represented by metropolitan areas and cities and census tracts within these and, in addition, occupation and years of schooling of the head of households. The intercity correlations tend to be suspect because of a possible correlation among cities between income of consumers and price of housing. The observations by occupation and years of schooling of the head are too few to be useful, especially since characteristics of households differ by schooling and occupation of the head, and some shifting among occupations, correlated with transitory income, seems likely to occur.

Such deficiencies or shortcomings of these instrumental variables can be eliminated through using them to derive estimates of difference between two subsets of consumer units for a set of places. The evidence from such differences indicates that interarea correlations yield fairly reliable estimates of value or rent of dwelling units with respect to normal income provided the effect of cyclical change is held constant.

Observations representing census tracts within cities or metro areas seem to be especially satisfactory. The number of observations is large and a housing market is fairly, if not entirely, homogeneous in price and general cultural setting. Users of data by census tracts provided for 1950 and 1960 are, however, handicapped by insufficient information on income and moderately handicapped by insufficient information on distribution of household types. It is hoped that later censuses will permit a more complete examination of housing-income relations among census tracts. These data have the great advantage of being readily understood by lay users as well as providing reliable estimates.

## Application to Other Consumer Products

This monograph has been concerned with housing. Nevertheless its findings bear on estimates of demand for other products. It has demonstrated that Friedman's permanent-income hypothesis provides a very useful frame of reference in investigating consumer behavior and that measured income of consumers tends to have a large transitory component. It seems not improbable that the importance of this component affects tendencies observed for housing more than those of other consumer products. Even so, the findings create the presumption that elimination of the effect of transitory income is likely to increase the reliability of cross-section estimates of consumption and of saving with respect to normal income. The techniques used to hold constant transitory income in order to estimate the relation of housing to normal income are applicable to other consumer products.

## Interpretation of Income Distributions

The findings also bear on the interpretation of income distributions now being poured out in large volume and variously interpreted. They indicate, for example, that short-run income changes together with variation in income with age accounts for much of the inequality of income observed, and unless these are taken into account more fundamental change in the equality of income may be obscured. It may well be that some stable component of consumption such as housing, that tends to be closely correlated with normal income, little affected by age of head and unaffected by short-run income change, represents a useful means of getting a better understanding of the degree of equality of normal incomes as these affect the general welfare of consumers.

The evidence brought to light in chapter v, dealing with housing and the income of consumers, again and again made me feel that I was not investigating the variation in housing with respect to income so much as the variation in income with respect to housing. It was the gyration of annual incomes, not the variability of housing that was determining the tendencies observed. With housing quite stable in the life of consumers it provides a benchmark for revealing how far off its norm the current income is likely to be.

## Net Effect of Change in Income and Price

For a population in general the two main conditions of change that affect housing consumption are normal income and relative price of housing. Rise in normal income tends to bring a marked improvement. And since further rise in such income seems likely, so also is further improvement in housing. Rise in price of housing may, however, offset the effect of rise in normal income. If the future is like the past, the secular rise in normal income appears likely to bring improvement in housing in spite of a greater rise in the price of housing than of other consumer products, and in spite of many new products entering the market to compete for a share of consumers' dollars.

Those who rely wholly on causal empiricism, on what they see around them en masse in modern cities, and who know something of the dwellings and their facilities of earlier generations, but whose ideas are unsullied by scrutiny of muddled data, may wonder what justification there is for this monograph. Tendencies described above and projected to the future may seem obvious. They represent, however, a break with the past as housing-income relations have usually been interpreted in the economic literature, and accordingly they merit careful scrutiny. Without such scrutiny, without determining the conditions accounting for variation in housing-income relations indicated by various surveys, it would not be possible to make a judgment as to which tendencies are the most reliable indicators of basic behavior. It is this scrutiny that accounts for the length of the monograph. Past judgments with few exceptions have been based on cross-section tendencies where a relatively small increase in housing with income is observed because much of the variation in income represented short-run income change or stages of the age-income cycle of household heads. On the other hand, secular change tends to be influenced by normal income. Difference in normal income is the dominant condition causing difference in housing consumption among areas within cities and among occupational groups. To understand variation in housing observed within any market or to predict secular change, or even the inflationary effect of rise in normal income in current dollars, it is essential to distinguish between income difference represented by age of head and by short-run income change, that is transitory income, from that represented by expected or normal income.

# Chapter Fifteen

# A REAPPRAISAL OF HOUSING CONSUMPTION IN RELATION TO INCOME

So far, the bearing of the evidence assembled on private or public decisions with respect to housing has largely been ignored. It has been assumed that understanding variation in housing-income relations indicated by various sets of observations and deriving measures of housing with respect to normal income would be useful. This in itself was an entertaining puzzle. The findings have, however, a bearing on the functioning of the housing market and on programs directed to raising the level of housing consumption. This chapter presents a restatement of main findings and comments briefly on their implications. The comments have to do only with basic tendencies. This monograph provides only a small portion of the information needed to make many policy decisions. The findings leave no doubt, however, that a new look at housing is called for.

The central evidence of the monograph deals with a seeming paradox: On the one hand, housing consumption tends to increase markedly with normal income, so that the higher is normal income the higher tends to be the housing-income ratio. On the other hand, housing consumption is little affected by short-run fluctuations in income or by change in income related to age of head of consumer units. Hence, to the extent that variation in income represents these, the higher is the income the lower tends to be the housing-income ratio. Thus, in interpreting housing-income relations for any set of observations, it is of the utmost importance to consider whether one is observing the effects of difference in normal income or of the difference in income related to age of head and short-run income fluctuations.

The Schwabe law of housing, that housing-income ratios tend to be lower for the rich than the poor, and hence to decline with rise in normal income, has long been accepted and many predictions and policies have been formulated with such expectation. The findings of this monograph imply the opposite tendency. They show higher housing-income ratios for the rich than the poor. In other words, the ratio of housing to income tends to rise with normal income. The findings imply an elasticity of housing with respect to normal income of around 2.0. Furthermore, it indicates that this relationship was quite stable between 1918 and 1960.

## Housing with respect to Normal Income

Normal income accounts for the difference in quality housing between owners and renters within cities and also that among places, occupational groups, and races. This has long been recognized, but opinion has been widespread that preference and other conditions also contributed to differences observed.

Where current income of consumers is the explanatory variable, owners appear to be willing to buy better housing than tenants with the same current income. This has led to the notion that owners tend to have a higher standard of, or preference for, housing than tenants. But this difference in housing between owners and tenants seems unlikely to represent preference. Instead, it is observed because current income is much influenced by a transitory or short-run income change. Because of this, where current income is the same, difference in housing of groups, such as owners and tenants, tends to be positively correlated with the average normal income of the groups compared. Where owners and tenants have the same normal income and are of the same household type, their housing appears to be very similar. Owner-occupancy appears to be preferred by a large part of the population. It tends to rise with normal income and so also does quality of housing. It is normal income, which determines ability to pay, that appears to account for the difference in housing between owners and tenants.

One important difference by tenure appears to occur, namely a lower mobility among dwelling units of owners than tenants. As a result, owners are less likely than tenants to change the dwelling unit occupied when number of persons in the household changes. From some points of view failure to make such changes results in diseconomies in the use of the housing stock. If there are extra costs involved in not changing one's dwelling when number of persons changes, owner-occupants seem to be willing to pay them.

Difference in average housing, similar to that described above between tenures, has been observed between regions, with consumers of the North appearing to have higher value or rent of housing than those of the South with the same current income. Similar difference has been observed among occupational groups, so that the notion is widespread that salaried and professional workers tend to be willing to buy a better quality of housing than wage earners of the same income. In addition, similar tendencies have been observed between white and non-white consumers. In other words, it has been observed, where non-white and white households have identical current income, that on the average the value or rent of dwelling unit occupied by non-white is less than that occupied by white households. The tendencies observed that give rise to this idea disappear where the subgroups compared have the same normal income and are of the same household type. The standard of housing, that is the place of housing in the standard of living, appears to be common to all parts of the United States, at least to all non-farm places, and to all important subgroups within them. Thus, the findings give no reason to suppose that housing with respect to normal income differs by occupation or by race or by national origin. In other words, the low quality of housing and the overcrowding of rooms of families of unskilled workers, of Negroes, and of Puerto Ricans appears to be mainly if not wholly the result of low normal income,[1] or to the recency of in-migration that tends to increase housing-income ratios and to be associated with room crowding.

Low quality of housing of these groups has at times been ascribed to low standards of living or to discrimination that prevented improvement in housing. To the extent that such conditions occur, they seem to

1. Large-scale surveys to permit extensive comparison by race among American consumers were those made during the thirties. The U.S. Bureau of Labor Statistics in summarizing its findings on housing of wage earners and lower-salaried clerical workers stated: "In Northern cities Negro families spent more for housing than white families at the same income level, and the reverse was found in the South" (see U.S. Bureau of Labor Statistics, Bul. 638, 1941, p. 8). Findings such as these were popularized by the book by Gunnar Myrdal, The American Dilemma (New York: Harper & Bros., 1944). They also appear to have influenced the study by Davis McEntire, Residence and Race (Berkeley: University of California Press, 1960). The findings of the survey of the thirties are consistent with the evidence presented in chap. v of this monograph, but they are not consistent with the evidence of chapts. vii and xii which show tendencies by race of housing with respect to normal income, with household type and migration status held constant.

be minor in their effect. The ability to pay that determines the housing of a consumer unit is, however, long-run expected or normal income rather than income of any one year.

## Response of Housing to Short-Run Income Change

Some situations call for recognition of response of housing to short-run income change. For example, public housing policies that require payment of a fixed proportion of income for rent irrespective of level of employment of members may be quite unrealistic. Families may be admitted to public housing when the employment level of their members is low. Under this condition they may be willing to pay a relatively high percentage of the income for rent. If they were in private housing, they probably would be doing so. They may, however, be unwilling to pay the same percentage of their income for housing when income rises with fuller employment of the members. Among households in general, a rise in income with fuller employment tends to bring a decrease in rent-income ratio, for this is a short-run increase that tends to bring little or no change in housing consumption.

Income below normal is also likely to characterize families seeking advice on budgeting or requesting public assistance. These are situations where housing-income ratios tend to be relatively high compared to those of other low-income families with members fully employed.

## Demand for Additional Dwelling Units

Increase in population and income tends to increase demand for new units.[2] If population growth and rise in per capita income coincide, the increase in demand for new units will be especially high. Rise in per capita income seems likely to increase the rate at which dwelling units of low quality are withdrawn from the stock and to reduce the likelihood that newly married couples are accommodated by reconversion. In addition, rise in income tends to reduce the importance of the doubling up of potential households. A reduction in their importance is one method of achieving a higher quality of housing for a given population, even though average quality of dwelling units is not thereby improved.

---

2. For extended discussion of conditions affecting household formation, see L. Jay Atkinson, "Factors in the Housing Market," Survey of Current Business, April, 1960.

The rise in real income has other indirect effects. It seems not unlikely that the recent rise in real income accounts for some of the decline in age of first marriage and some of the increase in birth rate that occurred during the fifties. These have stimulated formation of new households. There seems no reason to suppose that this trend will long continue to be an important factor. The interaction of income, age of marriage, and household formation may, however, continue to have a cyclical pattern.

The rise in real income affects the number of dwelling units in yet another way, namely through increase in the proportion of the population maintaining two or more dwelling units. The expansion of suburbs has been accompanied by an increase in the proportion of high-income families maintaining a suburban and a city dwelling unit. And increase in the proportion of the population with long vacations has resulted in more families owning or renting a vacation dwelling unit. Such units tend to be vacant during much of the year. The proportion of the population with an extra dwelling unit seems likely to increase, and it seems highly probable that this demand has a very high income elasticity.

## Who Demands New Dwelling Units?

Who demands new dwelling units has been explored to only a limited extent in this monograph. One general finding is, however, especially relevant. Current incomes do not represent ability to consume housing; hence the relation of current incomes to the average cost of new dwelling units gives little information as to who is likely to be a prospective buyer or a renter of a new unit.

Prior to the release of the 1950 census, the first to permit extensive insights into houseing-income relations, judgments on this basis were made. For example, Weinfeld writing in 1949 states: "In America today two of the essentials of life—food and clothing—are available in adequate supply at prices within reach of virtually all families. But in the third essential—shelter—the American economy is failing to meet minimum required. . . . Top brackets are being served as they always are." Weinfeld scrutinized the cost of housing and an annual income distribution of the late forties[3] and guessed at what people could afford to pay. He then concluded: "The moral is plain. Not only are the lowest reaches of the

3. Such income distribution has been reported annually since the mid-forties.

income level outside the market for housing today, but the great middle segment is also experiencing difficulty in finding housing at a price it can afford. Indeed, nearly 70 per cent of American families have incomes below $4,000 a year, the amount needed to buy the cheapest of the housing commonly being produced today."[4] Strauss, writing in 1952, expresses the opinion that "actually few new homes are built within the reach of middle-income families."[5]

Grebler[6] in 1950 presented quite different evidence. He quoted an estimate of the U.S. Bureau of Labor Statistics to show that in 1947 private enterprise was building homes within the reach of 75 per cent of the population. He further noted that new units entering the stock varied widely in quality, apparently reflecting the range in willingness of consumers to purchase or to rent them.

The 1950 census of housing, like that of 1940, shows a wide range in the value of dwelling units built in the last five or ten years. Neither of these censuses reports the distribution of such dwelling units by income of household. However, such information seems likely to tell very little about demand for new units. Better information seems likely to come from variation in importance of new units among subgroups differing in average income. Furthermore, such information is likely to be improved by taking into account the age of household heads.

A brief examination was made of census tracts of the 1960 census to determine who is likely to occupy the new units. The data of this census are of special interest because the volume of new units is large and also because special efforts were made during the fifties, through mortgage credit terms, to stimulate the purchase of new units by households able or willing to make only a small down payment. These indicate, for tracts high in owner-occupancy, that the greater is the importance of aged adult males the lower the importance and the higher is the average income the greater the importance of new units. Similar tendencies are observed among census tracts that represent households of the central city, irrespective of tenure (see Table 74).

---

4. Edward Weinfeld, "Can America be Adequately Housed?" American Journal of Economics and Sociology, October, 1949, pp. 77 and 84.

5. Nathan Strauss, Two-Thirds of the Nation (New York: Alfred A. Knopf and Co., 1952, p. 5).

6. Leo Grebler, Production of New Housing (New York: Social Science Research Council, 1950), pp. 149-52.

That demand for new units is negatively correlated with the importance of the aged is not surprising. Many of them doubtless demanded a new unit two or three decades earlier. Nor is it surprising that the demand for new units is positively correlated with normal income. Housing is one of the important durable goods, and houses like automobiles tend to pass down the economic hierarchy of consumers as they pass through various stages of obsolescence and depreciation.

### Housing and Cyclical Change in Income

Cyclical change in annual income represents a transitory component. In depressions the transitory component is negative and during periods of prosperity it is positive. Such changes have little effect on housing consumption as represented by the physical character of the stock, even though they bring changes in rent-income ratios. They are likely, however, to have a marked effect on additions to the housing stock. In this sensitivity of new stock to transitory income, housing is very similar to other consumer durable goods.

### Lag of Housing and Secular Change in Income

Secular increase in income brings improvement in housing.[7] There appears, however, to be a considerable lag. This lag may be related to the long horizon of consumers in gauging expected income as it relates to housing. It may also relate to the long production period, that is to the gap between registered or recognized demand and the availability of new units. Thus it seems likely that secular rise in income find expression in the market demand of later years. This monograph presents evidence of the presence of a lag in 1950 but does not indicate its distribution throughout the years following rise in normal income.

Secular rise in national income, other things held constant, can be expected to be accompanied by an increase in demand for housing. It may take the form of demand for more rooms or space per dwelling or for higher quality of structure and facilities or for undoubling of households so more privacy is possible. All these trends have characterized the demand for housing of the years since World War I, with the depression of the thirties and World War II providing interludes of stagnation.

---

7. For one experiment in forecasting demand see R. A. Gordon, "Population Growth, Housing and Capital Coefficients," American Economic Review, June, 1956.

## Price Effects

The notion that housing is little affected by price derives in part from the idea that housing quality is little affected by income, and products little affected by income tend to be little affected by price. Until very recently there has been a dearth of estimates of price elasticity of housing. The evidence presented in this monograph indicates a price elasticity of demand for housing around -1.0 (see, for example, Table 43). This is not inconsistent with estimates shown earlier by Muth using other types of observations (see p. 235). In addition, the evidence presented demonstrates that various components of housing have quite different price elasticities. For example, the price elasticity of demand for rooms appear to be around -0.3 (see chap. xii, p. 348). This would imply that the price elasticity of demand for housing, apart from the number of rooms, is much lower than -1.0.

The marked negative price elasticity of demand for housing indicates that technological changes that lower the cost of housing will tend to increase housing consumption appreciably. Consumers respond to reduced prices by buying or renting housing of higher quality. On the other hand, housing improvement tends to be checked by monopolistic practices of labor unions and of sellers of building materials and by building codes that impose unnecessary costs or limit the extent to which technological change reduces the cost of housing.[8] In addition, a rise in the interest rate[9] will serve to check housing consumption appreciably. This is an important part of the cost of housing to owners as well as renters.

Price tends to be an important regulator of consumption, and since rent control regulates price it tends to regulate consumption. The evidence on the price elasticity of demand for housing indicates that a rise in rent tends to reduce consumption. Hence, if there is a scarcity of dwelling units, a rise in rents will cause consumer units to share the space occupied with others or to seek less expensive space.

The rent control is, however, an obstacle to seeking less expensive space. It tends to reduce the mobility of tenants among dwelling units be-

---

8. For discussion of high cost of building codes, see Miles L. Colean, American Housing (New York: The Twentieth Century Fund, 1944).

9. For a recent discussion of the role of interest rates, see Leo Grebler, Housing Issues in Economic Stabilization Policy ("Occasional Paper," No. 72; New York: National Bureau of Economic Research), 1960.

cause to move is to give up the advantage of rent below market levels. Other space may involve paying someone key money for occupancy rights to another dwelling unit. If rent control tends to reduce the mobility of occupants among dwelling units, it will tend to reduce vacancy rates. Hence the existence of a low vacancy rate seems to be a very dubious test of when a housing market is ready for decontrol of rent.[10]

In that rent control tends to reduce the mobility of households among dwelling units, it reduces the adaptation of the dwelling unit to variation in number of persons in households. This number varies greatly with the age of head, for example. Thus rent control seems likely to increase the variability among tenant households in rooms per person. Thus rent control, merely because it checks mobility among dwelling units, may lead to serious inequities and diseconomies in the use of the tenant stock as judged by intensity of room use.

Since rent control tends to make some households willing to accept low quality of housing rather than to pay market rent for higher quality, it tends to restrict the demand for new units of higher quality. On the other hand, it seems likely to restrict the supply of second-hand units of low quality that free markets tend to make available to consumer units of low or moderately low normal income.

## Price Subsidies

Public housing programs are authorized on the grounds that those with low incomes cannot afford housing of a minimum standard and, therefore, that housing at less than market rents should be made available to them. Some of the housing occupied by those of low income supports this judgment. In order to minimize the cost of the program or to make a given subsidy contribute to improving the housing of most families, rents charged need to be based on families' willingness to pay for housing. And, presumably, willingness to pay is influenced by income and by the extent to which the rent is below that of housing of similar quality in the market.

The public housing act of 1949 requires that rent paid by low-income families should equal one-fifth of current income.[11] The rule probably

10. Such tests were used by various investigations made in the State of New York. See for example State of New York Temporary State Housing Rent Commission, <u>People, Housing and Rent Control in Syracuse</u>, November, 1956, p. iii, and <u>High Rent Housing and Rent Control in New York City</u>, April, 1958, p. 5.

11. For discussion of rent-income ratios in public housing pro-

evolved out of what surveys indicated that low-income families tend to pay and how families of low income respond to the rule. The evidence of this monograph indicates that 25 per cent is a relatively high ratio for those of low normal income if they are paying for market rents unless they are broken families or families with an aged or an unemployed head.

For example, annual contract rent of all urban tenant units in 1950 was 12.6 per cent of disposable income.[12] This level was undoubtedly depressed by rent control. However, I doubt that, under free market conditions, rent in 1950 would have been as much as 20 per cent of normal income of households in general. Several conditions may have contributed to the relatively high rent-income ratios that those in public housing are willing to pay: (a) a willingness to devote more of their income to housing because of higher quality of housing made available; (b) families in public housing are those with a relatively high preference for housing and hence are willing to spend a high proportion of their income for rent; or (c) the rule selects for public housing those household types or those households at the stage in their experience when housing-income ratios tend to be high, for example those with the chief earner unemployed or with head retired or a female. It may well be that these are the ones that should be assisted through public subsidy to make better housing possible. The bearing of the selective force of the rent-income ratio on community development, where public housing is highly concentrated, appears not always to have been recognized.

## Normal Income and Housing Improvement

The prospects are good for further rise in national income per person. Better housing on the average is thus to be expected unless a drastic increase occurs in the price of housing relative to other consumer goods or a drastic downward shift occurs in consumer preference for housing compared to other products. Nothing in the past would lead one to expect such a downward shift in preference. Raising the average level of housing is not enough. To many there is the much more important question as to whether rise in normal income of the nation will bring good housing to all consumer units. Those who believe that the upsurge in national income

---

grams, see Robert M. Fisher, Twenty Years of Public Housing (Harper & Bros., 1959, pp. 223-29).

12. In 1941 urban tenants were paying 15 per cent of their income for rent. See U.S. Dept. of Labor, Bul. 822, Appendix Table 22.

has tended to make the rich richer and the poor poorer see slums continuing unless large-scale housing subsidy is provided for those of low income.

Historical evidence, however, gives no reason to suppose that a rise in national income is not going to be widely shared within the population, and some conditions point to the likelihood of increased equality of normal incomes, such as a progressive income tax, the effect of which is intensified by inflation, greater equality in schooling, and a breaking down of race discrimination in job opportunities. If greater equality comes, it will contribute to the elimination of poor housing.

If the degree of equality of normal income increases, it will tend to reduce the range in the quality of dwelling units in the stock. There seems no reason, however, to expect complete equality of normal incomes; hence some range in quality of housing is likely to continue. Whether or not low quality housing, classed as slums, tends to disappear will depend on the yardstick used in judging whether housing is substandard. There has been some tendency in the administration of public relief programs to use a flexible yardstick, one that tends to move with the average achievement of the population. This kind of yardstick has certain merits. However, it should not be the only one used if the forces making for improvement and increased welfare are to be appraised. In the past all subgroups have shared in the housing improvement as represented by reduction in room crowding and by increase in preferred facilities, and most groups have had their housing environment worsened by the growing congestion of cities. Considerable improvement in housing could occur for all parts of the population without any reduction in the importance of slum or low-quality housing, if the yardstick for gauging minimum housing tends to move steadily upward.

Rise in normal income is an important condition but not the only one that tends to bring improvement in housing. Understanding its effect should make it easier to discover the effects of other conditions and to develop more realistic housing programs and more reliable projections of consumer demand for housing.

# DEFINITION OF VARIABLES AND THEIR SYMBOLS

Definitions of variables and their symbols are summarized here. The summary chiefly represents variables used in more than one chapter. One main set is omitted, those of chapter xi describing change between two years for sets of cities and time periods. Definitions of the variables and symbols of that chapter are summarized in Tables 41 and 42.

Some symbols are unique to a single analysis, such as those identifying the subsets of consumer units of households represented. These are not included here. The purpose of this summary is to assemble variables used in several correlations in order to facilitate comparison among estimates.

The summary has three parts (1) general characteristics of variables, (2) general characteristics of their symbols, and (3) definitions of basic variables and their symbols.

## General Characteristics of Variables

Some averages are means and others are medians or midpoints of income intervals. Where census data are used, the housing and income variables are either medians or midpoints of intervals. The use of such averages rather than means seems to have had only a minor effect on tendencies observed, and type of average represented is not always specified in the interpretation of evidence.

Many explanatory variables, in addition to income, are used. These represent conditions associated with housing or income that are suspected of influencing tendencies observed. Estimating their effect is not the prime interest of this monograph, and the type of variable used to represent a given condition is not uniform among the sets of observations used. For example, sets of observations differ in the variable representing the aged persons in the population. Some estimates represent males only, irrespective of their headship of a household, others represent only aged males who are heads of households, and still others aged heads of households, irrespective of sex. Much of this variation was imposed by the limitation of the data available. In addition, there is some variation in the definition of aged, both 60 and 65 years having been used as the lower limit. This occurs because of failure to standardize definitions early in the exploration of the various sets of data. One other difference in the variables relates to the type of measure used. For example, for some estimates the aged in the population are represented by a percentage, such as the percentage of adult males who are 65 years or more, and for others by a ratio, such as the number of all adult males per 100 adult males 21 to 65 years of age. Decision as to which of these forms to use was based on tendencies indicated by scatters.

Some minor differences in definitions, such as those illustrated, are ignored in the system of symbols used. Where the difference seems likely to affect the coefficient of income elasticity of housing, this likelihood is noted in the text.

Most variables are expressed in log form. Where equations are shown in the text, a variable in logarithmic form is symbolized by a lower-case x, and if in arithmetic form by an upper-case X. Where equations are summarized in tables, the variables are in logarithmic form unless otherwise stated.

## General Characteristics of Symbols Used

Where the relationship being measured is that among consumer units, the housing, income, and other variables describing consumer units are shown in lower-case letters. For example, income of consumer units is symbolized by y. On the other hand, where the observations are averages of subsets of consumer units, other than where they are ranked by y, the variables are shown in upper-case letters. For example, average income of places is symbolized by Y.

Where variables represent subsets of consumer units within a place, a superscript is used: For example, "*a*" is used to symbolize variables representing averages of subsets of census tracts or areas within a city and "q" is used to symbolize a variable representing subsets of consumer units by quality of housing. For example, average Y for these two types of subsets is symbolized by $Y^{a}$ and $Y^{q}$, respectively.

Where variables represent difference between two subsets such as the environs and central city of a metro area, the variable is symbolized by the superscript $^{*}$: for example, such difference in income is symbolized by $Y^{*}$.

Where variables represent change between two years, superscripts are used to represent the time period represented. Such measures are chiefly important in chapter xi. However, some measures of change are used in the cross-sections, notably to estimate change during the decade of the forties, such as population change and change in rent. In general such measures are symbolized by the superscript ''.

Where the variables are those of a time series the superscript t is used; for example per capita annual income is symbolized by $Y^{t}$.

Where a similar variable of an earlier period is introduced to test the effect of lag, the superscript is $^{-t}$; for example, rooms per dwelling unit in 1940 is symbolized by $R_{o}^{-t}$.

A system of subscripts is used. These largely signify a variant of a basic variable. For example, all variables representing housing, such as value or rent of dwelling units, are symbolized by h, and subscripts are used to indicate what measure of housing is represented, such as value of dwelling, contract rent, gross rent, and housing expenditure. Similarly all variables representing income are symbolized by y, and subscripts are used to indicate what income is represented. Thus subscripts are chiefly used to identify sets of variables that have much in common.

## Definition of Variables and Their Symbols

Where a variable represents separate consumer units, its symbols are expressed in lower-case letters. It may also be expressed in upper-case letters to represent the average of subsets derived through the use of an instrumental variable. Such variables, that is the upper-case form, are not shown here. Where variable as used represents only the average of such subsets, it is shown below in upper-case letters.

The variables are grouped as follows: (1) housing, (2) household size and type, (3) income, (4) price and cost, and (5) population and other. The variables of chapter xi are not shown and some of the general rules described do not apply to them.

| Symbol (1) | Definition (2) |
|---|---|
| **1) Housing** | |
| $h$ | Housing consumption as represented by residential structure and land area attracted to it, or by market value or estimated rent of owner units or space rent of all units. |
| $h_r$ | Contract rent of tenant units representing h plus additional services covered by the rent. |
| $h_{gr}$ | Gross rent of tenant units; that is, contract rent plus additional expenditure made for fuel, light, and refrigeration, with or without deduction for furnishings included in contract rent. |
| $h_s$ | Estimated space rent of tenant units; that is, contract rent less the cost of fuel, light, and refrigeration covered by rent. |
| $h_e$ | Expenditure for the main dwelling unit by owners, such as that for repairs, taxes, and interest on the mortgage. |
| $h_{er}$ | $h_e$ plus $h_r$; that is, housing expenditure for a main dwelling unit irrespective of tenure, exclusive of additional expenditure for fuel, light, and refrigeration or for household operation. |
| $h_o$ | All expenditure for housing and for household operation, irrespective of tenure. |
| $g/c$ | Gross rent per $100 of contract rent. |
| $r_o$ | Rooms per dwelling unit. |
| $r_p$ | Rooms per person in the household. |
| $r_c$ | Percentage of households with 1.01 or more persons per room. |
| B | The percentage of dwelling or housing units of the stock built in the last ten years, or the importance of all dwelling or housing units per 100 such units ten years of age or more. |

| Symbol (1) | Definition (2) |
|---|---|
| $B_1$ | The percentage of dwelling units in the stock of 1950 built in 1945 or later, or the number of all dwelling units in the stock of 1950 per 100 such units built prior to 1945. |
| $B_2$ | The percentage of dwelling units of the 1950 stock built in 1940 to 1945, or the number of all dwelling units of the 1950 stock per 100 of such units exclusive of those built in 1940 to 1945. |
| O | The percentage of households with owner-occupancy. |
| $o_y$ | A measure of the greater importance of owner-occupancy among consumer units of high than of low income. |

2) Household size and type

| Symbol (1) | Definition (2) |
|---|---|
| s | The number of persons in a household or other type of consumer unit. |
| $s_y$ | A measure of the increase in number of persons with income of consumer units. |
| ea | The number of earners of a consumer unit. |
| $ea_y$ | A measure of the increase in number of earners with increase in income of consumer units. |
| ag | The age of head of a consumer unit. |
| $ag_y$ | A measure of the difference in average age of head of consumer units between those of low and of high income. |
| Af | The percentage of the consumer units with an aged or a female head. |
| $Af^q$ | Af of dwelling units of the highest quality with Af of dwelling units of the lowest quality equal to 100. |
| $A_h$ | The number of all households per 100 with head under 65 years of age. |

| Symbol (1) | Definition (2) |
|---|---|
| $A_y$ | The number of all households exclusive of those with male head under 35 years of age and with wife but no non-relative present. |
| $A_m$ | The percentage of adult males 60 or 65 years of age or more, or the importance of aged adult males or of male heads 65 years of age or more. |
| Lo | The number of all households per 100 households without a non-relative present. |
| $Lo^q$ | Lo of dwelling units of highest quality with Lo of dwelling units of lowest quality equal to 100. |
| U | The importance of unrelated individuals per 100 families. |

3) Income

| Symbol (1) | Definition (2) |
|---|---|
| y | The theoretical construct of income as defined by economists as well as measured income of consumer units usually reported in surveys, such as money income received or disposable money income. |
| $y_n$ and $y_p$ | Permanent income as defined by Friedman and referred to in this monograph as normal income. |
| $y_t$ | Transitory income as defined by Friedman ($y = y_n + y_t$). |
| $y_k$ | y plus some income in kind as represented by consumer surveys. |
| $Y_o$ | Median income of the male labor. |
| $Y_{ov}$ | The standard deviation of the average income (log form) among occupational groups, for the most part represented by the male labor force. |
| $Y_m$ | The median income of males, either fully employed males or the entire male labor force or all males receiving income. |

| | Symbol (1) | Definition (2) |
|---|---|---|
| | c | Total expenditure by income interval or that of separate consumer units (assumed by some to be a suitable proxy for $y_n$). |
| | Le | Percentage of the male labor force of the spring of 1950 with less than 26 weeks of employment during 1949. |
| 4) Price and cost | | |
| | $P_r$ | Rent component of the Consumer Price Index from around 1940 to 1950. |
| | $P_c$ | The intercity residential (brick) construction cost index. |
| 5) Population and other | | |
| | Po'' | Population change increase in population from 1940 to 1950. |
| | Ip | Increase in population from 1949 to 1950. |
| | Cd | Importance of the population within a county changing residence from 1949 to 1950. |
| | Jt | Mean January temperature. |

# SELECTED BIBLIOGRAPHY

This bibliography of data on housing, the relation of housing to income, and associated characteristics is divided into two sections: (1) reports of federal agencies that provide data for estimates of housing in relation to income and (2) other sources of basic data. Unless otherwise stated, publications of the first type were issued by the U.S. Government Printing Office: Washington, D.C. The bibliography includes the sources represented in estimates shown of housing with respect to income and associated characteristics. In addition, it lists other publications that might be of interest to those wishing to have a fairly comprehensive bibliography of basic data available.

The publications cited do not include the monthly or quarterly publications that carry certain data of basic annual times series. Citations to them are given in the footnotes and reference to them is included in the index.

Only a few references to very early studies are included. Those wishing to assemble information on housing as described in family surveys made prior to 1930 will find useful the bibliography by Faith M. Williams and Carle C. Zimmerman, "Studies of Family Living in the United States and Other Countries," U.S. Department of Agriculture, Miscellaneous Publication 223 (1935).

## Publications of Federal Agencies

Publications of federal agencies listed are grouped in three categories: those of (a) the U.S. Bureau of the Census, (b) the U.S. Bureau of Labor Statistics and earlier labor agencies, and (c) other federal agencies. Within each category, unless otherwise stated, the publications are arranged chronologically.

U.S. Bureau of the Census

1) _Census of 1930_: _Population_, Vol. IV: _Families_, 1933.

2) _Census of 1940_

   a) _Housing_, Vol. II: _General Characteristics_, 1943, and Vol. III: _Characteristics by Monthly Rent or Values_, 1943.

   b) _Population_, Vol. II: _Characteristics of the Population_, 1943; Vol. III: _The Labor Force_, 1943; and Vol. IV: _Characteristics by Age_, 1943.

   c) _Population and Housing_ (special reports), _Statistics of Census Tracts and Community Areas_, 1943; _Families: Income and Rent_, 1943; and _Families: Tenure and Rent_, 1943.

3) _Census of 1950_

   a) _Housing_, Vol. I: _General Characteristics_, 1953; Vol. II: _Nonfarm Housing Characteristics_, 1954; Vol. III: _Farm Housing Characteristics_, 1953; and Vol. IV: _Residential Financing_, 1952.

   b) _Population_, Vol. II: _Characteristics of the Population_, 1953, and Vol. III: _Census Tract Statistics_, 1952.

   c) _Family Income and Rent Survey for Local Housing Authorities_ (separate volumes cover Baltimore, Md.; Boston, Mass.; East St. Louis, Ill.; Dallas, Tex.; Elizabeth, N.J.; Philadelphia, Pa.; and New York, N.Y.),[1] 1954.

4) _Historical Statistics of the United States: Colonial Times to 1957_, 1960. With the co-operation of the Social Science Research Council.

5) _1956 National Housing Inventory_, Vol. I: _Components of Change 1950 to 1956_, and Vol. III: _Characteristics of the 1956 Inventory_, 1959.[2]

6) _Census of 1960_

   a) _Housing_, Vol. I: _States and Small Areas_, 1961; Vol. II: _Metropolitan Housing_, 1962.

1. These are processed reports released directly by the U.S. Bureau of the Census. They illustrate rent-income relations among households of low economic status that seem likely to be very homogeneous with normal income.

2. These are processed reports distributed by the U.S. Bureau of the Census.

b) *Population and Housing*: *Census Tracts*, 1961.

c) *Population*: *General Economic and Social Characteristics*, *1962*.

U.S. Bureau of Labor Statistics and earlier labor agencies

1) U.S. Commissioner of Labor, *Seventh Annual Report*, 1891, and *Eighteenth Annual Report*: *Cost of Living and Retail Prices of Food*, 1904.

2) "Cost of Living in the United States," *Bul*. 357 (1924).

3) "Money Disbursement of Wage Earners and Clerical Workers," *Bulletins* 636-41 and 691 (1941).

4) "Consumer Purchases Study," Vols. I and II of Bulletins 642-49 (1941).

5) "Changes in Cost of Living in Large Cities of the United States, 1913-41," *Bul*. 699 (1941).

6) "Family Spending and Savings in Wartime," *Bul*. 822 (1945).

7) "Housing and Fuel Expenditures of City Families," *Monthly Labor Review*, May, 1947.

8) "Family Income, Expenditures, and Savings in 10 Cities," *Bul*. 1065 (1952).

9) "Family Income, Expenditures, and Savings in 1950," *Bul*. 1097 (1953).

U.S. Department of Agriculture

1) "Consumer Purchases Study," *Miscellaneous Publications* 396, 399 (1940), and 465 (1941).

2) "Family Spending and Saving as related to the Age of Wife and Number of Children," *Miscellaneous Publication* 489 (1942).

3) "Rural Spending and Saving in Wartime," *Miscellaneous Publication* 520 (1943).

4) *Farms and Farm People: Population, Income, and Housing Characteristics*, 1953. With the U.S. Department of Commerce.

5) *Farmers' Expenditures*, 1956. Vol. III, Part II, *1954 Census of Agriculture*. With the U.S. Bureau of the Census.

Other Federal Agencies

1) Wickens, Davis L., *Financial Survey of Urban Housing* (U.S. Bureau of Foreign and Domestic Commerce, 1937).

2) National Resources Planning Board, *Family Expenditures in the United States, 1941*.

3) U.S. Income and Output (U.S. Office of Business Economics, 1958).

Other Publications

Blakey, Roy G., and others, Analyses of Minnesota Incomes, 1938-39 (University of Minnesota Press, Minneapolis, Minn., 1944).

Menderhausen, Horst, "Changes in Income Distribution During the Great Depression," in Studies in Income and Wealth, Vol. VII (New York: National Bureau of Economic Research, 1947).

Study of Consumer Expenditures, Incomes and Savings. Statistical Tables, Urban U.S., 1950 (Philadelphia, Pa.: University of Pennsylvania, especially Vols. I (1956), II (1956), IV (1956), and XVIII (1957). Tabulated by the U.S. Bureau of Labor Statistics for the Wharton School of Finance and Commerce.)

# INDEX OF AUTHORS

# SUBJECT INDEX